W9-DIZ-411

RETRIBUTIVISM

Retributivism

ESSAYS ON THEORY AND POLICY

Edited by Mark D. White
COLLEGE OF STATEN ISLAND/CUNY

OXFORD
UNIVERSITY PRESS

OXFORD
UNIVERSITY PRESS

Oxford University Press, Inc., publishes works that further Oxford University's objective of excellence in research, scholarship, and education.

Oxford   New York
Auckland   Cape Town   Dar es Salaam   Hong Kong   Karachi   Kuala Lumpur   Madrid   Melbourne
Mexico City   Nairobi   New Delhi   Shanghai   Taipei   Toronto

With offices in
Argentina   Austria   Brazil   Chile   Czech Republic   France   Greece   Guatemala   Hungary   Italy
Japan   Poland   Portugal   Singapore   South Korea   Switzerland   Thailand   Turkey   Ukraine
Vietnam

Copyright © 2011 by Oxford University Press, Inc.

Published by Oxford University Press, Inc.
198 Madison Avenue, New York, New York 10016

Oxford is a registered trademark of Oxford University Press
Oxford University Press is a registered trademark of Oxford University Press, Inc.

All rights reserved. No part of this publication may be reproduced, stored in a retrieval system, or transmitted, in any form or by any means, electronic, mechanical, photocopying, recording, or otherwise, without the prior permission of Oxford University Press, Inc.

Library of Congress Cataloging-in-Publication Data
Retributivism : essays on theory and policy / edited by Mark D. White.
    p. cm.
Includes bibliographical references and index.
ISBN 978-0-19-975223-2 (hardback : alk. paper)
1. Punishment—Philosophy. 2. Retribution. I. White, Mark D., 1971-
K5103.R48   2001
303.3'6—dc22   2010045110

1 2 3 4 5 6 7 8 9
Printed in the United States of America on acid-free paper

Note to Readers
This publication is designed to provide accurate and authoritative information in regard to the subject matter covered. It is based upon sources believed to be accurate and reliable and is intended to be current as of the time it was written. It is sold with the understanding that the publisher is not engaged in rendering legal, accounting, or other professional services. If legal advice or other expert assistance is required, the services of a competent professional person should be sought. Also, to confirm that the information has not been affected or changed by recent developments, traditional legal research techniques should be used, including checking primary sources where appropriate.

(Based on the Declaration of Principles jointly adopted by a Committee of the American Bar Association and a Committee of Publishers and Associations.)

You may order this or any other Oxford University Press publication by
visiting the Oxford University Press website at www.oup.com

Table of Contents

Notes on Contributors

Thom Brooks is Reader in Political and Legal Philosophy at the University of Newcastle. He is also founder and editor of the *Journal of Moral Philosophy*. His recent books include *Hegel's Political Philosophy* and *Punishment*. Brooks is currently co-editing a book, *Rawls's Political Liberalism*, with Martha Nussbaum.

Michael T. Cahill is Professor of Law and Associate Dean for Academic Affairs at Brooklyn Law School. He is co-author, with Paul H. Robinson, of the treatise *Criminal Law* (Aspen, forthcoming) and the book *Law Without Justice: Why Criminal Law Doesn't Give People What They Deserve* (Oxford, 2006). Other work by Professor Cahill has appeared in the *Texas Law Review*, *Northwestern University Law Review*, *Washington University Law Review*, and *Hastings Law Journal*, among other publications. Before joining the Brooklyn faculty, Professor Cahill was the staff director for a project to rewrite the Illinois Criminal Code and also served as a consultant for the Penal Code Reform Project of the Kentucky Criminal Justice Council. He received a B.A. from Yale University and has M.P.P. and J.D. degrees from the University of Michigan.

Marc DeGirolami is an Assistant Professor at St. John's University School of Law in Queens, New York. His research interests are in criminal law and law and religion. His articles have been published or will be appearing in *Legal Theory*, *Constitutional Commentary*, *Ohio State Journal of Criminal Law*, *Boston College Law Review*, *Journal of Law and Religion*, and *Alabama Law Review*, among others.

Antony Duff is a Professor Emeritus in the Department of Philosophy, University of Stirling, and a Professor in the Law School, University of Minnesota. He has published two books on criminal punishment (*Trials and Punishments*, 1986; *Punishment*,

Communication, and Community, 2001), and has written widely on other aspects of the philosophy of criminal law (most recently in *Answering for Crime: Responsibility and Liability in the Criminal Law*, 2007). He is currently leading a four-year research project on *Criminalization*.

Gerald F. Gaus is the James E. Rogers Professor of Philosophy at the University of Arizona. His essay "On Justifying the Moral Rights of the Moderns," won the 2009 American Philosophical Association's Kavka award. Among his books are *On Philosophy, Philosophy and Economics* (Wadsworth-Thomson, 2008), *Justificatory Liberalism* (Oxford, 1996), and *Value and Justification* (Cambridge, 1990). His most recent book is *The Order of Public Reason: A Theory of Freedom and Morality in a Diverse and Bounded World* (Cambridge, 2011) and, with Julian Lamont, *Economic Justice* (Blackwell, forthcoming). With Fred D'Agostino, he is currently editing the *Routledge Companion to Social and Political Philosophy*.

Sarah Holtman is Associate Professor of philosophy at the University of Minnesota, Twin Cities. She specializes in moral and political philosophy and philosophy of law, with an emphasis on Kantian practical philosophy. Her Kant-based work, including several pieces on penal theory, includes both interpretive articles and extensions of Kant to contemporary issues.

Jane Johnson is a postdoctoral research fellow in clinical and public health ethics in the Department of Philosophy, Macquarie University. Her research encompasses an eclectic range of philosophical interests with current work focused on the ethical and epistemological issues generated in two fields, animal experimentation and surgical innovation. With respect to the latter, she is lead author on a paper published in *The Lancet*. Jane undertook her Ph.D. at the University of Sydney where her research investigated justifications of legal punishment using the resources of Kant and Hegel. She continues to work on German Idealism and hopes to develop a Hegelian approach to public health ethics.

Richard Lippke is Senior Scholar in the Department of Criminal Justice at Indiana University. He taught for many years at James Madison University and more recently at DePauw University. He is the author of *Rethinking Imprisonment* (Oxford, 2007) and of numerous articles in the philosophy of criminal law. His recent articles include "Punishing the Guilty, Not Punishing the Innocent," *Journal of Moral Philosophy* (2010); "Retributive Parsimony," *Res Publica* (2009); "Rewarding Cooperation: The Moral Complexities of Procuring Accomplice Testimony," *New Criminal Law Review* (2010); "The Case for Reasoned Criminal Trial Verdicts," *Canadian Journal of Law & Jurisprudence* (2009); and "Criminal Record, Character Evidence, and the Criminal Trial," *Legal Theory* (2008). He is currently working on a book on the philosophical issues raised by plea bargaining.

Dan Markel is the D'Alemberte Professor of Law at Florida State University and Scholar in Residence at the Center for the Administration of Criminal Law at New York University. He is the author of numerous articles, which can be found at http://www. danmarkel.com, and he is also a co-author of *Privilege or Punish: Criminal Justice and the*

Challenge of Family Ties (Oxford, 2009). He holds degrees from Harvard College, Harvard Law School, and the University of Cambridge.

Jeffrie G. Murphy is Regents' Professor of Law, Philosophy, and Religious Studies at Arizona State University. He is the author of numerous books and articles on Kant, punishment, forgiveness, mercy, and the moral emotions of guilt, remorse, shame, and resentment. His most recent book is *Getting Even—Forgiveness and its Limits*. He gave the Stanton Lectures ("Remorse, Apology, and Forgiveness") at Cambridge University in 2010.

Mark Tunick teaches political theory and constitutional law at the Wilkes Honors College of Florida Atlantic University, where he is Professor of Political Science. His publications include *Punishment: Theory and Practice* (University of California Press), *Hegel's Political Philosophy: Interpreting the Practice of Legal Punishment* (Princeton University Press), as well as articles on privacy, property rights, culture and the law, the moral obligation to obey law, and the political thought of Kant, Hegel, and J.S. Mill.

Mark D. White is Professor in the Department of Political Science, Economics, and Philosophy at the College of Staten Island/CUNY, where he teaches courses in economics, philosophy, and law. He is the author of *Kantian Ethics and Economics: Autonomy, Dignity, and Character* (Stanford, 2011) as well as numerous articles and book chapters, and editor of *Accepting the Invisible Hand: Market-Based Approaches to Social-Economic Problems* (Palgrave, 2010), *The Thief of Time: Philosophical Essays on Procrastination* (with Chrisoula Andreou; Oxford, 2010), *Theoretical Foundations of Law and Economics* (Cambridge, 2009), and *Ethics and Economics: New Perspectives* (with Irene van Staveren; Routledge, 2009), among others.

Introduction
Mark D. White

RETRIBUTIVISM—BROADLY DEFINED as the view that punishment is justified and motivated by considerations of justice, rights, and desert, rather than by personal or societal consequences—holds a long-standing yet controversial position in legal and political philosophy. Critics deride it as inhumane, backward looking, and dogmatic, a perverse rationalization of vicious sentiments such as revenge and hatred. Supporters argue that it alone respects the demands of justice, maintains the balance between sacrifices made by all citizens, and acknowledges the inherent dignity and equality of all rational persons. The contemporary debate over retributivist punishment has become particularly vibrant in recent years, focusing increasingly on its political and economic, as well as philosophical and practical, aspects. This volume offers innovative perspectives on this debate from twelve prominent scholars that, in the hopes of the editor, will further the discussion of the theory and practice of retributive punishment and promote new areas of expansion for its study.

The first part of the book deals with the basic concept of retributivism, such as how retributivism should be understood, interpreted, and justified. The first chapter, "Retrieving Retribution," by **R.A. Duff**, offers new perspectives on his position that punishment communicates the censure that the offender deserves for his crime, focusing on the challenge of explaining why penal "hard treatment" should be the appropriate means of communication. He meets that challenge by showing that appropriate kinds of penal hard treatment can serve as a vehicle for a *two-way* communication between offender and political community—the communication of formal censure from community to offender, and of formally apologetic recognition from offender to community—which is motivated by the offender's wrongdoing as ascertained during a fair trial, which Duff emphasizes as critical to the retributivist project. In this chapter, Duff goes beyond his last book (*Punishment, Communication and Community*, Oxford University Press, 2001) in developing the "apology" dimension and saying more about the relationship between retributive and restorative justice, bringing together ideas from some of the papers and book chapters that he has published since then (most in relatively obscure publications).

The second chapter, "Punishment Pluralism" by **Michael T. Cahill**, speculates that contemporary understandings of retribution have come to see it either as a good or as a deontological side constraint on action, rather than as an affirmative deontological duty as earlier versions saw it (or purported to see it). Yet, if retribution is formulated as a good or a constraint, it loses its centrality as a basis for punishment: under such a view, retribution may be one consideration, among others, favoring (or opposing) punishment, but it cannot justify punishment except in a very narrow sense. Accordingly, characterizing retributivism as a "theory of punishment," which was never entirely apt, now seems untenable. As an alternative, Cahill favors an overtly pluralistic scheme in which various principled and practical considerations, including retributivist considerations, may inform punishment policy at both the systemic and the individual level. To this end, Cahill surveys the most significant arguments for and against punishment, as a first step toward an account that properly balances the competing ends at stake instead of privileging one over the rest.

In the next chapter, "What Might Retributive Justice Be? An Argument for the Confrontational Conception of Retributivism," **Dan Markel** offers the first dedicated treatment of his Confrontational Conception of Retributivism, which is designed to show both the internal intelligibility of retributive punishment situated in a liberal democracy and the limits that attach to the pursuit of that social project of retributive justice. Similar to but distinct from Duff's account, the version of retributivism that Markel offers focuses on the confrontational (not just communicative) encounter that occurs when the state inflicts some level of coercion upon an offender who has been adjudicated through fair and reasonable procedures of violating an extant and justifiable legal norm. This is essentially a legal or institutional view of retributive punishment and thus necessarily concerned with the consequences of running such an institution alongside other important social projects, themes taken up by several other contributors to this volume.

Based on experiments in social evolution theory and game theory, the final chapter of the first section, "Retributive Justice and Social Cooperation" by **Gerald Gaus**, argues two points: (a) the success of social groups depends on having punishers, and (b) punishers are supplying a public good, since those who cooperate but do not punish outperform those who cooperate and do punish. If we were simply forward looking in our reasoning, as in the simple instrumental theory of rationality—if all payoffs are either current or anticipated, and not tied to past action—social cooperation would be a mystery. Gaus shows that for societies to thrive in the presence of noncooperative "free riders," it needs some members who are motivated to punish the free riders without instrumental justification—that is, as a matter of (evolved) sentiment or instinct rather than calculated, rational, utility-maximizing action. This, according to Gaus, accounts for both the existence of retributive "tastes" as well as their importance to social cooperation.

The second part of the book delves more into the philosophical foundations of retributivism, focusing chiefly on Kant and Hegel as well as modern legal philosophers. In the first chapter, "Some Second Thoughts on Retributivism," **Jeffrie G. Murphy** provides a reflection on his long career and esteemed body of work on retributivist punishment and details his current critical stance on the subject. After some prefacing remarks on legal moralism that lead to a brief discussion of the relevance of character to sentencing in a retributivist spirit, Murphy turns to his previous stances on retributivism and reassesses them, considering first the moral balance theory of desert (associated chiefly with Herbert Morris), and then his embrace of the retributive emotions (as reflected in his book co-authored with the late Jean Hampton), now finding them both lacking. He instead adopts and recommends a profound humility regarding retributive punishment in the face of human imperfection, frailty, and essential inequality, motivated in part by William Blake, Friedrich Nietzsche, and the Holy Bible. He concludes by exploring what he terms "The Two Faces of Retributivism," asserting values he still finds attractive in retributivism—such as its emphasis on human dignity—as well as ones he does not—such as the role of what he calls "deep character" in influencing our retributive judgments and actions—in the end, declaring himself a "reluctant retributivist."

The second chapter in this part, "Kant, Retributivism, and Civic Respect" by **Sarah Holtman**, focuses on recasting the retributivism of Immanuel Kant, grounding it in his demands for civic respect and political equality. Historically, many have thought of Kant's account of the purpose and justification of punishment for legal offenses as a paradigm example of thoroughgoing retributivism, but Holtman questions this interpretation. She offers a detailed examination of the justification that Kant provides for legal punishment, the purposes he recognizes, the protections he demands (for criminals, victims, and the accused), and the principles he enunciates to guide the structuring of a penal system. What Kant endorses, Holtman suggests, is a modern retributivist penal theory focused on civic respect for persons as citizens, with implications not only for institutions, laws, and policies, but for citizen attitudes and commitments (similar in spirit to Markel's account offered above). To illustrate significant differences between this view and the classical retributivism it rejects, she closes by applying it to the famous *Miranda* decision and warnings, as well as the case of Kirsten Driscoll, a recent example of punishment perceived to be overly lenient, and finds that the civic respect interpretation of Kant's retributivism explains both better than the classical version.

In the next chapter, "*Pro Tanto* Retributivism: Judgment and the Balance of Principles in Criminal Justice," **Mark D. White** suggests a way that deontological retributivists can accommodate the compromises to the ideal of just punishment made necessary in the real world by scarce resources and competing societal needs and goals (a context also emphasized by Cahill and Markel in their chapters). He considers recent work supporting consequentialist retributivism, in which trade-offs are allowed in order to maximize some measure of punishment or justice but finds the quantification of just punishment problematic due to the ideal or principled nature of justice inherent in the concept. Instead, he proposes a practical, deontological retributivism in which the principle of just punishment is balanced with other principles and goals according to a concept of judgment drawn from the moral philosophy of Immanuel Kant and the jurisprudence of Ronald Dworkin. After outlining the resulting "*pro tanto* retributivism," White compares it to other suggestions regarding how to balance competing interests within punishment, including Michael S. Moore's "threshold retributivism," and argues that his conception is more flexible while adhering to a deontological understanding of retributivism.

In the final chapter of this part, "Hegel on Punishment: A More Sophisticated Retributivism," **Jane Johnson** shifts our attention to G.W.F. Hegel's contributions to retributivist thought. Owing, perhaps, to his frequently obscure writing style and idiosyncratic terminology, Hegel's account of punishment has generally not received widespread attention or a favorable reception in English-speaking jurisprudence. This is in stark contrast to the space devoted to, and more ready acceptance of, Hegel's fellow German retributivist Immanuel Kant. However, Johnson argues that if one perseveres with Hegel's position and draws on the resources of his broader philosophy (including aspects of his logic regarding negation, contradiction and judgment, and his theory of recognition), a number of fruitful results will follow. Not only will a coherent and interesting account of punishment emerge that represents a much more sophisticated take on this institution than the one offered by Kant, but a revitalized Hegelian view of punishment can also furnish a solution to the otherwise elusive task of justifying legal punishment. Hegel's way of construing crime and punishment, in terms of the parties whose rights are infringed and in turn restored, seems in fact to be a tailor-made answer to the problem of punishment as set down so influentially in the twentieth century by H.L.A. Hart, and resembles other views presented in this volume (for instance, by Markel).

The third and final part of the book discusses the practical implications of retributivism for policy and practices in criminal justice. In the first chapter, "Entrapment and Retributive Theory," **Mark Tunick** addresses whether a retributivist can support an entrapment defense and, if so, under what circumstances, by considering the culpability of entrapped defendants. It is often argued that retributivists must oppose the entrapment defense for various reasons, such as that entrapped defendants have nonetheless broken the law, and this itself warrants punishment. Tunick explores some reasons why a retributivist *can* support an entrapment defense. First, entrapped defendants may be less culpable than the "privately enticed" insofar as they do not cause harm. Since the police control the situation, no actual harm is caused, and whether one actually causes harm may bear on one's culpability. Furthermore, if one's predisposition were weak and required substantial police coaxing to be triggered, we might say that the police action and not the defendant caused the crime in the relevant sense. Also, applying Robert Nozick's account of coercion in a novel way, Tunick considers the argument that entrapped defendants may be less culpable insofar as their action was not fully voluntary; unlike in private enticement cases, they necessarily underestimate the probability of being caught before making their choice.

In the second chapter of this part, "The Choice of Evils and the Collisions of Theory," **Marc DeGirolami** explores the relationship of retributivism to the another affirmative defense, that of "choice of evils" (also known as the necessity defense): where an actor is faced with a choice of evils—either break the law or allow something terrible to happen—the actor who breaks the law may be justified if the evil he chose outweighs the evil that he prevented. There are numerous side constraints on the availability of the defense, but it has generally been presupposed by legal scholars that the choice of evils defense is a paradigm example of a purely consequentialist calculation of the net social benefit achieved. An actor is justified, on this common view, if the scales of utility tilt in favor of the illegal action he chose. In nearly every jurisdiction, however, an actor who acted with purpose or knowledge in causing the necessity is barred from the defense; this bar has been rejected as illegitimate by many scholars. After summarizing his argument that only a deontological principle can justify the bar (because the actor who has purposely or knowingly created the necessity has not earned, and does not deserve, justification of his conduct), DeGirolami suggests that this connection between retributivism and the choice of evils defense has been overlooked because scholars have been overly fixated on the choice of evils as a purely consequentialist defense, without noticing (or by marginalizing) its retributivist features. Just as there may be mixed theories of punishment, so might there be mixed theories of justification and excuse. The reach of retributivism extends, then, even to those features of the criminal law where it has often been assumed that it had no place. More broadly, DeGirolami (like Cahill) argues for a pluralistic understanding of criminal doctrines such as the necessity defense and its myriad details, rather than attempting to find conceptual purity of theoretical explanation.

The next chapter, "Retributive Sentencing, Multiple Offenders, and Bulk Discounts," by **Richard Lippke**, considers the problem posed by individuals who have pled guilty or have been convicted of multiple criminal offenses at a given point in time but whose total punishment, if their sentences are served consecutively, seems excessive. One solution to the problem of the seeming disproportionality of consecutive sentences in such cases is to grant the offenders "bulk discounts" for their crimes. Concurrent sentencing policies, according to which multiple offenders are sentenced for the most serious of the crimes they have committed, with the sentences for their lesser crimes served concurrently, is one type of bulk discount. Yet other types of bulk discounts are conceivable, and the questions addressed in this paper are whether and how those who favor a retributive approach to sentencing can defend them. In particular, if we set aside appeals to parsimony or mercy, can bulk discounts be defended on grounds of proportionality? Lippke argues that they can, although different types of multiple offenders should not be eligible for the same kinds of bulk discounts. For instance, he urges smaller bulk discounts for serial offenders than those whose various crimes are organized around a central crime or crimes, especially in cases in which many of the supporting crimes involve violations of *mala prohibita*.

The final chapter of this part (and the book), "Retribution and Capital Punishment" by **Thom Brooks**, argues that contrary to popular wisdom (and clear pronouncements by classic retributivists such as Kant), retributivists should oppose capital punishment for murderers. He concedes that murderers may deserve to be executed, and that this can be carried out fairly and humanely. Rather, his argument focuses on epistemic problems with ascertaining guilt, which have been made more prominent and visible by recent advances in forensic science (such as DNA testing). Even after guilt was found beyond a reasonable doubt during a fair trial, and confirmed in all subsequent appeals, these scientific advances have been able to clearly demonstrate the innocence of dozens of convicted murderers on death row. Brooks rejects several other arguments against capital punishment offered as retributivist before outlining and defending his own against actual and potential criticisms.

My debts of gratitude are few but very heartfelt. I wish to thank Chris Collins and Michelle Lipinski at Oxford University Press for their support of this project; the contributors (especially Dan Markel) for their cooperation, enthusiasm, and brilliance; and Maryanne Fisher for personal support when I needed it most.

Conceptualizing Retributivism

RETRIEVING RETRIBUTIVISM

R.A. Duff

RETRIBUTIVISM NEEDS SAVING not only from its plentiful enemies, but from some of its would-be friends. More precisely, since there are so many different accounts of punishment calling themselves "retributivist" that we might wonder whether the term picks out a single school of thought,[1] what needs saving is what I take to be the core retributivist thought: that what gives criminal punishment its meaning and the core of its normative justification is its relationship, not to any contingent future benefits that it might bring, but to the past crime for which it is imposed. The challenge for a would-be retributivist is to explain that thought and that justificatory relationship in a way that makes them both intelligible and morally plausible: morally plausible, in particular, as an account of criminal punishment in a liberal democracy, since that is the context in which, for most likely readers of this book, criminal punishment operates. Retributivism needs saving, and the core retributivist thought needs retrieving, from those who interpret it in ways that fail to make it morally plausible. Such failures are found among advocates of retributivism as well as among its critics. They are found most obviously among political advocates, in the depressingly familiar penal rhetoric that makes it sound as if the sole aim of a system of criminal justice is to inflict harsh suffering on offenders. But they are also found among theoretical defenders of retribution, who are too prone to portray criminal punishment as consisting simply in the deliberate infliction of suffering on passive recipients who are said to deserve it.

This is not the place for a detailed critique of other retributivist accounts of punishment, partly because such a critique has been provided in detail by others;[2] but I will note (in the next section) the main problems faced by many such accounts. The following section will outline a framework for an adequate account of punishment as retribution, by proposing a conception of the criminal law and the criminal process that makes room for retributive punishment. Finally, the last section will sketch an account of criminal punishment within that framework.

Two initial clarifications are in order. First, my focus is on *criminal* punishment. There are important questions to be asked about punishment in other contexts—about the role it can play and the meaning it can have in our informal moral dealings with each other,[3] in child-rearing and education, and in a range of other institutional contexts. There are important questions to be asked about the relationship between extra-legal punishment and criminal punishment: can we illuminate criminal punishment by attending to these other kinds of punishment, or vice versa? There are obvious reasons for caution, for instance in the fact that parental and educational punishment deal with wrongdoers who are not yet fully responsible agents,[4] or the possibility that sanctions imposed by various other institutions are better understood as penalties rather than as punishments.[5] It would, however, be odd if there were no substantive connections of meaning or of value between these different contexts. I would argue that we can understand criminal punishment as (part of) a formalized legal version of our extra-legal responses to moral wrongdoing,[6] and that we can sometimes see the punitive activities of institutions outside the criminal law as close analogues of criminal punishment—as dealing in analogous ways with wrongs that belong not to the whole polity, as criminal wrongs do, but to the particular institution.[7] But I cannot develop these arguments here.

Second, my interest is in so-called positive retributivism, rather than in a less ambitious kind of negative retributivism, according to which retributivism sets side-constraints on the pursuit of the consequentialist goals that provide the positive aim of punishment.[8] Some version of negative retributivism has seemed to many to open the way to a rational reconciliation of retributivist and consequentialist concerns—to a taming of retributivism that leaves it a substantial role in the justification of punishment, but avoids the problems created by making retribution one's aim. It is not clear how far those side-constraints (do not punish the innocent, or punish the guilty unduly harshly) must be explained in retributivist terms—that is, whether they really do provide a place for retributivist thinking in penal theory.[9] Nor is it clear whether the resulting theory, so long as it posits a strictly consequentialist end for punishment—a goal to which punishment is instrumentally related as an efficient means—can avoid the objections brought against consequentialist theories in general: that they use, if not the innocent, then the guilty "merely as means" to that end.[10] Nor is it clear that the resulting structure of a further goal that must be in tension with the constraints that negative retributivism sets on its pursuit can be stable, or whether the insatiable goals that consequentialism typically posits will too often tempt us to throw off those constraints in what we perceive to be an emergency, or for the sake of some significant consequential benefit.[11] Whatever the strengths and weaknesses of a negative retributivism, however, my concern is with its more ambitious relative, which explains the positive justifying aim of punishment in retributive terms.

This is not to say that prospective consequences can play no role in a retributivist theory; let me mention three roles here. First, prospective consequences could play a constraining role analogous to that played by retributivist values in a side-constrained consequentialism: we should punish the guilty as they deserve, unless doing so is likely to bring about damaging consequences. Second, they could play a more positive but still subordinate role, as they do in "limiting retributivism," or in any theory that does not take desert to be the sole determinant of penal liability: within the limits (whatever they are) set by the demands of desert, we are allowed to attend to consequences in deciding on the precise sentence.[12] And third, they could play a yet more significant role as providing part of punishment's justifying aim: we could, for instance, hold that punishment is justified (at least at the level of a penal system, if not in individual cases) only to the extent that it is both deserved and consequentially beneficial.[13] My concern here, however, is to make sense of the idea of retribution as the core, if not the only, justifying aim of punishment.

1. Pitfalls for Retributivism

In this section, I note various pitfalls that make it harder to defend a retributive conception of punishment. First, if we talk of punishment simply as the infliction of suffering ("the guilty deserve to suffer"), or of a burden whose weight is determined only by a demand that it be proportionate to the seriousness of the crime for which it is imposed, and whose material mode or content is left unspecified, we invite the charge that we are advocating a primitive, morally unappealing enterprise of "pain delivery."[14] We also imply that any constraints on the material forms of punishments, or on their overall severity if we cannot find within our retributive theory the resources to "anchor" the penalty scales,[15] must come from outside rather than from within a retributivist conception of punishment: all that retribution requires is a proportionate quantum of punitive suffering. This then presents us with the puzzle of why suffering is an appropriate or required response to criminal wrongdoing, a puzzle to which retributivists have devoted a large amount of often unproductive energy.

If we are to get clearer about what "retribution" could amount to, we must attend to just what it is that wrongdoers may be thought to deserve, and to the significance of different modes of punishment. This should lead us to consider not just punishment's impact, the quantum of suffering that it imposes, but its meaning, or more precisely the meanings of different modes of punishment. That punishment has meaning is a familiar theme among theorists who highlight its expressive or communicative dimension.[16] What matters, however, is not just the meaning of punishment *qua* punishment, for instance as a general mode of censure, but the particular meanings of different modes of punishment. What does imprisonment, a fine, or a community service order say to the offender or to others about the offender and his crime; is it a message that punishment should convey? Is the reason why we should not use torture as a punishment (not even for torturers) that, while it might be deserved for their crime, it is ruled out by desert-independent moral demands of humanity; or is torture intrinsically inappropriate as a mode of punishment?

Second, retributivists (and others) too often tend to justify criminal punishment in purely moral terms, without attending adequately to its essential political grounding. If we begin by portraying the imposition of deserved penal suffering as an impersonal, universal demand of justice ("the guilty must be punished"), or as an intrinsic good, we then face the questions of audience and standing. To whom is that demand addressed; who has the standing to seek to satisfy it? Even if the imposition of deserved suffering on the guilty is an intrinsic good, who has the standing to pursue that good by imposing that suffering? Is that good great enough to warrant the material and moral cost that its pursuit incurs?[17] We must remember that criminal punishment is an aspect of the state, and is thus a political enterprise. If we are to understand its meaning and rationale, we must ask what proper state purposes it could serve and how the state could be warranted in imposing such burdens on its citizens; to answer such questions, we must clearly engage in political theory. If we are ambitious, we might hope to articulate the one true political theory and to draw from it the one true theory of punishment. If we are more modest, as we should be, we will ask what normative sense can be made of criminal punishment from within some more local political theory that is appropriate to our time and place—in our case, a theory of liberal democracy.[18]

An essential dimension of a political theory that is going to make sense of punishment is the matter of agency: when an offender is punished, by whom is he punished? If we begin, as theorists and preachers often seem to begin, with an impersonal demand from heaven or from justice that "the guilty must be punished" (the passive voice is significant), we must still ask who, if anyone, has the standing to meet that demand, and, in particular, why it should be a proper task for a liberal state. Some might say that if the demand is a moral demand of justice, then anyone could in principle satisfy it by imposing the right quantum of suffering on the guilty, so that even private enterprise "punishment" inflicted by a vigilante group could constitute just punishment. The state's claim to exclusive authority to punish breaches of the criminal law could then be justified only as a part of a wider justification of the state's monopoly over the use or authorization of coercive force. But if we begin instead, as we should, by asking how we should treat each other, and how a state should treat and address its citizens; if we recognize, as we should, that punishment is a relational activity (its simple manifestation is not A being punished, but A being punished by B), the question of how punishment can be justified is, from the start, the question of how B can be justified in punishing A. That question, however, brings with it the question of what the relationship is or should be between them.[19]

So when we talk of criminal punishment, we must ask not just who is being punished, but who is punishing whom, and in virtue of what relationship between them.

Furthermore, in the context of criminal punishment, our answer to that question must be not (merely) moral, but (also and essentially) political. It is not enough to say, for instance, that as moral agents we have a proper interest in seeing that retributive justice is done and the standing to ensure that it is done, for criminal punishment is a dimension not of our personal, informal moral lives, but of our political lives as members of a state; punisher and punishee must be related by the existence of some appropriate political structure that gives them these roles. Not only must the answer we give be political, which is to say that it must reflect some political theory: the nature of the answer will make a crucial difference to the kind of penal theory that we can go on to offer. If we take the punisher to be a Hobbesian sovereign, for instance, we will look to a deterrent conception of criminal punishment as our natural normative theory. A sovereign (at least a Hobbesian one), after all, issues orders or commands that she expects to be obeyed. She must therefore be able to answer the question that a subject might naturally put: "And what if I disobey?" Since the answer "I would be disappointed in you" is not likely to be persuasive, it will be natural to back such orders by the deterrent threat of sanctions.[20]

There is no puzzle about the role of criminal punishment in a Hobbesian state, but surely we aspire to something more and other than that. In particular, we surely aspire to a liberal polity—a republic, even—of citizens living together in equality, rather than one of subjects living under the command of a sovereign. If we begin, however, not with a sovereign and her subjects, but with citizens who owe each other equal concern and respect as fellow members of the polity,[21] matters should seem more problematic. We need now to ask how or on what basis citizens can punish each other: what kinds of punishment (if any), serving what kinds of goal (if any), could be consistent with that equal concern and respect for our fellow citizens?

That question should seem difficult, and its difficulty may be evidenced in the speed with which both politicians and (sometimes, to their shame) theorists start to deny the full status of citizen to those who commit crimes (or those who commit the kinds of crime that "we" do not commit—one does not often find speeding motorists or tax evaders described as anything less than full citizens). If we can honestly claim that someone who commits a crime thereby forfeits his standing as a citizen, it is of course much easier to justify punishing him, for instance in order thereby to reduce the incidence of future crimes.[22] So too, if we can portray criminals as outsiders or enemies against whom "we," the law abiding, must be protected (against whom the "war on crime" is to be fought), it will be much easier to punish them than if we still see them as fellow citizens.[23] Now it is, of course, absurd to suggest that anyone who commits any crime at all thereby forfeits his civic standing, as if failing to display a tax disc on my car, or even a "real" crime such as buying a stolen video recorder, is enough to forfeit my status as a citizen. On the other hand, there is a question, which I cannot pursue here, about whether a persistent enough career of serious criminality can warrant something like a suspension of civic status. Can citizenship be unconditional; or must it be to some degree conditional, if not on good behavior, at least on the absence of persistent and really serious bad behavior?[24] But if we take citizenship, and a proper concern and respect for our fellow citizens, seriously, we will at least be very reluctant to judge that a citizen has forfeited his citizenship, and very slow to deny him that status. Even if long persistence in the commission of serious crimes can lead us to ask whether we can continue to treat him as a fellow citizen, nothing short of that should raise this as a practical question. We must, that is to say, continue to see and to treat most if not all offenders as fellow citizens; we must thus ask how (if at all) we can punish them.

That "if at all" is to remind us that we cannot take it for granted that criminal punishment can be justified. Although philosophical theorists have begun to engage more seriously with the idea that punishment might not be justifiable,[25] they have not engaged seriously enough with the rich recent literature of abolitionism,[26] a literature now expanding enormously with the growth of interest in "restorative justice" as an alternative to "retributive" justice.[27] If we assume that criminal punishment is somehow inevitable (factually or normatively), and are sufficiently impressed by objections to consequentialist accounts of its rationale, we might think that some version of retributivism must be correct—if only we can find the right one. But that is just what we cannot assume, if we are seriously engaged in a normative inquiry into the justifiability of criminal punishment. (Furthermore, the thought that some system of criminal punishment is normatively inevitable, apart from betraying a lack of imagination, is more likely to favor a consequentialist theory, since what makes it appear inevitable is, most probably, the thought that its abolition would be consequentially disastrous.)

The third pitfall for those who would defend retributivism is to treat criminal punishment in isolation from the criminal process, in particular the criminal trial that precedes it. Divine punishment might require no prior process of divine investigation (given God's omniscience) or trial (although believers do talk of standing before the seat of judgment), for the hand of God strikes the sinner unerringly and without warning. Human criminal punishments, however, are (if they are distinct from lynchings) the outcome of a criminal process of investigation, trial, and conviction; we need therefore to examine the relationship between punishment and that prior process. If that relationship is simply instrumental, of course, penal theorists need pay it no close attention; punishment is justified only when inflicted on the guilty, not on the innocent, and the point of the criminal process is simply to ensure, as far as is practicable, that we do punish only the guilty. On this view, as far as the justification of punishment goes, if a guilty person is punished after a trial that was procedurally flawed (or without a trial at all), his punishment itself (if proportionate) is justified, although we might object to the unreliable process from which it emerged (the process has produced the right result, by unreliable means). This is, however, an inadequate conception of the criminal process. As I will argue in the third section of this chapter, we should see the criminal process, in particular the criminal trial, not in merely instrumental terms as a way of identifying those who, having committed crimes, are now eligible for punishment, but rather as having its own intrinsic significance as a process of calling to account. This will then open the way to a conception of punishment as normatively continuous with, rather than separate from, the criminal trial.

We also need an account of criminal law, since criminal punishment depends on criminal law. It depends on the penal law that authorizes it and provides for its formal administration; on the procedural law that governs the criminal process; and on the substantive criminal law that defines the offenses for which people are punished, and the defenses that can save them from punishment. If punishment is to be justified as a deserved response to crime, we need an account not just of punishment as such a response, but also of crime as that which makes such a response appropriate: what is it about crime that requires or deserves punishment?

All of which is to say that an adequate normative theory of punishment must be part of a normative theory of criminal law, which must itself be part of a political theory of the state. I cannot even sketch such larger theories here;[28] but in the following section, I will try to sketch enough of them to show what kind of retributivism I think we can and should defend. The key to this defense of retribution will be a contrast (analytically clear, though often blurred in practice) between "civil" and "criminal" responses to wrongdoing.

2. Criminal Law and Criminal Trials

Suppose that I have damaged your car. This causes you annoyance and inconvenience, and it will cost money to repair or replace. Two kinds of legal response are possible.[29] One is civil: if I refuse to accept liability to pay for your car's repair or replacement, or to compensate you for the inconvenience that I caused you, you might sue me in civil court for compensation. If you do so, you (as the plaintiff) will need to show not just that I did, through some action of mine, cause the damage to your car, but that I was at fault in doing so—minimally, that the damage resulted from my negligence, since liability to pay damages is typically fault-based. If you prove both causation and negligence, it is open to me to argue that while I was both at fault and causally responsible, so too were you: that your contributory negligence also played a role, and thus that I should not bear the whole cost of the harm. If I lose the case and am found wholly or partly liable to pay, I might have to pay the sum myself; or, if I prudently took out insurance, I may be able to pass the cost onto my insurers (with, of course, a likely impact on my future premiums). However, it is always open to you, as the plaintiff, not to bring a case, or to drop the case, or to decide not to enforce any award made by the court.

The other response is criminal. Perhaps I committed a criminal offense in damaging your car: I was driving carelessly or dangerously and as a result collided with your car; or I was knocking down my shed and was reckless as to the obvious, and actualized risk, that the wall would fall onto your car parked next door; or I damaged it on purpose, out of malice. It is not open to you to bring a criminal charge in the way that you could bring a civil case. But if the police become involved (perhaps, but not necessarily, because you call them), they might decide to charge me; and if the prosecution goes ahead (which is for the prosecuting authority to decide, not you), and I either plead or am proved guilty, I am liable to be convicted in a criminal court and punished. My punishment might be or include a fine whose amount might match what I would be ordered to pay by a civil court hearing your civil case—but that would be a coincidence, and the money would go not to you but to the state. Furthermore, though criminal courts do typically (controversially) base sentences partly on the actual outcome of the offense, so that someone who causes damage is likely to be punished more severely than he would have been had he luckily caused no damage, my fine would not be calibrated to the actual cost of repairing the damage to your car, in the way that a civil award (geared toward compensation) is set. Nor need my sentence be, or be limited to, a fine. I might be disqualified from driving if I caused the damage through bad driving, or given a noncustodial sentence, such as probation or community service, or even imprisoned. I cannot argue for a reduction in my sentence on the grounds that you were also at fault or partly responsible for the harm that you suffered (unless I can show that you provoked me): the victim's contributory negligence is not relevant to criminal sentencing as it is to a civil award of damages, as is shown by the justified criticism of judges who impose lighter sentences on rapists whose victims might be seen as having taken negligent or foolhardy risks.[30] Nor can I insure against being punished, even when the sentence is a fine: I must pay the cost myself, rather than passing it on to my insurer. Finally, it is not up to you, as the victim, to decide whether to pursue the case or to enforce the sentence imposed by the court: you can free me from my obligation to pay you the damages that the civil court has awarded you, but cannot free me from my obligation to pay my fine or to undertake any other sentence imposed by the criminal court.[31]

One way to put the key contrast between criminal and civil proceedings is to say that the civil case is focused on harm, and the criminal case on wrong. The criminal case is concerned with who is answerable and punishable for a wrong (even if, for those who accept a version of the Harm Principle, it must be a harmful wrong), whereas the civil case is concerned with who should have to pay to repair or to ameliorate some harm (even if, for those who eschew strict civil liability, it must be a wrongful harm). Wrongfulness might be relevant to the civil case, but it is relevant as a necessary condition for the just imposition of liability to pay for the harm that one caused: I am held civilly liable for that harm so long as I was at fault in causing it. By contrast, and even if the criminal law should be concerned only with conduct that causes or threatens harm, the wrongfulness of the (harmful) conduct is the very focus of criminal liability, rather than merely a condition of it.[32] This is just what some (in particular abolitionist) critics object to about criminal law: that it focuses on condemning and punishing wrongs rather than on the more productive, less oppressively harmful enterprise of trying to get harm repaired.[33] Such critics are right about this feature of criminal law but wrong to find it objectionable: we need a public institution that focuses on wrongdoing in something like the way that criminal law focuses.

An initial issue concerns the idea of compensation or repair. When I damage your car, we can try to work out what would be adequate compensation for the harm that you suffered. The car can be repaired or replaced; you can be reimbursed for additional costs that you incurred; you might be paid something for the time you had to spend organizing the repairs, or some of the organization could be done by the person who damaged your car or by his insurers. You might complain that what you receive does not sufficiently compensate you, that it falls short of what is required. But to say that it falls short implies that there is some level of payment or provision that would be adequate—that would constitute full compensation. It is a matter of controversy how we should understand the idea of full compensation: does it involve putting you into a condition in which you are no worse off than you would have been had your car not been damaged, or into a condition as between which and the condition you would have been in had your car not been damaged you are indifferent? But without trying to resolve that controversy, we can see how in cases like this we can make sense of the idea that full compensation could in principle be provided by monetary payment or by the provision of other services, even if in particular cases that is contingently impossible. Furthermore and crucially, that payment or those services could in principle be provided by the person who caused the damage or by others, in particular by an insurance company.

Even within the realm of civil compensation, matters become much less simple when we move from property damage to other kinds of harm, including physical injury. With relatively minor injuries causing no serious pain, something like full repair and compensation might be possible. With more serious injuries causing lasting impairment or disability, something can, of course, be done: help can be provided for tasks that the person can no longer do, equipment (including prosthetic limbs) can be provided, and money can be paid to cover the additional costs that will be incurred and to make up for lost income. We can then hope to get some idea of how close the various possible measures (which can again be provided by people or bodies other than the person who caused the harm) can come to full repair or compensation, or how far short they fall. This implies that they can be measured (roughly) on a scale at the top of which stands full compensation; they might fall far short, but they constitute movement toward full compensation.

In other cases, we cannot even make good sense of full compensation, or see what can be done as moving toward full compensation, even if it also falls short of it. If, as a result of the injury you caused me, I face a life of pain and serious disability, I might reasonably deny that what is provided amounts even to partial or incomplete compensation for my loss (as distinct from what might be complete compensation for some material aspects of that loss). I might, however, also say that "it helps," which is to say that it does to some degree offset my loss by making my life, taken as a whole, somewhat less drastically worse than it would have been without that payment or those services. We can still think, roughly, of a balance: one that is still weighed down on one side by the seriousness of my loss, but that can be tipped at least a little way back toward the center by the provision of this money or these services.

In other cases, however, we cannot properly talk of the payments or services that insurers could provide even as "helping." This is most evident in cases of death. Suppose that someone has lost a loved one—a parent, child, or spouse—through medical negligence. There might, of course, be financial costs and losses that could be compensated: expenses can be reimbursed, help can be provided with what needs to be done, and loss of earnings that one depended on can be made up. But the central loss, of one's beloved, is not addressed by such measures. This can become all too painfully clear when parents sue a hospital over the death of their child. Suppose a court awards them $10,000 damages against the hospital,[34] and they protest that this improperly values their child's life at (merely) $10,000. In one way, such a protest is fully justified: it would be an insult to suggest that this constitutes adequate compensation for the loss of their child. In another way, however, such a complaint is at least misleading, since it implies that the court would have come closer to providing full or adequate compensation had it awarded a larger sum. But that is surely not what the parents can believe; nor, surely, could they say that the money "helped" (beyond recompensing them for costs that they incurred), as if their grief could be to some degree assuaged by the money or what it could buy (a new car, a holiday, and so forth). What they mean, or should mean, is that a monetary payment is the wrong kind of response to what they have suffered: no such payment could address their loss. An obvious reason for this is that to regard a monetary payment as appropriate implies that one could put a price on the child's life and on their loss, or at least weigh the monetary award on the same scales. But there is a further reason: that the money is or could be paid not by the author of the careless death but by an insurance company. I will return to this point shortly.[35]

There are two dimensions to the parents' grief: that their child has died, and that the child died because the hospital and its employees were negligent. The child's death is, of course, the massively salient dimension, but that grief is aggravated by the knowledge that the death was avoidable, and would have been avoided had the doctors acted with due care. The loss of a child cannot be compensated whether or not the child died through another's negligence; the most that others can do is show sympathy and try to help the parents face life without the child. But something—something other than the kind of payment that an insurance company could fund—can be done to address the wrongfulness of the death, which is what concerns us here, since it helps us to see what kind of response to wrongdoing could be appropriate. There are, in particular, two things that the parents (or others who have suffered loss through another's faulty conduct) might seek: an explanation or accounting, and an apology. As we will see below, the provision of an appropriate service, or even a payment, by the person or body who caused the harm might then also be appropriate, not (merely) as compensation of the kind that an insurer could pay, but rather as a way of giving material expression to the apology.

The explanation that is sought includes a kind that could be provided by a third party, of how the harm was caused. But it will also require an explanation *by the person or body who caused the harm*, which is as much a matter of answering for what one has done as it is of providing an informative explanation: what we want is that those who harmed us or our loved ones be called to account for their conduct. That calling is in part a request for an explanation of what we do not already know about what happened and why. But the giving of such an explanation is not just a matter of providing new information, and matters even when the information is already known, since its value lies in its coming from the relevant agent as an expression of his recognition of what he has done and of what he owes to you as its victim. Such an explanation is owed even when the agent was not at fault: if your father died while in my care or at my hands as a surgeon, I owe you an explanation, even if the explanation shows that I did everything possible to save his life. I owe it to his family to own (up to) my role as an agent in his death and to explain myself to you. But when the agent was at fault, when the harm was due to his negligence, the explanation must also (if honest) take on a confessional, apologetic dimension. The account I give of my conduct is now an account of where and how I went wrong: an account that must, if it is to display the kind of concern that I should have for those whom my actions affect, be remorseful and not merely descriptive. The process of calling to account seeks to get the agent to face up to what he has done and to the necessity to answer for it to those with a proper interest in the matter. That answering might involve showing that he was not at fault (without, of course, simply washing his hands of the affair), or admitting (or being shown) that he was culpable in causing the harm, in which case an apology is also due. If we ask why this matters, the obvious, simple answer is that this is one of the central ways in which we recognize each other and our claims on each other.[36]

This is, I suggest, a central feature of our appropriate response to being wronged, whether or not that wrong is also harmful: that we want the person who wronged us (or whom we may think wronged us) to answer to us, either by explaining himself in a way that exculpates him, or by admitting his culpable wrongdoing and apologizing for it. Such a calling to account is a feature of our informal moral lives, of our institutional lives (many professions have formal procedures through which those charged with misconduct are called to account), and of some kinds of civil suit, when the aim is not so much to secure damages or compensation as to call to account the person or body who wrongfully harmed me.[37] It is also a central dimension of criminal law.

Criminal law and the criminal process are, I suggested above, focused on wrongs rather than on harms. The criminal law does not (it cannot) create norms, or make wrongful conduct that was not already wrongful independently of the criminal law; rather, it provides an appropriate formal response to wrongs that it defines as public wrongs, which are our business as members of the polity. The criminal trial, on this view, is a process through which an alleged wrongdoer is called to answer. He is to answer, initially, *to* the charge that he is guilty of a criminal wrong, by pleading "Guilty" or "Not Guilty." If he admits or is proved to have committed the offense charged, he must answer *for* that commission, either by accepting the conviction that follows a plea of "Guilty" or a successful prosecution case, or by offering a defense that shows why he should not be condemned for committing the offense.[38]

Criminal law differs from civil law partly in making wrongs rather than harms salient. It also differs in that a criminal case is pursued not by the direct victim but by the whole polity, acting through the prosecutor. To justify a system of criminal law, we thus need to justify an institution that is in this way both public and focused on wrongdoing. How can we do that?

According to traditional versions of legal moralism, it seems that the polity should create a system of criminal law as the agent of the moral law, in order to ensure that wrong-doers are condemned and punished as they deserve;[39] but that is not a plausible account of the aims of a liberal polity. Accounts that make the harm principle (in one of its versions) central suggest a different picture. A central task for any polity is to protect its members from various kinds of harm. Some such harms are caused (or preventable) by human action and could be averted by proscribing or prescribing the relevant kinds of action. The criminal law is sometimes an efficient way of doing this, since it backs its proscriptions and prescriptions by the prudential sanction of punishment as well as by the moral sanction of condemnation; and it is a means of harm-prevention that we can justifiably use so long as we use it only against conduct that deserves such condemnation because it is wrongful.[40] However, it is not clear whether or when the criminal law is a more efficient method of harm prevention than other modes of legal regulation would be.[41] More significantly, the reasons that we have to criminalize such core wrongs as murder, rape, and other attacks on the person do not depend on the contingent fact that criminal-ization will efficiently prevent them. Those reasons have to do, rather, with what it is for a polity to take its defining values seriously, and for its members to take each other seri-ously as participants in a shared civic life that is structured by those values.

There are, of course, many ways in which a polity can express its defining values, and its members can express their shared commitment to those values. But since an important aspect of those values will be that in their light certain kinds of conduct count as wrongs, one way to express the values will be to take public notice of such wrongs: to declare, formally, that they are public wrongs that merit condemnation. We can see the begin-nings of criminal law in such a declaration: a polity's criminal law identifies and defines the wrongs that must be recognized as public wrongs. This by itself takes us no further than a merely declaratory law, but a polity that takes its values seriously cannot just ignore violations of those values. Not only must it take such steps as it reasonably can to avert such violations:[42] it must respond to violations that occur. For consistently to ignore vio-lations would be to betray those values, and would fail to do justice both to the victims and to the perpetrators of such violations. We owe it to our fellow citizens to respond not just to harms that they suffer (by providing help, sympathy, support) but also to wrongs that they suffer. We also owe it to them, as fellow members of a normative community, to respond to the wrongs that they commit; simply to ignore a fellow member's wrongdoing is to imply that neither he nor his actions matter.

What form should such a response take? Liberal polities typically emphasize individ-ual responsibility, and an important aspect of individual responsibility is responsibility for one's own actions. That responsibility is in part prospective: I am left free to determine my own actions. But it is also retrospective: I am held responsible for what I have done.

Retrospective responsibility is answerability: to be held retrospectively responsible is to be called to answer for my actions by those who have the standing to do so; it is to be called to explain my actions, and if necessary to justify or excuse them, or accept censure for them. That is how we treat each other in extra-legal moral contexts: if another's wrong-doing is my business, I respond properly by calling her to answer for it, for that is how I take both her and her wrongful conduct seriously. That is what the criminal law does in relation to public wrongdoing: it calls alleged perpetrators of such wrongs to account, and holds them answerable for such wrongs through the criminal trial. To respond in this way to public wrongs is to do justice to both victims and perpetrators. We show that we take the victim's wrong seriously in part by seeking to bring its perpetrator to book: the common complaint by victims of crime that the perpetrators were allowed to get away with it has force when the failure to bring the perpetrator to book reflects a failure to take the crime seriously enough, especially if the failure to pursue and prosecute the perpetra-tor reflects discrimination against the group to which the victim belongs. We also thus treat the perpetrator as a fellow member of the polity, as someone who is entitled to the respect and concern that is due to all citizens, and thus also as someone who must answer for his public wrongdoing.[43]

This is only the start of an account of criminal law; its proper functions are not exhausted by the identification of public wrongs and the provision of a procedure through which alleged perpetrators of such wrongs are called to account. But these purposes are, I suggest, central to the criminal law as a distinctive legal institution, and central to its role in a liberal republic. This raises, of course, a number of further questions, notably about the role of the victim and the charge that the criminal law "steals" the case from the victim by taking it over as a public wrong over which he then loses control.[44] Instead of pursuing those questions, however, we must turn finally to the role that punishment can play in a criminal process of this kind: I will argue that we can now see how punishment can be justified as retribution.

3. Civic Criminal Punishment

The criminal process, understood in the way suggested above, treats victims and offenders as citizens; it takes seriously the wrongs that offenders commit against victims, as wrongs that are our collective business, by calling offenders to answer for them in a criminal trial. That process is already in a sense retributive, for although its aims are partly forward looking,[45] it looks back to the past crime, and its primary meaning and justification lie in its character as an appropriate response to that crime. Furthermore, it is something that we impose on the offender, in that he is required to face trial, and it is intended to be burdensome. For his trial subjects him to the judgment of his peers (his fellow citizens), and his conviction condemns him as a wrongdoer. While we cannot guarantee that the process will pain him, nor am I suggesting that we should so design the criminal process that it will be burdensome or unpleasant for all those subjected to it,[46] it is intended to be burdensome or painful for the guilty defendant in that it is intended to arouse (or endorse) his remorse for what he has done and his recognition of its implications for his relations with his fellows—something that it will do if he is open to such moral appeal, and that will be painful if he takes it with the seriousness with which it is intended. If the core retributivist thought is that the guilty deserve to suffer (something), and that a proper aim for the criminal law is to subject them to that suffering, the criminal trial is a mode of retribution: criminal wrongdoers deserve to be called to account in such a way by their peers and to be condemned for what they have done. The aim is not simply that they should "suffer" or be caused pain, but that they should undergo this particular process, which will be painful to them if they receive it as they should.

However, this is not yet to justify (what usually counts as) criminal punishment, let alone justify it in retributive terms. Nothing I have said so far shows that or why our formal public response to crime should not end with the offender's conviction and condemnation in court. Why should we go beyond that, and impose penal "hard treatment" on the offender: a burden that is (unlike the condemnation expressed in a conviction) intended to be onerous independently of any censorial message that it might carry?[47] How can the imposition of such hard treatment be consistent with a proper concern or respect for the offender as our fellow citizen; how can citizens properly aim to make fellow citizens suffer?

The account of the criminal law and the criminal process sketched in the previous section also provides the starting point for a plausible retributivist theory of criminal punishment: one that shows punishment to be continuous in its aims and meaning with the criminal trial that precedes it, and to be (like the trial) consistent with or even expressive of a proper regard for each other as citizens. Central to that theory is the familiar thought that punishment has an expressive or communicative dimension that is essential to its purpose: the penal burden that is imposed on the offender is not *merely* a meaningless burden, but it also aims to communicate the censure that the criminal trial showed to be justified and that his conviction then expressed. That is of course at best the starting point for a theory of punishment, since it at once invites the question, "Why should we choose this burdensome means of communication?" One obvious reply to this question is: "In order to deter those whom mere condemnation will not dissuade."[48] To offer such a reply is not to abandon retributivism altogether, since one could still insist that punishment must be justified as the communication of an appropriate degree of censure, and that its severity must therefore be proportionate to the seriousness of the crime. But it is to give up on the ambition to provide a more thoroughly retributivist account, since it brings this strong consequentialist dimension back into the picture. I will not discuss this line of thought further here, but will instead indicate how we might develop a more fully retributivist, though still also forward-looking, answer.

A key point for this possibility is that communication is a two-way rather than a one-way process, at least in intention or aspiration: when I seek to communicate with another,

I seek a response from her. Now communication is an active process: if punishment is to involve not just communication from the polity to the offender, but from the offender back to the polity, the offender must be, or at least have the chance to be, active in his own punishment. This is not something to which penal theorists often attend: punishment is more typically portrayed as something done to or imposed on the offender, with the implication that his role is purely passive.[49] Most punishments do, however, require the offender to be active: they are required of him, rather than merely inflicted on him. This is obviously true of such punishments as probation and community service; it is true of fines when the offender is expected to pay the fine himself (rather than, for instance, seeing it deducted from his wages); it is true of imprisonment in some jurisdictions, not just because the offender can be active within the prison, but because he is told when and where he should present himself to serve his prison term, rather than being simply taken, passively, from court to prison.

So can we explain criminal punishment in retributive-communicative terms as a process of communication in which the offender, as well as the polity, is meant to be a participant? I think we can, by thinking both about how the polity can properly seek to communicate to the offender, and about what the offender owes in return.

The first aspect of this communicative process is by now familiar (which is not of course to say that it is generally accepted). Punishment communicates censure from the polity to the offender, with a view to persuading him to attend to that censure, to face up to the wrong he has done, and therefore also to recognize the need to mend his ways. Merely verbal censure, as conveyed by a conviction or by purely symbolic punishments, is likely to be inadequate, because they are all too easily ignored. By imposing a burdensome punishment, we hope to make it harder for the offender to ignore the message, to keep his attention focused on what he has done, and to provide a structure within which he can face up to his wrongdoing and on what he must do to avoid its repetition.[50] The aim is not simply to "make him suffer," as some crude versions of retributivism imply, but if the sentence is to communicate the right message of censure and to provide an appropriate vehicle for the offender's remorse, it must involve something burdensome.[51]

The second aspect of communicative punishment draws on an idea, prominent in recent penal theory, that punishment has to do with the kind of apology that offenders owe to their victims, and to the wider polity (whose values and relationships they have violated).[52] For a wrongdoer to come to recognize the wrong she has done is also for her to come to recognize that she needs to communicate that recognition, in suitably remorseful terms, to those whom she wronged and others who have a proper interest in the matter. That is an essential part, the essential start, of a process of "making up," or making reparation, for what she has done, and thus also (unless the wrong was so serious as to create an irreparable breach) an essential start to the process of restoring or repairing her relationships with them. But words might not be enough for this purpose, especially between those whose relationships are relatively formal and distant rather than informal and intimate; something more may be needed to give material form, and thus greater social force, to the apology. That is one function served (albeit not adequately) by damages in civil cases: they provide a material currency in which apologies can be more forcefully expressed, though they can also distort that expression by implying that a monetary value could be put on what the plaintiff suffered. Analogously, in criminal cases, when the apology is owed both to the direct victim (when there is one) and to the wider polity, we can see the offender's sentence as a mode of moral reparation, a burden that he is required to undertake as a formal, forceful expression of the apology that is due. Perhaps community service orders, involving work done to benefit the community, display this kind of meaning most clearly, but other kinds of legitimate punishment can be understood in the same way.[53]

4. Conclusion

I have only gestured here at a way in which we could understand criminal punishment in a liberal polity whose citizens aspire to treat each other with equal concern and respect. My main aim has been to sketch the framework, in particular an account of the criminal law and the criminal process, within which we can see criminal punishment not as a mere imposition to which we subject offenders, but as part of an ongoing process of communication between citizens. Central to that framework is a focus on wrongdoing, which I have argued is essential for any polity that takes its defining values seriously; and on calling wrongdoers to account, which I have argued is essential for any polity that takes individual responsibility seriously. This then generates a conception of punishment (and of the whole criminal process of which punishment is part) that is firmly retributivist, in the sense that it finds the meaning and the primary justification of that process in its character as an appropriate response to criminal wrongdoing: a response that marks, and seeks to induce in the offender, a due recognition of the wrongdoing and of what is needed to make reparation for it.[54]

Notes

1 *See* Cottingham, "Varieties of Retribution."

2 See, for example, Shafer-Landau, "Failure of Retributivism"; Golash, *Case Against Punishment*; Boonin, *Problem of Punishment*.

3 See, for example, Bennett, *Apology Ritual*.

4 Which has not deterred theorists from portraying criminal punishment in educational terms; see, for example, Morris, "Paternalistic Theory of Punishment"; Hampton, "Moral Education Theory of Punishment."

5 On penalties as against punishments, see Feinberg, "The Expressive Function of Punishment." For present purposes, the key differentia are that penalties do not convey censure, whereas punishment does, and that penalties are to be justified pragmatically.

6 As I argued in *Trials and Punishments*.

7 Consider, for instance, the way in which an academic institution might deal with plagiarism. Plagiarism is sometimes a criminal offense, of obtaining material advantage by deception, but it is not typically dealt with by calling in the police; it is treated as an "internal" matter that concerns the distinctive significance that academic institutions attach to intellectual honesty.

8 See Dolinko, "Some Thoughts about Retributivism," 539–43.

9 For alternative grounds for the first constraint, see Hart, *Punishment and Responsibility*, chs. 1-2; Walker, *Why Punish?*, ch. 11. It is less clear whether the second constraint could be explained without recourse to retributive ideas of desert; see Feinberg, *Harmless Wrongdoing*, 144–55.

10 For an (overly) simple version of this objection, see Murphy, "Marxism and Retribution"; for further development, see my *Punishment, Communication and Community*, sections 1.2, 3.3.

11 For the charge of instability, see, for example, Goldman, "Paradox of Punishment"; Morison, "Hart's Excuses"; Lacey, *State Punishment*, 46–56. On insatiability and its dangers, see Braithwaite and Pettit, *Not Just Deserts*.

12 On "limiting retributivism," see Morris, *Future of Imprisonment*; Morris and Tonry, *Between Prison and Probation*. On the role of consequentialist considerations in more stringent versions of retributivism, see von Hirsch, *Censure and Sanctions*, ch. 7.

13 See, for example, von Hirsch and Ashworth, *Proportionate Sentencing*, ch. 2.

14 On delivering pain, see Christie, *Limits to Pain*. On whether retribution should be understood as a matter of inflicting deserved suffering, see, for example, Gray, "Punishment as Suffering," and Markel and Flanders, "Bentham on Stilts," arguing against Bronsteen, Buccafusco and Masur, "Happiness and Punishment," and Kolber, "Subjective Experience of Punishment."

15 On anchoring, and on how much harder it is to determine cardinal as opposed to ordinal proportionality, see von Hirsch, *Censure and Sanctions*, ch. 5.

16 A theme revived by Feinberg, "Expressive Function of Punishment"; on communication as against expression, see my *Punishment, Communication, and Community*, 79–80, and at note 49 below.

17 A question incisively emphasized by Husak, "Why Punish the Deserving?"

18 See the chapter by Holton in this book for an example of this approach.

19 A particularized version of this question is evident in international criminal law. By what right do domestic courts claim a "universal jurisdiction" over certain kinds of international crime (see Reydams, *Universal Jurisdiction*)? By what right does the International Criminal Court try "crimes against humanity" committed within a state by and against its own members (Rome Statute of the International Criminal Court, art. 7)?

20 Compare the conception of criminal law and punishment suggested by the classical positivist conception of law as a sovereign's threat-backed orders.

21 On equal concern and respect, see Dworkin, *A Matter of Principle*, ch. 8, and "Liberal Community." For versions of the republicanism being assumed here, see Dagger, *Civic Virtues*; Pettit, *Republicanism*.

22 See Goldman, "Toward a New Theory of Punishment"; Morris, "Punishment and Loss of Moral Standing."

23 The issue of the right to vote is symbolically important in this context: states which, like the UK, deny those serving prison terms the right to vote thereby declare them to be temporarily suspended from the full status of citizen; states which, like some American states, deny convicted felons the right to vote for the rest of their lives thereby declare them to have permanently forfeited their status as citizens; while states which, like many European states, impose no such

disenfranchisement on prisoners thereby symbolically preserve their citizenship. See Altman, "Democratic Self-Determination and the Disenfranchisement of Felons"; also, more generally, Whitman, *Harsh Justice*.

24 This connects to the controversy over the treatment of persistent "dangerous" offenders: see further my *Punishment, Communication and Community*, section 4.4.

25 See, for example, Golash, *Case Against Punishment*; Boonin, *Problem of Punishment*.

26 For key examples, see Christie, "Conflicts as Property," and *Limits to Pain*; Hulsman, "Critical Criminology and the Concept of Crime," and "Abolitionist Case"; Bianchi, *Justice as Sanctuary*.

27 For useful surveys, see Braithwaite, "Restorative Justice"; Johnstone, *Restorative Justice*; von Hirsch et al., *Restorative Justice and Criminal Justice*; Johnstone and van Ness, *Handbook of Restorative Justice*. I have argued elsewhere that restoration should be pursued through retribution; see my "Restoration and Retribution," and "Responsibility, Restoration and Retribution."

28 I have tried to explicate some of their central elements in *Punishment, Communication and Community*, *Answering for Crime*, and "Towards a Theory of Criminal Law."

29 Assuming, of course, that the law is involved at all: we could decide to settle the matter informally between us, as advocates of restorative justice would urge.

30 See Bergelson, *Victims' Rights and Victims' Wrongs*, for an argument that this contrast cannot be quite so sharply drawn; in response, see my "Responsible Victims and (Partly) Justified Offenders."

31 The analytical distinction drawn here between civil and criminal responses is in various ways blurred in our actual systems: for instance, by the provisions for compensation or reparation orders following a criminal conviction (see Walker and Padfield, *Sentencing*, 245–50; Crime and Disorder Act 1998, s. 67); by provisions for "punitive damages" in civil cases (see Markel, "Retributive Damages" and "How Should Punitive Damages Work?"); and by the provisions that exist for private prosecutions. See also Duff and Marshall, "Public and Private Wrongs."

32 In explanatory support of this claim, see my *Answering for Crime*, ch. 4.

33 See for example Walgrave, "Restoration and Punishment"; "Imposing Restoration Instead of Inflicting Pain."

34 The family of a man who died because of a negligent overdose accepted £40,000 compensation: while one of his sons said, "We always knew there was not much money involved. It is about making sure changes are implemented," the solicitor called the money "a derisory sum for loss of life" (http://www.guardian.co.uk/ society/2010/may/23/family-man-killed-gp-overdose-compensation).

35 There is of course very much more to be said about what can and what cannot be compensated; for a useful start, see Goodin, "Theories of Compensation."

36 Sometimes, as in the quotation from the son in note 34 above, the avowed aim is (also) to prevent any future recurrence of such accidents or errors.

37 Our libel laws can be understood, and criticized, in this light: although a libel suit must formally be a claim for damages for consequential harm that the plaintiff claims to have suffered, the proper aim of such legal actions is to defend one's good name by calling the libelers to account for what they have published.

38 For this normative conception of what the criminal trial should be, see Duff et al., *The Trial on Trial Vol. III: Towards a Normative Theory of the Criminal Trial*. On the distinction between offenses and defenses, see my *Answering for Crime*, especially chs. 1, 9.

39 See, for example Moore, *Placing Blame*, ch. 1.

40 Compare Feinberg's classic development of the harm principle (*Harm to Others*).

41 To which consequentialists would reply that we should use criminal law only when it is an efficient method of preventing the relevant harms, see, for example, Braithwaite, *Restorative Justice and Responsive Regulation*.

42 Including education and "situational crime prevention," for instance (but on the latter see von Hirsch et al, *Ethical and Social Perspectives on Situational Crime Prevention*).

43 "Critical" theorists (e.g., Norrie, *Crime Reason and History*) object that a focus on individual responsibility distortingly abstracts individuals from the social contexts which generated their crimes. The answer is that such abstraction is an important aspect of the limited ambitions of a liberal criminal law.

44 See Christie, "Conflicts as Property." For an interesting counter-argument in the context of prosecuting domestic violence, see Dempsey, *Prosecuting Domestic Violence*, especially chs. 8–9. On the idea that victims should have more say over whether "their" offenders are prosecuted, see Duff and Marshall, "Public and Private Wrongs," 80–85.

45 Not just in paving the way to punishment, but also in attempting to get the offender to confront what he has done, and thus to affect his future conduct.

46 On some of the ways in which this happens, see Feeley, *Process is the Punishment*.

47 On "hard treatment," see Feinberg, "The Expressive Function of Punishment." The label might mislead, if it suggests that what we impose must be something oppressively painful, like imprisonment: but punishment should more often involve less oppressive burdens, such as probation or community service.

48 See, for example, Lipkin, "Punishment, Penance and Respect for Autonomy"; Baker, "Consequentialism, Punishment and Autonomy." For a sophisticated revision of this idea, making deterrence firmly secondary to censure, see von Hirsch, Censure and Sanctions, ch. 2. For another subtle version, see Matravers, *Justice and Punishment*. For critical discussion, see Bottoms, "Five Puzzles in von Hirsch's Theory of Punishment," and my *Punishment, Communication and Community*, ch. 3.3.

49 For an interesting exception, see Adler, *Urgings of Conscience*. See also Markel, "State, Be Not Proud," "Executing Retributivism," and his chapter in this volume; Markel and Flanders, "Bentham on Stilts," for a retributivist account of punishment as communicative.

50 Punishment as thus understood is best exemplified by such sentences as probation and community service, rather than by imprisonment, especially when their content is focused on the implications of the crime or on the problems (such as drug addiction) that provided its immediate background.

51 For versions of this kind of account, see Garvey, "Punishment as Atonement"; Tudor, "Accepting One's Punishment as Meaningful Suffering"; my *Punishment, Communication and Community*.

52 See, for example, Bennett, *Apology Ritual*; Radzik, *Making Amends*; and further references cited in Smith, "Kantian Restorative Justice?" (discussing both Radzik and Bennett).

53 See further my *Punishment, Communication and Community*, ch. 4.

54 Thanks to Dan Markel for helpful comments on an earlier version of this paper.

Bibliography

Adler, Jacob. *The Urgings of Conscience*. Philadelphia: Temple University Press, 1992.

Altman, Andrew. "Democratic Self-Determination and the Disenfranchisement of Felons." *Journal of Applied Philosophy* 22 (2005): 263–73.

Baker, Brenda M. "Consequentialism, Punishment and Autonomy." In *Retributivism and Its Critics*, edited by Wesley Cragg, 149–61. Stuttgart: Franz Steiner, 1992.

Bennett, Christopher J. *The Apology Ritual: A Philosophical Theory of Punishment*. Cambridge: Cambridge University Press, 2008.

Bergelson, Vera. *Victims' Rights and Victims' Wrongs: Comparative Liability in Criminal Law*. Stanford, CA: Stanford University Press, 2009.

Bianchi, Herman. *Justice as Sanctuary: Toward a New System of Crime Control*. Bloomington, IN: Indiana University Press, 1994.

Boonin, David. *The Problem of Punishment*. Cambridge: Cambridge University Press, 2008.

Bottoms, Anthony E. "Five Puzzles in von Hirsch's Theory of Punishment." In *Fundamentals of Sentencing Theory*, edited by Andrew Ashworth and Martin Wasik, 53–100. Oxford: Oxford University Press, 1998.

Braithwaite, John. *Restorative Justice and Responsive Regulation*. Oxford: Oxford University Press, 2002.

Braithwaite, John. "Restorative Justice: Assessing Optimistic and Pessimistic Accounts." In *Crime and Justice: A Review of Research* 25 (1999): 1–127.

Braithwaite, John and Philip Pettit. *Not Just Deserts: A Republican Theory of Criminal Justice*. Oxford: Oxford University Press, 1990.

Bronsteen, John, Christopher J. Buccafusco, and Jonathan S. Masur. "Happiness and Punishment." *University of Chicago Law Review* 76 (2009): 1037–81.

Christie, Nils. "Conflicts as Property." *British Journal of Criminology* 17 (1977): 1–15.

Christie, Nils. *Limits to Pain*. London: Martin Robertson, 1981.

Cottingham, John G. "Varieties of Retribution." *Philosophical Quarterly* 29 (1979): 238–46.

Dagger, Richard. *Civic Virtues*. Oxford: Oxford University Press, 1997.

Dempsey, Michelle M. *Prosecuting Domestic Violence: A Philosophical Analysis*. Oxford: Oxford University Press, 2009.

Dolinko, David. "Some Thoughts about Retributivism." *Ethics* 101 (1991): 537–59.

Duff, R.A. *Answering for Crime*. Oxford: Hart Publishing, 2007.

Duff, R.A. *Punishment, Communication and Community*. New York: Oxford University Press, 2001.

Duff, R.A. "Responsibility, Restoration and Retribution." In *Retributivism Has a Past: Has it a Future?*, edited by Michael Tonry. Oxford: Oxford University Press, in press.

Duff, R.A. "Responsible Victims and (Partly) Justified Offenders." *Ohio State Journal of Criminal Law* 8 (2011), in press.

Duff, R.A. "Restoration and Retribution." In *Restorative Justice and Criminal Justice: Competing or Reconcilable Paradigms?*, edited by Andrew von Hirsch et al., 43–60. Oxford: Hart Publishing, 2003.

Duff, R.A. "Towards a Theory of Criminal Law?" *Proceedings of the Aristotelian Society* (Supplementary Volume) 84 (2010): 1–28.

Duff, R.A. *Trials and Punishments*. Cambridge: Cambridge University Press, 1986.

Duff, R.A, Lindsay Farmer, Sandra Marshall, and Victor Tadros. *The Trial on Trial, Volume 3: Towards a Normative Theory of the Criminal Trial*. Oxford: Hart Publishing, 2007.

Duff, R. A, and Sandra Marshall. "Public and Private Wrongs." In *Essays in Criminal Law in Honour of Sir Gerald Gordon*, edited by James Chalmers. Edinburgh: Edinburgh University Press, 2010: 70–85.

Dworkin, Ronald M. *A Matter of Principle.* Cambridge, MA: Harvard University Press, 1985.

Dworkin, Ronald M. "Liberal Community." *California Law Review* 77 (1989): 479–504.

Feeley, Malcolm M. *The Process is the Punishment: Handling Cases in a Lower Criminal Court.* 2nd ed. New York: Russell Sage Foundation, 1992.

Feinberg, Joel. "The Expressive Function of Punishment." In *Doing and Deserving,* 95–118. Princeton: Princeton University Press, 1970.

Feinberg, Joel. *Harm to Others.* New York: Oxford University Press, 1984.

Feinberg, Joel. *Harmless Wrongdoing.* New York: Oxford University Press, 1988.

Garvey, S. "Punishment as Atonement." *UCLA Law Review* 47 (1999): 1801–58.

Golash, Deirdre. *The Case Against Punishment.* New York: New York University Press, 2005.

Goldman, Alan H. "The Paradox of Punishment." *Philosophy and Public Affairs* 9 (1979):42–58.

Goldman, Alan H. "Toward a New Theory of Punishment." *Law and Philosophy* 1 (1982): 57–76.

Goodin, R. E. "Theories of Compensation." In *Liability and Responsibility: Essays in Law and Morals,* edited by R.G. Frey and Christopher W. Morris, 257–89. Cambridge: Cambridge University Press, 1991.

Gray, David. "Punishment as Suffering." *Vanderbilt Law Review* 64 (2010), in press/

Hampton, Jean. "The Moral Education Theory of Punishment." *Philosophy and Public Affairs* 13 (1984): 208–38.

Hart, H. L. A. *Punishment and Responsibility.* Oxford: Oxford University Press, 1968.

Hulsman, Louk. "The Abolitionist Case: Alternative Crime Policies." *Israel Law Review* 25 (1991): 681–709.

Hulsman, Louk. "Critical Criminology and the Concept of Crime." *Contemporary Crises* 10 (1986): 63–80.

Husak, Douglas N. "Why Punish the Deserving?" *Nous* 26 (1992): 447–64.

Johnstone, Gerry. *Restorative Justice: Ideas, Values, Debates.* Cullompton, Devon: Willan, 2002.

Johnstone, Gerry, and van Ness, Donald W. (eds.). *Handbook of Restorative Justice.* Cullompton, Devon: Willan, 2006.

Kolber, Adam. "The Subjective Experience of Punishment." *Columbia Law Review* 109 (2009): 182–236.

Lacey, Nicola. *State Punishment.* London: Routledge, 1988.

Lipkin, Robert J. "Punishment, Penance and Respect for Autonomy." *Social Theory and Practice* 14 (1988): 87–104.

Markel, Dan. "Executing Retributivism: Panetti and the Future of the Eighth Amendment." *Northwestern Law Review* 103 (2009): 1163–222.

Markel, Dan. "How Should Punitive Damages Work?" *University of Pennsylvania Law Review* 157 (2009): 1383–484.

Markel, Dan. "Retributive Damages: A Theory of Punitive Damages as Intermediate Sanction." *Cornell University Law Review* 94 (2009): 239–340.

Markel, Dan. "State, Be Not Proud: A Retributivist Defense of the Commutation of Death Row and the Abolition of the Death Penalty." *Harvard Civil Rights-Civil Liberties Law Review* 40 (2005): 407–80.

Markel, Dan, and Chad Flanders. "Bentham on Stilts: The Bare Relevance of Subjectivity to Retributive Justice." *California Law Review* 98 (2010): 907–88.

Matravers, Matt. *Justice and Punishment: The Rationale of Coercion.* Oxford: Oxford University Press, 2000.

Moore, Michael S. *Placing Blame: A Theory of Criminal Law*. Oxford: Oxford University Press, 1997.

Morison, John. "Hart's Excuses: Problems with a Compromise Theory of Punishment." In *The Jurisprudence of Orthodoxy: Queen's University Essays on H. L. A. Hart*, edited by Philip Leith and Peter Ingram, 117–46. London: Routledge, 1988.

Morris, Christopher W. "Punishment and Loss of Moral Standing." *Canadian Journal of Philosophy* 21 (1991): 53–79.

Morris, Herbert. "A Paternalistic Theory of Punishment." *American Philosophical Quarterly* 18 (1981): 263–71.

Morris, Norval. *The Future of Imprisonment*. Chicago: University of Chicago Press, 1974.

Morris, Norval, and Tonry, Michael. *Between Prison and Probation: Intermediate Punishments in a Rational Sentencing System*. New York: Oxford University Press, 1990.

Murphy, Jeffrie G. "Marxism and Retribution." *Philosophy and Public Affairs* 2 (1973): 217–43.

Norrie, Alan W. *Crime, Reason and History*. 2nd ed. London: Butterworths, 2001.

Pettit, Philip. *Republicanism: A Theory of Freedom and Government*. Oxford: Oxford University Press, 1999.

Radzik, Linda. *Making Amends: Atonement in Morality, Law and Politics*. New York: Cambridge University Press, 2009.

Reydams, Luc. *Universal Jurisdiction: International and Municipal Legal Perspectives*. Oxford: Oxford University Press, 2003.

Shafer-Landau, Russ. "The Failure of Retributivism." *Philosophical Studies* 82 (1996): 289–316.

Smith, Nick. "Kantian Restorative Justice?" *Criminal Justice Ethics* 29 (2010): 54–69.

Tudor, Steven K. "Accepting One's Punishment as Meaningful Suffering." *Law and Philosophy* 20 (2001): 581–604.

von Hirsch, Andrew. *Censure and Sanctions*. Oxford: Oxford University Press, 1993.

von Hirsch, Andrew and Andrew Ashworth. *Proportionate Sentencing: Exploring the Principles*. Oxford: Oxford University Press, 2005.

von Hirsch, Andrew, David Garland, and Alison Wakefield (eds.). *Ethical and Social Perspectives on Situational Crime Prevention*. Oxford: Hart Publishing, 2000.

von Hirsch, Andrew, et al. (eds.). *Restorative Justice and Criminal Justice: Competing or Reconcilable Paradigms?* Oxford: Hart Publishing, 2003.

Walgrave, Lode. "Imposing Restoration Instead of Inflicting Pain." In *Restorative Justice and Criminal Justice*, edited by von Hirsch et al, 61–78. Oxford: Hart Publishing, 2003.

Walgrave, Lode. "On Restoration and Punishment. On Favourable Similarities and Fortunate Differences." In *Restoring Justice for Juveniles: Conferencing, Mediation & Circles*, edited by *Allison Morris and Gabrielle Maxwell*, 17–37. Oxford: Hart Publishing, 2001.

Walker, Nigel. *Why Punish?* Oxford: Oxford University Press, 1991.

Walker, Nigel, and Nicola Padfield. *Sentencing: Theory, Law and Practice*. 2nd ed. London: Butterworths, 1996.

Whitman, James Q. *Harsh Justice: Criminal Punishment and the Widening Divide between America and Europe*. Oxford: Oxford University Press, 2003.

2

PUNISHMENT PLURALISM

Michael T. Cahill

THE PRESENT STATE of punishment theory is ambiguous but seems to hold the promise of a potential emerging consensus. It once seemed as if the two leading so-called theories of punishment, retributivism and utilitarianism, were fundamentally at odds, and support for each would rise and fall. To crudely generalize, the postwar generation of theorists were of a firmly utilitarian (specifically, rehabilitationist) bent, rejecting retribution as atavistic or uncivilized; the following generation witnessed a renaissance of retributivism, both defending its moral validity and critiquing the practical and normative failings of the utilitarian project. Scholarship in the most recent generation, however, has bridged or blurred what once seemed to be a firm boundary between these two basic orientations. On one side, theorists generally sympathetic to retributivism have questioned its ability to provide a comprehensive justification or agenda for punishment[1]; on the other, work focused on deterrence has shifted from a "law and economics" approach toward a "law and norms" approach that recognizes the importance of social norms or moral values (such as retribution or desert) to even a purely crime-control-based agenda.[2] In the middle, many have proposed a hybrid model of "limiting retributivism" that explicitly purports to combine aspects of both of the canonical theories.[3]

So perhaps we are entering a world where disagreements about the purposes of punishment, serious though they may be, exist within a broadly shared theoretical accord, recognizing some significant role for both retributive and preventive considerations. In other words, perhaps the ascendant view of punishment is more openly *pluralistic* about its purposes and its proper constraints.[4] I favor such a view and suspect at least some others do as well, yet there seems to be little current dialogue regarding exactly what considerations such an account is to weigh and how it is to weigh them. One purpose of this chapter, then, is to elaborate on various considerations that might inform such a pluralistic view—not for the sake of defending all (or any) of them, but merely for the sake of identifying them in a fairly comprehensive way, as a relatively modest first step toward assessing which concerns a pluralistic account should prioritize, maximize, deemphasize, or reject altogether. If we are all pluralists now, this provides one means of starting a further conversation about what form of pluralism is best.

Alternatively, however, perhaps pluralism is not (or not yet) the dominant view, even at the most basic conceptual level, which will make it harder to deal with the more obviously contentious issues of what a pluralistic account should value, and how much. Many theorists seem to resist any claim that we have reached a new era or that the divide between retributivism and utilitarianism has narrowed or been spanned—even while, in many cases, remaining somewhat coy about whether (and if so, why) they themselves remain committed to one or the other perspective.[5] Accordingly, another purpose of this chapter is to set out the pluralist position and see whether any response or opposition is forthcoming. If we are *not* all pluralists now, it would advance the conversation for any avowedly monistic theorists to identify themselves and explain why they find a unitary theory of punishment compelling or useful.

Given my uncertainty as to the current scholarly landscape, I am unsure whether to characterize this chapter's underlying premise as a descriptive speculation that we might indeed all (or mostly) be pluralists now or as a normative claim that we should be. In either case, it may be useful to step back and explain why a pluralistic account might be preferable to a unitary one.

First, a bit of clarification. Retributivism and utilitarianism are commonly labeled the two leading "theories of punishment," but this characterization is somewhat misleading.[6] Retributive and utilitarian concerns with, respectively, desert and crime control (or harm prevention) offer *justifications* for punishment, but a justification for a practice is not the same as a full-fledged theory of when and how to engage in that practice. Even the term "justification" can mislead, for neither retributivism nor utilitarianism offers a *complete* justification of punishment, either as a social practice or in individual cases. Rather, they provide responses to a particular objection to punishment: that it causes pain or suffering.[7] Against various other objections to punishment—say, that it violates fundamental rights, or that it exhausts resources better used elsewhere—the retributive or utilitarian "theories" have little to say.

Except where a contrary meaning is obviously intended, this chapter will typically use the term "punishment" as shorthand to refer to the state criminal-justice apparatus charged with defining and implementing rules for the imposition of punishment. In other words, "punishment" here means a set of actual institutions and practices rather than a conceptual category. In related fashion, the notion of a "punishment theory" as used here will mean a theory of *what, how,* and *how much* to punish as well as whether or why to do so. The position advanced here is that such a theory should be pluralistic as to each of these questions and is thus distinct from certain hybrid theories that would use different considerations to answer different questions.[8]

It seems more appropriate to say that desert and harm prevention are *reasons* to punish, and that their absence might provide a reason, strong or weak, *not* to punish. And they are both good reasons to punish: that is, I take it as a mark in favor of an instance of punishment that it either (1) gives an offender what he or she deserves, or (2) will prevent future harm. It is even better if an instance of punishment does both of these things— which is arguably the case in the vast majority of instances of actual punishment[9] and not by coincidence or accident. Yet even this (to my mind) trite observation is obscured by adopting or supporting a "theory" of punishment that looks solely to one or the other reason, effectively discounting to zero the value of the disfavored reason,[10] as a basis for defending punishment generally or for exploring particular issues relating to what or how or how much to punish.

There is nothing wrong with punishment being overdetermined in some cases, in the sense that there are multiple bases for pursuing it[11]: indeed, the criminal justice system should strive to recognize and to focus its efforts on exactly those cases. At the same time, even in those cases, there remain multiple reasons *against* pursuing punishment, including the "original" or fundamental objection that it causes suffering, which remains a noteworthy consideration even where it does not decisively militate against imposing punishment. No unitary theory can provide or, for that matter, tries to provide an all-things-considered account of when the state should punish and when it should refrain from punishing. Yet such an account is exactly what any sensible policy maker or discretionary agent in the criminal justice system would want to make sound decisions. What is needed is either a more comprehensive theory or an open embrace of incomplete theorization.

This chapter aims to take the first step toward an all-things-considered account by seeking to survey all the things that are to be considered, both at the systemic level and in individual cases. In doing so, it does not claim that every noted consideration should or must be taken seriously in all cases, or even in any case, but merely trying to get on the table all of the plausible candidates for criteria to inform decisions about punishment. Where necessary or useful, the discussion will also point out why it might be inaccurate or unhelpful to claim that a given consideration should be categorical or decisive, as opposed to being merely one factor among many that contribute to an assessment of the appropriateness or desirability of punishment.

The first section identifies and explains considerations favoring punishment, and the following section identifies and explains considerations opposing it. Both of these sections distinguish principled claims about the intrinsic goodness or badness of punishment from instrumental claims about its usefulness toward achieving some other goal and, as to the instrumental claims, identify the other goal (or goals) that punishment is thought to help achieve. The third section provides a preliminary analysis of some of the conflicts among these various concerns that a full-fledged, pluralistic account of punishment would need to adjudicate.

1. Reasons to Punish

Before surveying possible reasons in favor of punishment, it is worth noting that some features of a system of punishment do not truly provide reasons in favor of the erection of such a system. For example, though a criminal justice system requires employment of numerous workers, job creation is not itself a valid reason to establish or maintain such a system. Unless the criminal justice system is achieving some other worthwhile objective, its use for creating jobs is not enough to provide any basis for its existence, since the same purpose could be served simply by paying people to dig holes and fill them in again. This discussion aims to survey the considerations that might favor punishment, *qua* punishment, over some other possible practice. Yet even in situations where punishment itself may serve some genuine end, it is, of course, worth remembering that other means may be as, or more, effective in achieving that end. For example, the educational system may promote socialization or moral instruction as, or more, effectively (or cost effectively) as criminal punishment.

Like anything else, punishment may be "good" in two senses: it may be proper or desirable in and of itself (that is, intrinsically good), or it may be useful in promoting some other purpose (that is, instrumentally good). This section will discuss, in turn, the extent to which punishment may provide each of these types of good.

A. PUNISHMENT AS INTRINSIC GOOD

Some accounts of punishment assert that it is intrinsically good on the ground that, and only insofar as, it achieves *retributive justice*. The argument is typically, though not always, that punishment gives an offender what s/he deserves.[12] Punishment is not only a suitable but a necessary means of pursuing the goal of desert; the claim is that punishment is the *only* means of effectuating the relevant interest and providing a fitting response to the offender's wrongdoing. This claim is associated with so-called *positive* retributivism; the distinct claim of negative retributivism—which provides a reason *not* to punish rather than a claim favoring punishment—is discussed in the next section.[13]

A few introductory issues present themselves. First, it is not entirely clear whether the desert principle calls for wrongdoers to experience *punishment* or *suffering*.[14] Punishment tends to produce suffering but for the desert theorist, is this suffering only a side effect of punishment, or is it the very purpose of punishment? A wrongdoer may also suffer without being punished: if a reckless driver severely injures himself in an accident that also kills another (or, for that matter, is injured by another in a later accident), do we count those injuries on the desert ledger, or are they irrelevant? This question is not entirely resolved, though it has been noted recently that the desert-as-suffering claim seems to generate some troubling or dubious results.[15]

Second, if punishing the bad is meant to satisfy a principle of desert, shouldn't the same principle also demand rewarding the good?[16] If not, why not? The philosophy literature discusses various forms of desert, good and bad,[17] but retributivist criminal-law literature concentrates on punishment for ill desert with little discussion of whether legal or political systems also have a similar (or even conjoined) duty to reward positive desert.[18]

Finally, it is important to distinguish a few different reasons why retribution or desert is thought to be justified or desirable. Probably most self-proclaimed retributivists argue that desert is a moral principle, though of course they disagree about the exact demands or contours of that principle.[19] Others, however, offer a sort of political defense of retribution in which the practice of imposing retributive punishment is justified for its embodiment or fulfillment of certain aspects or goals of a flourishing polity. These two groups might roughly be associated with *moral retributivism* and *legal retributivism,* though the labels may be inexact.[20] Two additional positions favoring retributive punishment view it as an instrumental rather than an intrinsic good and are therefore discussed in the next section. One view is that retributive punishment promotes crime control; the other is that it provides pleasure or utility, much like the satisfaction of any other preference.

1. Retribution as Moral Commitment

Retributivist defenses of deserved punishment may claim that it is morally good or proper or, more strongly, that it is morally obligatory—in other words, that there is a moral duty to impose deserved punishment. The first of these characterizations does not itself justify punishment but fits naturally within a pluralistic account, providing a significant though not controlling argument in favor of it. The second characterization fits less comfortably with a pluralistic account insofar as it prioritizes the asserted moral duty to punish over other concerns—though it might note the significance of other concerns as well[21] and might not treat the duty to punish as indefeasible.

For reasons set out in more detail elsewhere,[22] I find the first characterization, retribution as good, compelling—and the second, retribution as duty, unpersuasive—for purposes of developing a theory of criminal justice. Stated simply, the moral-duty view seems patently unworkable and probably affirmatively undesirable as it leads to real-world outcomes that nobody would want. If a moral duty demands that we punish every known offender to the full extent of that person's desert, neither police nor prosecutors would be able to forgo some or all punishment of some known offenders, even for the sake of pursuing other more serious ones, which seems counterproductive in terms of the desert goal standing alone. Beyond the practical difficulties, the general nature of the absolutist moral obligation is such that it creates an odd prioritization of known, identified offenders (whom the state must punish) over yet-undiscovered offenders (toward whom no such obligation has formed). Basing the state's punishment agenda on the happenstance of those criminals it has already found versus those it might find later seems hard to defend in any principled way and also might lead to perverse or distorted enforcement or prosecutorial incentives. To the extent the retribution-as-duty view accommodates these concerns by rendering the putative duty to punish increasingly defeasible, it starts to resemble the retribution-as-good view, which more explicitly recognizes the need to balance retribution against other goods and values.[23]

2. Retribution as Political Practice

Retribution is sometimes presented as a sort of political good or practice rather than a purely moral good. For example, R.A. Duff describes a communicative model in which punishment is a "calling to account" before the community, as embodied by the relevant governmental institutions charged with imposing criminal justice, which then helps reintegrate the offender into that community—partially by means of the offender's acceptance of the punishment itself. Punishment also communicates social norms and the state's authoritative support of them to victims and the community generally, strengthening social and political bonds.[24] Dan Markel's theory posits liberal democracy as a precondition to legitimate retribution but also says that retribution can, in turn, bolster and fulfill the ideals of liberal democracy. From his account, offenders are held *morally* responsible for violating a *legal* norm (at least so long as the norm is consistent with liberal values), rather than the other way around, and are also punished to vindicate interests in equality (similar to those discussed in the next subsection) and to preserve the authority and legitimacy of the state.[25]

Note that although Duff and Markel have particular views about the nature and justification of both retribution and legitimate government, the nature and validity of those views are not significant for present purposes. Whatever is thought to make political institutions legitimate, or however the relevant community is defined, the point here is that one possible defense of punishment is as a practice that advances political values. (Indeed, even Duff and Markel or others advancing the same view need not articulate an explanation of what makes state institutions legitimate but may simply assert that punishment can protect and advance the stability or authority of a state or community stipulated to be legitimate. Of course, they are also free to provide an explanation of what, in their view, generates such legitimacy.)

This consideration only justifies punishment if the community decides it is appropriate; it does not seem to offer an independent account that would support punishment where the community opposes it. That is, it provides a defense of punishment without saying much, if anything, about what in particular to punish—that question is to be answered by the community, through the political process. Where the community itself takes the position that retribution is not important or that some other nonpunishment mechanism or remedy can achieve the community's goals just as well, it is unclear whether any "outside" reason, extrinsic to the community's own preferences, could be relied on to support punishment. Unlike a pluralistic account of punishment, which might offer a basis for judging the substantive merits of various punishment decisions, this account focuses on the legitimacy of the process generating those decisions.

At the same time, however, this view of retribution need not simply ratify any community decision about what to punish. It might still recognize that some or all of the considerations set out in the next section might provide valid reasons *not* to punish, either in individual cases or across the board, notwithstanding the considerations favoring punishment. Indeed, for example, Markel's liberalism-constrained view of retributivism commits him to endorsing some of those limitations.

3. Corrective Justice (Restitution)

A final way in which punishment might serve as an intrinsic good is if it achieves some form of corrective justice or restitution, as opposed to retributive justice. One version of this sees punishment as correcting the balance between the offender and the victim s/he has wronged. (Of course, this would only apply to crimes with one or more identifiable victims.) This is sometimes called *restorative justice*,[26] but that term seems to capture a combination of the intrinsic good asserted here (assuming such a good exists) and a purely instrumental good of making victims feel better; the latter component is discussed below. A second version sees punishment as correcting the balance between the offender and other members of society generally: by violating the rules that others respect, acting as if those rules do not apply to him, the offender has usurped power or status that is not properly his and must right the situation by accepting punishment, thus restoring the offender's equality to others.[27] The latter account is sometimes labeled a version of retributivism by its adherents or others, though it has a different flavor, as it seems rooted in a principle of "fair play" or political equality under law, rather than moral desert. The offender must make restitution to the community for a violation of the legal rules that all have agreed to respect, rather than for committing a moral wrong. This account might offer a better basis for treating punishment as an intrinsic good, even for *malum prohibitum* offenses.

B. PUNISHMENT AS INSTRUMENTAL GOOD

1. Harm Prevention

A *consequentialist* agenda is one that orients itself toward achieving some future goal, as opposed to redressing or correcting a past wrong, which is one common motivation— though, as noted below, not the only possible motivation—of a desert-based system of criminal law. The classic consequentialist is the *utilitarian* or welfarist, for whom justice is important, if at all, not as an end in itself but only as a means of increasing social welfare; specifically, criminal rules and their enforcement are expected to promote welfare by reducing the amount of crime in society. Ideally, under this view, the mere threat of punishment would be enough to minimize crime, for this would secure the benefit of prevention without necessitating the cost of punishment. But where the threat fails, punishment itself might in appropriate instances generate some marginal contribution to crime reduction. Note that the threat of punishment might also be supported as a means of promoting compliance with noncriminal rules. For example, failure to obey certain civil regulatory requirements might be criminalized, not because the failure is itself thought worthy of punishing, but as leverage to induce compliance with or facilitate enforcement of the civil rules.[28] Perhaps even more than with other rules, the threat here is more valuable and more defensible than any actual punishment that would need to be imposed: in this case, the punishment would be purely for the sake of maintaining the threat's credibility.

In the area of criminal law, three methods have traditionally been relied on as tools to advance the broad overall goal of crime reduction. *Deterrence* seeks to dissuade, in advance, those who may contemplate committing a crime in the future. An ideal, per-fectly effective system of deterrent rules would need no enforcement, as the mere threat of sanction would prevent potential crimes from ever occurring. *Rehabilitation* aims to transform those who were formerly motivated to commit crimes into law-abiding citi-zens. Unlike deterrence, rehabilitative efforts are typically applied, after the fact, to people who have already committed crimes, although in principle, there is no reason they need be so limited. Failing those two goals, a utilitarian system will also pursue *incapacitation*, to remove from society those who have shown themselves to be dangerous, undeterred by threat of punishment, and resistant to rehabilitation. Here again, the usual method is to incapacitate those who have already offended and are likely to do so again. But in the abstract, there is no reason this method could not be used to incapacitate dangerous people before they commit any crime at all (indeed, such a tactic would be superior from a utilitarian perspective, as it would avoid the social cost of the first crime).

More recent work has argued that a distribution of punishment in accordance with lay intuitions of desert might achieve greater crime control than reliance on the classic utili-tarian tools. The claim of this *desert-utilitarian* school is that the greatest power to gain compliance with society's rules of prescribed conduct lies not in the threat or reality of official criminal sanction but in the power of social and individual moral norms.[29] The law, criminal law in particular, plays a central role in creating and maintaining the social consensus necessary for sustaining those moral norms, thereby contributing to and har-nessing the compliance-producing power of interpersonal relationships and personal morality. Further, if the criminal law gains a reputation for being just, people are more likely to defer to its commands as morally authoritative and appropriate to follow in those borderline cases where the propriety of certain conduct is unsettled or ambiguous. The extent of the criminal law's effectiveness in promoting compliance and controlling crime depends greatly, according to this view, on the degree of moral credibility that the criminal law possesses for the citizens it governs—that is, the extent to which it accords with their own sense of just punishment.

Imposing what is seen as deserved punishment may also prevent crime or harm in a more direct way, not by encouraging compliance and law-abiding behavior but by obviating vigilantism or preventing some other harmful outraged response to the very failure to impose punishment in a particular case. Indeed, the practice of entrusting punishment to the state may have arisen because it was simply thought more effective or efficient than the preexisting scheme of private retaliation—all too often followed by reprisal and escalation.[30]

2. Moral Education

A different account of punishment sees it not merely as a means of promoting good *behavior* but, perhaps more aspirationally, as a means of promoting good *character*. This position is sometimes described, by its proponents or critics, as a *virtue-ethics* or an *aretaic* account of punishment.[31] The benefit of character development might inure to the person being punished, or to others, such as the public generally. The idea of punishment as a mechanism for advancing virtue, or good character, might seem to merely replicate the utilitarian goal of discouraging harmful or criminal conduct—or perhaps the stronger, but still utilitarian, goal of promoting socially beneficial conduct. This need not be the case, however; aretaic theories can and do claim—and if they are to provide a truly independent basis for punishment must claim—that punishment can be desirable for reasons other than its promotion of social welfare.

Jean Hampton has suggested one version of such a theory, defending punishment (including specifically retributive punishment) as a means for advancing goals external to the punishment itself: specifically, moral education.[32] This view, as least as endorsed by Hampton, is nuanced and complex, for she adopts a "pluralist approach" that also involves a commitment to retribution as an intrinsic good.[33] Yet of course it is also clear that this view provides an instrumental rather than intrinsic reason to punish. There are other means available to promote the end of moral education, and this account does not offer a basis for pursuing punishment where another means will effectuate the moral-education objective just as well.

On some civic-republican accounts, the overall process of determining what kinds of conduct are sufficiently wrongful to merit punishment—the conversation, as distinct from the rules or individual instances of punishment resulting from that conversation—might itself provide a form of moral education for the community. It might also, somewhat in keeping with the Duff or Markel accounts of retribution, generate societal cohesion or better governance: social virtue, perhaps, as distinct from the virtue of individual members of society. Whether such a thing exists, of course, might be open to debate. It is possible, however, that other such conversations about how the law should address various social issues could serve the same or a similar function without discussing or implicating punishment.

Punishment may also enable not only moral education but also plain old education or training in a skill. Such rehabilitative efforts might make offenders more productive, just as moral education makes them better citizens (or better people). Yet education and training do not seem to be a benefit of punishment *qua* punishment; such benefits could presumably also be provided to the same population or others outside the context of punishment. Indeed, there are those who say it is unfair or inappropriate to provide such benefits in the context of punishment without making them equally available to others who are not being punished.[34] Education and training are benefits of punishment only insofar as punishment enables the education of people (1) who otherwise would resist it, and (2) derive additional marginal benefit from it relative to those who could obtain similar education outside the context of punishment.

3. Punishment as a Source of Pleasure

A final reason to punish is that it simply feels good. This is still an instrumental basis for punishment because the claim is that punishment is a means of creating pleasure, utility, happiness, or some other state considered normatively desirable. A version of this claim is perhaps most commonly made in the context of victims' rights or interests in punishment: that it gives the victim (or his or her family, etc.) satisfaction, or "closure," or some other benefit sometimes described as "justice," though it seems improper to use that term in an agent-relative way, as if justice is directed at, or exists for, someone in particular. Yet nonvictims may also obviously share this benefit or even enjoy the benefit where the victim does not: anyone might have a "taste" or preference for punishment.[35] Indeed, even the person being punished might take some satisfaction in it, whether it be a masochistic pleasure or a contemporaneous or retrospective sense that the punishment was appropriate or desirable.

The "taste" for punishment need not be a taste for justice. People might take pleasure in another's suffering or misfortune for good or bad reasons, and there might be a principled basis for arguing that such pleasure should be discounted or ignored entirely where its basis is objectionable. Yet there is at least some reason to think that, here as elsewhere, the utility or pleasure that a practice generates is at least a prima facie reason in favor of it—just as the displeasure or pain it generates is a prima facie reason against it, as the next section shall discuss.

2. Reasons Not to Punish

Some of the justifications for punishment set out in the first section also imply constraints or limitations on it, insofar as punishment is worthwhile if and only if it advances one or more of those justifications and not otherwise. Of course, this is just another way of saying that punishment is painful or costly, and that such pain or cost requires justification. Indeed, such pain or cost may provide a valid reason not to punish, even in some situations where punishment would generate one or more of those benefits, for punishment would be appropriate only in the absence of any alternative means of achieving a similar benefit without bearing the cost.

This section identifies the various potential negative aspects of imposing punishment, which bear not only on the question of whether to punish at all but on how much to punish since they are pertinent to decisions about any increment of punishment, whether the first or the last. Just as punishment (or anything else) may be intrinsically or instrumentally good, it may be intrinsically or instrumentally bad. I shall refer to arguments that punishment directly violates some normative principle as claims that it is *wrong* and to arguments that it generates some normatively undesirable outcome or effect as claims that punishment is *harmful*. One initial question raised by this organizational scheme is whether the standard "suffering objection" (the claim that punishment is presumptively improper because it causes suffering, which forms the basis for the hypothesized need to justify punishment[36]) fits into the former or latter category. It seems that retributivist and utilitarian accounts presuppose, or respond to, different formulations of that objection, one of which frames punishment as wrong and one of which frames it as harmful. That is, the retributivist defense of punishment essentially makes the claim that "punishment is *not* wrong" (where it satisfies the desert principle),[37] and the utilitarian defense essentially makes the claim that "punishment is justified *although* harmful," which are answers to two different questions. Retributivists would shrug at the objection that "punishment is harmful, though admittedly not wrong"— though it may be debatable whether this is because retributivism is untroubled by, or inadequate to address, that claim—while utilitarians would shrug at the objection that "punishment is wrong, though admittedly not harmful," finding it incoherent or preposterous. For present purposes, it is quite easy to treat these two formulations of the suffering objection as two different (and both legitimate) arguments against punishment, to be noted separately. Indeed, one possible advantage of a pluralistic account is that it need not get hung up on terminological questions of whether a negative attribute of punishment should be called a harm, or pain, or cost, or wrong—any downside of punishment is relevant, however labeled.

It is worth noting at the outset that the potential for *inaccuracy* might appear to provide a reason not to punish, but in fact does not. This is not an independent concern with punishment but must be derivative of some other concern; wrong outcomes are problematic only insofar as they generate one or more of the costs indicated below. If punishment were otherwise costless, its errors would be no more problematic than a consumer-preference algorithm that sometimes offered poor suggestions about what to add to one's Netflix queue. Of course, inaccuracy *is* a concern both in individual cases and in the aggregate, because (and to the extent that) punishment *does* involve serious costs of the varieties described below—including costs that arise specifically, or are more pronounced, in cases of wrongful punishment—and also because inaccurate results might reduce or eliminate the benefits of punishment (though some benefits, such as general deterrence, may be generated even by inaccurate instances of punishment). The same is true for *uncertainty* about the accuracy of punishment: its costs depend on the presence and degree of the various costs described below, including the costs that arise only when the system "gets it wrong." As uncertainty rises, the expected costs rise, and the expected benefits may diminish, but uncertainty is not itself a cost of punishment or of having a criminal justice system.

A. PUNISHMENT AS WRONG

1. Violation of Desert Principle

The principle of *negative retributivism* opposes imposition of undeserved punishment. The view is that punishing an innocent (in the sense of undeserving) person is not only harmful but morally wrong and, perhaps, categorically forbidden. In fact, the sense that negative retributivism imposes a categorical duty remains strong and apparently widely shared, even while, as discussed in the first section, the view of positive retribution as a duty (at least, as a categorical or indefeasible duty) appears to be on the wane. Mitchell Berman has recently noted that "retributivism has increasingly morphed into an account that rests upon a justificatory structure that is plainly consequentialist," but at the same time, even many who are consequentialists or instrumentalists about punishment "routinely accept that it is impermissible to knowingly punish the innocent."[38]

Does it make sense to view avoiding undeserved punishment as an absolute duty, or, like the goal of imposing deserved punishment, is it better seen as a good? The categorical-duty view has met with the critique that because any real-world system of punishment—even one based purely on desert—will inevitably have errors resulting in innocents being punished, the absolutist is bound by her own principles to refrain from creating a system of punishment.[39] Some retributivists have responded to this critique,[40] though their responses sometimes seem to soften the absolutist position and adopt some other version of retributivism, under which the duty to avoid undeserved punishment would no longer be categorical.[41] Further, the basis of the standard retributivist defense to this critique— that if the system did not knowingly or intentionally punish the innocent, it would violate no moral duty and would remain acceptable[42]—has been met with some skepticism.[43] There might be reason, then, to treat the negative-retribution goal, like the positive-retribution goal, as a (perhaps especially important or valuable) good rather than an absolute obligation. Importantly, even if negative-retribution considerations are held to impose a side constraint on permissible actions, this would limit the set of options available to a pluralistic scheme but would not contradict the possibility of such a scheme.[44]

2. Affront to Liberty, Dignity, or Autonomy of the Person Punished

Punishment might also violate other rights of the person punished, aside from the right to be free of undeserved punishment. For example, one might oppose the death penalty on

the ground that even if it is consistent with an offender's desert, it violates some independent commitment to human liberty, autonomy, or dignity. Some such basic rights may be
inalienable in that they may not be waived by the person whose rights are violated.[45] Such
independent values might oppose punishment of certain kinds of behavior (say, consensual sodomy), or oppose punishment of certain types of individuals (say, the incompetent),
or oppose use of some methods of punishment (say, torture), or oppose certain practices
or procedures as part of the investigative or adjudicatory process (say, invasions of privacy
or coerced confessions). Claims relating to the last of these considerations do not provide
reasons against punishment per se but reasons not to do other things that might lead to
punishment later—though often these considerations too are cashed out, via remedies
such as the Fourth Amendment exclusionary rule, in ways that have the transparent effect
of preventing punishment of a known offender. Further, privacy considerations may differ
from liberty interests in that avoidance of privacy violations ensures the rights of all, not
just those who avoid punishment. Privacy is thus not just a reason to avoid punishing a
particular person but a reason to organize the entire system in a certain way.

Again, these competing interests might be seen simply as considerations to be factored
into an overall analysis, or they might be seen as creating categorical obligations that,
where they apply, forbid punishment (or other rules or actions) without regard to its
potential benefits or to other concerns. If adopted, this position would have the same
effect as taking a categorical view toward negative retributivism: the relevant competing
interest(s) would impose a side constraint on the set of choices available within what
would remain a pluralistic approach to making punishment decisions.

3. Violation of Equality or Distributive Justice

Even if it does not violate the rights of the person punished directly, punishment may
violate a broader principled commitment to social equality or distributive justice.[46] For
example, although a person deserves punishment, and the punishment would not
improperly infringe on his human rights, it might be troubling that the punishment to be
imposed has the effect (or intent) of discriminating among different social groups. The
famous crack-versus-powder cocaine sentencing disparities provide an example: the issue
is not (exactly) that any individual convicted of possessing crack does not deserve the
allowed punishment, but that (1) the amount of punishment is disproportionate given
how others are treated,[47] and (2) the disparities lead to severe and unwarranted disparities
between the sentences imposed on members of different ethnic groups. Perhaps more
subtly, punishment may generate undesirable inequities by defining a category of individuals as "other," as the "criminal element," ineradicably different from the rest of us
law-abiding folk.

Measuring the relation between punishment and distributive justice may be more
complex than its relations to the desert principle or other rights, for those interests implicate the act of punishment itself, whereas a troubling inequity might be an *outcome* of
punishment that can be anticipated but cannot be measured in advance. To the extent the

concern is with a discriminatory or otherwise unjust *intent* rather than an *effect*, however, this complication does not arise.

4. Unwarranted Exercise of State Power

Other limitations on punishment might follow from a sense of the boundaries of state power. Often these boundaries are dictated by interests in personal freedom, as noted above. Some procedural protections are also designed to promote accuracy for the sake of avoiding other costs of punishment, such as the negative-retributive cost of punishing the innocent, also noted. Yet some of these limitations, or others, might also reflect an independent rationale that democratic self-governance requires certain rules and preconditions either for punishment to be legitimate, or for the state itself to be legitimate, or both. Whether or not they protect the innocent, promote individual rights, or help secure the various benefits of punishment, these rules may be thought necessary for the integrity of the system.

For example, the Fourth Amendment exclusionary rule has sometimes been defended as a means of deterring misconduct and sometimes as a necessary means of preserving the integrity of the judicial system. Likewise, rights to a speedy trial, rules against double jeopardy, and statutes of limitation might (or might not) promote accuracy but also might be considered necessary for the criminal justice system to be legitimate in some basic way. It has also been argued that the right to a jury trial should not be seen as an individual right but as a public right, a feature of democracy.[48] Some other rights may also be held unwaivable on the ground that they promote social interests that transcend the interest of the affected individual.[49]

Such concerns with the proper scope of governmental power are also reflected in the *legality principle*, which bars criminal prosecution in the absence of a prior written definition of the prohibited conduct expressed with some minimum of clarity and conciseness. This principle does not define a single legal rule but rather is the overarching rationale that forms the basis for a collection of related rules: the constitutional prohibition against ex post facto laws, the constitutional invalidation of vague offenses, the rule of strict construction of penal statutes (also called the rule of lenity), the statutory abolition of common-law offenses, and the bar to judicial creation of offenses.

To a certain extent, the justifications of the legality principle overlap with the goals of desert, deterrence, efficiency, and freedom already discussed. Clear, preexisting rules make citizens aware of the ones promoting deterrence; predictability in law makes it easier to administer. A sense that the system is playing fair may promote compliance for reasons similar to those supporting the desert-utilitarian position.[50] Yet legality may also reflect a distinct concern with the proper distribution of state power. Requiring a clear ex ante declaration of the law, typically through codification, allocates criminalization authority to the legislature, the most democratic branch of government, rather than enabling ex post lawmaking by the courts or granting undue discretion to executive-branch actors.

B. PUNISHMENT AS HARM

In addition to the various principled objections, punishment may be opposed or disfavored on the ground that it generates some real-world harm or cost, whether tangible or intangible.

1. Pain and Suffering

Whether the person being punished is innocent or guilty, punishment typically, and by design, will cause that person to experience harm, pain, and/or suffering. Whether such suffering is an intrinsic feature, central to the very conceptualization of punishment, or merely a (perhaps unfortunate) side effect of punishment, has been debated and can depend on one's position regarding the underlying purposes of punishment. As noted above, if punishment is motivated by the offender's ill desert, imposing pain and suffering may be the whole point; if punishment is motivated by crime prevention, suffering is an unfortunate cost that can and should be avoided or mitigated if possible.

Punishment can also cause pain and suffering to third parties, such as the family and friends of the person punished. Under any theory, this is seen as an unfortunate side effect that does not provide any benefit or fulfill any purpose, at least not directly; of course, it may generate ancillary positive effects such as additional deterrence if, say, potential criminals avoid crime not for their own benefit but for the sake of shielding their families from the pain of seeing them punished. This pain and suffering might also have additional ancillary costs, however, if family members' painful encounter with the criminal justice system undercuts its credibility or ability to impart useful moral education.

2. Economic or Other Social Cost

Punishment is not free; it costs money. Whether to punish, and how, and how much, are all questions that might be influenced by the financial cost of punishing. The adjudicative system that determines punishment and the correctional system that imposes it create direct costs and also opportunity costs, as time and money are dedicated to criminal justice rather than other things. Depending on its form, punishment may also create opportunity costs for the person punished: someone serving a prison sentence loses the chance to be a productive worker. On a broader level, if the costs of punishment are imposed overwhelmingly or disproportionately on specific communities, as by incarcerating and thereby removing some critical mass of their populations, a generalized social or economic breakdown or destruction of social capital might ensue. Of course, not all incarcerated offenders would be gainfully or productively employed if free, and unpunished criminality can also obviously generate broad social disorder in a community. Further, some offenders might have generated other costs, such as the cost of civil institutionalization, if they were not within the correctional system, which may offset the costs of their punishment.

The system for investigating offenses that would merit punishment is also costly, again in both direct and indirect ways. In addition to the direct and opportunity costs, law enforcement may lead to greater investment in privacy than would otherwise occur. Of course, law enforcement also creates deterrent crime-control benefits quite apart from the deterrent effect of punishment itself, obviating the need for private expenditures on personal safety that would otherwise be required, and facilitating social interaction that might not take place in its absence. (Perhaps, however, a purely preventive police force could generate similar benefits ex ante even if there were no system in place to punish offenses ex post.)

Punishment (or the threat of it) or the threat of investigation might also have a chilling effect on some socially useful conduct or otherwise make it more difficult for people to do their jobs, generating additional inefficiencies. For example, some government officials are typically granted immunity from criminal prosecution on the ground that subjecting them to potentially malicious investigation or punishment would impede the government's effectiveness. Diplomats are similarly granted immunity from suit so that they will be able to perform their duties without fear of hostile or retaliatory prosecution.

3. Criminogenesis

Punishment might cause crime instead of (or in addition to) preventing it. (More broadly, punishment might lead to other forms of harmful or undesirable, though noncriminal, behavior.) This refers not to the mere failure to detect or prevent crime, which merely adds to the cost of the system (that is, increasing the per-unit price of crime control), but to the possibility that the criminal justice system will itself make a counterproductive contribution to the crime rate. This might occur if the system of punishment makes the populace, or parts of it, more disaffected and rebellious rather than more compliant; if its apparent failings or injustices provoke violent, outraged reaction or retaliation; or if, as has been asserted (and debated), punishment modalities such as incarceration increase the likelihood or ability of offenders to recidivate following release (or, for that matter, to commit additional crimes while incarcerated).[51]

3. Making Trade-offs

Having identified the various positive and negative aspects of punishment, this section considers some issues that arise in the course of weighing those aspects to arrive at a decision about whether to punish. Accounts that privilege one or a few considerations suffer from either or both of two shortcomings: they may become too closed minded or too open ended. The first concern is that a unitary theory may oversimplify, reducing a complex balancing act to a predetermined, and possibly myopic, viewpoint. Alternatively, the theory may try to avoid this problem by expanding to embrace all of the same considerations that an overtly pluralistic account would, but seeking to fit all those considerations within the potentially uncongenial framework of the chosen theory, reducing whatever conceptual elegance the theory might have had and also possibly distorting the underlying issues. For example, utilitarian or welfarist theories often show a tendency to subsume any potentially competing value, such as a "preference" for equality or desert, into the welfare function, but this seems to result in a distorted representation of both the value thus incorporated and the notion of welfare itself.

An overtly pluralistic account eschews any favoritism toward or against particular purposes of punishment and also explicitly acknowledges the existence of multiple, possibly incommensurable principles or goals and the difficulty of adjudicating among them. It does not simplify the decision-making process—indeed, it might make it harder—but it clarifies that process. Given that punishment can serve multiple ends and generate multiple harms, which may conflict in ways that demand second-best solutions, reasonable minds can disagree about the proper resolution. But at least a pluralistic perspective openly and honestly reminds us that multiple answers *are* reasonable—rather than one being right and the others all ludicrous—and can increase the odds of realizing a better accommodation of our conflicting, often incompatible objectives instead of distorting the result by placing a thumb on the scale.[52]

This section raises just a handful of the important trade-offs that a pluralistic account needs to confront. Indeed, these are some of the easy ones, in that they have less of an apples-and-oranges quality than some other trade-offs (e.g., balancing retribution against financial cost). Each of these conflicts, at least, revolves around a common concern or locus. First is the conceptual issue of how to weigh two different principled commitments—positive versus negative retribution—as considerations in the punishment equation. Second is a brief discussion of how to balance the various effects of punishment on the individual being punished. Finally, this section discusses the balancing of punishment's overall social effects.

A. PRINCIPLE

A challenge within principled accounts of punishment—before practical issues such as effective crime prevention or financial cost are considered—is how to trade off positive and negative retribution.[53] The relative values of punishing the guilty and not punishing the innocent will have powerful implications for, among other things, the optimal standard of proof in criminal cases.[54] Past efforts to address the issue have typically treated it as if only the costs of error, and not also the benefits of success, were relevant, seeking to determine the relative harm of "false positives" (undeserving people who are punished) as opposed to "false negatives" (deserving people who fail to be punished). Another way to frame the question is to focus on the total costs and benefits of instances where punishment is imposed, rather than those where it is not, balancing the benefit of "true positives" (the value of punishing the guilty) against the cost of "false positives" (the harm of punishing the innocent). One cost of a false positive is that it often simultaneously generates a false negative, creating the opportunity cost of missing out on a possible true positive: where a crime has clearly taken place, and only one person is responsible, the cost of convicting the wrong person includes the forgone benefit of convicting the right one. (This will not be true, however, where a person is wrongly convicted of a crime that did not occur or in conspiracy cases that end up punishing the guilty along with the innocent.) In any event, further exploration of the relative values of these possible outcomes, whether based on principled considerations, practical considerations,[55] or empirical research into popular preferences,[56] is a significant avenue for future research.

B. EFFECTS ON THE OFFENDER

Can criminal penalties make people better without making them suffer? Would this be desirable even if it were possible, or is suffering an ineradicable feature of punishment and hence of criminal liability? Can retributive goals be achieved without suffering? Recent work asserts that the nature of the retributive desert claim is that wrongdoing calls for *punishment*, not that it calls for *suffering*.[57] If this account is viable—and in such a way that punishment can be meaningfully distinguished from suffering, as opposed to constituting a particular subset of experiences of suffering—presumably the hunt should be on for penalties that can constitute a satisfactory objective form of punishment while minimizing the amount of the offender's subjective suffering. One possibility is to rely on "shaming" sanctions that might express the proper condemnation of the offender's wrongdoing and reinforce the social norms that the law reflects, without causing undue pain or hardship. Even these sanctions are controversial, however.[58]

C. THIRD-PARTY EFFECTS

A final level at which to consider the trade-offs of punishment is the social level, weighing the overall costs of crime against the costs of crime prevention—including an analysis of whether the criminal justice system itself is the most cost-effective means of crime prevention. Unlike the other two categories of trade-off, here the issues are empirical rather than principled, and a great deal of work has been done to investigate them. The research does not always point to clear prescriptions, but at least a robust effort is already underway to assess the situation and offer guidance.

More recent work has begun to incorporate some other, principled concerns—such as a desire for fairness or for retributive justice—into the social-scientific analysis, engaging in empirical research to determine what informs people's moral judgments and how those judgments, in turn, affect their attitudes toward law and willingness to obey it.[59] Such work holds open the promise of offering some indication of how people actually value different abstract principles relative to each other, how they value those principles relative to practical goals such as crime prevention, and how the system's principled and pragmatic commitments interact (for example, whether pursuing justice also promotes compliance). This work may not satisfy some theorists, who would hold that our moral commitments should be determined in a more intellectually rigorous way rather than merely looking to possibly unreflective and uninformed lay intuitions, but at least it represents an initial effort to bridge the gap between normative analysis and descriptive observation.

4. Conclusion

I have proposed that the criminal justice system should be overtly and unashamedly pluralistic in its aims and its implementation and have sought to identify the considerations that such a pluralistic view would need to take into account. One way to codify such a pluralistic framework for law and enforcement might be to adopt an administrative-law model explicitly directing lawmakers or discretionary agents to consider and balance, in some specified fashion, the various benefits and costs of a given punishment intervention before enacting a new offense, changing enforcement priorities, imposing sentence, or the like. Of course, it would almost certainly be unworkable or unwise to grant actors at all levels the discretion to engage in their own individual weighing of all relevant considerations. Substantial regulation (that is, law) is necessary to guide their decisions, but that law itself, and our thinking about it, should be expansive in its approach and explicit about its compromises.

Notes

1 For example, see Berman, "Punishment and Justification" and "Two Kinds of Retributivism"; Cahill, "Retributive Justice in the Real World"; Markel, "Are Shaming Punishments Beautifully Retributive?"

2 For example, see McAdams and Ulen, "Behavioral Criminal Law and Economics"; Meares, "Norms, Legitimacy and Law Enforcement"; Nadler, "Flouting the Law"; Robinson and Darley, "Utility of Desert."

3 For example, see Frase, "Limiting Retributivism"; Reitz, "American Law Institute, Model Penal Code, Sentencing."

4 By pluralism, I primarily mean a recognition that there are multiple valid reasons to engage in the practice of punishment. The discussion here is also pluralistic in the sense that it recognizes punishment as just one of many things that are valuable, even within the confines of the criminal justice system specifically, but I assume this type of pluralism is widely shared and uncontroversial; see, for example, the chapters in this book by Markel and White.

5 As an anecdote, I was present at a conference (hosted by Rutgers–Newark School of Law) where Mitchell Berman presented a draft of a paper (titled "Are We All Consequentialists Now?") opining that what he called "desert-constrained pluralistic consequentialism" (DCPC) had become the dominant contemporary view of the justification of punishment. This claim met with considerable resistance among those present, although those who contested Berman's empirical observation never (in my recollection) seemed to assert or defend their own personal normative objections to the view Berman described. In the face of this skepticism, Berman quite sensibly abandoned the assertion of theoretical consensus in the published version of the paper ("Two Kinds of Retributivism"). But it's not at all clear to me that Berman's initial assertion was incorrect,

or who exactly opposes DCPC itself (as opposed to the claim of contemporary consensus around DCPC), or the nature of the opposition.

6 Huigens, "On Commonplace Punishment Theory," pp. 439–44.

7 Berman, "Punishment and Justification."

8 See Hart, *Punishment and Responsibility*, pp. 3–13; Rawls, "Two Concepts of Rules."

9 Whether a specific practice or case achieves either or both goals may (and likely will) be ambiguous or contestable in many cases; people may differ about what desert demands, and the empirical evidence of preventive effects may be conflicting or nonexistent. I am claiming only that in most cases, there is a reasonable basis for believing punishment will advance both objectives.

10 Compare to Moore, *Placing Blame*, p. 153.

11 Compare to Nietzsche, *On the Genealogy of Morals*, pp. 80–81.

12 Berman, "Punishment and Justification."

13 Though I use the term "intrinsic good," both forms of retributivism are probably more often conceptualized as describing a duty or a claim about the right as opposed to the good; more on this, though not much more, in a moment. (See also the chapter by White in this book.)

14 Berman, "Two Kinds of Retributivism"; Gray, "Punishment as Suffering."

15 Markel and Flanders, "Bentham on Stilts"; Gray, "Punishment as Suffering." These pieces respond to the critique offered in Kolber, "Subjective Experience of Punishment." For another discussion supporting the position that wrongdoers deserve suffering, not punishment per se, see Husak, "Retribution in Criminal Theory," pp. 971–74.

16 Husak, "Holistic Retributivism," pp. 995–96.

17 For example, Feinberg, *Doing and Deserving*; Sher, *Desert*.

18 For discussion of the issue and its implications for the relation between desert and punishment, see Markel, "Retributive Damages," pp. 259–60; Markel and Flanders, "Bentham on Stilts."

19 Moore, *Placing Blame*; Alexander and Ferzan, *Crime and Culpability*.

20 In their "Bentham on Stilts," Markel and Flanders propose a different distinction, between what they call *comprehensive* and *political* retributivism (they favor the latter).

21 Compare to Moore, *Placing Blame*, pp. 172, 186 (noting that retributive justice is not the only intrinsic good, and that other goods may override it in some cases).

22 Cahill, "Retributive Justice."

23 See the chapter by White in this book for an approach to balance duties to punish with other societal concerns and obligations.

24 For example, see Duff, *Trials and Punishments* and *Punishment, Communication, and Community*.

25 For example, see Markel, "State, Be Not Proud," pp. 426–37.

26 Braithwaite, *Restorative Justice and Responsive Regulation*.

27 Morris, "Persons and Punishment."

28 Robinson and Cahill, *Law without Justice*, pp. 186–91.

29 Robinson and Darley, "Utility of Desert."

30 For discussion of the private system of "blood feuds" in medieval Iceland, see Miller, *Bloodtaking and Peacemaking*.

31 Arenella, "Character, Choice and Moral Agency"; Huigens, "Virtue and Inculpation."

32 Hampton, "Correcting Harms Versus Righting Wrongs," pp. 1659 n. 2, 1701 n. 65.

33 Ibid., pp. 1659, 1701; Hampton, "Retributive Idea," pp. 129–33.

34 Moore, *Law and Psychiatry*, pp. 234–35; Rafter and Stanley, *Prisons in America*, p. 27.

35 Polinsky and Shavell, "Fairness of Sanctions."

36 Berman, "Punishment and Justification."

37 As noted in the first section, stronger versions of retributivism would say that punishment is not only "not wrong" but affirmatively good (or, stronger still, obligatory), where dictated by the desert principle.

38 Berman, "Two Kinds of Retributivism," pp. 2, 21.

39 Kaplow and Shavell, *Fairness Versus Welfare*, pp. 340–41; Christopher, "Deterring Retributivism," pp. 869–88. Note also, however, that negative retribution does not always, or only, arise as an issue in cases involving erroneous verdicts. First, it does not concern itself with Type II errors, where the deserving go unpunished. Second, it is not concerned with factually inaccurate but with morally improper punishment, opposing even legally authorized punishment supported by incontrovertible evidence where it would exceed the offender's desert.

40 Moore, *Placing Blame*, p. 158; Alexander, "Retributivism and the Inadvertent Punishment of the Innocent."

41 Moore, *Placing Blame*, pp. 156–57.

42 Ibid., p. 158; Alexander, "Retributivism," p. 245.

43 Kaplow and Shavell, *Fairness Versus Welfare*, p. 344 n. 6; Christopher, "Deterring Retributivism," pp. 869–70, 887–88.

44 Berman, "Two Kinds of Retributivism."

45 For example, the Eighth Amendment protection against cruel and unusual punishment is thought to be unwaivable; see Kirchmeier, "Let's Make a Deal."

46 For a discussion of the relationship between retributive and distributive justice, see Green, "Just Punishments in Unjust Societies."

47 In some cases, a claim of disproportionate punishment is equivalent to the claim that the desert principle has been violated. Here, however, even if one agrees that the punishment for crack possession is proportionate to the offense, given the available sentences for all other equivalent crimes, one might oppose the inequality of giving crack offenders what they admittedly deserve while giving powder-cocaine possessors an unfair "break."

48 Appleman, "Lost Meaning of the Jury Trial Right."

49 For discussion of constitutional criminal justice rights that protect persons other than the accused, see Stuntz, "Waiving Rights in Criminal Procedure." For other discussions of whether and when criminal defendants should be able to waive rights, see King, "Priceless Process"; Mazzone, "Waiver Paradox."

50 Robinson and Cahill, *Law without Justice*, pp. 137–39, 183–85.

51 Pritikin, "Is Prison Increasing Crime?"

52 See the chapter by White in this volume, discussing approaches to achieving such a balance.

53 Kaplow and Shavell, *Fairness Versus Welfare*, p. 342 n. 103; Bierschbach and Stein, "Mediating Rules in Criminal Law," p. 1208; Christopher, "Deterring Retributivism," pp. 912–13.

54 For the most sophisticated recent efforts to weigh the various costs and benefits of accurate and inaccurate verdicts, and to consider the implications of these costs and benefits (coupled with rates of error) for burdens of proof, see Laudan, *Truth, Error, and Criminal Law*; Laudan and Saunders, "Re-Thinking the Criminal Standard of Proof."

55 For a summary of the practical consequences, good and bad, of each possible outcome, see Laudan and Saunders, "Re-Thinking the Criminal Standard of Proof," p. 20.

56 *See* ibid., pp. 22–24 (describing a framework for eliciting information about popular attitudes toward relative values of these possible outcomes).

57 Gray, "Punishment as Suffering"; Markel and Flanders, "Bentham on Stilts."

58 Markel, "Are Shaming Punishments Beautifully Retributive?"

59 Lind and Tyler, *Social Psychology of Procedural Justice*; Nadler, "Flouting the Law"; Robinson and Darley, *Justice, Liability, and Blame*; Robinson and Darley, "Utility of Desert"; Skitka and Mullen, "Dark Side of Moral Conviction"; Thibault and Walker, *Procedural Justice*; Tyler, *Why People Obey the Law*.

Bibliography

Alexander, Larry. "Retributivism and the Inadvertent Punishment of the Innocent." *Law and Philosophy* 2 (1983): 233–46.

Alexander, Larry and Kimberly Ferzan, with Stephen Morse. *Crime and Culpability: A Theory of Criminal Law*. New York: Cambridge University Press, 2009.

Appleman, Laura I. "The Lost Meaning of the Jury Trial Right." *Indiana Law Journal* 84 (2009): 397–446.

Arenella, Peter. "Character, Choice and Moral Agency: The Relevance of Character to Our Moral Culpability Judgments." In *Crime, Culpability, and Remedy*, edited by Ellen Frankel Paul Fred D. Miller, Jr., and Jeffrey Paul, 59–83. Cambridge, MA: Blackwell, 1990.

Berman, Mitchell N. "Are We All Consequentialists Now?" Unpublished manuscript.

Berman, Mitchell N. "Punishment and Justification." *Ethics* 118 (2008): 258–90.

Berman, Mitchell N. "Two Kinds of Retributivism." In *The Philosophical Foundations of Criminal Law*, edited by R.A. Duff and Stuart P. Green. New York: Oxford University Press, forthcoming.

Bierschbach, Richard A., and Alex Stein. "Mediating Rules in Criminal Law." *Virginia Law Review* 93 (2007): 1197–258.

Braithwaite, John. *Restorative Justice and Responsive Regulation*. New York: Oxford University Press, 2002.

Cahill, Michael T. "Retributive Justice in the Real World." *Washington University Law Review* 85 (2008): 815–70.

Christopher, Russell L. "Deterring Retributivism: The Injustice of 'Just' Punishment." *Northwestern University Law Review* 96 (2002): 843–976.

Duff, R. A. *Punishment, Communication, and Community*. New York: Oxford University Press, 2001.

Duff, R. A. *Trials and Punishments*. New York: Cambridge University Press, 1986.

Feinberg, Joel. *Doing and Deserving: Essays in the Theory of Responsibility*. Princeton: Princeton University Press, 1970.

Frase, Richard S. "Limiting Retributivism: The Consensus Model of Criminal Punishment." In *The Future of Imprisonment*, edited by Michael Tonry, 83–119. New York: Oxford University Press, 2004.

Gray, David C. "Punishment as Suffering." *Vanderbilt Law Review* 63 (2010): 1619–93.

Green, Stuart P. "Just Deserts in Unjust Societies." In *The Philosophical Foundations of Criminal Law*, edited by R. A. Duff and Stuart P. Green. New York: Oxford University Press, forthcoming.

Hampton, Jean. "Correcting Harms Versus Righting Wrongs: The Goal of Retribution." *UCLA Law Review* 39 (1992): 1659–1702.

Hampton, Jean. "The Retributive Idea." In *Forgiveness and Mercy*, by Jeffrie G. Murphy and Jean Hampton, 111–61. New York: Cambridge University Press, 1988.

Hart, H. L. A. *Punishment and Responsibility: Essays in the Philosophy of Law*. New York: Oxford University Press, 1968.

Huigens, Kyron. "Virtue and Inculpation." *Harvard Law Review* 108 (1995): 1423–80.

Huigens, Kyron. "On Commonplace Punishment Theory." *University of Chicago Legal Forum* (2005): 437–58.

Husak, Douglas N. "Holistic Retributivism." *California Law Review* 88 (2000): 991–1000.

Husak, Douglas N. "Retribution in Criminal Theory." *San Diego Law Review* 37 (2000): 959–86.

Kaplow, Louis, and Steven Shavell. *Fairness Versus Welfare*. Cambridge, MA: Harvard University Press, 2002.

King, Nancy Jean. "Priceless Process: Nonnegotiable Features of Criminal Litigation." *UCLA Law Review* 47 (1999): 113–82.

Kirchmeier, Jeffrey L. "Let's Make a Deal: Waiving the Eighth Amendment by Selecting a Cruel and Unusual Punishment." *Connecticut Law Review* 32 (2000): 615–52.

Kolber, Adam J. "The Subjective Experience of Punishment." *Columbia Law Review* 109 (2009): 182–236.

Laudan, Larry. *Truth, Error, and Criminal Law: An Essay in Legal Epistomology*. New York: Cambridge University Press, 2006.

Laudan, Larry, and Harry D. Saunders. "Re-Thinking the Criminal Standard of Proof: Seeking Consensus about the Utilities of Trial Outcomes." *International Commentary on Evidence* 7 (2009): No. 2, article 1.

Lind, E. Allen, and Tom R. Tyler. *The Social Psychology of Procedural Justice*. New York: Plenum Press, 1988.

McAdams, Richard H., and Thomas S. Ulen. "Behavioral Criminal Law and Economics." In *Criminal Law and Economics*, edited by Nuno Garoupa, 403–36. Northampton, MA: Edward Elgar, 2009.

Markel, Dan. "Are Shaming Punishments Beautifully Retributive? Retributivism and the Implications for the Alternative Sanctions Debate." *Vanderbilt Law Review* 54 (2001): 2157–242.

Markel, Dan. "Retributive Damages: A Theory of Punitive Damages as Intermediate Sanction." *Cornell Law Review* 94 (2009): 239–340.

Markel, Dan. "State, Be Not Proud: A Retributivist Defense of the Commutation of Death Row and the Abolition of the Death Penalty." *Harvard Civil Rights-Civil Liberties Law Review* 40 (2005): 407–80.

Markel, Dan and Chad Flanders. "Bentham on Stilts: The Bare Relevance of Subjectivity to Retributive Justice." *California Law Review* 98 (2010): 907–88.

Mazzone, Jason. "The Waiver Paradox." *Northwestern University Law Review* 97 (2003): 801–78.

Meares, Tracey L. "Norms, Legitimacy and Law Enforcement." *Oregon Law Review* 79 (2000): 391–416.

Miller, William Ian. *Bloodtaking and Peacemaking: Feud, Law, and Society in Saga Iceland.* Chicago: University of Chicago Press, 1990.

Moore, Michael. *Law and Psychiatry: Rethinking the Relationship.* New York: Cambridge University Press, 1984.

Moore, Michael. *Placing Blame: A General Theory of the Criminal Law.* Oxford, UK: Clarendon Press, 1997.

Morris, Herbert. "Persons and Punishment." *Monist* 52 (1968): 475–501.

Nadler, Janice. "Flouting the Law." *Texas Law Review* 83 (2005): 1399–442.

Nietzsche, Friedrich. *On the Genealogy of Morals.* Translated by Walter Kaufmann. New York: Vintage Books, 1969.

Polinsky, A. Mitchell, and Steven Shavell. "The Fairness of Sanctions: Some Implications for Optimal Enforcement Strategy." *American Law and Economics Review* 2 (2000): 223–37.

Pritikin, Martin H. "Is Prison Increasing Crime?" *Wisconsin Law Review* (2008): 1049–1108.

Rafter, Nicole Hahn, and Debra L. Stanley. *Prisons in America: A Reference Handbook.* Santa Barbara, CA: ABC-CLIO, 1999.

Rawls, John. "Two Concepts of Rules." *Philosophical Review* 64 (1955): 3–32.

Reitz, Kevin R. "American Law Institute, Model Penal Code: Sentencing, Plan for Revision." *Buffalo Criminal Law Review* 6 (2002): 525–672.

Robinson, Paul H., and Michael T. Cahill. *Law without Justice: Why Criminal Law Doesn't Give People What They Deserve.* New York: Oxford University Press, 2006.

Robinson, Paul H., and John M. Darley. *Justice, Liability, and Blame: Community Views and the Criminal Law.* Boulder, CO: Westview Press, 1995.

Robinson, Paul H., and John M. Darley. "The Utility of Desert." *Northwestern University Law Review* 91 (1997): 453–99.

Sher, George. *Desert.* Princeton: Princeton University Press, 1987.

Skitka, Linda J., and Elizabeth Mullen. "The Dark Side of Moral Conviction." *Analyses of Social Issues and Public Policy* 2 (2002): 35–41.

Stuntz, William J. "Waiving Rights in Criminal Procedure." *Virginia Law Review* 75 (1989): 761–842.

Thibaut, John, and Laurens Walker. *Procedural Justice: A Psychological Analysis.* Hillsdale, NJ: L. Erlbaum Associates, 1975.

Tyler, Tom R. *Why People Obey the Law.* New Haven, CT: Yale University Press, 1990.

Tyler, Tom R., and John M. Darley. "Building a Law-Abiding Society: Taking Public Views About Morality and the Legitimacy of Legal Authorities into Account when Formulating Substantive Law." *Hofstra Law Review* 28 (2000): 707–40.

3

WHAT MIGHT RETRIBUTIVE JUSTICE BE? AN ARGUMENT FOR THE CONFRONTATIONAL CONCEPTION OF RETRIBUTIVISM

Dan Markel

THERE ARE MANY conceptions of retributive justice. This chapter is designed to articulate and defend a particular kind of retributive justice, one that I call the "Confrontational Conception of Retributivism," or the CCR. This particular conception is political, not comprehensive, and thus is interested in defending the claim that *state* punishment is, as a general matter, warranted as a response to *legal* wrongdoing. Accordingly, the focus is on the legal manifestations of punishment, particularly within a liberal democracy; it is not concerned with justifying punishment in other spheres such as parent-child relations. Related to this account of state punishment is that its contours should be devised principally ex ante and that such punishment should be distributed through actors upon whom there are checks with respect to their remaining discretion.

1. The Confrontational Conception of Retributivism

As I conceive and defend it, retributive punishment is a form of humane but condemnatory communicative state action directed at the offender. Action is communicative when directed to a designated recipient in a way "meant to convey thoughts done through means reasonably recognizable as serving that end."[1] The action is undertaken in a way that the *sender* of the message *thinks* will make sense to the recipient and is performed in a way that the thought conveyed can be made sense of, or effectuated, through the free will of the recipient.[2] This communicative goal is realized even when the offender rejects the message, that is, he refuses to coordinate his actions or values in accordance with the message sent to him. Moreover, this communicative goal is distinct from the goals of more familiar instrumental approaches to punishment, which include, but are not limited to, the government's "expression" of messages through the medium of an offender's punishment to an undefined public at large.[3]

The discussion below sketches an account of this communicative understanding, one that explains and justifies the intrinsic goodness of retributive punishment independent of the external social ends it might serve. It also justifies *punishing* mentally competent offenders for their *crimes*, as opposed to "treating" the offenders or ignoring them in search of cheaper measures of harm reduction. That said, for reasons advanced below, such a view does not entail indifference to the consequences and costs of retributive punishment.[4] In this respect, the project is designed to (a) reveal the internal intelligibility of retributive justice as a practice and in individual cases where we have good reason to believe other legal constraints have been abided by, (b) explain why the pursuit of such justice is an imperfect duty upon state officials, and (c) argue that, notwithstanding that imperfect duty, there are various internal and external limits that may and properly should be placed on such a social obligation.

While this account builds upon prior accounts of retributive justice ranging from Kant and Hegel all the way to Duff, Finnis, Hampton, Moore, Morris, Murphy, and Rawls, it also departs from them in various ways. The point here, however, is not to trumpet or explicate these differences or claim complete originality. Rather, my goal is more modest: to present a sketch of retributive justice that illustrates the basis for a noninstrumental, communicative conception of punishment. The bare claim is that states are justified in and have positive, though not inflexibly demanding, reasons for censuring and punishing legal wrongdoing in a manner shaped by law. I now turn to elaborating what underlies this claim: that is, to describing what retributive punishment seeks to communicate.

John Rawls once proffered the view that retributive justice rests on the idea that

> wrongdoing merits punishment. It is morally fitting that a person who does wrong should suffer in proportion to his wrongdoing . . . and the severity of the appropriate punishment depends on the depravity of his act. The state of affairs where a wrongdoer suffers punishment is morally better than the state of affairs where he does not; and it is better irrespective of any of the consequences of punishing him.[5]

Similarly, Michael S. Moore once summarily described retributivism as "the view that punishment is justified by the moral culpability of those who receive it."[6] Underlying this description is a sense that imposing punishment for moral wrongdoing is a self-evident obligation.[7]

The problem with this capsule characterization, however, is that the nature of this obligation requires further explanation. Imagine Jack. He has spitefully run over Jane, his neighbor's prize-winning child. If the state seeks to punish Jack on account of his purported moral desert, several questions arise. First, why does Jack deserve *punishment*? And is that the same thing as deserving *suffering*?[8] Moreover, why shouldn't Jack undergo some form of treatment that can cure or ameliorate his antisocial condition?[9] Skeptics might also ask why one *should* embrace the pursuit of retributive justice through authorized coercive condemnatory deprivations, and not just solemn declarations of denunciation. Even if one agrees that Jack deserves to endure some punishment in the form of a coercive condemnatory deprivation, it does not follow that the state has a right or a duty to punish Jack. Why is the state, rather than the victim or her allies, adjudicating and punishing Jack? Liberal democracies must understand what it is about Jack's past offense that might entail the state's prima facie right and obligation to punish him. These issues animate the following account, which tries to describe retributive justice as a socio-legal practice whose value is internally intelligible when the state inflicts some level of coercion upon an offender whose violation of an extant legal norm has had fair and reasonable adjudication. In other words, the preconditions for this account's attractiveness are that the laws being vindicated are reasonable and democratically enacted, and the adjudicative procedures are appropriately conceived and reliably applied.

A. HOLDING AGENTS RESPONSIBLE FOR CHOOSING UNLAWFUL ACTIONS

Retributive punishment for legal wrongdoing is justified in part because in treating the offender as a responsible moral agent it communicates to him a respect for his dignity as an autonomous moral agent. When the state adjudicates and punishes a person's unlawful wrongdoing, it affirms her moral agency through that process because she can express remorse, recognize her wrongdoing, and endeavor to avoid that conduct in the future. Or, in the alternative, during the adjudicative process, the offender may give reasons why the conduct was not wrongful under the circumstances.[10] The retributive encounter of adjudication and punishment involves a cognitive process possessing moral weight.[11] The public, through the state, conveys respect for an offender by holding him responsible as a moral agent capable of choosing to act unlawfully and thus in a blameworthy manner. In maintaining credible institutions of criminal justice, the state communicates to offenders that their unlawful actions matter to this community of shared laws, and that it will hold them responsible for these actions.

Recall Jack, who maliciously killed Jane's child. If the state, in its ordinary course of business, knowingly did nothing to respond to Jack's unlawful action, its inaction here could convey two messages: first, the polity's indifference to the legal rights of its citizens; and second, a statement of condescension by the polity toward Jack, suggesting that the public does not take his actions seriously, even though Jack chose to commit the wrongdoing (arguendo) without excuse or justification.

Retributive punishment is a way in which the public holds Jack responsible for his unlawful choices and blames him for them. When the state creates credible legal institutions to advance retributive justice, it expresses certain commitments ex ante to the public and communicates these commitments ex post to the offender through retributive punishment. In this way, punishment—the censure manifested through coercive sanction—communicates to offenders that they are autonomous agents capable of responsibly choosing between lawful and unlawful actions, and that they can and must be held responsible for the actions they choose and thus blamed for them. To borrow from C.S. Lewis, retribution "plants the flag of truth within the fortress of a rebel soul."[12] The punishment of a competent criminal instantiates a belief in the ideal that one is morally responsible, that is, blameworthy, for one's unlawful actions; importantly, to punish someone is to recognize that flouting the law cannot simply be fixed by compensation or an acknowledgment of causation alone. Punishment communicates condemnation by the polity to an offender who is a worthy interlocutor.[13]

I noted earlier the view that retributive punishment is justified as a communicative practice. In other words, the value of retribution lies in the criminal's ability to understand rationally the polity's desire to repudiate his wrongful claim to be above the law. Imagine a perpetrator who is mentally impaired, such that during his last dinner before execution, he tells the prison guard, "I want to save my dessert for tomorrow night." Would retributive punishment make sense in this context? Not in my view. In that situation, the retribution would not be internally intelligible if the offender could not understand the meaning of the state's condemnatory action. Importantly, though the offender must be able to rationally understand the communication, he need not be persuaded by it. For example, he may proclaim his innocence notwithstanding the evidence to the contrary. However, if he cannot comprehend that he is being punished for his offense, then the punishment is not retributive but merely a coercive deprivation whose condemnatory character is lost on the offender.

Although this argument may seem similar to a justification for punishment based on moral desert alone, it is not the same. First, moral desert may stand outside the law. Thus, a theorist focused strictly on moral desert may oppose punishing someone who is proven to have eaten on the subway (absent justification or excuse) and thus in violation of the law prohibiting eating on the subway. My account of retribution distinguishes between moral and legal desert in this way: I might oppose as a legislator criminalizing silly things but nonetheless proceed (as a judge or corrections official) with punishing someone who violates a democratically enacted law that is not itself illiberal (or otherwise unconstitutional) but simply, by my lights, unwise.[14] One does this out of respect for the idea of democratic authority, about which more will be said later.

A second way this account differs from traditional or familiar notions of moral desert is by emphasizing the significance of communication over expression, which itself illuminates how we should think about punishing persons across a timeline. For example, imagine that on Monday, Jack kills Jane's child, but then on Tuesday, he bangs his head in a horrible accident, thereby losing the capacity to understand why he would be punished. Even though the question of whether to punish him may arise on Wednesday, arguably nothing has happened to change his moral desert, which according to some, may have "congealed" on Monday.[15] However, what I take to be the retributive point of punishment—communication of condemnation by the state to the offender through coercive sanction—would be lost if he were punished on Wednesday, not because he has already suffered a trauma and thus deserves leniency, but rather because he could no longer comprehend the punishment's *communicative* significance, even if the state might still realize its *expressive* goals to others.[16] In other words, the good achieved by retributive punishment is internal to the practice of punishment itself, though the state must weigh the pursuit of that good in all situations and contexts against the pursuit of other goods. In making these claims, however, we can still see that the point of retributive punishment is not to achieve psychological satisfaction for victims or their allies, or to reduce private violence, or to educate the public about norms of rightful conduct; all of these are contingent goals attainable through a variety of means.[17]

Notwithstanding the internal intelligibility (and intrinsic value) of retribution's *communicative* practice, retributive punishment also performs important coinciding *expressive* functions. That is, when the state creates institutions to communicate reprobation of the offender, the existence of these institutions signals that individuals' actions and interests matter to the state and its citizens. The expressive function of punishment (sending signals to the public), however, derives its legitimacy only when the state has properly achieved its primary communicative function to a culpable, competent offender.

Of course, in some instances one might think punishment could be unnecessary to communicate to particular offenders the value of being held responsible. For example, think of an offender who, immediately after committing her misconduct, comes forward, attempts to make restitution, and evinces her awareness of this ideal of moral accountability through her own sincere repentance. Such a situation, where an offender has ostensibly internalized the significance of the ideal of moral responsibility, illustrates that the justification for state sanction needs to run deeper. This is because one way to manifest acceptance of responsibility and repentance is through a willingness to endure punishment to help secure the regime of equal liberty under law.[18]

B. EFFECTUATING EQUAL LIBERTY UNDER LAW

Even against a quickly repentant offender, retributive punishment is warranted to effectuate a liberal democracy's commitment to the principle of equal liberty under law. In a liberal democracy, punishment serves to fulfill part of the promise of equality because each citizen is burdened by an obligation to obey those laws that have been reasonably crafted, enforced, and applied. When someone flouts a legitimate law, he elects to untether himself from the common enterprise of living together peaceably under a common law. He is not merely flouting a particular law with which he may disagree, but rather he is also defecting from an agreement about the basic structures of liberal democracy that he (would have) made as a reasonable person in concert with other reasonable people. By his act, the offender implicitly says, "I have greater liberty than you." He cuts himself off from the social order and elevates himself above his fellow citizens, notwithstanding that all should enjoy equal liberty under the rule of law in a liberal state.[19] What matters is that, ex ante, the offender can be seen as defecting from a legitimate legal order to which she has good reason to give allegiance,[20] and that in defecting, she demonstrates that she has taken license to do what others are not entitled to do. If the state establishes no institution to threaten punishment credibly, the offender's implicit or explicit claim to superiority over others commands greater plausibility than it would if the state had created such an institution.[21]

By making credible its threat to impose retributive punishment, the state makes its best reasonable efforts to reduce the plausibility of individuals' false claims of superiority over their specific victims, if there are any,[22] or claims of superiority vis-à-vis the public. In other words, the state's coercive measures against an offender communicate society's fidelity to the norm that all enjoy the same package of liberties under law.[23] Moreover, these sanctions communicate a message of condemnation to the person most in need of hearing that message—the offender who violated the law. This rationale helps explain both the notion of equal liberty under law and the subsequent personal obligation of self-restraint.

C. DEMOCRATIC SELF-DEFENSE

The two rationales discussed so far—effectuating responsibility and instantiating equal liberty under law—address why punishing an offender for his unlawful action is internally intelligible under the right conditions. However, they do not explain why the *state* should decide and implement matters of punishment. In this subsection, I examine why the state should play the central role in meting out retributive justice.

One reason for the state's role here has to do with the notion of *democratic self-defense*. Recall from the previous subsection how an offender's misconduct implicitly or explicitly serves to substantiate a claim of superiority. That claim of superiority is not merely a claim against his victim—indeed, for some offenses, there may not even be an identifiable victim. Rather, the claim of superiority is also against the *political order* of equal liberty under law. Each time an offender commits an offense, she effectively tries to shift where the rules of property, liability, and inalienability lie, at least with respect to her.[24] In so doing, the offender, in a sense, revolts against both society's determinations of what those primary rules are and also against the secondary or meta-rules governing who gets to adjust the primary rules. In other words, the offender usurps the sovereign will of the people by challenging their decision-making structure.[25] The misconduct, then, is not merely against the victim but also against the people and their agent, the state, whose charter mandates the protection of not only the persons constituting the political order but also the decision-making authority of the regime itself.[26]

The principle of democratic self-defense is embodied in the oath that federal officers take, which obligates them to protect the nation's decision-making structure.[27] The oath illuminates the idea that these officials must defend the Constitution against attack by those who shift the rules unlawfully and thus reveals offenses as, to some degree, a form of rebellion.

But one might ask: why *democratic*, rather than simply *political*, self-defense? As mentioned earlier, this account does not purport to justify punishment for all laws broken under all regimes. Its appeal lies in, and for now is restricted to, trying to understand what is condemnable about breaking reasonable laws passed fairly in liberal democracies that are generally respectful of persons' rights and liberties.[28] If we replace "democratic" with a broader word, such as "political," the principle could lend itself to justifying punishment even for breaking laws that reinforce tyranny or oppression.

One might also wonder if the account of democratic self-defense might seem inaccurate, even grandiose, with respect to the state of mind of most offenders. Surely, the typical offender who commits a "smash and grab" would deny that he is making any implicit or explicit "claim" against the victim or the state. He might further deny that he is trying to shift the rules or usurp the will of the democratic apparatus. Rather, he might assert that he is merely violating the law and hoping to get away with it because he wants the money. Consequently, imputing to criminal conduct a greater rebellion against the state or one's fellow citizens may appear implausible.

It only looks implausible, however, if retributivists are expected to justify punishment to a person who already knows he's an offender. Such an expectation is misplaced because it lacks impartiality and a commitment to reasonableness.[29] On my view, retributivist theory must explain the attractiveness of punishment to one who is reasonably trying to secure the conditions for human flourishing ex ante. At that point, such a person knows he will be punished only for misconduct reasonably proscribed by law and subject to his control but does not know whether he will be rich or poor, an offender or a victim.[30] It would seem plausible that a person in this position would understand such misconduct as warranting punishment because the offense is a rebellion against the public order.[31]

Of course, prior to imposing sanctions, we must also decide whether sanctions for particular conduct are appropriate as against a particular defendant. The modern liberal democratic state serves to regulate and thereby to permit the pursuit of diverse ends by citizens within a heterogeneous society. Accordingly, what justifies the state's involvement over some alternative private ordering arrangement? Because private citizens rarely know who will violate their rights—and thus cannot decide ex ante upon a dispute resolution mechanism—the state has a strong coordinating claim to serve as an impartial authority in resolving disputes among its citizens both in imposing and enforcing sanctions against wrongdoers. Moreover, the state also establishes, through its deliberative bodies, the scope of one's protected rights and interests; that also cannot be left up to private asseveration. So, the state not only has a strong claim, but the *sole* claim to be able to do these things with some degree of legitimacy in a "social union of social unions."[32]

The state's involvement in both the adjudication and the sanction of wrongful misconduct is thereby warranted—so long as the judiciary is independent and capable of reviewing abuses.

Taken together, commitments to the ideals of moral responsibility, equal liberty under law, and democratic self-defense explain why certain individuals should be punished and not others and why some persons (authorized officials) and not others should do the punishing. Importantly, one can see why—without reliance upon mere intuitions or emotions of vengeance, anger, or hatred—the authorized state officials must take care to punish only the guilty and not the innocent. After all, only a convicted offender has been judged to have made claims through his criminal actions that deny his responsibility, his status as an equal under the law, and his proper role in the chain of democratic decision making. Those found guilty *should* be punished, making this account more than a justification for so-called negative retributivism.

Indeed, it provides a positive but not absolute (or unyielding) obligation for state officials to punish the right persons in the right way, because a willful failure to punish the putatively guilty signals that the state does not care about the offender's misconduct, the rights and interests justifying the breached rule, or the integrity of the democratic decision-making structure. Such inaction wrongly conveys a lack of concern for reducing Type II (false negative) errors of nonpunishment for those laws whose underlying values society has committed to protect through state punishment. And it is only violations of those laws, and not simply generic moral vices such as smugness or a nasty demeanor, that themselves warrant punishment under law.

Seeing the practice of punishment through a political lens helps us also see that the framework above further explains why the innocent should *not* be punished, for they have not made claims of legal superiority through their actions, nor can they plausibly be deemed to have usurped power from the decision-making structure, which they have good reason to obey ex ante. Knowingly punishing the innocent presents a classic false positive, or Type I error, within the criminal justice system.

Finally, the framework here explains why to under-punish or over-punish relative to comparable offenders in the same jurisdiction exposes the state to (rebuttable) claims that it favors some people and disfavors others, thereby violating basic liberal commitments to equal concern and respect under the law and to consistent application of the law. One of the principal reasons we punish, as we just saw, is to maintain the regime of equal liberty under law. The way in which we punish must also cohere with that set of principles, ensuring that the values of consistency and evenhandedness are respected to the greatest extent reasonably possible. And that means evidencing some concern for ensuring the reduction of errors involving under- and over-punishment relative to comparable offenders. These errors frequently arise from institutions permitting excessive and unreviewable discretion, rather than making officials stay within some roughly proportionate band of sanctions for the particular misconduct.[33] Retributive theory provides good reasons to reduce errors both of under- and over-punishment in a liberal democracy. Balancing the reduction of one sort of error against that of another obviously involves difficult, even tragic, choices; but, at the very least, retributive theory clarifies the deficiencies associated with both kinds of errors. This is a point that has been largely lost on those courts and commentators who try to understand retribution strictly through a victim vindication or social denunciation model of punishment.

D. RETRIBUTIVISM'S INTERNAL LIMITS

Understanding retributive punishment as communicative action presents reasons not only for imposing punishment but also for limiting the availability, amount, and kind of punishment. Obviously, the real world of retribution poses significant risks of error and abuse by authorities. Occurrences of errors or abuses stand at odds with the animating principles of retributive justice and the rationales for reducing Type I and II errors. Consequently, retributive punishment is commendable only when authorities take reasonable and sufficient measures to reduce substantially or eliminate those risks.[34] This means, in other words, the state must conduct its rites of retribution with a degree of modesty and with assurances that those risks of error and abuse are tolerably minimal.[35]

Additionally, embedded in this account of retributive justice is a particular requirement of communicative intent on the part of the state's punishing agents. To insist only on the offender's perception of her defeat, to the exclusion of the *potential* internalization of correct values that the confrontation encourages, would stand in tension with our first interest—affirmation that society recognizes its members as autonomous dignity-bearing agents. To realize this vision in the concrete practice of punishment, the state should carry out its denial of the offender's false value claims in a manner conducive to fostering the internalization of the values that the retributive encounter is meant to uphold.[36] To be clear: the retributive punishment need not *guarantee* the offender's internalization of those values, but the polity ought not to take measures that, in the course of punishment, directly *preclude* the opportunity for internalization. Accordingly, the state's imposition of punishment not only denies the offender's false claim of superiority but also invites her transformation.[37] To borrow Robert Nozick's memorable and apt phrase, "The hope is that delivering the message will change the person so that he will realize he did wrong, then start doing things because they are right."[38]

2. Five Key Contrasts

The preceding discussion will benefit from some further clarification and amplification. Importantly, this conception of retributivism focuses on the *punishment* of the offender and not on his *suffering*, in part because of the focus on legal institutions and their limited capacities and the proper normative constraints upon those institutions and capacities. Justified retributive punishment entails a legal institution, one that exists to enforce legal rules; it is not to assess the moral goodness or badness of an offender in toto.

A. RETRIBUTIVISM AS DISTINCT FROM REVENGE

Contrary to various courts and commentators,[39] we can see how retributive justice, especially in its institutional form as described here, might usefully contrast with revenge—at least as an ideal type.[40] To begin with, what induces retributive punishment is the offense against the legal order. Therefore, where the law runs out, so must retribution. By contrast, revenge (and perhaps also other conceptions of what I call "comprehensive retributivism") may address slights, injuries, insults, or nonlegal wrongs. Nozick identified five other distinctions between retribution and revenge: (a) retribution ends cycles of violence, but revenge fosters them; (b) retribution limits punishment so that it is in proportion to the wrongdoing, whereas revenge is not necessarily limited by this principle; (c) the state administers retribution impartially, while revenge is often personal; (d) retributivists seek equal application of the law, whereas the avenger is not attached to such a principle; and (e) retribution is cool and unemotional, while revenge (often) has a particular emotional tone of taking pleasure in the suffering of another.[41]

There are a few other important distinctions that an account like the CCR can draw. Retributivists, on this account, always seek to attach the punishment to the offender directly, because it is the offender who makes the claims that the state seeks to reject, whereas revenge may target an offender's relatives or allies.[42] Second, retributivism, distinct from revenge (or some forms of comprehensive retributivism), is uninterested in making the offender experience unvariegated suffering, that is, negative experiences as such; it instead seeks to communicate certain notions (typically of condemnation) through the state's power to coerce the offender.[43] Third, retributivism (*qua* CCR) is interested in, and speaks to, the moral autonomy and dignity of the offender, whereas revenge may be indifferent to those qualities. This indifference accounts for the crucial fact that certain defenses—justifications and excuses—might limit retribution but fail to stem revenge. Finally, the CCR's communicative intent requirement, discussed above, requires that the punishment not preclude the offender's internalization of a "sense of justice" that would allow her to demonstrate her respect for the norms of moral responsibility, equal liberty under law, and democratic self-defense, whereas revenge has no such requirement. Often enough, it is sufficient for an avenger to have the target suffer or die, perhaps even without receiving a message regarding who the author of that misfortune is. (Obviously, this is not always true as some avengers want that suffering to be known to the target as the result of his prior actions.) The CCR, by contrast, encourages the offender to buck up and engage in moral reconstruction—even if the offender were to spend the rest of his days in a prison.

The value of retributivism, on this particular account, is realized when the state makes reasonable attempts to communicate its commitment to these ideals through the use of its coercive power against the offender. In contrast to those who might be tempted to view retributivism as merely an "expressive theory" reducible to its success at projecting norms onto society, the account here reveals retributivism's intelligibility even if we focus strictly on the relationship between state and offender.[44]

An important aspect of this type of retributivism is the emphasis placed on the distinction between punishing the *acts* of a person and the *person* herself.[45] The CCR's focus is on punishing people *for their particular acts* and not punishing the person because of who the person is—to the extent this line can be drawn.[46] Revenge and perhaps even "comprehensive" retributivism make no such fine distinction, for they are directed not just against a particular act done by a person but rather against the *person* herself—the person must suffer and usually or ideally through the agency of those wronged or their allies.[47] The appropriate punishment for a person is the appropriate punishment for the *culpable* act committed; the CCR does not take that action to represent something deeper, something corrupt, about the personhood of the offender.

Nor does the CCR necessarily aim at the *rehabilitation of* the offender for society's future and contingent benefit. The CCR limits how much the state can punish; it cannot continue to punish an offender beyond his sentence, even if he refuses to internalize society's message of condemnation. But the CCR also represents a key shift in emphasis. If the focus were on rehabilitating the offender or on deterring him, we might have to take into account the kind of person he or she was in order to fix the person. If our focus is on acts, however, we just look at the offender's offense (and adjudicated criminal history) and match the legislatively appropriate condemnatory sanction for that. We need not tailor our punishments to the bad *offender* and the unique sensibilities he or she might possess. That said, there might be a range of social self-defense mechanisms that the polity should undertake to reduce the risk of crime, such as subsidized drug or alcohol addiction treatment, skills training, and so forth. But all these programs could theoretically be made available to all persons, regardless of a criminal past.

B. THE CCR AS DISTINCT FROM UTILITARIANISM

A second contrast exists, one that focuses on juxtaposing the CCR with "thoroughgoing utilitarianism" in punishment. Thoroughgoing utilitarianism in punishment focuses on realizing states of affairs that are theoretically indifferent to communicating particular messages to the offender. On the conventional and perhaps overly simplistic utilitarian account, the state punishes a person merely to prevent him and others from committing crimes in the future. The "pure" utilitarian will be indifferent to whether this deterrence comes about through communicating to the offender the wrongness of his action, holding him responsible, or some other means. The goal of deterrence is compatible with treating the offender not as an *autonomous agent* but rather, as Hegel contended, like a dog that responds to threats and incentives but not to reasons.[48] While deterrence discourse need not be crudely understood as impervious to *reasons* for action, utilitarians are principally indifferent to choices among the various *causes* of harm reduction. Thus, on the utilitarian view, one could simply administer shock treatment to competent offenders if that would better or more cheaply prevent them from committing crimes in the future.

By contrast, the CCR finds its intelligibility and attractiveness through its effectuation of certain intrinsic goods associated with the practice of communicating condemnation to those found guilty of offenses against the legal order: treating the offender as a responsible agent; effectuating the offender's equal status under a democratic legal system; and, most important, communicating to him that he has broken the law. In other words, the goods of democratic self-defense, moral accountability, and the maintenance of equal liberty under law are goods *intrinsic* and integral to the (correct and fair) punishment of an offender; they are not goods achieved merely by means of his punishment.

That said, because the CCR is less concerned with *maximizing* "just deserts" above all other social priorities than it is with developing the claim for retributive punishment's internal intelligibility, it is better able than prior retributivist accounts to pay heed to the important costs and consequences of institutions of retributive justice.[49] Punishment realizes many goods—while also, of course, causing some bads—but these goods (fidelity to accountability, equality, and so forth) are not always at every moment the most important goods that a polity should pursue. For one thing, there are hard choices within the criminal justice system—how much to spend on policing, on prisons, on the court system, etc.—and of course more hard choices arise between criminal justice and other moral priorities, such as health care or national security. As a result, no persuasive justificatory account of punishment can be ignorant of the real-world trade-offs that our democratic institutions inevitably have to make. The best we can hope for an account like the CCR is to furnish a "tailored" justification to the "demand" claim that punishment is an intentionally imposed sanction that otherwise requires justification.[50] It can explain why the intrinsic goodness of retributive justice is, to borrow Berman's phrase, an always available and weighty reason for punishment.[51] It need not and should not be relied upon to justify the unsound proposition that every last unit of scarce social resources must be applied to the pursuit of retributive justice.[52]

C. THE CCR AS DISTINCT FROM A RETRIBUTIVISM OF BALANCING PAIN AND SUFFERING

Third, although the CCR fits snugly within the family of retributive theories, it has disagreements with various elders within that larger family. As alluded to earlier, some versions of retributive theory directed attention at the infliction of suffering in the offender—in some cases, emphasizing that such inflictions of suffering should follow *lex talionis* and thus be equal to the pain and suffering he has caused (or, under some views, threatened). Those accounts, however, have often stumbled on explaining *why* the offender deserves pain and suffering,[53] as well as whether to address wrongful actions that do not actually cause any harm. Hand-waving references to intuition or "fittingness" were often the only support that the pain and suffering version of retribution could muster.[54] Thus, relying on cultural leitmotifs dating back to the Bible, it somehow made cosmic sense that the wicked should suffer and that the good be made happy.[55] This view is not only embraced popularly but even by some modern retributive theorists who use or endorse the language of inflicting pain and suffering on offenders.[56]

My sense is that this desire to cause the offender suffering is misguided. The goal should not be to cause suffering as such but rather to communicate condemnation to the offender and, simultaneously, to express society's shared disapproval. Where the older versions obscurely referred to the fittingness of retributive punishment, the more modern accounts of state retribution, including the CCR, note the intrinsic goods that retributive punishment may secure through a communicative account and thus without reference to the contingent benefits of crime control (or other extrinsic ends). In these modern versions, the goal is not to vindicate an agent-neutral duty to cause the offender unvariegated suffering but to implement punishment that is conceived in a relational manner, one that allows and encourages the *polity* to communicate to the offender the wrongness of her action, using particular deprivations to signal that condemnation.[57] In other words, these versions treat the offender as an agent who can understand the point of her punishment, not merely as a body that can suffer pain in return for the harm she has wrongfully caused or threatened. Punishment is a good, then, not because it is fitting in some cosmic sense that harms be balanced out between victim and offender, but because punishing the offender treats her as an agent, equal to the other members of society, and communicates the polity's disapproval of her actions *to* her. Consistent with this reduced focus on the offender's suffering as the goal is a corresponding defense of *objective liberty deprivations*, and not physical pain per se, as the means of communication.

D. THE CCR AS POLITICAL, NOT COMPREHENSIVE

The fourth contrast to note is that the CCR's version of retributive justice is political, not comprehensive. Here I invoke but also tweak John Rawls's famous distinction between a political conception and a comprehensive (or metaphysical) conception of justice.[58] Political values, according to Rawls, are those that are universally, or at least very widely, shared in a liberal political culture.[59] Comprehensive values, by comparison, are those that are tied to a "controversial" metaphysical system and therefore could not be the basis by which the state legitimately exercises coercive power over a heterogeneous population.[60]

For example, the idea that the wicked should suffer because they are wicked or have what Kant called "inner viciousness" is a metaphysical conception of "divine" or "poetic" justice.[61] This is a comprehensive conception of retributive justice that is predicated on a desert commitment that proves to be a controversial ideal. To my mind, I doubt such a view could serve as the political basis of the institution of punishment, if only because so many people might disagree about what counts as wickedness, or about the measure of suffering, or even about whether the wicked should endure suffering or therapy.

Moreover, though there is a rich philosophical literature about the nature of moral desert and its relationship to punishment,[62] my sense is that retributivists should frame their argument differently to convey why punishment against legal wrongdoers is justified in liberal democracies. Someone who is industrious, wise, and kind may *deserve* plaudits, after all, but liberals (among others) tend not to believe that it is the state's responsibility to bestow those plaudits as a matter of social programming. Conversely, one might be miserly and indolent, but one's inner viciousness in this regard is generally not a compelling reason for the state to condemn that person through punishment. A person's moral desert, whether negative or positive, is generally insufficient by itself to motivate state action in a liberal democracy.

For this reason, desert should not be the key focus as we talk about retributive justice. Instead, recall the values at the core of the CCR: accountability for unlawful choices, equal liberty under the law, and commitment to protecting the channels of democratic decisionmaking in the impartial administration of justice. All of these are properly political values and can be the basis of an overlapping consensus among diverse groups of citizens of a liberal democracy.[63] At its heart, the CCR does not rely on a controversial and comprehensive notion of global just deserts; rather, it insists that retributive punishment against those who offend against the liberal legal order is internally intelligible and attractive in a prima facie sense. The state holds people responsible through punishment for what they do, but only for those actions that constitute offenses against reasonably enacted laws. All of this stays (much more) on the surface, philosophically speaking, and avoids the metaphysical puzzles associated with linking political institutions too closely to any controversial comprehensive notion of desert.[64]

E. RETRIBUTIVISM AS A THEORY OF JUSTIFICATION, NOT PRIMARILY OF SENTENCING

Theorists of criminal justice often divide their interests into a series of questions. Without addressing all of them, let me highlight two. One question is: what might justify the state's creation of legal institutions of punishment? This is the "justification" question. A second question is: once the state has determined someone's liability for a crime, how much and what kind of punishment should the state mete out in response? This is the "sentencing" question. That a retributivist theorist gives a retributive (or, specifically, communicative) answer to the justification question does not require her to offer a *precise* answer for each sentencing question. Instead, she can simply say that the precise answer to a sentencing question should not be inconsistent with the values underlying her answer to the justification question. Thus, retributivists may offer a range of permissible modes and amounts of punishment without committing to one specific prepolitical or "moral" notion of the correct punishment for each specific offense.[65]

Importantly, the punishment appropriate on this account arises as a *choice of the public* exercised through the state's democratic institutions, implemented through law, and most reasonably done in a way that resonates with rule of law values that facilitate the even-handed treatment of similarly situated offenders and offenses. Ideally, these choices would cohere with some kind of metric of objective proportionality, but we live in a world where these issues are subject to immense contestation, and so we must muddle through issues of objective proportionality in a way that respects our obligations to each other as citizens within a democratic framework trying to work these answers out through deliberative and fairly representative political institutions. That does not mean there ought not be judicially enforced limits that reflect concerns about cruelty, incompetence, or gross disproportionality, but it does mean that the discussions about these sentencing issues should be addressed with more modesty. Moreover, because of the concerns of error and abuse adverted to earlier, the state should itself punish with modes of punishment that are both consistent with the underlying values of the CCR and that reflect a modest understanding of the state's power, for example, by not punishing in a way that renders impossible the state's ability to apologize to the offender when the offender was mistakenly punished.

That said, a retributive perspective should give relatively little consideration to the preferences, experiences, and capacities of the offender vis-à-vis her punishment because, after all, the nature of punishment is *coercive*. No doubt, most offenders would choose no punishment if they could. They might alternatively be willing to have two pinkies cut off to avoid having to spend a year in prison away from their family. Such preferences neither necessitate that the state must punish people by cutting off fingers nor signify that such punishments are inherently less cruel than, say, incarceration. The polity has to make its decisions on how to punish based on the values and considerations the public's representatives deem vitally important,[66] not on the tastes, preferences, and individual baselines of the offenders who come into the system.

Pure theorizing, of course, might trigger an abstract question such as "what is the proper punishment for X crime?" Proportionality is often invoked and yields the bland assertion that the punishment should "fit" the crime. The answer is often indeterminate. Some might suggest it is an empty principle. But to my mind, we should not confuse indeterminateness with emptiness.

First, retributive theory emphatically has something to say about the question of sentencing. At the lower end of the scale for any offense, retributivists may plainly criticize punishments that do not adequately and sufficiently communicate and express condemnation. So too may they criticize punishments that communicated and expressed too much condemnation in proportion to the crime. But how much is too much condemnation for a given crime? Is our only benchmark that the death penalty for parking tickets is objectively disproportionate? Such questions bedevil proportionality analysis, both in theory and in our constitutional praxis.[67] That principles of proportionality cannot give us a certain answer in every case does not mean we can say that proportionality (or retributive justice) is never able to give answers about what is too little or too much. But the better way to approach this substantive question is one that squarely appeals to ideas of democratic authority limited by liberal constraints.

Thus, to the challenge of whether proportionality is empty, one should answer in a Bickelian vein: "no answer is what the wrong question begets."[68] In other words, the main problem in determining proportionality is not to figure out what the absolute "right" punishments are for each crime but to figure out who is in the best and most legitimate position to do the determination, based on a range of considerations. In this respect, and I will elliptically stop here and leave the argument for another day, picking up on themes earlier argued,[69] my sense is that legislatures in conjunction with accountable commissions are better positioned to reach these decisions than an array of unconstrained judges or parole commissions, whose untrammeled discretion often creates risks of random, arbitrary, or discriminatory punishment choices. So a better answer may be to determine the right institutions to fix proportionality. As John Finnis has emphasized, punishment presents a good example of "the need for *determinatio*, a process of choosing freely from a range of reasonable options none of which is simply rationally superior to the others."[70] The problem with discretion is not in how to eliminate it entirely (for, in this case, it is ineliminable) but in finding out *who* is in the best position to wield it. These kinds of challenges are more fairly and often better worked out through democratic authorities subject to outer and somewhat deferential constitutional limits.

3. Conclusion

This paper has tried to articulate and, to some extent, defend a particular conception of retributive justice that I have called confrontational because it emphasizes the confrontation the state initiates when it accuses, convicts, and punishes an offender for a legal offense. This confrontational relationship between state (or better, polity) and offender provides again, to paraphrase Berman, an always available and substantially weighty reason for certain kinds of punishment against certain persons for noninstrumental reasons. Unlike other accounts of retributive justice, however, this one is political and not comprehensive, and thus rejects the claim that state punishment is or should be tied to the suffering of the offender, to the satisfaction of desires for vengeance by victims or their allies, or even to hatred of the offender. The account has some oddities, to be sure, and more could certainly be said to clarify or illuminate its meaning in particular contexts. Indeed, some questions I hope to take up (and invite others to also consider) include, first, to what extent can an account such as this one be used to reform our existing punitive practices; and second, to explore whether an account like this one has much of anything to say to people unfortunate enough to live in polities that are not governed by liberal democratic institutions. Unfortunately, I will have to leave those questions, among others, for another time.[71]

Notes

1 Greenman, "On Communication," p. 1341.
2 Ibid., pp. 1344–45.

3 For my purpose, the term "expression" signifies that an action (including speech) may emit certain views or attitudes but does not require that a particular member of the audience for the action understands the basis for or purpose behind the action. The actor may intend the expression to benefit other members of the audience or even only the actor herself. To illustrate the expression-communication distinction, consider, for example, the following: when Mariah calls her brother, Nathan, at home and speaks in a language Nathan can understand to tell him, "Dad is coming home for dinner at 8 p.m. tonight," that is a communication. When Nathan writes an entry in his private diary, he is expressing his opinions without communicating them to anyone. Similarly, when the Blues Brothers drive around a neighborhood with a giant speaker strapped to their car rooftop, broadcasting details of their upcoming show to all and sundry, that too is expression. State punishment can also communicate messages to offenders and express messages to the public. The message to the public may be "do not do X" or "we are keeping our promise to punish X." But when punishments emit messages to the public, the messages have an unspecified target; it is not important that one person in particular have a rational understanding of that message. For that reason, I call those signaling goals to the public "expressive" goals instead of "communicative" goals.

4 The state's pursuit of retributive justice can be thought of as a prima facie duty. Such duties cannot be denied as obligations, but since the determination of how and when to discharge those obligations is a prudential matter, these obligations may be set aside when other duties of justice supersede. Phrased differently, the obligation to create and maintain institutions of retributive justice must be balanced against other social obligations and moral duties. For an instructive elaboration on reconciling competing obligations, see generally Cahill, "Retributive Justice in the Real World"; see also the chapter by White in this volume.

5 Rawls, "Two Concepts of Rules," pp. 4–5. Rawls later changes his focus from suffering to punishment.

6 Moore, "Moral Worth of Retribution," p. 179. For Moore, moral culpability is the same as desert (pp. 181–82).

7 See, for example, Blecker, "Rethinking the Death Penalty."

8 For the most part, I will assume that the state's interest is in punishing the offender to communicate condemnation effectively, not in having the offender suffer. I have elsewhere explained why this should be the case; see Markel and Flanders, "Bentham on Stilts"; see also Gray, "Punishment as Suffering," and Berman, "Two Kinds of Retributivism."

9 For example, Menninger, *Crime of Punishment*.

10 See von Hirsch, "Penal Theories."

11 Moore, *Placing Blame*, p. 133.

12 Lewis, *Problem of Pain*, p. 94.

13 Importantly, on this view, one cannot say that the obligation to respect another as a morally responsible agent ceases as soon as a court has rendered a (correct) judgment; it must continue throughout the retributive encounter.

14 A law prohibiting eating on the subway by pain of a criminal fine would probably pass muster with me. By contrast, a law criminalizing adult intimate conduct between two men would not because it prohibits something closely and fundamentally connected to individual liberty.

15 Garvey, "As the Gentle Rain from Heaven," p. 1030.

16 Of course, if Jack lobotomized himself intentionally after the crime, the state might have a deterrence-based reason to punish him for his self-created condition of ill-repair notwithstanding

that the punishment would at that later point lack communicative significance. (See generally Robinson, "Causing the Conditions of One's Own Defense," as well as the chapter by DeGirolami in this volume.) I treat this as an open question, however. I am admittedly unsure to what extent concerns about making sure people are not able to "escape" their punishments can trump the fact that communication with the offender was no longer possible. This is, of course, an extreme case.

17 See Moore, *Placing Blame*, p. 90.

18 Kant put the point somewhat differently; he thought someone who endured punishment for his wrong was perfecting his autonomy (see, for example,*Metaphysics of Morals*, p. 335). The claim that even a repentant offender should experience equal punishment with a defiant but otherwise similarly situated offender runs contrary to the views of some other prominent punishment theorists. See Murphy, "Legal Moralism and Retribution Revisited," p. 10 (noting that Joel Feinberg, Jean Hampton, and Herbert Morris embraced the idea of lower punishments based on true repentance).

19 See Murphy and Coleman, *Philosophy of Law*, p. 124.

20 Or at least, so I will assume for purposes of this paper.

21 A lack of at least a threatened state response would leave the offender's claim to superiority unchallenged, a situation that a society committed to equal liberty under law should wish to avoid.

22 On the point of diminishing the plausibility of an offender's claims to superiority, see generally Hampton, "Retributive Idea" and "Correcting Harms Versus Righting Wrongs." Hampton was focused on repudiating false messages emitted by offenders toward victims; my own concern expands the focus to the false messages of superiority emitted by the offender against the polity through a disrespect for democratic authority.

23 Bradley, "Retribution," pp. 25–26; Finnis, "Retribution," pp. 99–101. Of course, this does not assume that, in fact, everyone has the same likelihood of enjoying the same liberties; clearly, tastes and various constraints—economic, geographic, and so forth—influence the patterns resulting from the provision of equal liberty under law.

24 Calabresi and Melamed, "Property Rules, Liability Rules, and Inalienability."

25 Murphy and Coleman, *Philosophy of Law*, p. 116. It could be argued that violations of all legal norms (that is, both civil and criminal) would be sufficient to trigger the democratic self-defense argument, making it seem that this argument proves too much in the context of a justification for punishing violations of criminal laws. This is a plausible argument, but democratic authorities get to decide which rules will be criminal or civil in nature. Consequently, one might see the violation of a criminal law as a greater and more salient form of rebellion than a violation of a rule simply establishing potential exposure to tort liability when a plaintiff brings a claim on his own volition.

26 Ibid., p. 124.

27 See 5 U.S.C. § 3331 (2010).

28 See, for example, Christiano, "Authority" (section 7.2): "To the extent that the democratic assembly's claim of authority is grounded in the public realization of the principle of equal respect, the authority would run out when the democratic assembly makes law that undermines equal respect. This establishes, at least for one conception of democratic authority, a substantive set of limits to that authority."

29 Compare to Feldman and Lifshitz, "Behind the Veil of Legal Uncertainty."

30 Compare to Murphy, "Marxism and Retribution," p. 228: "The criminal himself has no complaint, because he has rationally consented to or willed his own punishment. That is, those very

rules which he has broken work, when they are obeyed by others, to his own advantage as a citizen. He would have chosen such rules for himself and others in the original position of choice."

31 Furthermore, to see the offense as a rebellion is not to say that all rebellions need be quashed with maximum resources. We might wish to empower private citizens to address some rebellions through tort and to empower the public to address other rebellions through criminal law and the administrative state, and some others through a number of responses, including public and private law. Importantly, the scarcity of social resources in a society committed to pursuing various projects of moral significance requires a principle of frugality in the use of retributive punishment, such that the state pursues and punishes only those acts that are necessary for securing the conditions conducive to human flourishing.

32 The phrase here is borrowed from Rawls, *Theory of Justice*, p. 527.

33 See generally my "Against Mercy." As explained there, the more discretion over sentencing one confers on victims (or juries, or trial judges), the greater the likelihood of creating Type I and II errors based on vindictiveness or unwarranted compassion.

34 As Allen and Laudan demonstrate ("Deadly Dilemmas," pp. 81–84), however, an "innocentristic" social concern eliminates only Type I errors, that is, those false positives involving mistaken punishment. As a matter of social policy, we have very strong reasons, on retributive and nonretributive grounds, to be concerned with Type II error reduction—that is, reducing the false negatives associated with failing to punish the guilty—as well.

35 While invoking a principle of modesty may seem theoretically vague, it actually has substantial policy implications. Elsewhere, for example, I have argued that a commitment to modesty entails forbearing from the death penalty or shaming punishments; see my "Are Shaming Punishments Beautifully Retributive?," "State, Be Not Proud," and "Executing Retributivism."

36 Hampton, "Correcting Harms."

37 Markel, "Are Shaming Punishments Beautifully Retributive?" Compare to Ezekiel 33:11: "I have no pleasure in the death of the wicked; but that the wicked turn from his way and live." A similar point is developed in Duff, *Punishment, Communication and Community*, and Nozick, *Philosophical Explanations*.

38 Nozick, *Philosophical Explanations*, p. 377.

39 Markel, "State, Be Not Proud," p. 410 n. 13 (providing citations to Supreme Court cases that crudely equate retributivism with revenge, the desire to make criminals suffer, or both).

40 This discussion by reference to ideal types is necessary because there have often been cultures or social norms involving revenge that fall somewhere in between. For an illuminating and entertaining discussion of this cultural history, see Miller, *Eye for an Eye*.

41 Nozick, *Philosophical Explanations*, pp. 366–68.

42 This is not to deny that retributive punishment may result in third-party harms, nor to suggest that revenge is always targeted at third parties close to the offender. The point is narrow: retributive punishment does not aim to harm third parties, and in some cases, the kind of retribution imposed should take into account innocent third-party harms. *See* Markel, Collins and Leib, "Criminal Justice and the Challenge of Family Ties" (urging greater use of time-deferred incarceration to mitigate innocent third-party harms).

43 An avenger who sees his antagonist experience suffering from some other source, such as disease, may decline to follow through on the revenge, whereas the state's retributive interest would not be satisfied merely by having an offender suffer.

44 This notion might be enhanced for some through the thought experiment of the "secret and fair punishment." See my *Shaming Punishments*, pp. 2211–12; compare to Moore, *Placing Blame*, p. 90.

45 For discussions of this principle, see Nussbaum, *Hiding from Humanity*, p. 233 ("Punishments may treat the act very harshly, while still expressing the sense that the person is worthy of regard and of ultimate reintegration into society"); Whitman, *Harsh Justice*, p. 51 (discussing Beccaria's view that punishment should focus on acts, not offenders); and Whitman, "Making Happy Punishers," p. 2711 (noting Christian and liberal roots of person/act distinction).

46 Whitman, "Making Happy Punishers," p. 2711: "[N]o legal system has ever succeeded in focusing entirely on acts rather than on persons. . ." This difficulty is especially true because CCR cares both about the offender's competence as a fit interlocutor for the message of punishment and also considers that the offender's actions may be read as more pernicious or reprehensible as a result of having previously been adjudicated and punished for a prior criminal act.

47 Recent debates over the propriety of "shaming punishments" have also centered on this distinction. With shaming sanctions, it is hard not to convey the impression that the whole person is tainted, corrupted, and "lower," rather than that he has done a bad thing, which must be condemned. See generally my "Shaming Punishments."

48 Hegel, *Philosophy of Right*, p. 71; see the chapter by Johnson in this book for more on Hegel's views on crime and punishment.

49 Cahill, "Retributive Justice in the Real World," p. 834.

50 Berman, "Punishment and Justification," pp. 278–84.

51 Compare to Berman, "Two Kinds of Retributivism," draft p. 12 (using this phrase in a different context).

52 See the chapter by White in this volume for more on balancing retributivist concerns against others.

53 Adler, *Urgings of Conscience*, p. 80 (discounting the view that punishment's defining characteristic is pain).

54 Compare to Berman, "Punishment and Justification," p. 270 (rehearsing the objection that "the proposition that wrongdoers deserve to suffer on account of their blameworthy wrongdoing is mere ipse dixit," but concluding that "this charge does not stick").

55 Ross, *Right and the Good*, p. 56 (noting that "[m]ost intuitionists would take the view that there is a fundamental and underivative duty to reward the virtuous and punish the vicious").

56 *See* Husak, "Holistic Retributivism"; *see also* Berman, "Two Kinds of Retributivism," draft p. 8 (noting the inclination among some philosophers to think that offenders deserve suffering and not simply punishment).

57 Duff, *Punishment, Communication, and Community*.

58 Rawls, *Political Liberalism*, pp. 154–56. The point here is not to fully defend Rawls's distinction between the political and the comprehensive but rather simply to make the more modest point that CCR is not "comprehensive," something which may help to distinguish it from other, more metaphysically fraught versions of retributivism. This is something I see as an advantage, but others may not.

59 Ibid.

60 Ibid.

61 For example, Kant writes (*Metaphysics of Morals*, p. 333) that "[t]his fitting of punishment to the crime, which can only occur by a judge imposing the death sentence in accordance with the

strict law of retribution, is shown by the fact that only by this is a sentence of death pronounced on every criminal in proportion to his inner wickedness."

62 Shafer-Landau, "Retributivism and Desert," p. 189 n. 1 (providing citations to the relevant philosophical literature); McLeod, "Desert."

63 These political values are, of course, also moral values. But they are moral values that are thought to be implicit in the public political culture of a democracy. In this respect, the familiar distinction between moral retributivism and legal retributivism is perhaps more helpfully understood as differentiating between political versus comprehensive forms of retributivism.

64 The account in the text, albeit brief, stands as a short summary of my views regarding the debate between Jean Hampton and Jeffrie Murphy, among others, over the precise character of punishment in a liberal democracy. It also points to a compromise of sorts for persons torn between perfectionist and anti-perfectionist liberal worldviews. Agreeing with Murphy, I see punishment as needing to have a political, and not a comprehensive, justification and shape (see Murphy, "Retributivism, Moral Education, and the Liberal State," pp. 15–30). Agreeing with Hampton, I see this account as unproblematically retributive—our emphasis remains, after all, on the core claim that punishment for legal offenses is internally intelligible assuming that the content and application of the laws is suitably liberal and fairly enforced. But, *contrary to* Hampton, retributivists need not be thoroughgoing perfectionists and need not abandon their commitment to a Rawlsian-style political liberalism that emphasizes reasons for punishment that are grounded in the state's legal grievances against offenders who flout the reasonable legal norms established and enforced fairly by the polity. See generally Hampton, "Comments on Legal Moralism," pp. 105–15.

Indeed, given the risks, costs, and consequences associated with error and abuse in the criminal justice system, it might be permissible or desirable to promote a greater intolerance of perfectionism within the criminal justice system while giving the state more democratic (or perfectionist) flexibility outside the criminal justice system. By this logic, criminal law and enforcement (including sentencing) must hew closer to the core liberal values of individual liberty and equality under the law (for example, not discriminating on the basis of family status or religious affiliation) than, say, tax law or social policy, which might be used to create a civic culture that promotes certain values (related to, for example, patriotism or volunteerism). An illustration of this perspective can be viewed, with respect to the use of family status in criminal law or noncriminal laws, in Markel, Collins, and Leib, *Privilege or Punish*.

65 Indeed, this should help dislodge any quick sense of a natural relationship between retributive justice and *lex talionis*. Though I am not committed at all to *lex talionis* (because it is not essentially a retributive principle), it is worth noting how capacious (and nonretributive) even the *lex talionis* approach can be. (*See generally* Waldron, "Lex Talionis.")

66 Antony Duff makes a related point about punishment being concerned with crimes as primarily wrongs implicating public concern: "What matters about crimes is not just their seriousness but their character as public wrongs. What matters about punishments is not just their severity but their character as responses to such wrongs" (*Punishment, Communication and Community*, p. 139).

67 For some initial thoughts on the relationship between the CCR and the Eighth Amendment, however, see my "Executing Retributivism."

68 Bickel, *Least Dangerous Branch*, p. 103.

69 Markel, "Against Mercy" (arguing against unreviewable sites of sentencing discretion).

70 Finnis, "Retribution," p. 103.

71 While innumerable persons have, over the years, helped me think through the issues discussed in the chapter, I owe special thanks to Chad Flanders for help with the account in this particular essay, which draws on and revisits some of my earlier work cited in the bibliography. Thanks also to Philip Kovoor, Meg Powers, Will Ourand, and Holly Griffin for invaluable editorial assistance with this chapter and to Mark White for editorial guidance. Comments and questions are invited; please send them to markel@post.harvard.edu.

Bibliography

Adler, Jacob. *The Urgings of Conscience: A Theory of Punishment*. Philadelphia: Temple University Press, 1992.

Allen, Ronald J., and Larry Laudan "Deadly Dilemmas." *Texas Tech Law Review* 41 (2008): 65–92.

Berman, Mitchell N. "Punishment and Justification." *Ethics* 118 (2008): 258–90.

Berman, Mitchell N. "Two Kinds of Retributivism." In *The Philosophical Foundations of Criminal Law*, edited by R. A. Duff and Stuart P. Green. Oxford: Oxford University Press, 2011 (in press).

Bickel, Alexander M. *The Least Dangerous Branch: The Supreme Court at the Bar of Politics*. 2nd ed. Binghamton, New York: Vail-ballou Press, Inc., 1986.

Blecker, Robert. "Rethinking the Death Penalty: Can We Define Who Deserves Death?" *Pace Law Review* 24 (2003): 107–86.

Bradley, Gerard V. "Retribution: The Central Aim of Punishment." *Harvard Journal of Law & Public Policy* 27 (2003): 19–31.

Calabresi, Guido, and A. Douglas Melamed. "Property Rules, Liability Rules, and Inalienability: One View of the Cathedral." *Harvard Law Review* 85 (1972): 1089–128.

Cahill, Michael T. "Retributive Justice in the Real World." *Washington University Law Review* 85 (2007): 815–70.

Christiano Tom. "Authority." *Stanford Encyclopedia of Philosophy* (http://plato.stanford.edu/entries/authority/).

Duff, R. A. *Punishment, Community and Communication*. Oxford: Oxford University Press, 2001.

Duff, R. A. *Trials and Punishments*. Cambridge: Cambridge University Press, 1986.

Feldman, Yuval, and Shahar Lifshitz. "Behind the Veil of Legal Uncertainty." Bar-Ilan University Public Law and Legal Theory Working Paper No. 11-August 10, 2010. Available at http://papers.ssrn.com/sol3/papers.cfm?abstract_id=1633429.

Finnis, John. "Retribution: Punishment's Formative Aim." *American Journal of Jurisprudence* 44 (1999): 91–103.

Garvey, Stephen P. "'As the Gentle Rain from Heaven': Mercy in Capital Sentencing." *Cornell Law Review* 81 (1996): 989–1048.

Gray, David. "Punishment as Suffering." *Vanderbilt Law Review* 63 (2010): 1619–93.

Greenman, John. "On Communication." *Michigan Law Review* 106 (2008): 1337–78.

Hegel, G. W. F. *Philosophy of Right*. Edited by Allen W. Wood. Translated by H. B. Nisbet. Cambridge: Cambridge University Press, 1991.

Husak, Douglas N. "Holistic Retributivism." *California Law Review* 88 (2000): 991–1000.

Hampton, Jean. "Correcting Harms Versus Righting Wrongs: The Goal of Retribution." *UCLA Law Review* 39 (1992): 1659–1702.

Hampton, Jean. "How You Can Be Both a Liberal and a Retributivist: Comments on Legal Moralism and Liberalism by Jeffrie Murphy." *Arizona Law Review* 37 (1995): 105–116.

Hampton, Jean. "The Retributive Idea." In *Forgiveness and Mercy*, by Jeffrie G. Murphy and Jean Hampton, 111–61. Cambridge: Cambridge University Press, 1988.

Kant, Immanuel. *The Metaphysics of Morals*. Translated and edited by Mary Gregor. Cambridge: Cambridge University Press, 1996.

Lewis, C. S. *The Problem of Pain*. New York: Harper Collins, 2001.

Markel, Dan. "Against Mercy." *Minnesota Law Review* 88 (2004): 1421–80.

Markel, Dan. "Are Shaming Punishments Beautifully Retributive? Retributivism and the Implications for the Alternative Sanctions Debate." *Vanderbilt Law Review* 54 (2001): 2157–242.

Markel, Dan. "Executing Retributivism: Panetti and the Future of the Eighth Amendment." *Northwestern University Law Review* 103 (2009): 1163–222.

Markel, Dan. "State, Be Not Proud." *Harvard Civil Rights-Civil Liberties Law Review* 40 (2005): 407–80.

Markel, Dan, Jennifer M.Collins, and Ethan J. Leib. "Criminal Justice and the Challenge of Family Ties." *University of Illinois Law Review 2007* (2007): 1147–227.

Markel, Dan, Jennifer M. Collins, and Ethan J. Leib. *Privilege or Punish: Criminal Justice and the Challenge of Family Ties*. Oxford: Oxford University Press, 2009.

Markel, Dan and Chad Flanders. "Bentham on Stilts: The Bare Relevance of Subjectivity to Retributive Justice." *California Law Review* 98 (2010): 907–88.

McLeod, Owen. "Desert." *Stanford Encyclopedia of Philosophy* (http://plato.stanford.edu/entries/desert).

Menninger, Karl. *The Crime of Punishment*. Bloomington, Indiana: Authorhouse, 2007.

Miller, William Ian. *Eye for an Eye*. Cambridge: Cambridge University Press, 2006.

Moore, Michael S. "The Moral Worth of Retribution." In *Responsibility, Character and the Emotions: New Essays in Moral Psychology*, edited by Ferdinand Schoeman, 179–219. Cambridge: Cambridge University Press, 1987.

Moore, Michael S. *Placing Blame: A General Theory of the Criminal Law*. Oxford: Oxford University Press, 1997.

Murphy, Jeffrie G. "Legal Moralism and Retribution Revisited." *Criminal Law and Philosophy* 1 (2007): 5–20.

Murphy, Jeffrie G. "Marxism and Retribution." *Philosophy and Public Affairs* 2 (1973): 217–43.

Murphy, Jeffrie G. "Retributivism, Moral Education, and the Liberal State." *Criminal Justice Ethics* 4 (1985): 3–11.

Murphy, Jeffrie G., and Jules L. Coleman. *Philosophy of Law: An Introduction to Jurisprudence*. Boulder, CO: Westview Press, Inc., 1990.

Nozick, Robert. *Philosophical Explanations*. Cambridge, MA: Harvard University Press, 1981.

Nussbaum, Martha C. *Hiding From Humanity: Disgust, Shame, and the Law*. Princeton: Princeton University Press, 2004.

Rawls, John. *Political Liberalism*. New York: Columbia University Press, 1993.

Rawls, John. *A Theory of Justice*. Cambridge, MA: Harvard University Press, 1971.

Rawls, John. "Two Concepts of Rules." *Philosophical Review* 64 (1955): 3–32.

Robinson, Paul H. "Causing the Conditions of One's Own Defense: A Study in the Limits of Theory in Criminal Law Doctrine." *Virginia Law Review* 71 (1985): 1–63.

Ross, W. D. *The Right and the Good*. Oxford: Oxford University Press, 1930.

Shafer-Landau, Russ. "Retributivism and Desert." *Pacific Philosophical Quarterly* 81 (2000): 189–214.

von Hirsch, Andrew. "Penal Theories." In *The Handbook of Crime and Punishment*, edited by Michael Tonry, 659–82. Oxford: Oxford University Press, 1998.

Waldron, Jeremy. "Lex Talionis." *Arizona Law Review* 34 (1992): 25–50.

Whitman, James Q. *Harsh Justice: Criminal Punishment and the Widening Divide Between Europe and America*. Oxford: Oxford University Press, 2003.

Whitman, James Q. "Making Happy Punishers." *Harvard Law Review* 118 (2005): 2698–724.

4

RETRIBUTIVE JUSTICE AND SOCIAL COOPERATION

Gerald Gaus

1. The Bishop and John Stuart Mill

IN RESPONSE TO American criticisms of the Scottish ministers' decision to release the Lockerbie bomber on compassionate grounds, Cardinal Keith O'Brien, the Roman Catholic Archbishop of St. Andrews and Edinburgh, "launched a scathing attack" on American politicians and, in general, the "culture of vengeance" in the United States. It was reported that he proclaimed that "many Americans were more interested in retribution than justice."[1] For Cardinal O'Brien, retribution and vengeance are closely related—and to be disparaged—and are opposed to an interest in justice. John Stuart Mill offered a rather different analysis; as he saw it, an "essential" ingredient in the "sentiment of justice" is "the desire to punish a person who has done harm."[2] Mill traces the idea of justice back to "authoritative custom," composed of social rules enforced through punishment.[3] "It would always give us pleasure, and chime in with our feelings of *fitness*, that acts which we deem unjust should be punished. . . ."[4] Like the bishop, Mill is worried that the desire for retaliation or vengeance—which, along with sympathy he sees as providing the emotional foundations of justice[5]—is not itself moral and must be directed to moral ends, but he insists that the desire to punish is fundamental to the very idea of justice.

The bishop talks about "retribution," Mill about "punishment."[6] What is their relation? We should distinguish three levels at which "retributivism" is a "theory of punishment." At what I shall call the *shallow* level, retributivism is an account of genuine punishment. As Kurt Baier—very much in the spirit of Mill's analysis—argued, "'punishing' is the name of only a part-activity belonging to a complex procedure."[7] Punishment is part of the complex idea of a system of justice, which is a "whole 'game,' consisting of rule-making, penalization, finding guilty of a breach of a rule, pronouncing sentence, and finally administering punishment."[8] On Baier's analysis, punishment is part of this complex— the idea that hardship is inflicted on a person for an infraction of the rules:

> A method of inflicting hardship on someone cannot be called "punishment" unless at least the following condition is satisfied. It must be the case that when someone is found "not guilty" it is not permissible to go on to pronounce sentence on him and carry it out. For "punishment" is the name of a method, or system, of inflicting hardship, the aim of which is to hurt all and only those who are guilty of an offense.... To say that it is of the very nature of punishment to be retributive, is to say that a system of inflicting hardship on someone could not be properly called "punishment," unless it is the aim of this system to hurt all and only those guilty of an offense.[9]

In this shallow but important sense, there is a large body of evidence that most people *are* "retributivists": they believe that people who do wrong should have hardship inflicted on them just because they have done wrong. They believe that, as Mill said, it is *fitting* that wrongdoers should be punished. Stanley Benn appeared to think that Kant was such a retributivist when he maintains "that the punishment of a crime is right in itself, that is, that it is *fitting* that the guilty should suffer, and that *justice... requires the institution of punishment.*"[10] Benn charges that this, "however, is not to justify punishment but, rather, to deny that it needs any justification."[11] Benn is right that so understood, this is not a special justification of the practice of punishment; it expresses, rather, the Millian-Baierian observation that the idea of a just system of rules includes punishment, and such punishment is inherently retributive in the sense that Baier indicates above.[12]

Many philosophers find this unsatisfying because they understand "retributivism" in a much stronger sense: as a theory of *why the practice of (retributive) punishment is justified rather than some other practice of rule enforcement.*[13] Retributivism in the shallow sense is a backward-looking doctrine that says that one should be punished if and only if one is guilty of an offense. What are called "retributivist justifications of punishment" are typically doubly backward looking: they hold that this backward-looking practice is justified because of some other backward-looking consideration, such as the importance that people get what they deserve, where desert itself is a backward-looking consideration apart from guilt according to the rules of justice.[14] In contrast, a utilitarian justification of the practice of punishment seeks to give a forward-looking justification of this backward-looking practice of punishment, with all the obvious problems that entails.[15] In this deeper sense, most people are *not* retributivists, for most do not have a justificatory theory of the practice of punishment at all.[16] In between the shallow and this deep understanding is retributivist theory understood as an account of the appropriate severity of punishment: *lex talionis*, the idea that the punishment must have a certain proportionality to the evil of the offense.[17]

In this chapter, I provide an analysis of why the game that Mill and Baier observe, that the practice of justice includes the idea of "retributive punishment"—the idea that the guilty should have hardships inflicted on them just because they are guilty—is one that solves the problem of stable human cooperation in ways that theories of "telishment" or forward-looking enforcement, cannot.[18] In the case of telishment, the institution of enforcing rules via sanctions is not retributive: telishment explicitly aims at a "*telos,*" or an end, and so is forward looking in its decision whether harm or costs are to be inflicted as a way to enforce conformity to our rules of social cooperation. The idea that the shallow conception of retributivism is uninteresting because it simply identifies retributivism with punishment overlooks the really interesting question: why do we have a game of justice in which rules are enforced via the backward-looking idea of retributive punishment rather than some forward-looking strategy? On the face of it, there would seem strong reasons why we should enforce in a forward-looking way—that we should "telish" rather than punish. As Mill stressed, justice is crucial to utility[19]: if the aim of a system of justice is to allow humans to cooperate on mutually beneficial terms, it would seem that when applying sanctions, such a system should have an eye toward promoting cooperation rather than turning our back on the effects of our sanctioning and crying over spilled milk. If we conceive of humans as being devoted to pursuing their own ends and reasonably believe that the game of justice is conducive to this, why are we (or at least most of us) shallow retributivists? Why, *pace* the good bishop, is a culture of justice a culture of retribution?

2. Why Being Nice Is Not Enough

Let us begin by rounding up the usual suspect, in this case the Prisoners' Dilemma in Figure 4.1. The Prisoners' Dilemma is an example of a family of games, all of which model a conflict of motives. As I have constructed the game in Figure 4.1, the best payoff is 4, and the worst is 1. On the one hand, we can see the benefits of mutual cooperation: if Alf and Betty cooperate, they both receive a payoff of 3, which is better for both of them than the payoff of 2 that they will receive if they both defect. On the other hand, each has an incentive to defect. If Betty cooperates, Alf receives a payoff of 3 if he cooperates but 4 if he defects, so he does better by defecting. If Betty defects, Alf receives 1 by cooperating but 2 by defecting, so again he does better by defecting. Whatever Betty does, Alf does best by defecting, making defecting his *dominant* strategy: no matter what Betty does, he should defect. And Betty's reasoning is *mutatis mutandis*, the same. But this leads to mutual defection and, as we have seen, they can do better by mutual cooperation.

More generally, we can see how social interactions with this structure are an impediment to mutual advantage. If we suppose that individuals are solely devoted to their own ends, the development of mutually advantageous market exchange—which depends on trust— seems difficult to explain. As Hobbes so effectively showed, individuals who are solely devoted to their private ends will be sorely tempted to renege on "covenants": if the other

FIGURE 4.1 A Prisoners' Dilemma in Ordinal Form

party performs first and so gives the second party what she wants, there seems to be no incentive for the second party to perform her part of the bargain.[20] Rather than exchanging, she will be tempted to snatch the goods and flee.[21] Given sufficiently narrow, self-interested utility functions, she will often be tempted to snatch—getting the good without paying for it.

Clearly, the development of a system of rules of justice that requires each to cooperate would be beneficial to each, but, so long as they reason simply in terms of their own interests, they will be tempted to violate the rules. For Hobbes, once we recognize this, we see why a system of punishment is necessary to secure justice: there must be an authorized punisher who can inflict such hardships on defectors that once they tally up the gains from defection but subtract the costs of the imposed hardships, they will see that their interests align with cooperation.

As we will see, this is indeed a fundamental insight and one of the reasons anyone who grapples with the problem of cooperation in such "mixed motive" interactions must come to terms with Hobbes. But we might think that Hobbes's conclusions about the necessity of enforcement only follow because the Prisoners' Dilemma supposes that people are pretty nasty. According to Prisoners' Dilemma preferences, given a chance to cheat on Betty when she has already done her part of the bargain, Alf prefers to take advantage of her rather than do his part. We can imagine the bishop saying that it is precisely such an individualist (American?) culture that breeds the culture of vengeance. But people are nicer than that. The people modeled in the Prisoners' Dilemma game order the options like this: (1) the other cooperates and I cheat; (2) we both cooperate; (3) we both cheat; (4) I cooperate, and the other cheats. But nice people would not wish to cheat; they would prefer to cooperate if the others do so.

So suppose we reorder the outcomes so that the best option for both is mutual cooperation. But neither should we suppose that Alf and Betty are saintly: they still think the worst outcome is to be played for a sucker, cooperating while the other defects. This gives us a "Stag Hunt" as in Figure 4.2. In this game, rational individuals are pulled in two directions: mutual benefit points to cooperating (each gets 4), but risk aversion points to defecting (a guarantee of getting 3 is better than a chance of getting 0). There are two equilibria in this game: mutual cooperation and mutual defection. Under some conditions, it is remarkably easy to end up in social states in which everyone defects. Suppose first, a very simple iterated (repeated) game in which individuals randomly encounter each

	Betty	
	Cooperate	Defect
Alf Cooperate	4 4	3 0
Defect	0 3	3 3

FIGURE 4.2 A Stag Hunt

other, playing a series of games, and suppose (now using cardinal payoffs) that defecting has a payoff of 3 and mutual cooperation 4, but cooperating alone gives a 0 payoff. If less than 75 percent of the population begins with cooperating, the population will gravitate over time to all defectors; only if the initial cooperating population is over 75 percent of the total will the group evolve into all cooperators.[22]

So it is not only important that lots of people have "nice" Stag Hunt outlooks to assure that they will abide by the rules of cooperation. Alf must be confident that Betty is nice too, and, moreover, he must know that she knows he is nice (and that he knows she knows this, and so on). If they are cautious and start out by playing "defect," even a population of all "nice" people can end up *all* defecting. If the conversion process is incomplete—if most but not all of us have adopted "nice" preferences such as those in Figure 4.2, but some remain unreformed, Prisoners' Dilemma players—and this fact is generally known—the prospects for social cooperation seem quite dim. Gregory Kavka introduced the game of an "Assurance Dilemma" to model interactions in a Hobbesian state of nature, according to which some agents have nasty Prisoners' Dilemma orderings while others have nicer, more cooperative orderings (as in Figure 4.3).[23] Assume that parties do not have perfect information about each other's preferences. When Alf encounters another, the question facing nice Alf is whether he is playing another nice person—in which case he essentially will be playing the game in Figure 4.2—or whether he is playing a nasty person, as in Figure 4.3. Here, even a nice Alf should defect, for his cooperative move will be met with defection from Betty, giving him his worst outcome. Note that the sole equilibrium in this game is the same as that in the Prisoners' Dilemma: mutual defection.

Peter Vanderschraaf has recently developed a far more sophisticated version of this game in which players have a range of possible payoffs (rather than just two types), and ways of estimating (based on past performance) what the payoffs of the other player are. Players are uncertain about the payoffs of others but have ways of learning and updating their probability estimate that the others are prone to attack. In computer simulations of anarchy under these conditions, Vanderschraaf finds that "[t]he presence of only a few 'nasty' individuals gradually drives all, including those inclined to be 'nicer,' to imitate the 'nasty' conduct of these few. This dynamic analysis suggests that the Hobbesian war in anarchy is indeed inevitable in most realistic circumstances."[24] Under conditions of imperfect information and a range of parties' preferences, the uncertainty created by

		Betty (Nasty)	
		Cooperate	Defect
Alf (Nice)	Cooperate	3 / 4	4 / 1
	Defect	1 / 2	2 / 2

FIGURE 4.3 An Assurance Dilemma

the presence of a few nasty agents (that is, with Prisoners' Dilemma-like preferences) leads to universal war (or defection).

Vanderschraaf's analysis is important as it illustrates a deep flaw in a long line of theorizing that has supposed that social cooperation emerges from people reasoning themselves into, or adopting, more cooperative preferences. It has often been thought that the core task in explaining the rise of cooperation is to show the reasonability of preferences for conditional cooperation ("I'll cooperate if you do"). That is, at best, only the first step. Having a large majority of the population with preferences for conditional cooperation (such as in Figure 4.2) by no means guarantees social cooperation or even makes it likely. Although we began with the Prisoners' Dilemma, with "nasty" preference orderings, we now see that the problem is not only the character of the preferences but also uncertainty about what others' preferences are. Even interactions that are "objectively" cooperative—that is, under perfect common knowledge, we would all see that we are conditional cooperators—may easily end up at noncooperative equilibria. Indeed, under full common knowledge and cooperative preferences, cooperative equilibria are by no means certain; as Cristina Bicchieri stresses, firm first-order expectations about what others will do are required.[25] It turns out that the problem of social cooperation is difficult for even a population of cooperative people.

3. Minimal Enforcement: Boycotts

In addition to being nice, perhaps it will suffice if people are also discriminating. If cooperators can distinguish other cooperators from defectors, and interact with the former and boycott the latter, they could gain the benefits of cooperation without opening themselves up to be suckers. More formally, we can say that when cooperation is correlated—when there is a tendency for cooperators to seek out, identify, and interact with other cooperators—cooperative interaction can flourish.[26] We can think of this as a strategy of boycotting defectors, a relatively mild form of sanctioning for noncompliance with cooperative norms. Boycotting is effective *if* a cooperator has sufficient information about the dispositions of others—and, of course, that's the rub. Defectors have a good incentive to appear cooperative, so without a good deal of widespread, accurate, and shared information about who is a cooperator and who is a defector, boycotting will be an inefficient mechanism to produce compliance.

Hume and Hobbes thought that one's *reputation* as either a cooperator or defector—the public knowledge of one's past behavior—would serve as an effective way to enforce contracts. Again, Vanderschraaf's work has enlightened us about the conditions for compliance with covenants through reputation. Vanderschraaf focuses on what he calls "the covenant game," seeking to model Hobbes's and Hume's proposal that rational agents would not cooperate with those who have reputations as defectors, and this knowledge should itself provide a sufficient incentive for would-be defectors to refrain from double-crossing on covenants.[27] In his iterated (repeated) "covenant game," one has a choice to (1) boycott the other party by refusing to make an agreement; (2) promising and performing; or (3) promising and then double-crossing; as in the Prisoners' Dilemma (which forms a subgame of Vanderschraff's more complex game) there is an incentive to double-cross rather than perform. The parties know that they would gain in the present stage by double-crossing but also may gain a bad reputation by double-crossing, and those with bad reputations would be boycotted in future stages of the game and so would not gain in those stages the fruits of social cooperation.

The novel and insightful idea in Vanderschraff's analysis is modeling types of information available to the parties. If we possess accurate common knowledge of the trustworthiness of potential partners—we all know about who is trustworthy and all know that we all know this—reputation effects can indeed secure cooperation. But public, accurate, common knowledge is seldom available. Vanderschraaf thus models information produced by gossip: individuals letting other individuals know what they think of certain parties, taking account of the effects of false gossip as well as true gossip. As ethnographic studies of cooperation via reputation have shown, there are strong incentives to exaggerate and fake one's cooperative history.[28] Once we model information as gossip (true and false) and allow defectors to adopt slightly more sophisticated strategies (such as only double-crossing half the time rather than always), Vanderschraaf shows that such defectors "can fare better than Humeans in a community that must rely upon private information or 'gossip' only to spread information."[29]

4. Getting Tougher: Deterrence

Perhaps it is time to get a little tougher on defectors. Robert Axelrod is widely understood to have shown that cooperation can emerge among "egoists" (people with Prisoners' Dilemma-type orderings) playing repeated Prisoners' Dilemmas.[30] To see this, assume that although you are in a Prisoners' Dilemma with Alf, both of you know that every day from here on in, you will play one Prisoners' Dilemma after another. Axelrod has shown, using a computer simulation, that you often would do best by adopting a very simple strategy: tit for tat. According to tit for tat, your first move is the cooperative one. But if Alf defects rather than cooperates, the next time you meet Alf, you will be uncooperative, too. In short, except for the first move of the game, you decide whether to cooperate or act aggressively with respect to any person by a simple rule: "I'll do to him on this move whatever he did to me the *last* time we met." Essentially, a tit for tat player says to others, "If you defect on me in this game, you will get away with it, but I guarantee that in the next game, I will defect so that we will both be losers. But I am forgiving: if you start cooperating again, I'll begin cooperating again on the move after your cooperative move." Axelrod constructed a computer program specifying a game with hundreds of moves and a variety of actors employing different strategies. Some always act cooperatively no matter what others do, while some always defect. Each strategy played a 200-move game with each other strategy, making for over 100,000 moves: tit for tat won every time.

Many believe that tit for tat is somehow the correct strategy for all repeated Prisoners' Dilemmas, but this is not so.[31] Whether tit for tat is the correct strategy depends on the strategies of the other players. There is no single solution to an infinite (or indefinite) series of Prisoners' Dilemmas; indeed, repeated Prisoners' Dilemmas have infinitely many equilibrium "solutions." Two tit for tatters are indeed in a Nash equilibrium—neither will benefit from a unilateral change of move—when cooperating in such a series. Recall that a tit for tatter cooperates on the first game in a series of Prisoners' Dilemmas and then will do to its opponent in game n whatever its opponent did to it in game n-1. So if one tit for tatter defects in game n-1, the other tit for tatter responds by "punishing" the defector in game n. If one tit for tatter unilaterally defects from cooperation, the other tit for tatter will also "punish" and so lower the payoffs of the defector. Knowing this, neither tit for tatter can gain by unilateral defection, so they are in a Nash equilibrium.

But it is not just two tit for tatters that are in equilibrium—consider "the Grim strategy." Grim cooperates on the first move, but if its opponent defects, Grim will "punish" for every move after that—forever. Two Grim players are also in equilibrium: neither would benefit from defection. The important thing here is that what are generally called "punishing strategies" can achieve equilibrium: if I can inflict hardship on you I can deter you from defecting in cooperative interactions. Repeated Prisoners' Dilemmas allow what are essentially "self-policing contracts" to cooperate. Since we are playing infinitely or indefinitely many games, I can afford to inflict hardships on you now to bring you around, and, seeing that, you will not unilaterally defect. Indeed, any cooperative outcome that gives each player more (or, more formally, at least as much) as the minimum he might receive if the other player acted in the most "punishing" way can be an equilibrium: if we are each above this minimum point, then one party still has room to inflict hardship on the other for a deviation from the "contract." This is the baseline, the payoff a person could get if her opponent was intent on making sure she got as little as possible. As long as the agreement (the coordinated payoffs) is above this minimum, there is room for "punishment," and so unilateral defection will not pay, and thus there will be a Nash equilibrium. This result is known as "the folk theorem."

I have referred to these as "punishing" strategies since that is the common term in the literature, but we can see that they are not engaging in retributive punishment—such strategies adopt a form of deterrence. They make the following threat: if you defect at time t_1, I will inflict costs at a later time t_2 *as a way of securing future cooperative behavior.* As rational individuals, each player is solely devoted to maximizing her payoffs; but given that, "punishment" is simply an investment *now* so as to secure better behavior *later*. In these sorts of iterated interactions, a player is taking account of two factors: (1) how well he can do in this game, and (2) whether he can deter the other from defecting in the future. The second consideration is sometimes called the "shadow of the future." The longer it is—the further the future extends—the more people engage in deterrence and cooperative behavior. However, as the shadow of the future shortens—as people come to believe that they are coming near to the end of their interactions, and so there is less opportunity to be "punished" and less likelihood that one's inflicting "punishment" on them will affect their behavior, people switch from cooperative to defecting behavior.[32] Given this, such deterrence is effective in securing cooperation only when the deterring person has expectations for extended future interactions. If I am a defector, and I know we will never play any more games, I know that you will not incur additional costs to punish me for defecting in this interaction because it would just make you even worse off. As social organization expands, we are constantly encountering people whom we have never met before and whom we are uncertain whether we will meet often again, and so very often, it will not be rational to invest in deterrence behavior. Sophisticated models indicate that deterrence (like tit for tat) allows the development of cooperation in small groups but not in larger ones.[33]

5. Retaliation: Its Virtues and Puzzles

As we just described, cooperation among tit for tatters (or people playing related strategies) unravels as the end of the game approaches; the less certain we are of future interactions, the less incentive we have to sanction noncompliers, and so the less incentive for them to comply. The clear problem is the resolutely forward-looking nature of such telishing strategies: only if the expected benefits of the sanction exceed its costs will rational tit for tatters telish. Would a "culture of vengeance" help?

Call tit for tatters who are resolutely backward looking—who punish rather than telish—*vengeful*: they engage in true punishment because they impose sanctions at t_2 *just because* of the defection of another at t_1, regardless of the shadow of the future. Consider the famous case of private enforcement in medieval Iceland.[34] The rules of social cooperation were enforced by the victims of defection: injured individuals had the right to extract fines (socially fixed at different levels for different offenses) from those who had harmed them through a violation of the rules. A victim could either pursue the fines himself or transfer (by contract) the right to exact them to a third party. The system sought to reduce the costs of self-enforcement; for instance, society as a whole did become involved if the offender refused to pay, declaring the offender an outlaw, which affected what others could do. But the offender might resist; if he did so, any harm done in wrongful resistance was considered yet another offense, which could be the grounds for yet another self-enforcement action, and so on.

Anarchists tend to be fans of the Icelandic system, and they insist that the records do not show that it led to escalating feuds (as vengeance apparently did in the Hatfield–McCoy feud of 1878–1891). The key feature of the system is that the total costs of enforcement were put onto the victim. Suppose the costs of the violation to the victim are c, the costs of enforcement to the victim are d, the fine is f, and the probability of successfully exacting the fine is p.[35] So, unless the expected fine pf equals or exceeds the total costs $c + d$, the victim loses out. The problem is that if p is low (the fine is unlikely to be exacted), and if d is high (and increases in d do not sufficiently raise the possibility of successful enforcement), then unless the fines are set very high (which, one would think, would increase the tendency of defectors to resist, which would itself lower p), the victim will be faced with a double loss: she already has lost c due to the offense, and now she will incur an additional loss of d on the enforcement.

It is reported that the Icelandic system sought to increase p by only including crimes with a probability of detection near unity, and the threat of being declared an outlaw would reduce the probability of stiff resistance.[36] Nevertheless, even an advocate of the system such as David Friedman allows that in some cases it may have been that $pf < c + d$, and so the victim would except to lose out.[37] Friedman argues that enforcement would nevertheless occur because one wished to have a reputation as an enforcer, but we have already seen that reputation is an unreliable mechanism, at least in larger groups (which, admittedly, medieval Iceland was not). Here is the crux of the problem: economists such as Friedman wish to show that victims generally acted as good rational economics agents, only engaging in retaliation if $pf \geq c$, but it is very hard to think an enforcer will be confident that this will be so, at least in large societies where defectors may resist.

To stabilize cooperation in the face of defection, it would seem two things are required. First, enforcers must have a strong incentive to engage in retaliatory action even when the gains from retaliation are less than the costs. If enforcers were not so calculating and rational, they would retaliate even when it was a net loss for them to do so; the probability of enforcement would then clearly go up. Thus, if instead of being a rational policy, retaliation was a basic emotion or desire—if we enjoy retaliation—the certainty of enforcement would rise. But given that all the weight of enforcement is put on the shoulders of the victims (or their designated agents), it might seem that they would have to *really* enjoy their lone enforcement activity. To use Shaun Nichols's quip, they would have to think that retribution was very *yummy* indeed![38] It would help if the desire to retaliate was not just personal, so third parties would share some of the costs with the victims. This is the second of the two sentiments that Mill thought was required for punishment: sympathy for the wronged and a desire to strike back on their behalf.[39]

To show that these two sentiments of punishment would stabilize cooperation in larger groups is not to say that there is any reason to believe that these sentiments would arise. Just because they would be useful does not mean that we would acquire them. Moreover, their acquisition seems especially perplexing. Up to now, we have been considering enforcement mechanisms that are part of a rational system of cooperation—a system in which people are adding up the costs and benefits and deciding to cooperate and enforce. We have been investigating the limits of calculating instrumentalist enforcement. But through the last sections, we have been led to the conclusion that the more we think of enforcement in terms as an investment to obtain the future goods, the less certain we are of securing it. The enforcement of cooperative norms is a great public benefit to the group as a whole, but it often does make sense for an individual to incur the costs of enforcement herself. What we need, it seems, is an account of how it can be good in terms of cooperative order for people not to think about enforcement in these calculating terms.

6. A Simple Evolutionary Model

Instead of supposing that we are confronted with rational agents calculating the most efficient ways to achieve their ends, suppose instead we take an evolutionary perspective. Suppose, that is, we think of a society as populated by fixed strategies: some always cooperate, some always defect, and so on. In this sort of model, agents do not change their moves (as I said, they are fixed). Rather, the model is based on *replicator dynamics* in which those strategies that tend to have higher average payoffs increase their share of the population and so displace lower payoff strategies.[40] So what "moves" is the percentage of the population employing a certain strategy, as some replicate faster than others.

Let us begin with a very simple model, according to which these people are all Unconditional Rule Followers: they are unconditionally disposed to follow rules that dictate cooperation in mixed motive games such as the Prisoners' Dilemma, regardless of the strategy of other actors. Now a group with a preponderance of Unconditional Rule Followers will outperform groups of purely instrumental agents: as we have seen, instrumentally rational agents have considerable difficulty stabilizing cooperative interactions. In Prisoners' Dilemmas, a population of Unconditional Rule Followers will always receive their second highest payoffs. Thus, if we consider things from the level of group competition, social groups composed of Unconditional Rule Followers will do much better than groups of instrumentally rational agents. The people in them will have more of their ends satisfied, and they will generally achieve higher standards of living. In competition with other groups, we would expect them to displace less efficient groups.[41] Perhaps more importantly, we can expect their forms of social organization to be copied by other groups, as useful norms tend to spread.[42] It must be stressed that this need not be a story about genetic fitness and natural selection. There is considerable evidence that copying the activities of the more successful members of one's group is fundamental to culture.

The problem is that Alf's being an Unconditional Rule Follower easily detracts from his overall fitness within the group, at least if we think that his fitness is well correlated with his achieving his own individual goals. Although individuals in groups dominated by Unconditional Rule Followers will, on average, do better than individuals in groups where, for example, everyone is a Defector, groups of Unconditional Rule Followers could always be invaded by simple Defectors (who always defect on cooperative arrangements), each of whom would do better than the group average, since they would receive the group benefits of social cooperation as well as the individual advantages of cheating in all their personal interactions. But this means that despite their intergroup strengths, groups of Unconditional Rule Followers are not stable, as they are liable to be invaded by nasty types.

This appears to reaffirm from a different perspective our general lesson thus far: how difficult it can be to secure cooperation in the face of defectors! Let us introduce a slightly more complex model. Following Boyd et al., suppose that the benefit to the group of each act of cooperation through following norms is b, and a contributor incurs a cost of c to produce these benefits.[43] Defectors in the group produce no benefits and incur no costs, though by living in a cooperative group, they enjoy the group benefits of cooperation. To simplify matters, assume that all the benefits of each act of cooperation accrue to the entire group. Whatever a person gains by her own b (her contribution to the group's welfare) is less than c (its cost); otherwise there would be no temptation to defect. If there are x Unconditional Rule Followers in the group (where x is less than the total population of the group), the expected benefits to an Unconditional Rule Follower is $bx - c$: the total benefits of x cooperative acts minus the cost of her own cooperation. The expected benefit to Defectors is simply bx, and so the Defector will always have a higher expected payoff than the average in any group of Unconditional Rule Followers. So far it seems that while groups with large numbers of Unconditional Rule Followers will thrive, within those groups, they will always be less fit—do less well—than Defectors. Given this, Defectors would provide a model of someone "doing better," and so imitators would tend to copy them, spreading defection throughout the group.

Now suppose that "Rule-Following Punishers" enter the population. As the name indicates, Rule-Following Punishers unconditionally follow cooperative rules and *always* punish those who do not (in the spirit of Kant, even if their society were about to be dissolved, they would still punish the last Defector). Again following Boyd et al., we can say that a punisher reduces the benefit of an act of defection by punishment p at a cost of k to the punisher. Suppose that there are y punishers who punish each act of defection. It follows that:

1. The expected benefits to a nonpunishing Easygoing (unconditional) Rule Follower (an x-type person) are: $b(x + y) - c$. Each Easygoing Rule Follower gets the full advantages of cooperative acts performed by both her own x-types and well as the Rule-Following Punishers (y-types) and, in addition, she receives the social advantages of punishment of Defectors by Rule-Following Punishers and incurs only the cost of her own cooperative act.

2. The expected benefits to a Defector are $b(x + y) - yp$. A Defector still receives the full benefits of cooperation generated by x and y types (with no cost of cooperation) but incurs a punishment of p from each of the y punishers.

3. The expected benefits of being a Rule-Following Punisher (a y-type) are: $b(x+ y) - c - [k(1 - x - y)]$. Each y receives the full benefits of cooperation generated by x and y types, and like Easygoing Rule Followers, each incurs the costs of cooperation. In addition, each punisher must incur a cost of k for punishing each Defector; if there are x Easygoing Rule Followers, and y Rule-following Punishers in a group, then the number of Defectors (normalizing the population to one) is $1 - x - y$.

Therefore, if the costs of being punished are greater than the costs incurred in cooperating—that is, if $yp > c$—Defectors will decline in the population.

So this solves our long-standing problem: groups with Rule-Following Punishers are not liable to invasion by nasty types. Have we shown how social cooperation can be stabilized? Not quite. Unfortunately, they are liable to invasion by nicer types! The problem is that Rule-Following Punishers have a fitness disadvantage relative to Easygoing Rule Followers. Groups of Rule-Following Punishers can be invaded by Easygoing Rule Followers, who reap all the benefits of social cooperation and the elimination of nasty types but do not incur the costs of inflicting punishment. On the face of it, just as the superior fitness of Defectors within the group undermined Generalized Rule Followers, the superior fitness of Easygoing Rule Followers undermines the Rule-Following Punishers. However, as Boyd et al. show, the crucial difference between the two cases is that in the first, since the Generalized Rule Followers incur a constant cost c, they are always less fit by c in relation to Defectors—they can never, as it were, close the gap. However, the gap in fitness between Easygoing Rule Followers and Rule-Following Punishers reduces to zero if Defectors are eliminated from the population; it is only the punishing of Defectors that renders Rule-Following Punishers less fit than Easygoing Rule Followers.

We would not expect the fitness gap to reduce to zero—mutations, errors in determining defection, and immigration from other groups will result in above zero rates of punishing. Nevertheless, under a large range of values of the relevant variables, the discrepancy in relative fitness is small enough so that Rule-Following Punishers remain a high proportion of the population, and defection thus declines. Moreover, cooperation on the basis of Rule-Following Punishers is stabilized if we introduce n-level punishments by which a person is punished at the level n for failing to punish at level n-1. Now the Easygoing Rule Followers are also subject to punishment for their failure to punish. It can be shown that, although those who punish at the nth level are always less fit that those who do not punish *at that level*, the difference in fitness is diminishing at each level. At some point, the difference in fitness is sufficiently small that a slight tendency to conform to the majority retributivist practice can switch everyone over to being a punisher.[44]

It is important that in such group selection models, the survival of a strategy depends on two factors: (1) its individual fitness within the group, and (2) its inclusion in a group that has group-wide advantages over competing groups. In pure individual fitness accounts, of course, only the first factor is relevant. In our first group selection account with only Generalized Rule Followers and Defectors, the former enhance group fitness, but their serious individual deficit drives them to extinction within the group, and the result is that Defectors take over. Interestingly, although Defectors take over and, indeed, a group of all Defectors cannot be invaded by Generalized Rule Followers, the group would be driven to extinction in a competition with more cooperative groups. In the case of a mixed population of Easygoing Rule Followers, Defectors, and Rule-Following Punishers, the Rule-Following Punishers reduce the number of Defectors; during an initial period, they are less fit than Easygoing Rule Followers, but as Punishers succeed in eliminating Defectors, their fitness converges with their more easygoing comrades, and the group's overall fitness is enhanced. The more the Rule-Following Punishers must punish (say, because of high rates of mutation that constantly reintroduce Defectors into the population), the greater will be the gap between the fitness of the Punishers and the Easygoing Rule Followers.

This discussion has been rather complex, but the core point is straightforward. The evolutionary model we have been examining shows how individuals who possess Mill's two sentiments of punishment—a desire to retaliate on the basis of past wrongs and sympathy with wronged others, resulting in a desire to seek revenge against wrongdoers— are more apt to form social groups in which the population's goals are satisfied than are groups of agents who only see enforcement in instrumental terms, and which are resistant to invasion by nasty types. The groups populated by such individuals do much better than groups without them (they are bad news for Defectors), and within these groups, the Rule-Following Punishers may be nearly as fit as the cooperative free riders, and they also keep Defectors from invading the group. Plus, they can pretty much eliminate Easygoing Rule Followers by punishing those who fail to punish Defectors. To be a member of a society dominated by Rule-Following Punishers is the most effective way to advance one's ends.

7. The Critic, the Retributivist, and the Evolution of Social Order

Our punishers are genuinely "altruistic" agents in the sense that they engage in activities that do not best maximize their own goals but are advantageous for the group. Purely instrumental agents could never reason themselves into being strictly altruistic— performing acts that, all things considered, set back their own values, goals, and ends.[45] We thus have a powerful model for one of the most perplexing of evolutionary phenomena: the selection of altruistic traits which, by definition, reduce the individual fitness of those who possess them. Punishing violators is a public good; because the Easygoing Rule

Followers share the benefits of such punishment but do not incur the costs of contributing, they do better. And, of course, an agent solely devoted to her own goals will defect if she is not punished; Rule-Following Punishers will not. Thus, if we focus on simply instrumental rationality in terms of promoting one's goals narrowly understood (that is, apart from a taste for retribution), Rule-Following Punishers are not instrumentally rational.

Under some configurations of payoffs, models of the evolution of social cooperation show a mixed equilibrium of populations split between punishing and easygoing cooperative strategies (perhaps with some Defectors as well).[46] I began by noting the conflicting views of the bishop and John Stuart Mill: for one retaliation is distinct from, and often opposed to, justice; and for the other, retributive punishment and its accompanying sentiments are part and parcel of the very idea of justice. It has long been the case that people are divided in this way. Evidence indicates a majority with retributivist views about justice, almost always with a spirited dissent by some. The interesting possibility arises that *this* is our evolutionary stable outcome: a mixed population whose members have different views of the relation of justice and retribution.

It is easy for intellectuals to dismiss the shallow retributivism of the *hoi polloi*. It is not based on the deep philosophical justifications to which intellectuals are so drawn and which they love to construct (and destroy); it is a competency about the "game" of justice on which our cooperative order is based. If asked, "why *this* conception of a just order?" rather than one based on boycotts, deterrence, or Icelandic private enforcement, the *hoi polloi* will be unable to answer. Like so much of our social world, this system was not the product of philosophic construction but of social and biological coevolution: it is a crucial element in solving the absolutely fundamental problem of stabilizing social cooperation. If we did not have a "culture of vengeance," the good bishop probably would not be in the position to insist on compassion (a society of easygoing types can be invaded easily by nasty types). Yet, as Mill so clearly recognized, shallow retributivism needs to be moralized. We have a taste for punishment and, like all tastes, we may indulge it excessively. We need critics like the bishop to remind us that punishment imposes hardships for what is already done and in the past. A just and humane society seeks to stay fit and trim in satisfying such tastes.[47]

Notes

1 *Financial Times* (U.S. edition), Monday August 9, 2010, p. 2 (News Digest).

2 Mill, *Utilitarianism*, ch. V, ¶18.

3 Ibid., ch. V, ¶12.

4 Ibid., ch. V, ¶13 (emphasis added).

5 Ibid, ch. V, ¶20.

6 Mill also refers to "retribution" twice in chapter V of *Utilitarianism*. In paragraph 29, he uses "retribution" to describe a particular principle of justice—*lex talionis*—concerning how *much*

punishment is appropriate (so not a general justification of punishment itself); in paragraph 34, it is linked more generally to the sentiment of vengeance.

7 Baier, "Is Punishment Retributive?"

8 Ibid., p.26.

9 Ibid., p. 27.

10 Benn, "Punishment," p. 30 (emphasis added).

11 Ibid.

12 Benn concurs, I think, that retributivism can be understood in such a way that it is a definition of punishment. See Benn and Peters, *Social Principles and the Democratic State*, p. 184.

13 See ibid., p. 175ff.

14 If it is not distinct, it collapses into the shallow idea that justice requires that the guilty be punished. I defended a version of this deeper understanding of retributivism in "Taking the Bad with the Good." For an extended justification of deep retributivism, see Moore, "Moral Worth of Retribution."

15 For what is still a good account of these, see Benn, "Punishment."

16 As Nichols shows in "Brute Retributivism."

17 See Benn, "Punishment," p. 32, and Mill's view in note 6 above. Moore insists that retributivism is *only* a deep theory, and so denies that this "*lex talionis*" sense, or the shallow sense, are retributivist theses at all ("Moral Worth of Retibutivism," pp. 188–89).

18 This term derives from Rawls, "Two Concepts of Rules," p. 27.

19 Mill, *Utilitarianism*, ch. ¶37.

20 Hobbes actually thinks a person has some reason to perform second, but this is usually too weak to outweigh her selfish passions (see *Leviathan*, ch. 14).

21 On the game of snatch, see Schwab and Ostrom, "Vital Role of Norms and Rules," p. 205ff.

22 See Skyrms, *Stag Hunt and the Evolution of the Social Structure*, ch. 3.

23 The "Assurance Games" is a slight variation on the Stag Hunt in Figure 2. While in the Stag Hunt, I am indifferent between "both of us defecting" and "me defecting while the other cooperates," in the Assurance Game I prefer "I defect while the other cooperates" to "both of us defecting." The difference is not important here. Vanderschraaf ("War or Peace?") reports this is Kavka's view on the basis of the latter's unpublished 1989 manuscript on "Political Contractarianism."

24 Vanderschraaf, "War or Peace?," p. 245.

25 Bicchieri, *Grammar of Society*, p. 37.

26 See Skyrms, *Evolution of the Social Contract*, ch. 3.

27 Vanderschraaf, "Covenants and Reputations."

28 Henrich and Henrich, *Why Humans Cooperate*, ch. 6.

29 Vanderschraaf, "Covenants and Reputations," p. 184.

30 See Axelrod, *Evolution of Cooperation*.

31 See Binmore, *Natural Justice*, p. 78ff.

32 This is a well-established finding; see, for example, Selten and Stocker, "End Behavior in Sequences of Finite Prisoner's Dilemma Supergames."

33 See Richerson and Boyd, *Not by Genes Alone*, pp. 199–201. For an analysis showing the difficulty for reciprocity developing when larger groups face iterated N-person Prisoners' Dilemmas, see Boyd and Richerson, *Origin and Evolution of Culture*, ch. 8.

34 I am following here Friedman, "Private Creation and Enforcement of Law."

35 The variables p and d are not independent; one can increase p, the probability of success, by increasing d, say by purchasing weapons.

36 Friedman, "Private Creation and Enforcement of Law," p. 592.

37 Ibid.

38 Nichols, "Brute Retributivism." Nichols cites brain imaging evidence that people enjoy punishing norm violators.

39 Mill, *Utilitarianism,* ch. V, ¶19.

40 See Skyrms, *Evolution of the Social Contract.*

41 A striking example of how more efficient forms of social organization can lead one group to displace another is that of the Dinka and the Nuer. For an explicitly evolutionary account, see Richerson and Boyd, *Not by Genes Alone,* pp. 23–5. For an empirical study of how group functional norms can evolve by cultural group selection see Boyd and Richerson, *Origin and Evolution of Culture,* ch. 11.

42 See Boyd and Richerson, *Origin and Evolution of Culture,* ch. 12. Both group displacement and copying the norms of more successful groups are important to Hayek's account of social evolution; see my "Evolution of Society and Mind," pp. 238–46. After a long period of disfavor, group—or more generally, multilevel—selection is again respectable in genetic evolutionary theory. For a helpful analysis, see Okasha, *Evolution and Levels of Selection.* It is more than respectable in accounts of cultural evolution.

43 Boyd et al., "Evolution of Altruistic Punishment," 215–27.

44 Boyd and Richerson, *Origin and Evolution of Cultures,* ch. 10.

45 Sober and Wilson strenuously argue for group selection accounts of altruistic behavior in their *Unto Others: The Evolution and Psychology of Unselfish Behavior.*

46 See Boyd et al., "Evolution of Altruistic Punishment"; Skyrms, *Evolution of the Social Contract,* ch. 2.

47 I greatly benefited from a long conversation one hot Tucson summer day over cold beers with Shaun Nichols. I also have learned a great deal from graduate students in my seminar in moral and social evolution at the University of Arizona—special thanks to Keith Hankins, John Thrasher, and Kevin Vallier. Some of the material in this chapter is drawn from my forthcoming book, *The Order of Public Reason: A Theory of Freedom and Morality in a Diverse and Bounded World* (Cambridge University Press), chapters 3 and 4. My special thanks to Mark White for helping me avoid some errors.

Bibliography

Axelrod, Robert. *The Evolution of Cooperation.* New York: Basic Books, 1974.

Baier, Kurt. "Is Punishment Retributive?" *Analysis* 16 (1955): 25–32.

Benn, Stanley I. "Punishment." In *The Encyclopedia of Philosophy,* vol. 7, edited by Paul Edwards, 29–36. New York: Macmillan and the Free Press, 1967.

Benn, Stanley I and R.S. Peters. *Social Principles and the Democratic State.* London: Allen and Unwin, 1959.

Bicchieri, Cristina. *The Grammar of Society.* Cambridge: Cambridge University Press, 2006.

Binmore, Ken. *Natural Justice.* Oxford: Oxford University Press, 2005.

Boyd, Robert, Herbert Gintis, Samuel Bowles, and Peter J. Richerson. "The Evolution of Altruistic Punishment." In *Moral Sentiments and Material Interests: The Foundations of Cooperation in Economic Life*, edited by Herbert Gintis, Samuel Bowles, Robert Boyd, and Ernst Fehr, 215–28. Cambridge, MA: The MIT Press, 2005.

Boyd, Robert, and Peter J. Richerson. *The Origin and Evolution of Culture*. Oxford: Oxford University Press, 2005.

Friedman, David. "Private Creation and Enforcement of Law: A Historical Case." In *Anarchy and the Law*, edited by Edward P. Stringham, 586–601. New Brunswick, NJ: Transaction Publishers, 2007.

Gaus, Gerald. "The Evolution of Society and Mind: Hayek's System of Ideas." In *The Cambridge Companion to Hayek*, edited by Ed Feser, 232–58. Cambridge: Cambridge University Press, 2006.

"Taking the Bad with the Good: Some Misplaced Worries about Pure Retribution." In *Legal and Political Philosophy*, edited by Enrique Villanveua, 339–62. Amsterdam: Rodopi, 2002.

Gintis, Herbert. *Game Theory Evolving*. Princeton: Princeton University Press, 2000.

Henrich, Natalie, and Joseph Henrich. *Why Humans Cooperate: A Cultural and Evolutionary Explanation*. Oxford: Oxford University Press, 2007.

Hobbes, Thomas. *Leviathan*. Edited by Edwin Curley. Indianapolis, IN: Hackett, 1994.

Mill, John Stuart. *Utilitarianism*. In *The Collected Works of John Stuart Mill*, edited by John M. Robson. Toronto: University of Toronto Press, 1985.

Moore, Michael S. "The Moral Worth of Retribution." In *Responsibility, Character, and the Emotions: New Essays in Moral Psychology*, edited by Ferdinand Schoeman, 179–220. Cambridge: Cambridge University Press, 1987.

Nichols, Shaun. "Brute Retributivism." In *The Future of Punishment*, edited by T. Nadelhoffer. New York: Oxford University Press, forthcoming.

Okasha, Samir. *Evolution and Levels of Selection*. Oxford: Clarendon Press, 2006.

Rawls, John. "Two Concepts of Rules." In *Collected Papers of John Rawls*, edited by Samuel Freeman, 20–46. Cambridge, MA: Harvard University Press, 1999.

Richerson, Peter J., and Robert Boyd. *Not by Genes Alone: How Culture Transformed Human Evolution*. Chicago: University of Chicago Press, 2005.

Schwab, David, and Elinor Ostrom. "The Vital Role of Norms and Rules in Maintaining Open Public and Private Economies." In *Moral Markets: The Critical Role of Values in the Economy*, edited by Paul Zak, 204–27. Princeton: Princeton University Press, 2008.

Selten, Reinhard, and Rolf Stocker. "End Behavior in Sequences of Finite Prisoner's Dilemma Supergames." *Journal of Economic Behavior and Organization* 7 (1986): 47–70.

Skyrms, Brian. *The Evolution of the Social Contract*. Cambridge: Cambridge University Press, 1996.

Skyrms, Brian. *The Stag Hunt and the Evolution of the Social Structure*. Cambridge: Cambridge University Press, 2005.

Smith, John Maynard. "The Evolution of Behavior." *Scientific American* 239 (1978): 176–92.

Sober, Elliot, and David Sloan Wilson. *Unto Others: The Evolution and Psychology of Unselfish Behavior*. Cambridge, MA: Harvard University Press, 1998.

Vanderschraaf, Peter. "Covenants and Reputations." *Synthese* 157 (2007): 167–95.

Vanderschraaf, Peter. "War or Peace? A Dynamical Analysis of Anarchy." *Economics and Philosophy* 22 (2006): 243–79.

Philosophical Perspectives on Retributivism

5

SOME SECOND THOUGHTS ON RETRIBUTIVISM

Jeffrie G. Murphy

WHEN, IN THE mid-1960s, I first began working on the philosophy of punishment, two related issues tended to dominate the discussion: legal moralism and explorations of the degree to which, if at all, a retributive justification of punishment could be rendered consistent with a consequentialist justification. The legal moralism controversy had, at its core, the Hart-Devlin debate. Lord Patrick Devlin, in his influential 1959 Maccabaean Lecture titled "The Enforcement of Morals" had challenged the liberal idea that as a matter of *principle*, some things are simply not the legitimate business of the criminal law.[1] In particular, he challenged the famous "harm principle" that John Stuart Mill had introduced in *On Liberty*. According to this principle, the only purpose that justifies society in coercing any one of its members is to prevent harm to others, where harm is understood as posing what Justice Oliver Wendell Holmes would later call a clear and present danger to the rights or interests of others. Coercion for a person's own good or coercion for the perceived general long-range moral good of society are in most cases to be ruled out.

Devlin's own view came to be called "legal moralism" because of his belief that one legitimate use of the criminal law is to enforce the widely shared moral values of the community—deep moral disapproval of homosexual sodomy, for example—even if these values have little or nothing to do with the kinds of harm that Mill had in mind. In Devlin's view, widely shared moral values constitute a kind of glue that binds society together, and a failure to enforce those values has a tendency to undermine social stability—a serious kind of social harm. (Devlin was as concerned with harm as was Mill, but the two men had very different understandings of what constitutes relevant harm.) Devlin argued that the appeal to Mill's harm principle—or indeed, to any other totally general and abstract principle—obscures rather than clarifies the values that are at stake in criminal punishment, and he suggested that the limits on the scope of the criminal law should be thought of primarily in pragmatic terms.[2] In his book *Law, Liberty and Morality*, Herbert Hart mounted a sustained attack on almost every aspect of Devlin's account. My first publication in legal philosophy was an uncritical endorsement of Hart's critique and a muddled expansion of that critique—a publication so truly dreadful that I no longer list it on my CV (and will not cite it here). And since I have expressed in detail my current thoughts on legal moralism elsewhere,[3] I will address it in this essay only insofar as it has a bearing on retribution—namely, with respect to the relevance of *character* in criminal sentencing.

Devlin explicitly raises the issue that I have elsewhere called "character retributivism in criminal sentencing" and argues that liberals such as Mill and Hart probably want to count such virtuous states of character—such as remorse and repentance—as relevant factors in sentence reduction. And this is certainly true of such later liberal theorists as Joel Feinberg, Herbert Morris, and the late Jean Hampton, since they have all argued that the truly repentant criminal in general *deserves* less punishment than the unrepentant criminal, a moral claim quite different from the empirical (and possibly false) utilitarian claim that repentant criminals tend to be less dangerous (likely to cause harm) than unrepentant criminals. But if such beliefs about personal virtue and vice are legally relevant here—at this point in the criminal law—how could it be in principle wrong to make all questions of personal virtue and vice relevant to deciding what to criminalize in the first place? So if a certain sexual practice is regarded as a moral vice and the liberal seeks to argue against criminalizing the practice on those grounds, he cannot in consistency give as his reason the general principle "issues of personal vice and virtue have no place in the criminal law"—not, at any rate, unless he wants to give up his belief that they are relevant in criminal sentencing.[4]

Hampton and Morris are two liberal theorists who embraced a version of Feinberg's view that the criminal law should be grounded in what he called "grievance morality": a morality solely concerned with protecting the rights and interests of others, rights that give rise to a legitimate grievance on the part of those who find them violated. Yet, all three of these philosophers also claimed that remorseful and repentant criminals should receive less punishment than remorseless and unrepentant ones. According to Hampton, to quote just one of these philosophers, "what makes a state liberal... is its rejection of the idea that any enforcement of moral behavior should include punishment of immoral behavior that nonetheless has no victim other than the offender himself."[5] But if a sentencing judge, after giving the criminal a punishment properly proportional to the injury he has inflicted, adds on a little extra because of the defendant's vicious character—his smug unrepentance, say—is that not simply to punish him for an aspect of his character that has no victim? If so, is not the liberal who approves this inconsistent when he crusades against using the criminal law against victimless immorality? What does repentance have to do with grievance or rights violation?

Now there is one way in which one might attempt to make repentance relevant to grievance (at least with respect to some crimes) and thereby keep alive at least a part of the argument defended by Feinberg, Morris, and Hampton. But this way would still have to concede to Devlin the criminal law relevance of certain virtues and vices of character—embracing a view of harm closer to Devlin's than to Mill's. I have defended such a view in other writings, and I will sketch it here.[6] For at least some crimes (rape is perhaps a good example), part of the injury itself (and thus the grievance) may be a function of the *symbolic message* that the criminal act conveys: "I matter in a way that you do not and can use you, like a mere thing or object, for my own purposes." This is a degrading and insulting message, one that the victim would surely want to reject. If the wrongdoer manifests sincere repentance, however, then the evil message is being withdrawn—the wrongdoer is now standing with the victim in condemning the act—and the victim might now, for example, forgive the wrongdoer without fearing a compromise of self-respect. There are problems with this view; to the degree that it does work, however, then to that same degree will victim grievance be less as a result of repentance, and thus repentance could count toward sentence reduction even in a theory of criminal punishment, based entirely on grievance. In short, repentance could reduce the harm and culpability and thus the *penal desert* of the offender and would be relevant, on retributive grounds, to criminal sentencing. Indeed, I have argued elsewhere that on *all* plausible versions of retributive desert, counting remorse and repentance is in principle a relevant factor justifying some reduction in sentence, so I will not pursue this matter any further here.[7]

Having introduced the idea of retributive punishment in the context of the legal moralism debate, I would now like to discuss it as an issue in its own right. In particular, I am here going to sketch some of the reasons why I no longer have the unqualified enthusiasm for the theory that I once did. I hope that the reasons will reveal not just my own personal anxieties but matters that really do deserve more thought from all of us.

Put in the simplest terms, a retributivist is a person who believes that the primary justification for punishing a criminal is that the criminal *deserves* it. The devil (or maybe the angel) is in the details, of course, and so what is really needed to defend retributivism is a persuasive answer to three questions: (1) What is desert, (2) Why is it morally important that punishment be based on desert, and (3) Why should the *state* (which does not seek, after all, to promote all moral values) be concerned with moral desert as an aim in its system of criminal punishment? I have written on the third question elsewhere, and so I will not discuss it here.[8]

The characterization of desert given by some writers who wanted to render retributivism consistent with consequentialism—Rawls and sometimes Hart, for example—made consistency easy to achieve: desert is simply *legal guilt*. On this view, one becomes a retributivist simply by adopting the principle that the state should never intentionally punish the innocent.[9] Of course, it would surely lead to very bad consequences if the state made a practice of punishing those who were innocent of legal wrongdoing, since this, rendering it impossible for individuals to plan so as to avoid punishment, would leave all citizens in a state of great insecurity and would make it impossible for the criminal law to be an effective tool for social control through individual rational choice. (As Rawls noted, this would be like a price system in which a person could learn the price of an item only after buying it.) So if one sees retribution as a principle for deciding merely who receives punishment—what Hart called a "distributive principle"—one can see its legitimate, although subordinate, role in a system of punishment justified by the general utilitarian consequence of crime control. Consequentialism and retributivisim are thus reconciled.

The problem with this, of course, is that it buys reconciliation between retributivism and consequentialism at too high of a price: a totally unsatisfactory analysis of the concept of retributive desert that fails to capture the robust views of such classic retributivists as Kant and Hegel.[10] It is the robust versions of retributivism that will concern me in the remainder of this essay—versions that do not analyze desert merely as legal guilt and will not regard desert merely as a side constraint on a system that has, as its primary purpose, the utilitarian objective of crime control. To use Hart's language, the robust retributivist will see desert as central in answering not merely the question of how punishment is to be distributed but the more basic question, "what is the general justifying aim of punishment?" And the retributivist answer to this question is this: to give criminal wrongdoers the punishment that they *deserve*. A practice designed for the very purpose of giving criminal wrongdoers what they deserve will, of course, entail a prohibition against intentionally punishing the innocent, but such a prohibition will not be the core of the theory. The core will be a nonconsequentialist account of why we are justified in having a practice of punishment at all, a nonconsequentialist account of the very concept of desert itself.

According to the robust retributivist, the substantive offenses of the criminal law should be designed to target moral evil, and the punishments mandated by such a system should be proportional to the personal evil displayed by the criminal in what he has done and by his reasons and motives for doing it. Kant defended such a version of retributivism in terms of the classic principle of *lex talionis*, a principle that is often unhelpfully rendered as "an eye for an eye." What Kant actually advocated was that punishment be proportional to the moral iniquity that the crime represents, and he saw this iniquity as a function both of the injustice of the criminal's act and of what he called the "inner viciousness" (*inneren Bösartigkeit*) of the criminal in performing that act.[11] There will, of course, be very welcome crime control benefits from such a system, but those benefits are—for the true retributivist—secondary to the primary purpose of imposing on criminals the suffering that they deserve.

If so much weight is going to be placed on the concept of desert, then we need a very clear understanding of exactly what we are going to mean by desert. If desert is not simply to be understood as legal guilt, then what is it? We know that for the retributivist, the desert in question must be moral desert. But what is that? In seeking to answer this question, I was once very charmed by a version of retributivism that analyzes desert in terms of the concept of a debt owed for free riding and which has sometimes been referred to as a theory of *moral balance*. Instead of taking retributive justice as a foundational primitive in one's moral and legal theory, the moral balance theory seeks to derive a justification of retributive punishment from a more general moral principle—a principle of fairness. The best defense of this view is to be found in Herbert Morris's 1968 essay "Persons and Punishment." This essay, one of the classics of twentieth-century jurisprudence, almost single-handedly rescued robust retributivism from obscurity and rendered it philosophically respectable again.

The essence of the moral balance version of retributivism is this: every citizen benefits from living under the rule of law, a benefit that is possible only because most citizens, most of the time, give the law their voluntary obedience. This compliance involves assuming the burden of self-restraint—refraining, simply because the law requires it, from doing things we would very much like to do or that would benefit us. The criminal, on this model, violates a basic principle of fairness by being a free rider on this cooperative scheme since he derives the benefits without making the appropriate sacrifice. His punishment is thus a debt that he owes to those of us who have been law abiding, for without it the unfair advantage he has taken of us will be allowed to stand—a result that is clearly unfair and explains why the criminal deserves punishment. To this fairness-based theory, Morris also adds the important Hegelian idea that criminals have a *right* to punishment, since punishing them is a way of showing that we respect them as free and responsible beings rather than viewing them as sick and nonresponsible.[12]

As anyone familiar with my 1973 essay "Marxism and Retribution" will recall, I very early in my career expressed grave doubts about the legitimacy of *applying* this version of retributivism to a society of great inequality. In that essay, I drew on some insights from Marx, but I could have made my main point just as well by drawing on Rawls's idea of luck on the natural and social lottery or even on some wonderful lines from William Blake. (It will give you some idea of how old I am that I was actually required in school to memorize these and many other passages from plays and poems.) The lines are these:

Every night and every Morn
Some to Misery are Born.
Every Morn and Every Night
Some are Born to sweet delight.
Some are Born to sweet delight,
Some are Born to Endless Night.[13]

Although I realize that this is an overly simplistic way of putting my concern, societies of radical inequality often seem to be societies in which the Sweet Delight folks are imposing punishment on the Endless Night folks and adding insult to injury by justifying this to the Endless Night folks by telling them that they owe this sacrifice to the community as a kind of debt. Unless they pay this debt, so the story goes, they will be unfair free riders on a mutually beneficial scheme of social cooperation, receiving all the benefits of the society in which they live without making the sacrifice of obedience to law required to make the system work. This might make a kind of sense for corporate criminals or other members of the Sweet Delight Club, but it strikes me as rather indecent to say this sort of thing to those who might understandably have a difficult time naming all the wonderful benefits that have supposedly put them in debt to the rest of us.

Given the worries about inequality that I expressed in that 1973 essay, for quite some time I remained committed to the debt/moral balance version of retributivism at the ideal theoretical level, even if not at the level of concrete application. Eventually, however, under the sharp criticism of Richard Burgh, David Dolinko, Joshua Dressler, Antony Duff, Robert Nozick, and others, I came to doubt this and certain other versions of retributivism at the theoretical level. With respect to moral balance retributivism, I came to find problematic the idea that one could acquire such important obligations merely from the passive receipt of benefits and thus became suspicious of any debt model of crime and punishment. Also, I came to think that the theory could not provide a plausible ranking of criminal offenses on a scale of severity. Murder and rape, for example, should surely be ranked as much more serious crimes than tax evasion, but I—like most decent, well brought up, and (let's face it) lucky people—am conscious of exercising no self-restraint in not raping or not murdering while being very conscious of great self-restraint in being honest in filing my tax returns. Others may have different priorities here, of course, but even that would illustrate the radical and unpredictable subjectivity that would be introduced into ranking offenses if one tried to do it in terms of some notion of the burden of self-restraint. Finally, it struck me that the moral balance theory at least flirts with explaining the obvious in terms of the controversial. If someone asks me why a murderer deserves to be punished, I would be far more inclined to answer this question simply by saying with emphasis, "because he is a *murderer*" rather than by saying "because he is a free rider."

So I moved away from regarding desert merely as legal guilt and also from regarding it as merely owing a debt. But I still had very strong retributivist intuitions—and was even prepared to defend some degree of vengeance and, in the book *Forgiveness and Mercy* that I joint authored with Jean Hampton, to defend an emotion that I called "retributive hatred."[14] Gradually, I began to realize that what had always really drawn me to retributivism was some version of Kant's idea of punishing not just wrongdoing, but human *evil*— vile deeds performed by people of "inner viciousness." I learned that such a notion had even found its way into American homicide law where phrases such as "cruel, heinous, and depraved" and "flowing from a hardened, abandoned, and malignant heart" occurred in statutes and in sentencing guidelines. This appealed to me.

Such a strong notion of just deserts is, of course, in some ways a secular analogue to traditional notions of divine justice—the judgment that God will administer in the Last Assizes. Indeed, Michael S. Moore (the legal philosopher, not the maker of propaganda films) defends a robust version of retributivism very like the one that I am sketching here but claims that if he believed in God, he would not be so concerned to organize secular systems of criminal law around retributive values. As an atheist, however, he sees no other way to target moral desert in punishment and regards this value as too important to leave unrealized.[15] This analogy with divine punishment is interesting; but it should, I now believe, alert us to some dangers of thinking of secular punishment along these lines. It is not for nothing that we often find ourselves condemning people who—as we put it— "play God," and even Scripture famously teaches, "Judge not that ye be not judged."

The *Living Bible*, that wonderful source of unintended theological humor, once rendered (if I recall correctly) that biblical recommendation as "Don't criticize, and then you won't be criticized." But the true point of the passage is surely not a prohibition against making any critical moral judgments at all, but is rather a caution against making final judgments of deep character, against presuming to declare any fellow human being as simply vermin or disposable garbage—evil all the way down—and a legitimate object of our hatred. And why should we be reluctant to make such judgments? There are two reasons: (1) we do not know enough ("only God can read the heart" as Scripture puts it), and (2) we are not ourselves good enough to presume such a sharp us/them distinction. This, I take it, is at least part of the point of Jesus's remark, "let him who is without sin among you be the first to cast a stone at her."

Jesus's remark can, I think, be taken as potentially applicable to cases other than that of a woman caught in adultery. According to Moore, however, Jesus's remark—when thus generalized—may be an inspiring slogan but is, as he puts it, "pretty clumsy moral philosophy." He writes as follows:

> It is true that all of us are guilty of some immoralities, probably on a daily basis. Yet for most people. . . the immoralities in question are things like manipulating others unfairly; not caring deeply enough about another's suffering; not being charitable for the limitations of others; convenient lies; and so forth, Few of us have raped and murdered a woman, drowned her three small children, and felt no remorse about it.[16]

Moore's point seems to be this: in the relevant sense most of us are without sin, and so we might as well feel free to pick up some stones and cast away.

Is this an adequate answer to the concern raised by Jesus? I think not. The response is too shallow, for it fails to reflect the kind of serious introspection that the passage should provoke.[17] The point is not to deny that many people lead lives that are legally and morally correct. The point is, rather, to force such people to face honestly the question of *why* they have lived in such a way. Is it (as they would like to think) because their inner characters manifest true integrity and are thus morally superior to those people whose behavior has been less exemplary? Or is it, at least in part, a matter of what Rawls has called "luck on the natural and social lottery"? Perhaps, because of favored circumstances, they have never been adequately tempted, for example. Perhaps, if they imagined themselves possessed of the Ring of Gyges (a ring that in Plato and Herodotus makes its wearer invisible) they might—if honest with themselves—have to admit that they might use the ring—not to perform anonymous acts of charity—but to perform some acts of considerable evil: acts, if not identical to, then still comparable in evil to those for which they seek the punishment of others. "There, but for the grace of God, go I," is a thought that might well occur to them at this point.

Many persons will, of course, associate the perspective that I have just been outlining with a kind of sloppy sentimentality about crime and criminals. In an attempt to lay such associations to rest, let me call your attention to passages from two writers—Immanuel Kant and Judge Richard Posner—who can hardly be regarded as bleeding heart soft on crime sentimentalists.

Those who know only Kant's rather bloodthirsty passages on retribution from *The Metaphysics of Morals* may be surprised by this passage on blame and self-deception from his *Religion Within the Limits of Reason Alone*:

> [People] may picture themselves as meritorious, feeling themselves guilty of no such offenses as they see others burdened with; nor do they ever inquire whether good luck should not have the credit, or whether by reason of the cast of mind which they could discover, if they only would, in their own inmost nature, they would not have practiced similar vices, had not inability, temperament, training, and [non imputable] circumstances of time and place which serve to tempt one, kept them out of the way of these vices. This dishonesty, by which we humbug ourselves and which thwarts the establishing of a true moral disposition in us is, if not to be termed wickedness, at least deserves the name worthlessness, and is an element of the radical evil in human nature which constitutes the foul taint of our race.[18]

And here is Judge Posner writing in dissent in *Johnson v. Phelan*, a case dealing with prison conditions:

> I do not myself consider [the inmates of prisons and jails] as a type of vermin, devoid of human dignity and entitled to no respect. We should have realistic conceptions [of these people] before deciding that they are scum entitled to nothing better than what a vengeful populace and a resource-starved penal system chooses to give them. We must not exaggerate the distances between "us," the lawful ones, the respectable ones, and the prison and jail populations; for such exaggeration will make it too easy for us to deny that population the rudiments of humane consideration.[19]

Finally, as a further step on the road to my increasing lack of enthusiasm for robust retributivism, vengeance, and retributive hatred, I was pulled up short when, in teaching my undergraduate course in Existentialism (a recent interest of mine), I had my students reflect on Nietzsche's claim that we should mistrust any person in whom the urge to punish is strong.[20] It seemed to me that Nietzsche had a potentially profound insight here, one that made me uncomfortable about my own long-standing defense of a retributive theory of punishment—uncomfortable because of a fear that my defense of such a theory perhaps in part grew out of my own strong and unexamined urge to punish, rather than exclusively from objective moral and intellectual considerations. If Nietzsche was in part justified in his skepticism about the conscious rationales of justice, rights, and desert that we generally give for retribution, and if he was partly correct in diagnosing the retributive urge as *ressentiment*—an ugly emotional brew of malice, spite, envy, and cruelty—then one will, to put it mildly, want to rethink one's own urge to punish and any theories one builds on that urge. Surely, I needed at least to consider the possibility that the retributive theory had put me and many others in what Rawls called "reflective equilibrium," in part because our pretheoretical intuitions about punishment and wrong-doing were corrupt. Those who embrace, as I do, reflective equilibrium as an important test for the adequacy of a moral theory must be willing to explore the deep psychology of their pretheoretical intuitions and not simply dismiss such explorations as examples of the genetic fallacy.

I now come to the final section of this brief essay where I will address what I call "The Two Faces of Retribution." I will note one face that draws us, in its stress on moral desert, toward the recognition of human dignity and responsibility, and another face that tempts us to self-deceptive cruelty. It is this second face that has given me second and even third thoughts about retributivism. And where do these second and third thoughts leave me? They leave me as what I will call a "reluctant retributivist": I still hold a variety of retributivist convictions, but I hold many of them much more cautiously than was once the case for me.

To the degree that a retributive outlook on punishment involves a respect for the dignity of human beings as free and responsible agents—even if it sometimes tempts us to overstate their degree of responsibility—then retributivism surely makes an important point and is, as Herbert Morris has persuasively argued, dramatically preferable to some alternatives, such as advocacy of a therapeutic state in which wrongdoing is regarded as illness, and criminals are subjected to involuntary chemical and other personality destroying intrusions in order to turn them into compliant members of the social order. Some concept of desert, if not what might be called "desert all the way down," is vital to our conception of ourselves and others as responsible beings, having the value that Kant called "dignity." This insight by itself is sufficient to keep me somewhere within the retributivist camp.

Also consider this: A retributive outlook on punishment is often identified with excessive harshness in punishment. This is a mistake, however. Such an outlook can, of course, sometimes urge us toward harsh punishments, but it can just as frequently urge us to greater concern with the humanity of criminals and thus to greater justice, goodness, and decency in our punitive practices. For example, surely one of the most powerful ways to confront the conditions of terror, assault, and rape that are common in the pest holes of many American jails and prisons is to remind ourselves that the people in those facilities are our fellow human beings, possessed of the basic human rights that attach to such a status. As such, they simply do not *deserve* to be treated in such inhumane ways—no matter how much criminal deterrence society gets (and perhaps subconsciously welcomes) from such abusive treatment. Many of the people in these facilities have committed crimes for which such a level of abuse is radically disproportionate; for example, on what theory of *lex talionis* is it just to ignore repeated gang rapes inflicted on persons who have been convicted of drug possession or criminal fraud? And in cases where we may be tempted to think that the inmate has done such malicious evil that an environment of rape is properly proportional punishment for him, the Kantian retributivist will surely be guided by Kant's own injunction that all punishments, even those directed at the worst criminals, must be kept free of any maltreatment that would degrade the humanity of the criminal or of those administering the punishment. If the worst criminals are not human beings possessed of basic human rights, then the whole language of desert and just punishment would not even apply to them—as it does not apply to beasts. Thus, in spite of the deviation from strict proportionality, a decent society will not, according to Kant, torture the torturer or rape the rapist.

Given that I acknowledge some considerable virtues present within a retributive outlook on punishment—virtues that represent a very good face—why have I qualified my endorsement of retributivism and called myself a "reluctant retributivist"? To answer this question, let me briefly explore the bad face of retribution.

One of Nietzsche's great insights, I think, was his realization that our abstract theorizing—at least in moral theory—cannot fully be divorced from its social setting and from our own personal human psychology, a psychology that may affect us in ways of which we are not fully conscious. He claimed that all philosophy should be seen as the psychological autobiography of its writer, and—following in his footsteps—Iris Murdoch said that the first question that should be asked of any philosopher is, "What is he afraid of?" C. D. Broad put a similar point in his characteristically flip way simply by observing that "we all learn our morality at our mother's knee or at some other joint." All of these statements are obviously exaggerations, but they still contain important insight.

Although, like any decent philosopher, I try to get some critical distance from all these social and psychological and autobiographical factors, I am sure that to some degree I remain a prisoner—in ways of which I am often unaware—of my own resentful and vindictive Irish nature, some tendencies toward self-righteousness, a certain rigidity of character, and my lifelong back and forth struggle between the gospel of love stressed in my Christian upbringing and my not-always-loving personality. At the very least, these factors surely influence the framework I choose for discussion—the questions that I decide to ask first. At most and at worst, these factors may have inclined me to favor philosophical accounts for less than fully honorable reasons, especially those that may reveal that my enthusiasm for settling scores and restoring balance through retributive justice may in part have been extensions of what Nietzsche called "a soul that squints"—the soul of a shopkeeper or an accountant. If I had been a kinder person, a less angry person, a person of more generous spirit and greatness of soul, would robust retributivism have charmed me to the degree that it at one time did? I suspect not.

Let me emphasize, by the way, that this observation about my character is not a narcissistic confession of some unique and perhaps even perversely heroic depravity on my part. I do not think that I am at all unique in the way in which some of my principled intellectual views may at least, to some degree, be an extension of less than admirable aspects of character. If what is now usually called virtue ethics teaches us to worry about such matters, then I think that it teaches a good lesson and should be welcomed by those of us who might have mistakenly thought that their Kantianism could proceed without such introspective reflection.

Let me take the slippery slope of retributive thinking as an example to illustrate the concerns that I have expressed above. The transition from "because your act and your mental state at the time of your act were blameworthy, you deserve punishment" to "you have a vicious character" to "you have a hardened, abandoned, and malignant heart" to "you are evil and rotten to the core" to "you are scum" to "you deserve whatever cruel indignity I choose to inflict on you" is, of course, not a logical transition. No single step logically follows from its predecessor. I fear, however, that the transition is *psychologically* a rather common and in some ways compelling one, one that ultimately may tempt us to endorse cruelty and inhumanity. I fear that I have myself sometimes succumbed to this temptation while talking the grand abstract language of just deserts, and I know that others have—and always will—succumb to this temptation as well. As recent reports of torture and humiliation of prisoners—both by "our side" and by "their side"—have reminded us, there are enormous subterranean reservoirs of terrifying cruelty within the human personality just waiting to be tapped. An overly confident retributive outlook on crime and punishment—particularly one that would presume to target deep character—has great potential to tap those resources, and this is why my commitment to a retributive theory of punishment has now become reluctant and cautious.

Judgments about deep character and responsibility for it go far beyond the mere attribution of intention and other *mens rea* mental states. My worries about such judgments are to some degree applicable at all points in the criminal justice system, but they are most obviously applicable at the time of sentencing—most dramatically in capital sentencing. And it is these judgments—judgments about what Kant called "inner viciousness"—that will, I fear, both exceed our epistemic capacities and risk engaging the cruelty latent in all of us.

Symmetrical obstacles will also be present, of course, if we seek to reward good character—for example, by imposing less punishment on a criminal whom we believe manifests the character virtue of deep and sincere repentance. This problem is obviously logically similar to the problem about punishing inner viciousness, but I tend to find it less practically worrisome because it will have no tendency to engage our capacities for cruelty.

I tend to worry more about engaging these capacities than I do about engaging our capacities for trust, generosity, and kindness—in part, I suppose, because I think that there is already too much of the former in the world and precious little of the latter. Excessive generosity can be dangerous, of course, if it leads us to free dangerous people to prey again upon the public. But we can surely accomplish the legitimate goal of just crime control with concepts of blameworthiness and desert that do not, as do ultimate negative judgments of deep character, invite hatred and the denial of the human dignity and worth of even the worst among us.[21]

I realize that closing a chapter with expressions of uncertainty and unease is something of a philosophical disappointment. However, such lack of total clarity and comfortable confidence may be a moral and political good. To the degree that we are nervous and unsure of exactly what we are doing when we punish our fellow human beings, then I am inclined to think that to that same degree we will, at the very least, be less cruel.

I know, of course, that there are dangerous, even monstrous, people in the world—both within and outside our national borders—and that they do not become less dangerous or monstrous simply because they are often our creatures, to some degree products of how we have treated or ignored them. I say "ignored them" because, as Simone Weil noted, the poor and other outsiders are invisible to most of us unless seen, as they rarely are, with the eye of love. Because of this and our (at least partial) responsibility for it, we should, of course, seek to correct when we can the conditions that breed such dangerous people. In the meantime, however, we must, for the survival of our communities, find ways to contain the threats posed by these people; and sometimes criminal punishment, even very severe criminal punishment, will emerge as the method of choice. But even when it comes to that, I think that it is probably wise not to be too charmed by such retributive slogans as "giving them what they deserve" and not to be too enthusiastic in the belief that one is on a righteous retributive crusade. Better, I think, that Nietzsche be given the last word here: "He who fights with monsters should look to it that he himself does not become a monster."[22]

Notes

1 Devlin, *Enforcement of Morals*, which contains a reprinting of his 1959 Maccabaean Lecture.

2 Devlin had doubts that it is, on pragmatic grounds, a good idea to use the criminal law to enforce a society's shared moral convictions about homosexual sodomy. Enforcement of such laws might, for example, lead to overly intrusive invasions of privacy or might consume police resources better used on other matters. He was mainly concerned to argue that such enforcement was not *in principle* a wrong objective of the criminal law.

3 See my essays "Legal Moralism and Retribution Revisited" and "Legal Moralism and Liberalism."

4 For an excellent presentation of the challenge that Lord Devlin (and, earlier, James Fitzjames Stephen) present to Millian liberals who claim that the harm principle should control all criminal

law policy, see Feinberg's "Some Unswept Debris from the Hart-Devlin Debate." Feinberg argues that the Millian can make a place for counting blameworthiness, repentance, and other retributive values by appealing to a principle of fairness. I argue (in the essays cited in the previous note) that this fairness argument does not work.

5 Hampton, "How You Can be Both a Liberal and a Retributivist."

6 See my chapters 1 and 3 in *Forgiveness and Mercy*.

7 See my "Repentance, Mercy, and Communicative Punishment." Although I think that repentance is in principle relevant to retributive penal desert, I am skeptical on practical grounds about counting expressions of repentance in criminal sentencing. See my "Remorse, Apology, and Mercy."

8 See my "Retributivism, Moral Education, and the Liberal State."

9 Rawls, "Two Concepts of Rules"; Hart, "Prolegomenon to the Principles of Punishment."

10 See, for example, the chapters by Holtman and Johnson in this volume for more on the retributivism of Kant and Hegel, respectively.

11 For the most detailed discussion of Kant on punishment that I am able to provide (with full textual references and citations), see my "Does Kant Have a Theory of Punishment?"

12 Again, see the chapter by Johnson in this volume for more.

13 Blake, "Auguries of Innocence."

14 Chapter 3.

15 Moore, "Moral Worth of Retribution."

16 Ibid., p. 188.

17 I first developed my argument against Moore in my essay "Moral Epistemology, the Retributive Emotions, and the 'Clumsy Moral Philosophy' of Jesus Christ."

18 Kant, *Religion Within the Limits of Reason Alone*, pp. 33–4.

19 No. 93-3753, United State Court of Appeals, Seventh Circuit, 1995 WL 621777 7th Cir. [Ill.].

20 *Thus Spoke Zarathustra*, ch. 29 (The Tarantulas). See Moore, "Moral Worth of Retribution," for a rich discussion of Nietzsche's views on punishment and for extensive relevant quotations and citations.

21 For an exploration of this issue see my "The Case of Dostoevsky's General: Some Ruminations on Forgiving the Unforgivable."

22 *Beyond Good and Evil*, Aphorism 146.

This chapter was adapted from the retribution section of my 2006 Presidential Address to the American Philosophical Association, Pacific Division ("Legal Moralism and Retribution Revisited").

Bibliography

Blake, William. "Auguries of Innocence." http://www.online-literature.com/blake/612/

Devlin, Patrick. *The Enforcement of Morals*. Oxford: Oxford University Press, 1965.

Feinberg, Joel. "Some Unswept Debris from the Hart-Devlin Debate." *Synthese* 72 (1987): 249–75.

Hampton, Jean. "How You Can Be Both a Liberal and a Retributivist: Comments on *Legal Moralism and Liberalism* by Jeffrie Murphy." *Arizona Law Review* 37 (1995): 105–16.

Hart, H. L. A. *Law, Liberty and Morality*. Stanford: Stanford University Press, 1963.

Hart, H. L. "Prolegomenon to the Principles of Punishment." In *Punishment and Responsibility*, 1–27. Oxford: Oxford University Press, 1968.

Kant, Immanuel. *Religion within the Limits of Reason Alone*. Translated by T. M. Greene and Hoyt Hudson. New York: Harper and Row, 1960.

Moore, Michael S. "The Moral Worth of Retribution." In *Responsibility, Character, and the Emotions: New Essays on Moral Psychology*, edited by Ferdinand Schoeman, 179–219. Cambridge: Cambridge University Press, 1987.

Morris, Herbert. "Persons and Punishment." *The Monist* 52 (1968): 475–501.

Murphy, Jeffrie G. "The Case of Dostoevsky's General: Some Ruminations on Forgiving the Unforgivable." *The Monist* 92 (2009): 556–82.

Murphy, Jeffrie G. "Does Kant Have a Theory of Punishment?" *Columbia Law Review* 87 (1987): 509–532.

Murphy, Jeffrie G. "Legal Moralism and Liberalism." *Arizona Law Review* 37 (1995): 73–94.

Murphy, Jeffrie G. "Legal Moralism and Retribution Revisited." *Proceedings and Addresses of the American Philosophical Association* 80(2) (2006): 45–62, reprinted with revisions in *Criminal Law and Philosophy* 1 (2007): 5–20.

Murphy, Jeffrie G. "Marxism and Retribution." *Philosophy and Public Affairs* 2 (1973): 217–43.

Murphy, Jeffrie G. "Moral Epistemology, the Retributive Emotions, and the 'Clumsy Moral Philosophy' of Jesus Christ." In *The Passions of Law*, edited by Susan Bandes, 149–67. New York: New York University Press, 1999.

Murphy, Jeffrie G. "Remorse, Apology, and Mercy." *Ohio State Journal of Criminal Law* 4 (2007): 424–53.

Murphy, Jeffrie G. "Repentance, Mercy, and Communicative Punishment." In *Crime, Punishment, and Responsibility: The Jurisprudence of Antony Duff*, edited by R. Cruft, M. Krause, and M. Reiff. Oxford: Oxford University Press, 2011 (in press).

Murphy, Jeffrie G. "Retributivism, Moral Education, and the Liberal State." *Criminal Justice Ethics* 4 (1985): 3–11.

Murphy, Jeffrie G., and Jean Hampton. *Forgiveness and Mercy*. Cambridge: Cambridge University Press, 1988.

Nietzsche, Friedrich W. *Beyond Good and Evil*. Translated by Walter Kaufmann. New York: Vintage Books, 1966.

Nietzsche, Friedrich W. *Thus Spoke Zarathustra*. Translated by Walter Kaufmann. New York: The Modern Library, 1995.

Rawls, John. "Two Concepts of Rules." *The Philosophical Review* 64 (1955): 3–32.

6

KANT, RETRIBUTIVISM, AND CIVIC RESPECT

Sarah Holtman

THOSE IN THE business of classifying penal theories use the term "retributivist" in varying ways and so capture a shifting class of theories under this heading. Nevertheless, few would hesitate to place Immanuel Kant's account of just punishment squarely in the retributivist camp. This remains true despite recent work by Kant specialists, several of whom argue that Kant offers at most a mixed or modified retributivism.[1] More, even these specialists (myself included) have yet fully to capture the more and less basic tenets of Kant's penal theory or the relationship among them, much less its proper classification.

This failure is not surprising. Kant's central discussion of punishment occupies only a few pages near the close of the *Rechtslehre*, his most thoroughgoing contribution to political philosophy. It is placed among the general remarks "On the Effects with Regard to Rights that Follow from the Nature of the Civil Union" and hardly offers the kind of careful and systematic discussion that one associates with a full-blown penal theory.[2] Indeed, as we will see, his account of just punishment includes claims as characteristic, for example, of deterrence and rehabilitative theories as of the classical retributivism with which he is typically associated. Consequently, it is not always clear from Kant's texts how his claims regarding just punishment relate to each other, much less what support they find within his larger theory of the just state.

Kant's account of justice, though, is itself what we might call hierarchical, an account whose more concrete principles are to follow by argument from the more fundamental. One consequence of this structure, and of the method of argument that Kant uses to construct it, is that we best interpret more concrete elements by appeal back to the more basic.

Thus, we might hope to resolve apparent conflicts in the penal theory, and perhaps to uncover a more satisfactory justificatory principle, by exploring the larger account.

There is, of course, much room for reasonable disagreement about the details of such an interpretive task. Textual interpretations inevitably will differ, as will conclusions about the relationship among elements of the penal theory and of the whole to the larger account. So my aim here is, and reasonably can be, only to offer a reading that specialists will find worthy of serious consideration, though certainly not the last word. More important, I hope to spark discussion (or more fervent and far-reaching discussion) regarding our classification of penal theories and of what we can and should demand of them.

To this end, I begin by examining the usual classification of Kant's theory, asking what aspects have led interpreters to term it "retributive," and to what extent this label initially seems justified. I then offer a fuller reading of Kant's discussion of just punishment, and, especially important here, an account of what we lose by classifying such a view as "retributive." This includes consideration not only of ways in which Kant's theory differs sharply from classical retributivism, but of the failure even of a more contemporary version to capture the richer and more appealing aspects of Kant's approach. I close with contemporary examples to drive home the point that we do better by Kant's theory, and it by us, when we see it for what it is and not through the lens of an inadequate label.

1. Evidence for Kant's Retributivism

Although reasonable summaries differ, I will take the central tenets of classical retributivism to be: (1) that the only justification for state-sponsored punishment is that the person suffering it has committed a crime, and (2) that the only state punishment that is justifiable is one proportional to the crime committed in manner and degree. Retributivists who are more strict, or thoroughgoing, add to these that every criminal must be punished and that justifiable punishments must accord with a strict interpretation of *ius talionis*. With some limits dictated by what is possible and humane, that is, just punishment imposes the same treatment on the convicted criminal that he or she has inflicted on the victim. As for the justifying aim or purpose of punishment, it is in some sense to restore moral balance or to right the scales of justice.[3]

Given this characterization, it is easy to see why Kant receives a retributivist label. His discussion of just punishment opens by characterizing the right to punish as: "the right a ruler has against a subject to inflict punishment upon him because of his having committed a crime" and never, for example, for the good of the convict or the state.[4] Later in his discussion, the requirement regarding guilt appears still more demanding, for Kant announces that even if a society decided to dissolve itself "the last murderer remaining in prison would first have to be executed. . .; for otherwise the people can be regarded as collaborators in this public violation of justice."[5]

As for the question of type and degree of punishment, Kant famously endorses *ius talionis*, or the law of retribution: "whatever undeserved evil you inflict on another within the people, that you inflict upon yourself. If you insult him, you insult yourself, if you steal him, you steal from yourself; if you kill him, you kill yourself."[6] As we will see shortly, Kant acknowledges that variations will be necessary to capture the spirit of this principle and cautions that every punishment must "be freed from any mistreatment that could make the humanity of the person suffering it into something abominable."[7] In some cases, for example, rape, the state may not morally do to the criminal precisely what he or she has done to the victim. He hastens to add, though, that there can be no just substitute or variation in the case of murder because "[t]here is no *similarity* between life, however wretched it may be, and death."[8]

The question that immediately comes to mind, of course, is what rationale undergirds Kant's claims about just punishment. The answer might appear to lie in some kind of cosmic justice or balancing of the moral scales. Certainly, Kant sometimes seems to suggest this. His description of *ius talionis* as a principle of equality that does the work of "the needle on the scale of justice" readily brings such a rationale to mind. The same is true of the language he uses to explain why a society preparing to disperse must put to death the last murderer "so that each has done to him what his deeds deserve and blood guilt does not cling to the people for not having insisted on this punishment."[9] But other, and especially more recent, interpreters have suggested that Kant endorses a richer and less mysterious rationale, although their characterizations differ, sometimes substantially.[10]

2. Uncooperative Passages

Whatever their disagreements regarding the ultimate interpretation and characterization of Kant's penal theory, those who question the standard retributivist reading largely agree on the supporting evidence. In particular, several passages seem to warrant skepticism about the usual interpretation and to provide the foundation for nonretributive alternatives.

The most important of these passages, because it is most basic to Kant's theory of justice more generally, concerns the connection between justice and coercion. For Kant, as a conceptual matter, justice concerns situations in which the choices and actions of one person influence those of another. He emphasizes that justice thus concerns only external relations between persons. In contrast to morality, then, one can satisfy the demands of justice merely by acting as they require. One's grounds, reasons, or motivations in so acting are irrelevant because justice asks only whether one person's choice can be "united with that of the other" under a "universal law."[11]

Without explaining the argument that gives rise to it, Kant then states what he terms the "universal principle of right":

> Any action is right if it can coexist with everyone's freedom in accordance with a universal law, or if on its maxim the freedom of choice of each can coexist with everyone's freedom in accordance with a universal law.[12]

Stated in the form of a command or law, this becomes the universal law of justice:

> So act externally that the free use of your choice can coexist with the freedom of
> everyone in accordance with a universal law.[13]

Importantly for our purposes, Kant holds that those whose actions comply with these
standards are wronged by the hindering actions of others. Moreover, coercion, itself "a
hindrance or resistance to freedom," is right whenever it opposes such impediments to
permissible actions.[14] Indeed, such coercion is "authorized" against those who infringe on
right action and serves as the incentive to such action when others are absent or
inadequate.[15] Although this coercion might take a variety of forms, punishments for
criminal offenses provide an obvious instance. Attached to public laws, they can dissuade
both convicted criminals, who otherwise might commit further crimes, and potential
criminals, who are deterred by the threatened penalty.

The prominence of coercion in Kant's account of the just state and its laws must give
us pause in classifying his views on punishment as unalloyed retributivism. Indeed, they
suggest that, in Kant's view, the underlying justification for state punishment might be
deterrence. This conclusion would remove him from the ranks of true retributivists and
not merely from those of retributivism's most staunch adherents.

Although they do not so clearly implicate the very foundations of Kant's view, further
passages bolster the conclusion that Kant departs, perhaps dramatically, from the tenets
of classical retributivism. For example, in discussing the "right of necessity," he contends
that, where one person must sacrifice another to save himself, his act, though morally
wrong, is not punishable. This is because a penal law that sought to punish such an action
"could not have the effect intended, since a threat of an evil that is still uncertain (death
by a judicial verdict) cannot outweigh the fact of an evil that is certain."[16] Again, Kant's
view seems to be that the intended, and appropriate, effect of a penal law, unavailable here,
is deterrence.[17] Much later, in condemning those who suggest that criminal punishments
serve some useful purpose for the criminal or the state, it appears that Kant does not
absolutely reject the view that punishments can or should serve such purposes. Rather,
the offender "must *previously* have been found *punishable before* any thought can be given
to drawing from his punishment something of use for himself or his fellow citizens."[18]

3. Further Complications

Perhaps Jeffrie Murphy is correct in suggesting, based on these and similar passages, that
Kant simply has no coherent penal theory.[19] I believe that the situation is, in fact, even
more confusing than we have seen so far (or, as I will suggest, richer). In my view, though,
this gives us reason to attribute a fuller and more coherent penal theory to Kant and not
the reverse.

To get a sense of the further, and apparently conflicting, strands in Kant's penal theory, first consider one of several passages that address difficulties in shaping punishments to achieve appropriate equality among offenders:

> Now it would indeed seem that differences in social rank would not allow the principle of retribution. . .; but even when this is not possible in terms of the letter, the principle can always remain valid in terms of its effect if account is taken of the sensibilities of the upper classes.[20]

Kant goes on to give examples suggesting, for instance, that a violent person of high social rank could be required both to apologize for striking a social inferior and to serve a term in solitary confinement accompanied by other hardships. This, he believes, would satisfy the demands of equality that inspire the law of retribution because "in addition to the discomfort he undergoes, the offender's vanity would be painfully affected, so that through his shame, like would be fittingly repaid with like."[21]

Absent this discussion, one might have thought that strict application of *ius talionis* was by itself sufficient to achieve punishment's appropriate aims in Kant's view. This passage suggests, though, that the offender must feel or experience the same pain or hardship that he has inflicted. Perhaps Kant merely intends that this felt equivalence is what is needed to balance the cosmic scales of justice. Two other aims, familiar in contemporary work on punishment, seem to offer at least as plausible an explanation though. The first is that the criminal comes to appreciate the harm done to the victim and their similarity in terms of needs, interests, and vulnerability, and through these the nature and significance of the injustice for which he is responsible. Punishment, in short, should be designed to educate the criminal regarding moral agency and moral responsibility.[22] The second is that, through the punishment imposed, civil society expresses its equal regard for victim and criminal as citizens by condemning the wrong the victim has suffered.[23] While we are not yet in a position to reject commitment to cosmic justice or moral balance as the basis for the views that Kant voices here, we must at least acknowledge that others are equally plausible and warrant closer scrutiny of Kant's penal theory itself and its relationship to his larger political theory. This is not to suggest that Kant views punishment chiefly (much less only) as justified by aims of moral education or the expression of equal regard, but that one cannot understand or properly characterize his theory without due attention to these strains.

Although arguably there are other indications of Kant's antiretributivist (or perhaps *non*retributivist) leanings, I will address only two here. They will allow us to identify further connections to familiar justificatory arguments and to establish an interpretation that could be tested against other aspects of Kant's penal theory. The first of these concerns society's obligations to the criminal himself. It is clear that Kant recognizes such obligations; they are most evident in the caution, mentioned earlier, that when death is the appropriate punishment for a crime, "it still must be freed from any mistreatment that could make the humanity in the person suffering it into something abominable."[24] While this language seems peculiarly detached from the offender as a person, it nevertheless acknowledges both ongoing humanity and the demand for respect that falls on the state and fellow citizens.

Although less direct, we find a similar acknowledgment in Kant's discussion of the death penalty as a means of recognizing variations in the "inner wickedness" of murderers. The man of honor (perhaps one who killed from a sense of obligation to his house or family) would choose to die rather than live as a prisoner condemned to hard labor, says Kant. The scoundrel (perhaps one who killed to advance his political position or reap monetary gain) would prefer to live in shame than not to live at all.[25] This passage suggests that Kant's account of just punishment (fully explicated) maintains a place for *mens rea*, at least as a factor in determining the severity of a crime and what is necessary to maintain proportionality in punishment. It also makes clear that, for Kant, the offender remains very much a player as we attempt to determine what justice demands. He or she must not be punished more severely than deeds deserve. Yet more telling, an offender maintains at least the potential to pass judgment on his or her own deeds, and not only to accept the appropriate punishment, but to embrace it insofar as it is an acknowledgment of the capacity to choose and to be deemed the author of choices and fully responsible and accountable for them.[26]

The remaining passage I consider seems, at first blush, to adopt the opposite view. Here, Kant takes up problem cases that result from faulty codes of honor. The first is a mother's murder of her illegitimate infant and the second a soldier's slaying of a fellow officer in a duel. The cases present a difficulty for Kant, given his claim that capital punishment is the only response to murder "that will satisfy justice," for he doubts that they warrant the death penalty.[27]

Kant's attempt to argue that his theory supports exceptions includes an unsavory comparison of the illegitimate child to "contraband merchandise" that has no claim to the commonwealth's protections, as well as reflections on the consensual nature of the duel. These features, he suggests, are part of what justifies removing such killings from the class of murders. The claim most central to Kant's conclusion, though, is that the social "incentives of honor" at work in these cases render unjust those laws that classify the killings in question as murders. These killings would properly be deemed murders and so would appropriately be punished by death, according to Kant, in a society where social norms were consistent with justice. This cannot be the case, though, in society as Kant knows it. For here, the woman who gives birth to an illegitimate child and the soldier who refuses to fight for his honor after insult can expect to live permanently in shame. The fear of this shame becomes an incentive to kill that outweighs, or at least blinds sufferers to, the demands of just laws. Until social norms align with justice, then, laws that seek to punish these offenders as murderers are unjust, and the state must impose a lesser penalty.

Unlike earlier passages suggesting that we wrong the criminal if we do not punish his crime, this discussion seems to suggest that some offenders are best "treated" as, at least partly, the products or victims of social failure rather than as fully responsible for their actions. While this is not explicitly a case of seeing an offender as the victim of a "social disease" for which he or she is not responsible, it addresses a very similar case and arrives at a similar conclusion.

4. A Multifaceted Political Freedom and a Conception of Civic Respect

Before we attempt to make sense of the puzzling Kantian landscape that has now emerged, we need to take stock of its features. In the most famous (or notorious) of Kant's passages on punishment, we have seen commitments to proportionality, guilt, *ius talionis*, and the punishment of each and every offender. These seem to signal a thoroughgoing classical retributivism that takes punishment to be justified and shaped, at bottom, by a concern for moral (or cosmic) balance. Elsewhere, and most importantly in foundational discussions of the place of coercion in the just state, we have found reason to believe that, for Kant, punishment instead is justified (and within limits also shaped) by a commitment to deterrence.

On yet more careful reading, we have identified apparent concerns to educate the offender so as to awaken an understanding of the nature and moral gravity of the wrong done, to publicly acknowledge or express respect for the victim as a citizen and agent due the state's protection, to respect the offender as a responsible agent, and to acknowledge the sometime role of society in undermining or thwarting the realization of that agency. Among these last four concerns, some might best be thought of as constraints on the nature and severity of punishment and others as considerations that may sometimes justify imposing or foregoing it. Apparently aimed at properly shaping the institution, they may not (or not always) address its underlying justification. Since many of Kant's remarks are vague, though, and the number, variety, and sometimes contradictory nature of the considerations suggests confusion (on our part or on Kant's), we perhaps do best to withhold judgment even on the question of their role.

In the face of such chaos, the appropriate course is to ask whether we have missed some connecting thread that would reveal a pattern or coherent line of thought where none so far has been apparent. Given the structure of Kant's political theory, which again proposes to build more concrete elements on the foundation of first principles, we most reasonably look to the latter. Although our sights initially might rest on the standards of justice discussed earlier, we should recall that each of these references "freedom" in a way that requires further explanation. This is both freedom "of choice" and freedom "in accordance with universal law."[28] It is the analysis of Kant's conception of freedom, I suggest, that may offer initial insight into his account of just punishment:

> This principle of innate freedom already involves the following authorizations, which are not really distinct from it (as if they were members of the division of

some higher concept of right): innate *equality*, that is, independence from being bound by others to more than one can in turn bind them; hence a man's quality of being *his own master* (*sui juris*), as well as being a man *beyond reproach* (*iusti*), since before he performs any act affecting rights he has done no wrong to anyone; and finally, his being authorized to do to others anything that does not in itself diminish what is theirs, so long as they do not want to accept it. . . . [29]

For Kant, freedom is not only the one foundational right of each person; it is best conceived as encompassing distinct, though related, interests. The last mentioned of these, which I will term freedom of action, likely would come most readily to mind for most of us in the context of punishment: provided I do not interfere with others' rightful claims, I may choose my actions as I please. The limits that rightful claims can place on my own freedom of choice, though, cannot obligate any one person to more than they do another. If enforcement mechanisms, presumably in the form of coercive laws, are unequal, they limit the freedom of some unduly. Similarly, such laws and the institutions from which they derive, must acknowledge each persons' independence, his capacity to use his own judgment not only to choose a course of action but to participate in and evaluate proposed state actions (for example, by voting on policies or representatives). One consequence of such independence is that each must be held accountable for, but only for, those of his own chosen actions that inappropriately limit the rights of others. Not only freedom of choice, but also civil equality, civil independence, and a conception of citizen responsibility thus are aspects of the political freedom that just laws properly protect and regulate in Kant's view.

Importantly for our purposes, Kant ultimately describes his ideal, or conception, of citizenship by appeal to this account of civic freedom:

In terms of rights, the attributes of a citizen, inseparable from his essence (as a citizen), are: lawful *freedom*, the attribute of obeying no other law than that to which he has given his consent; civil *equality*, that of not recognizing among the *people* any superior with the moral capacity to bind him as a matter of Right in a way that he could not in turn bind the other; and third, the attribute of civil independence, of owing his existence and preservation to his own rights and powers as a member of the commonwealth, not to the choice of another among the people. From this independence follows his civil personality, his attribute of not needing to be represented by another where rights are concerned. [30]

Given this, connections we uncover between Kant's penal theory and his account of political freedom are also connections with his account of what is required to honor or respect citizens as he conceives them. Thus, Kant's penal theory, I suggest in what follows, seeks to describe what is required for the state and its citizens to demonstrate civic respect and concern in the realm of punishment.

With Kant's accounts of political freedom and civic respect in hand, then, and recalling that these are multifaceted, we can attempt a more coherent interpretation of his penal theory. Deterrence concerns are perhaps most easily connected to citizens' freedom of action as we now understand it. The threat of punishment, attached to penal laws, can work to discourage unjust interference by one citizen with the choices and actions of others where a commitment to justice itself may not motivate reliably and, in any case, cannot be demanded by law. Determining what actions warrant such a penalty requires separate analysis, based on consideration of which freedoms require protection via criminal as opposed to other standards.

Simply deterring undue interference with citizen choice and action, though, will not be sufficient to address the freedom-related concerns arising in penal contexts. In particular, the protection the law offers must redound equally to each citizen, and the burden of compliance must be equally borne by each. What precisely equality amounts to here—for example, mere applicability of laws to all citizens, every citizen being subject to the same demands or something yet more robust—is a large topic and one we need not address to answer questions now at issue. It is enough to recognize that several Kantian demands regarding just punishment could reasonably be thought of as stemming from equality concerns, including demands that every criminal offender be punished and that punishments for the same type of crime be proportional to the wrong in question. These address demands for equality as between similarly situated offenders, between offenders and their victims, and among victims themselves. We may certainly question Kant's own conclusions, among them the claims that equality typically is best achieved through a close approximation to *ius talionis* and that nothing but capital punishment can be sufficiently similar to death to justify a substitute. Our objections, though, do not alter the relationship of punishment-related concerns to requirements of equality.

Connections to citizen independence may not be as readily apparent. Considerations of what will lead the offender to appreciate the harm he has done and of the appropriateness of leniency where society's own failings substantially contribute to criminal action, though, do seem well explained by such appeal. The first of these, we might think, stems from the view of punishment as appropriately concerned to achieve in offenders a recognition of the citizenship of their fellows and from a view of the state itself as charged with expressing that recognition. The discussion of leniency in cases of infanticide and dueling arguably has its source in a similar perspective, but now the subject is the offending citizen and not the victim. For such leniency would acknowledge the role of society in undermining independent judgment through faulty codes of honor (e.g., those requiring citizens innocent of legal or serious moral wrongdoing to choose between murder and a life of shame and accompanying social exclusion). It thus would encourage those who support or tolerate those codes to recognize both the citizenship of those who violate them and, perhaps, the vulnerabilities that threaten realization of independent judgment in citizens generally. Institutionalized as a legal standard, lesser penalties in such cases would also express the state's recognition of the citizenship of every member and a commitment to addressing threats to the realization of citizen capacities.

Beyond these examples, we might see the demand to put every murderer to death (the above exceptions aside) as likewise recognizing independence, and not merely the equality concerns mentioned earlier. For this regularity in punishment might seem necessary not only to achieve equality among similarly situated offenders and victims, but to acknowledge the offender as the responsible author of actions. Finally, both the requirement that only the guilty be punished and the observation that every criminal is in some sense owed his punishment seem clearly connected to the independence-related concern to acknowledge individual responsibility. The persons punished under just laws must be seen and addressed as originators of actions. More, they must be understood and addressed not merely as followers of just laws but as legislators, at least in the sense that they can recognize the warrant for such laws and commit themselves to them. A penal system that includes, as a necessary tenet, a commitment to punishing only the guilty (or at least those who have been determined by reliable means to be guilty) arguably honors this aspect of citizen freedom.[31]

5. The Merits of a Civic Respect Account

My suggestion thus far, then, is that we understand Kant's account of just punishment as one that seeks to give voice to his multifaceted accounts of political freedom and of civic respect and concern. Still, those inclined toward a traditional classification scheme will remind us, Kant's views concerning the demands of civic respect and concern in penal contexts certainly resemble those of classical retributivism in important respects. At moments, we should recall, they seem to endorse the most virulent version of that branch of penal theory. Granted, Kant seems at other moments to endorse deterrence and perhaps other familiar considerations as main (or at least important) aims of punishment. Thus, he is not well described as a classical retributivist. But it may nevertheless be appropriate and useful to place him generally in the retributivist camp.

Indeed, these traditionalists might continue, the analysis provided so far lends support to this position, for it shows that troubling divergences from the retributive line are not what they first seem. They are not based, in the end, on a concern to prevent or reduce harm or to reform the wrongdoer but on an account of the appropriate relationship of the wrongdoer in particular, and of society more generally, to moral understanding and commitment. Classical retributivism may cash out this concern by appeal to notions of moral or cosmic balance. More contemporary adherents, however, might be understood to see this balance as internal to the offender, or to political society, or both. Thus, some more recent proponents have suggested that just punishment removes unfair advantages that criminal offenders gain over fellow citizens or is called for by, or in harmony with, moral emotions that are appropriate responses to criminal wrongdoing (including resentment on the side of victims and guilt on that of offenders).[32] We can think of the first as an appeal to moral balance in society as a whole and the second as an appeal to balance internal to victims and offenders respectively. For the critic I now have in mind, the reading based in civic respect that I have offered is just another version of this sort of contemporary interpretation of moral balance. I may have provided a reading that is more sophisticated and satisfying than those that cast Kant as a classical retributivist, but I have not removed him from retributivist ranks.

I do not deny that we might understand Kant in this way and even see the foregoing sections as nicely supporting such a classification. But I suspect that much would be lost and little gained by going this route. The argument I will offer to this effect appeals to two examples: the first more closely tied to legal theory and the second to legal practice. My strategy is to show that, understood as a civic respect account, Kant's theory offers greater practical enlightenment than it can if simply seen as an example of what we might term contemporary (not classical) retributivism. Importantly, my argument in these last sections does not concern the historical Kant and what he himself endorsed. It instead explores the richness of that theory and possibilities for its extension beyond issues that Kant himself considered. It is thus perhaps best thought of as an exploration of Kantian theory—theory based in the civic respect account of punishment that I have just attributed to Kant.

A. *MIRANDA V. ARIZONA*

I turn first to what is now an aging legal decision, one that might be seen as the product of another day and an outmoded line of thought. We know *Miranda v. Arizona* best, of course, as the source of the famous *Miranda* warnings. These have been rendered especially familiar by police officers in movies and television dramas, who mimic reality as they rattle off these reminders that those under arrest have rights to "remain silent" and to be represented by legal counsel. From the perspective of conservative legislators and citizens, the demand for such warnings in custodial settings has been the cause of much rancor, another way to trip up the officer devoted to getting criminal offenders off the streets and for those offenders to walk free. From the perspective of defense attorneys and advocates for the rights of the accused, they are one step toward adequate protection of the rights and interests of these individuals.

Given our unusual familiarity with the warnings—for few legal standards are so firmly embedded in the mind of the average citizen—and the frequent focus of critics on their potential for helping the guilty avoid just punishment, many think little about their aim, much less what might be said for or against them from the perspective of a theory of punishment. For present purposes, we are most interested, first, in what might be said from the perspective of retributivism. From this viewpoint, the justification for *Miranda's* demands would seem to lie most importantly in a concern to prevent punishment of the innocent. If the police are permitted to engage in tactical custodial questioning of the sort that the *Miranda* majority describes at length, some who are innocent will make incriminating statements, either from confusion or desperation. These may lead to jail sentences or worse for those who in fact have done no wrong, creating moral imbalance in political society.

Those familiar with the decision, however, know that concern to protect the innocent was not the primary one advanced in *Miranda*. Instead, Chief Justice Warren's majority opinion rests on the constitutional right against self-incrimination and describes the significance of that right in this way:

> the constitutional foundation underlying the privilege is the respect a government—state or federal—must accord to the dignity and integrity of its citizens. To maintain a "fair state-individual balance," to require the government "to shoulder the entire load"..., to respect the inviolability of the human personality, our accusatory system of criminal justice demands that the government seeking to punish an individual produce the evidence against him by its own independent labors, rather than by the cruel, simple expedient of compelling it from his own mouth... In sum, the privilege is fulfilled only when the person is guaranteed the right "to remain silent unless he chooses to speak in the unfettered exercise of his own will."[33]

Classical retributivism, with its focus on guilt and proportionality, does not seem well suited to argue for the merits of such reasoning, but a more contemporary version might be able to. It could, for example, advocate either harmony between the offender's convictions or commitments and the act of giving testimony or an appropriate balance in the burdens placed on a powerful state and a comparatively weak individual. But these might seem, as the Court's own reasoning indeed has seemed to many, to be at best mysterious.

Without exploring now what is the best interpretation of the *Miranda* majority's reasoning, or whether there is some retributive account that could make it less mysterious and more compelling, I want to suggest that the Kantian alternative of civic respect and concern provides an especially fruitful approach. As I have interpreted it, Kant's penal theory appeals to a rich conception of political freedom and a related account of citizenship to determine the aims, contours, and limits required for justice in state punishment. In particular, as we have seen, it appeals to notions of freedom of choice and action, citizen equality, and citizen responsibility and independence of judgment, and demands that penal laws and institutions be designed so as to honor or respect each citizen as essentially possessed of these.

What could be said about the implications of such basic commitments for the questions at issue in *Miranda*? From this Kantian perspective, when we design our interrogation practices to trick, deceive, outwit or exhaust a suspect in the hope of evoking inculpatory statements, we view that person not as a citizen to be reasoned with but as a tool to be manipulated or an impediment to get around. Moreover, we view the state, and ourselves as its self-governing members, as properly in the business not of understanding, reasoning, and co-legislating with our fellow citizens but of manipulating them for useful purposes. Of course, some will object that engaging in such practices and taking such a viewpoint on ourselves and our fellow citizens is acceptable when there is danger that a crime, perhaps serious, will go unpunished and an offender, perhaps dangerous, will walk free. To this, the Kantian civic respect theory responds that we are dealing not with offenders but with mere suspects and that, in any case, there are equally grave dangers involved in many of our institutional interactions. If the viewpoint of justified manipulator, not fellow citizen, is appropriate here, it is appropriate in a multitude of other contexts, threatening (indeed almost promising) to become our default.

The civic respect account, moreover, allows us to recognize a link between protecting the innocent from unwarranted punishment (which is, at the least, a byproduct of *Miranda* warnings) and concerns to insure the voluntariness of statements and appropriate state (versus citizen) burden. As we have seen, punishment must have its basis in the commission of a criminal offense if we are to acknowledge fellow citizens as responsible agents. Since they are among the means by which we determine whom to punish, police tactics that measurably increase the likelihood of incarcerating, convicting, and formally punishing the innocent thus run afoul not only of the earlier-mentioned demand to recognize the independence of fellow citizens but also of the demand to acknowledge responsible agency.

After further analysis, of course, we may conclude that the risks of punishing the innocent are only marginally increased by a given procedure or that we can substantially reduce such a risk via other means (for example, by shaping rules of evidence to help insure that judges and juries will recognize and discount unreliable inculpatory statements). We may also conclude that, once these precautions are in place, the reliable evidence obtained by these methods, in fact, importantly answers demands for civic respect, especially in the guise of equality and freedom from force, by allowing us to identify and punish offenders who might otherwise have gone free. Indeed, based on careful evaluation of the best information available to us, we may conclude, after discussion and debate, that these procedures, perhaps reshaped, better address all relevant aspects of citizen respect than other means presently available.

This last analysis fills out an explanation of the connection from a Kantian perspective between police procedures, punishment of the innocent, and citizen respect. It also offers an example of the kind of discussion and debate that Kantian civic respect theory would seem to require if its multiple concerns are to be addressed across citizens. So viewed, it allows us to grasp the ways in which civic respect bears on all of those concerns potentially addressed by *Miranda* warnings. More, it offers us a way to see *Miranda's* most concrete outcome—its demand for warnings in custodial settings—as effecting the very kind of reshaping toward greater respect suggested above. For *Miranda* does not call a halt to interrogation practices that may encourage unreliable inculpatory statements or be unduly manipulative. Rather, it insists that those in custody be provided information about the availability of representation, an opportunity to obtain that representation, and a caution about the potential significance of statements made. In short, Kantian civic respect theory allows us to appreciate the demand for custodial warnings as one that reshapes extant police procedures to serve the multifaceted concern to achieve citizen respect across persons in complex circumstances. So conceived, the Kantian civic respect theory is a valuable explanatory and normative account with resources that go far beyond those apparently offered by retributivism in its classical or contemporary form.

Viewed as a theory of civic respect, then, Kant's account of just punishment not only provides a basis for explanatory work that is not obviously open to a retributive theory, it offers us a perspective on, or better yet, a perspective of citizenship that might profitably reshape our political lives. This, I suggest, provides us reason to reject a retributivist label for Kant's theory. For doing so at best masks what is distinctive and valuable in it.

B. THE CASE OF KIRSTEN DRISCOLL

I turn now to a case that is not famous, although the questions it raises will be familiar. I choose it not because it is more significant than similar cases, but because it provides a clear practical example with which to work. In June 2009, Kirsten Driscoll, a wealthy Minneapolis woman from a socially and economically affluent part of the city, attended a party to celebrate her daughter's graduation from an elite private high school. By her own account, she had had an exhausting and commitment-filled day and had eaten little, and at the evening party, she drank more than she intended or realized. Driving home through a working class neighborhood, she fell asleep at the wheel, ran into a bus shelter, and killed a neighborhood resident who had stopped to chat with a friend on his way to buy a pack of cigarettes. Her blood alcohol level was well over the legal limit in Minnesota.

Driscoll pleaded guilty to criminal vehicular homicide. At sentencing, her attorney noted that she had never been arrested or cited for drunk driving before, much less for any other crime, that she was an active volunteer for worthy causes, and that she had accepted full responsibility for her actions and committed herself to working to solve or prevent alcohol abuse in middle-aged women like herself. To the distress of the victim's family, she was sentenced only to a year in the workhouse. The judge, in evident distress himself, explained that the sentence was typical of those given similarly circumstanced offenders and followed Minnesota sentencing guidelines.[34]

The tension in the case, of course, is all too familiar. On the one hand, we can recognize the importance of treating like cases alike and of acknowledging the relevance of factors that suggest an offender's remorse, the likelihood of rehabilitation, and similar mitigating elements of the situation. On the other, we can see the enormous loss that Driscoll caused, recognize the importance of preventing similar devastating losses in the future, and appreciate the underlying sense that the victim's family and friends may well have had that the difference in the social status of the offender and her victim played a role in the relatively lenient sentence, despite the judge's assurances to the contrary. As before, I want to ask what the retributivist can say to help us evaluate such a case and whether any richer evaluation is available to Kantian civic respect theory.

With questions of Driscoll's guilt and actual (as opposed to perceived) special treatment to one side, the classical retributivist will ask whether the usual sentence is here, or in general, out of keeping with the demand that the punishment be proportional to the wrong done so that moral balance is achieved. Since we are dealing first and foremost with the application of extant rules (in particular the Minnesota sentencing guidelines) and not with regulatory reform, part of the inquiry into proportionality must presumably be an inquiry into what has been done in like cases. This provides a kind of default standard or judgment about appropriate fit between penalty and wrongdoing. Another part of any proportionality inquiry, though, will surely include the observation that a year in the workhouse is hardly comparable to the harm done. This point will remain salient even if we acknowledge that the wrong cannot be analyzed solely in terms of the harm it occasioned but requires appeal, for example, to the offender's *mens rea* (in this case, gross negligence). Further matters typically taken to be relevant here—for example, Driscoll's past record and present remorse, as well as deterrence concerns—cannot be a part of the classical retributivist's analysis of the case.

From the perspective of a more contemporary retributivism, the main question will remain one of proportionality. Now, though, one might attempt to balance punishment and wrong done by appeal to notions of remedy for unfair advantage or a match with the offenders' appropriate feelings of guilt or victims' appropriate moral resentment. Here, past record or present remorse might be relevant in determining the level of such feelings already present. These realizations about proportionality, whether from a classical or a contemporary perspective, may not outweigh equality considerations in the case at hand. It is (again) important to recognize, though, that beyond what past cases suggest about our judgments regarding proportionality, retributivism alone has relatively little to say in favor of equal treatment.[35] In particular, if mistakes have been made in the past, moral balance seems to suggest that it is best to right them now. What does seem clear is that retributivism, in either classical or contemporary form, would warrant an inquiry into legal reform in light of the outcome in Driscoll and similar cases.

Our query is whether a Kantian civic respect account can yield a more satisfying or enlightening analysis. From this perspective, the issue at hand is whether the law, as it stands, treats Driscoll, her victim, and others harmed by her actions (such as the victim's family), as well as those similarly situated, with due respect and concern for their status as free, equal, and independent citizens. As before, this inquiry sends us beyond questions of guilt and proportionality and also beyond vague notions of moral balance or of internal or social harmony.

Especially noteworthy, understood as a civic respect view, Kantian theory has the power to integrate and enrich our approach to the several questions that complicate this and similar cases. These include the questions of what penalty (1) appropriately takes account of the fact that the offender was grossly negligent but not a knowing or intending murderer, and duly acknowledges past record, present remorse, and the likelihood of rehabilitation; (2) acknowledges the loss to the victim and those who loved and relied on him, without becoming a vehicle for revenge or for venting grief and anger; (3) demonstrates and communicates that the state and fellow citizens equally value all offenders and all victims; and (4) adequately deters Driscoll and future similarly situated offenders from the harmful activity in question. As was true of our *Miranda* discussion, what follows is not a textual analysis meant to determine how Kant himself would have viewed a decision like Driscoll or dealt with the issues just identified, but rather an investigation into the possibilities for enlightening analysis and subsequent implementation that exist when we extend the civic respect approach that I have argued is implicit in those texts.

From this perspective of Kantian civic respect, the first set of considerations above demands a penalty that acknowledges the extent, but also the limits, of the offender's responsibility. Like all citizens, she is a human being with the capacity for varying intentions and with limitations that incline her to errors with negative consequences far beyond the level of ill will or motivation involved. Also, she is an integrated person with capacities for commitment and judgment that make her past choices as well as her demonstrated commitments for the future relevant to present evaluation. These indicate the level of her own appreciation of citizen obligations, the depth of her commitment to fulfilling them, and something about the likelihood that she will do so in the future.

Turning to our second question, we recognize that citizens depend on and value each other in myriad life-affecting ways. We are part of one another's plans and projects and possessed of our own. An appropriate penalty must take these relationships duly into account in its severity but also recognize that the grief and anger of loved ones, like the consequences of our actions, is likely to exceed what it is appropriate to countenance in determining just penalties. The very fact of the importance of our relationships to our lives as persons and citizens means that, absent further evaluation to determine its relevance to civic respect, our judgment from the inside is not the proper gauge to employ in assessing penalties.

Third, the civic respect approach not only demands that we treat all involved citizens with equal regard but focuses our inquiry and our attention in crucial ways. We cannot diverge significantly from past practice while extant rules remain fixed not merely because this practice identifies what we have deemed proportional punishment in the past, but because to do so is to treat some citizens as more or less worthy of respect than others and to send the message to all that we judge them so. Moreover, in choosing and enforcing a penalty, we must ask whether we are, or reasonably appear to be, guided, for example, by inappropriate considerations like the social status of the victim or offender. All of this is required to treat every citizen as properly conceived and to make clear to all that this is our commitment.

Finally, the concerns raised by our fourth question require that the above conclusions be shaped by a commitment to preventing similar actions and losses in the future. Respect for vulnerable citizens cannot adequately be shown by recognizing harm and fault after the fact if steps can be taken to prevent these consistent with other demands of citizen respect. Punishment has a deterrence-based role, though this is always to be limited and shaped not only by broad commitment to citizen respect but also by its more particular demands—for example, to honor human limitations, to avoid creating a vehicle for vengeance, and to treat like cases alike.

When we apply these considerations more directly to the Driscoll case, it appears, first, that Kantian theory would largely approve the inquiries regarding offenders that are required by relevant Minnesota statutes and sentencing guidelines and acknowledged in the Driscoll decision itself. Viewed from this perspective, Minnesota statutes attempt to take account of human capacities and limitations by distinguishing among several levels of manslaughter. (For example, punishing criminal vehicular homicide less harshly than manslaughter that occurs "in the heat of passion" or as a consequence of the malicious punishment of a child.[36]) In further distinguishing among cases of criminal vehicular homicide itself, the guidelines seemingly recognize the integrated lives of responsible human agents by acknowledging the relevance of past offenses (or their absence) and of signs of willingness to accept responsibility for past wrongdoing and to take action to prevent similar future errors.[37] Likewise of merit from the Kantian perspective, the Driscoll verdict explicitly noted not only her (previously) "clean" record but also her apologies and acceptance of responsibility, as well as the fact that she had already undertaken preventive steps in the form of treatment for alcoholism and a promise to work with other women like herself at risk of abusing alcohol.[38]

This analysis gives further substance to the implications of Kantian civic respect theory for matters often deemed relevant in judging not only the severity of a crime but the level of offender culpability and likelihood of rehabilitation. In particular, with its focus on offenders as free and independent citizens, Kantian theory endorses appeal to considerations (for example, willingness to accept responsibility and to take preventive measures for the future) beyond retributive concerns regarding criminal intent. Indeed, it recommends considerations that go beyond the indicators of guilt feelings that may be relevant in insuring proportionality between punishment and wrong or some other appropriate moral balance. Moreover, it provides an integrated approach to issues of intent, past record, and the like that is often lacking in discussions of sentencing criteria, viewing each through the multifaceted lens of freedom, equality, and independence.

Our second question raises the concern that statutes, guidelines, and the verdict at hand may not impose penalties severe enough to appropriately acknowledge losses to the offenders' fellow citizens, especially the victim's family. Viewed in light of the general Kantian approach already sketched and applied directly to the Driscoll case, this warrants further attention to relevant sentencing provisions and their application. The relevant Minnesota statute provides for a maximum sentence of ten years, a fine of $20,000, or both.[39] Sentencing guidelines emphasize the importance, from a standpoint of justice, of treating like cases in like manner. Indeed, they announce that ensuring that this occurs is their very purpose and highlight certain characteristics as ones that cannot justify any change in the severity of a sentence, such as race, gender, and socioeconomic status.[40] In a case like Driscoll's, the guidelines provide for a maximum prison sentence of four years and a minimum of one year. Finally, the presiding judge in the Driscoll case emphasized that "from 2001 to 2008 in Hennepin County [where Driscoll resides and where her crime was committed], 23 defendants were sentenced for the same crime and 13 of them received the same sentence. The others had prior criminal convictions or fled the scene of the crash."[41]

Kantian civic respect theory would applaud not only the attention that these standards and legal analyses give to equality among similarly situated citizens, but also the kind of careful public reasoning contained in these various provisions as well as in the judge's announcement of the verdict. Such reasoning is required if we are to address citizens both as self-governing agents and as joint participants in the government of the state. Nevertheless, the theory might also recommend, first, that the judge himself further emphasize not only recent sentencing statistics but the aim and cautions of the sentencing guidelines. Explanation of this sort provides one means of alerting citizen-victims, citizen-family-members, and others to the many considerations at issue and the careful reasoning at many levels that lies behind any appropriate verdict.

At the same time, partly in light of the reaction of victims and the district attorney (who vigorously argued that the maximum of four years was appropriate in this case), the theory likely would also support a revisiting of both statute and guidelines to consider whether the minimum sentence for criminal vehicular homicide is indeed appropriate from the perspective of civic respect and whether judges are properly applying it. For reasons already noted, the theory would not countenance reevaluation merely on grounds of victim outrage. Here, however, that outrage is accompanied by an obvious gap between the punishment and the harm done that any reasonable citizen can appreciate. This suggests that it is an outrage at least partly sparked by an appropriate sense that civic respect has not been shown rather than the outrage that naturally accompanies the loss of a loved one at the hands of another. Indeed, we can see the district attorney, who himself expressed such outrage, as properly a representative of such a "reasonable citizen" perspective. Absent grounds for believing that he departed from his appropriate role, his reaction provides further evidence that reevaluation is appropriate from the perspective of Kantian civic respect. Importantly, not only a change in recommendation, but the very revisiting of standards, serves to demonstrate respect for citizens from the standpoint of Kantian theory. For such revisiting takes seriously those expressions of outrage that appear, on analysis, to indicate citizen commitments to joint civic respect, without allowing what we might call personal (rather than civic) emotion improperly to decide this or that particular case.[42]

Our detailed discussion of these first two questions makes it easy to appreciate the way that Kantian civic respect theory likely would treat our remaining questions in the concrete circumstances of Driscoll. In particular (with regard to our third question), the theory will not endorse a dramatic divergence from past practice in one case simply because we believe that practice may err with regard to proportionality. Proportionality between punishment and wrongdoing is one way in which we acknowledge victims' losses and offenders' responsibility. But these are not the only considerations relevant in determining just punishment on the civic respect view, and proportionality between penalty and wrong is not the only vehicle available to us to demonstrate respect. As we saw in our discussion of *Miranda*, Kantian civic respect theory requires that we take account of a rich set of considerations and explore the routes that may be open to us for properly attending to each. One way of showing due respect for both victims and offenders may be carefully ensuring proportionality between punishment and wrong in the case at hand. Another may be ensuring similar (though perhaps inadequate) punishments for similarly circumstanced offenders (thus also ensuring equal treatment for their victims) coupled with an announcement of the grounds for so doing and action to revisit and revise standards for the future. This kind of multifaceted and nuanced inquiry and response is not open to retributivism in either its classical or contemporary form. Neither is any inquiry into the deterrent function of punishment. Kantian civic respect theory would treat a deterrence inquiry in much the same way as it does proportionality, giving due regard to the equal treatment of those similarly situated but acknowledging that deterrence (important to demonstrating proper regard for present and potential victims) may demand a revisiting of present standards and their application.

One response to this analysis might be that, in the end, it offers little that the retributivist approach cannot. After all, it recommends many of the same considerations and likely arrives at the same broad outcome in the case at hand: an acceptance of the Driscoll verdict with the recommendation for possible future legislative reform. But so concluding would be a mistake. The retributivist, whether classical or contemporary, does not have the wherewithal to explain, by appeal to a single rich set of commitments, for example, why and in what way issues of criminal intent and remorse, victim reaction, and equal treatment are at once relevant in determining penalty. The retributive inquiry into these matters is guided at best by vague and incomplete standards. Not only may these lead to extreme judgments, whether in the direction of leniency or severity, but they will cause us to miss central issues—for example, ones regarding the importance of clear and public reasoning at all stages and levels of the legal process. They also reject consideration of deterrence and of like treatment for like cases (except as linked to an underlying commitment to proportionality).

With its focus on achieving balance or an equal weighing, the retributive approach may also result in our failing to see that we may sometimes avoid conflicts among our penal aims by reshaping our response rather than by merely increasing or decreasing the severity of the penalty. In cases like Driscoll's, for instance, a Kantian civic respect approach has the means to recommend, with full consistency, that we maintain past practice (thus affording like treatment for like cases) but also admit inadequacies and pursue reforms. Also, with its focus on every involved party as a citizen due full regard as such, it is far less likely than retributivism to bend to calls for vengeance that are too sensitive to emotions appropriate in mourning but inappropriate as sentencing standards. Yet it can also acknowledge the relevance of emotions based in appropriate civic commitment to determining, say, when reform efforts or inquiries are required. This greater richness, I have suggested, is implicit (and often explicit) in Kant's own theory once we read it as a civic respect account.

6. Conclusion

I have argued that Immanuel Kant's penal theory, often cited as a paradigm example of thoroughgoing classical retributivism, is poorly represented by this classification. Although its many and sometimes seemingly contradictory elements at first seem a confusing mix (or an outright confusion), we can see the method in Kant's apparent madness by appealing to the larger political theory in which his account of just punishment is embedded. When we do, we find that Kant's theory of punishment is what we have called a civic respect theory. It offers an account of punishment that is justified and properly shaped by the demands of civic respect on citizens themselves and on the state as their representative. While we could nevertheless understand this account as an example and through the lens of a more contemporary retributivism, there is little justification for doing so. For the label offers little insight into the theory and easily could blind us to what is most valuable in it, not only from a theoretical but from a practical perspective. Finally, although I have concentrated on Kant's theory and have not attempted to defend a more global claim about the retributivist label, I hope also to have created a bit of unease about the usefulness of that label and its merits in general.

Notes

1 See, for example, Byrd, "Kant's Theory of Punishment"; Scheid, "Kant's Retributivism"; Murphy, *Kant: The Philosophy of Right*, 109–49; Holtman, "Towards Social Reform"; Ripstein, *Force and Freedom*, 300–24.

2 The *Rechtslehre* is the first part of *The Metaphysics of Morals*, Kant's most significant work in political philosophy. Page references herein provide the page numbers of the German Academy edition of Kant's work, found in the margins of most translations.

3 As Joel Feinberg points out, the term "retributivism" is often used to classify a much broader range of theories, essentially including those that oppose a utilitarian account of punishment. Kant would belong to this broad class of theories, but classifying him as a retributivist in this sense tells us nothing interesting about his penal theory or its relationship to other views. For discussion of retributivism and utilitarianism, see Feinberg, "Classic Debate."

4 Kant, *Metaphysics of Morals*, p. 331.

5 Ibid., p. 333.

6 Ibid., p. 332.

7 Ibid., p. 333.

8 Ibid., emphasis in original.

9 Ibid.

10 See, for example, Byrd, "Kant's Theory of Punishment," pp. 157, 184–98; Scheid, "Kant's Retributivism," pp. 262–65; Brooks, "Kant's Theory of Punishment," especially pp. 215–18, 223. For an excellent discussion of various views by an author who himself advocates closer attention to passages suggesting Kant's retributivism, see Hill, "Punishment, Conscience, and Moral Worth," pp. 237–38.

11 Kant, *Metaphysics of Morals*, p. 230.

12 Ibid.

13 Ibid., p. 231.

14 Ibid., p. 232.

15 Ibid.

16 Ibid., p. 235.

17 For fuller discussion, see Brooks, "Kant's Theory of Punishment," p. 214.

18 Kant, *Metaphysics of Morals*, p. 331.

19 See Murphy, "Does Kant Have a Theory of Punishment?"

20 Kant, *Metaphysics of Morals*, p. 332.

21 Ibid., p. 332–33.

22 One well-known example of such a view is Hampton, "Moral Education Theory of Punishment."

23 Joel Feinberg famously discusses expression of condemnation for wrongdoing as one function of punishment, though not the link with equality that I suggest is part of Kant's view. See his *Doing and Deserving*, pp. 95–118.

24 Kant, *Metaphysics of Morals*, p. 333.

25 Ibid., pp. 333–34.

26 Among the more contemporary authors who share the view that punishment shows regard for the offender as responsible agent is Herbert Morris; see, for example, his "Persons and Punishment."

27 Kant, *Metaphysics of Morals*, p. 333.

28 Ibid., p. 230–31.

29 Ibid., pp. 237–38.

30 Ibid., p. 314.

31 Although I will not pursue the question here, I take it that good Kantians need not automatically accept Kant's own concrete views about what punishments appropriately demonstrate civic respect. There are, in particular, strong arguments that neither the death penalty, nor *ius talionis* more generally, can fulfill the demands of civic respect in real-world circumstances.

32 For examples of the unfair advantage view, see Morris, "Persons and Punishment," and Sher, *Desert*. For examples of views advocating a balance between punishment and appropriate moral feelings or responses, see Murphy and Hampton, *Forgiveness and Mercy*, chs. 1 and 3, and Moore, *Placing Blame*, ch. 4.

33 Miranda v Arizona, 384 U.S.436, 460.

34 Olson and Brown, "Driver's Apology not Enough for Family."

35 For a discussion of these features of retributivism, see Shafer-Landau, "Failure of Retributivism."

36 Minnesota Statutes, 609.20, Manslaughter in the First Degree (2009); Minnesota Statutes, 609.21, Criminal Vehicular Homicide and Injury (2009).

37 Minnesota Sentencing Guidelines and Commentary, "Statement of Purpose and Principles" and "Determining Presumptive Sentences," (revised 2009), 1–50.

38 See Olson and Brown, "Driver's Apology not Enough."

39 Minnesota Statutes, 609.21, subd. 1a, Criminal Penalties (2009).

40 Minnesota Sentencing Guidelines and Commentary, "Statement of Purposes and Principles," 1.

41 Olson and Brown, "Driver's Apology not Enough."

42 On the capacity of Kant-based theory to acknowledge the moral relevance of the emotions, see, for example, Hill, "Punishment, Conscience and Moral Worth," pp. 242–53, and Baron, *Kantian Ethics Almost Without Apology*, chs. 5 and 6.

Bibliography

Baron, Marcia. *Kantian Ethics Almost Without Apology*. Ithaca: Cornell University Press, 1995.

Brooks, Thom. "Kant's Theory of Punishment." *Utilitas* 15 (2003): 206–24.

Byrd, Sharon. "Kant's Theory of Punishment: Deterrence in its Threat, Retribution in its Execution." *Law and Philosophy* 8 (1980): 151–220.

Feinberg, Joel. "The Classic Debate." In *Philosophy of Law*, edited by Joel Feinberg and Jules Coleman, 799–804. Belmont, CA: Wadsworth, 2004.

Feinberg, Joel. *Doing and Deserving*. Princeton: Princeton University Press, 1970.

Hampton, Jean. "The Moral Education Theory of Punishment." *Philosophy & Public Affairs* 13 (1984): 208–38.

Hill, Thomas E., Jr. "Punishment, Conscience, and Moral Worth." In *Kant's Metaphysics of Morals: Interpretive Essays*, edited by Mark Timmons, 233–53. New York: Oxford University Press, 2002.

Holtman, Sarah. "Towards Social Reform: Kant's Penal Theory Reinterpreted." *Utilitas* 9 (1997): 3–21.

Kant, Immanuel. *The Metaphysics of Morals*. In *The Cambridge Edition of the Works of Immanuel Kant: Practical Philosophy*, translated and edited by Mary Gregor. Cambridge: Cambridge University Press, 1996.

Moore, Michael. *Placing Blame: A Theory of Criminal Law*. Oxford: Oxford University Press, 1997.

Morris, Herbert. "Persons and Punishment." *The Monist* 52 (1968): 475–501.

Murphy, Jeffrie G. *Kant: The Philosophy of Right*. London: Macmillan, 1970.

Murphy, Jeffrie G. "Does Kant Have a Theory of Punishment?" *Columbia Law Review* 87 (1987): 509–32.

Murphy, Jeffrie G., and Jean Hampton. *Forgiveness and Mercy*. Cambridge: Cambridge University Press, 1988.

Olson, Rochelle, and Curt Brown. "Driver's Apology not Enough for Family." Minneapolis Star Tribune, January 27, 2010, available at http://www.startribune.com/local/82700112.html.

Ripstein, Arthur. *Force and Freedom: Kant's Legal and Political Philosophy*. Cambridge, MA: Harvard University Press, 2009.

Scheid, Donald. "Kant's Retributivism." *Ethics* 93 (1983): 262–82.

Shafer-Landau, Russ. "The Failure of Retributivism." *Philosophical Studies* 82 (1996): 289–316.

Sher, George. *Desert*. Princeton: Princeton University Press, 1987.

7

PRO TANTO RETRIBUTIVISM: JUDGMENT AND THE BALANCE

OF PRINCIPLES IN CRIMINAL JUSTICE

Mark D. White

IT IS NOW widely acknowledged that in practice, any positive conception of retributivism—that is, one that demands punishment of the guilty while also prohibiting punishment of the innocent—must be tempered by real-world considerations of resource scarcity and conflicting principles of justice, equality, and fairness.[1] This poses a problem for traditional retributivists (such as Immanuel Kant, according to common interpretations) who regard punishment as a categorical duty that does not allow compromises within the ideal of absolute punishment or with other societal principles or goals of similar (or greater) importance.[2]

But given that compromises need to made, how can (positive) retributivists accommodate them? One proposal that is gaining some traction among legal scholars is *consequentialist retributivism*, which (in some forms, at least) recommends identifying the intrinsic good in just punishment and then quantifying it (even if only roughly) so that it can be maximized (or optimized with respect to other goals). If successful, this would allow officials to make trade-offs within the criminal justice system (such as making a deal with one defendant to help secure prosecution of a more sought-after one), as well as with other societal principles and goals (such as devoting less resources to criminal justice to devote more to national defense or education).

But there are significant problems with this approach to retributivism, some of them well known and acknowledged. For instance, it is notoriously difficult to identify the "good" in just punishment, and even if it is identified, it is just as difficult (if not more so) to quantify it. Retributivism stands as an ideal (based on more basic ideals such as justice and desert) rather than a goal, a principle rather than a policy (in the rough sense in which Ronald Dworkin defined them).[3] It cannot easily be represented as a variable that can be maximized or optimized, much less traded off for other goals according to some exchange rate. How many car thieves are we willing to punish less harshly to build another junior high school or medical clinic? How much are we willing to lessen the punitive justice applied to a lower-tier member of a street gang in order to increase the chances of seeing justice served on a leader of the gang? Such considerations are unproblematic to a standard consequentialist with regard to punishment, of course, but hardly so to a deontologically oriented retributivist, which poses a problem to such a person in a world of limited resources in which such trade-offs must be made. Nonetheless, it does not seem that a consequentialist approach to such issues can adhere to the spirit of retributivism; it would be seen as an unacceptable compromise, if a well-motivated one.

I propose a different approach to the problem, one that remains true to a deontological orientation to retributivism—a Kantian approach, even, but relying upon a more subtle understanding of Kant than the standard caricature entails. Kant's moral philosophy is normally portrayed as demanding and absolute, allowing no exceptions whatsoever to duties such as "do not kill," "do not steal," and "do not lie" (not to mention "do not let wrongdoers go unpunished"). It is certainly accurate in that such duties do not allow for individual exceptions for purely prudential or personal concerns. However, obligations implied by different duties can conflict, and since there may only be one duty binding on an agent in any particular situation, a choice must be made between the competing obligations. Kant is clear that there is no "higher" rule governing choice in such situations, which instead requires judgment.

Once the importance of judgment to Kantian ethics is acknowledged, given the pervasiveness of conflicts between obligations, his system becomes much less of a rigid system of rules and more of a system of contributory (nonconclusive), *pro tanto* principles that must be balanced against each other, similar to the practical ethics of W.D. Ross.[4] This also bares significant resemblance to Ronald Dworkin's theory of judicial decision making, in which competing and perhaps inconsistent principles must be weighed and balanced to arrive at a decision.[5] If we assume that a similar description of choice would hold for the state, where competing principles would be just as common, if not more so, than in individual choice situations, then the imperative to punish wrongdoers can be seen as simply one principle or contributory reason among many. As Cahill writes,

> The application of a retributive-justice scheme might give rise. . . to conflicts between retribution and other *principled* commitments. For example, a commitment to certain aspects of procedural justice or fairness may sometimes frustrate the system's ability to impose punishment on those who deserve it. . . . Ultimately, resolution of such conflicts between principled commitments depends on some decision about which principle merits priority in the abstract.[6]

As such, the pursuit of the retributive principle can be imperfect internally, and can also be compromised in the service of other principles, without rejecting the principle outright. In the framework I will outline below, consequences are considered only at the balancing stage, not as a goal in themselves, which should satisfy deontologists troubled by quantifying and maximizing (or optimizing) concepts that are properly considered as ideals.

In a sense, my version of retributivism bears some resemblance to Michael S. Moore's *threshold retributivism*, which holds that retributivist principles should be upheld unless the costs reach some prohibitively high level, at which point the consequences become the operative factor in the decision. In my version (again drawing on Dworkin's jurisprudence), retributivist principles would also be balanced against other principles (including ones supporting goals and policies competing for scarce resources), and this balancing could be conducted along consequentialist lines (motivated by budget constraints, for instance). This is not contrary to Kant, who places no bounds on the basis of judgment when duties or obligations conflict (aside from assessing the "stronger ground of obligation"). For instance, if a police offender is apprehending two suspects each of whom runs in a different direction, and she can only follow one, the choice of which one to follow may certainly be made according to which apprehension would be more beneficial to the criminal justice system or society as a whole (as well as which one was more deserving of punishment or other reasons), or simply which one the officer is more likely to catch. Consequentialism enters into the balancing process but in a secondary way only, for the principles themselves are the focus. This is to be contrasted with consequentialist retribution, which reduces the principle of just punishment to a quantifiable good, or threshold retributivism, which places the primary focus on consequences once they reach the threshold level. The end result of my proposal and consequentialist (or threshold) retributivism may be very similar—they may "cash out" the same way— but I hope mine is more palatable to deontological retributivists who wish to retain the idealized conception of just punishment and are hesitant to admit consequentialist logic into it at the primary level.

This chapter will proceed as follows. First, I will discuss the conception of just punishment as an intrinsic good, arguing that it is better understood as an ideal to aim toward rather than as a quantitative goal. Then I will explain how the ideal of just punishment can be balanced with other concerns (consistently with Kant but also drawing on Dworkin and Ross). This, I believe, mirrors an important criticism of consequential retributivism made by David Dolinko; he critiques consequentialist retributivism for having too narrow of a conception of consequences, when rather, I would argue, retributivists have too narrow a conception of ideals.[7] The point here is to expand the range of ideals pursued by officials and to seek a balance between them, perhaps along consequentialist lines, rather than quantifying them and directly subjecting them to consequentialist calculation and thereby losing sight of their nature as incalculable principles. Finally, I compare my "*pro tanto* retributivism" with Moore's threshold retributivism, framing the latter as a specific instance of the former and arguing that my proposal answers several of the criticisms made of Moore's by other scholars.

1. Just Punishment: A Principle, Not a Good

Proponents of consequentialist retributivism characterize just punishment as an intrinsic good, which can then be maximized internally or optimized with respect to other societal goals that draw on common scarce resources.[8] I agree with the intrinsically desirable nature of just punishment; rather, it is the implication of the word "good" that troubles me.[9] Essentially, it implies quantification; in fact, Moore described a consequentialist retributivist as one who "regards the state of the guilty receiving punishment as a good state to be maximized."[10] If something is a good, or is described as good, then naturally more good must be better. This is not very controversial—after all, more of the something described as "right" would be better (or "more right"). However, if good can be increased in one area by sacrificing a lesser amount of good in another so that the total good rises, this must be a better state of affairs. Of course, this assumes commensurability, which is more appropriate if the "good" in question is truly some comparable, homogenous quantity (you have to spend money to make money, for instance). But just punishment is not an easily quantifiable thing, for it is not simply the number of guilty persons punished or the total number of years for which guilty persons are imprisoned; if it were, it would be a simple matter to trade off less just punishment for more. "Just punishment" is a narrower version of justice—to say one was justly punished (or received his just deserts) is a specific instance of justice being done. So while the "punishment" aspect of just punishment, by itself, seems like a measurable concept (according to length of prison term, size of fine, number of persons punished, and so forth), it is the "justice" in just punishment that makes it difficult to envision it as a (quantifiable) good.

In this sense, justice is a characteristic of the imposition of punishment: given that a particular person was punished, was it *just* punishment? This judgment has several dimensions, the most basic ones being: (a) is the person guilty; and (b) if he is guilty, how much punishment does he deserve? For punishment to truly be just, it needs to be deserved per se and also in degree. Of course, these are the main concerns of retributivism, and indeed they may be intrinsic concerns, insomuch as justice or desert are taken to be intrinsically valuable. (I chose to use the term "value" rather than "good," for I feel the former lacks the quantitative connotation so problematic in the latter. Value, of course, can also be taken quantitatively, but I hope it stirs in the reader the idea of Kant's incalculable dignity, rather than a Benthamite scalar.) But this concern with justice nonetheless rests on vague and uncertain ideas of guilt and desert (hence the word "judgment" above). We never actually *know* if the defendant is truly guilty and even if we did (and even if he were), it is widely recognized that there is nearly (or completely) impossible to equate the evil he committed with the punishment we should exact.[11] (After all, even "an eye for an eye" assumes eyes are of equivalent value to all, which depends as much on what one chooses to look at as how well one sees.) Likewise, we will never *know* that a given instance of punishment is just; we can only argue for its justice, given what we did know (or did believe) and our reasons for the punishment we chose.

I am being deliberately vague regarding the justification of retributivist punishment; I do not think my thesis depends on why one feels punishment is just or why it is of intrinsic value, only that one does think it so.[12] My point is that just punishment should not be thought of as a "good" as any sort, whether intrinsic or instrumental. Rather, it should be thought of as an ideal or a principle: when we punish, the principle of retributive justice provides us with a strong reason to punish according to its dictates. When the justice of a punishment is questioned (as it should be), the officials responsible for the decision should be able to give reasons for it. And when justice is compromised—when a punishment other than the just punishment is given, whether too harsh or too lenient in degree or kind—there must be a reason for that as well.

In other words, I am claiming that justice is similar in form to Kantian dignity, not to be compared or traded off internally or externally, and each instance of just punishment (or implemented justice) is invaluable in and of itself. Retributive justice cannot be represented quantitatively, much less aggregated and maximized; it manifests itself in instances of just punishment. If retributive justice in one case is to be compromised—as it often must, in a world of scarce resources—it must be in the service of another principle (such as corrective justice or equality), even if that principle supports another instance of retributive justice. Imagine a case in which justice dictates that a violent criminal be imprisoned for several decades, which will prevent him for compensating his victims pending a decision in civil court. If the demands of retributivist justice are given precedence, the legitimate demands of corrective justice will be neglected. Of course, the opposite may happen as well, and the choice between the principles is not an obvious one; in fact, this dispute may be seen to be at the heart of debates over the role and importance of the victim in criminal cases. But if both principles are held to be important, and neither one clearly more important than the other, then some balance must be achieved.

More common is the case in which prosecutorial discretion must be exercised in light of resource constraints. The principle of retributive justice—if it is held to apply at the level of prosecution—demands that each suspect regarded as guilty must be prosecuted (in order to be punished). But what if not all suspects so regarded can possibly be prosecuted? Here we have the principle of retributive justice confronting itself—as in the earlier case of the police officer being able to pursue only one suspect. But we do not simply trade off "less" justice for "more"; rather, we recognize that the principle of retributivist justice demands we prosecute both, but since we cannot, we must make a choice on other grounds, including a comparison of the consequences of foregoing either prosecution (as well as other options available).

This is similar to a case in which two people are dying but only one can be saved; they both have an incalculable, incomparable dignity, and there may be a duty or obligation to save each of them, but a choice must be made. We do not describe our choice in terms of trading off one life to save another, or letting one die as a means to letting the other live; we would not want to instrumentalize the loss in this manner.[13] Rather, we have to make a tragic choice in which the loss is acknowledged as necessary but is nonetheless regretted. In the same way, we do not represent exercises in prosecutorial discretion as trading off just punishment of one suspect to catch or prosecute the other; or the more abstract problem of the inevitable, inadvertent punishment of the innocent in an imperfect trial system as sacrificing the innocent to promote the end of punishing the guilty.[14] It serves retributive justice equally to punish a guilty shoplifter and a guilty murderer (according to the immeasurable culpability of each rather than the harm each caused), but the justice in punishing the shoplifter may have to be compromised to serve other principles (including the denunciation of a greater wrong). We tolerate but regret the compromise of our ideals due to the constraints of the real world, but this is not to treat such necessary compromises as a means to an end (though the result is the same).

There is no formula or algorithm for achieving the proper balance between principles in such cases; this is where judgment necessarily comes into play. If all instances of just punishment were quantifiable and commensurable, balancing would not be an issue; but principles, as ideals, do not work like that. Nonetheless, as illustrated in the last example, one obvious concern in determining the "best" balance is scarcity of resources relative to the numerous principles and goals facing any complex society. As recognized, a criminal justice system that punished every wrongdoer according to his desert would soon consume all of society's resources, leaving nothing for national defense or the civil court system (in systems of minimal government) or education and social welfare programs (in more expansive versions of the state). Unless one feels criminal justice is the only legitimate role of the state, one would not want that system to dominate governmental budgets completely.

So the principle of retributivist justice in any particular case may be compromised in the service of other principles (even other instances of just punishment), where the balance may be achieved according to economic (or another sort of consequentialist) reasoning, as well as other balancing techniques.[15] But there is no higher, determinate, second-order principle to pronounce on the superiority of one or the other; that, of course, is the desire of those who wish to devise an overall punishment formula that incorporates all concerns and criticisms. It is my contention that no such formula exists in general terms; the balancing of principles comes down to judgment, judgment that must be reasoned and defensible and which will produce different—and controversial—results in different cases. This does not deny, however, the possibility that results of judgment in individual cases, if deemed especially sound, can be formalized in lasting precedent or punishment guidelines. One example would be the standard leniency granted first-time offenders in misdemeanor cases, in which the principle of just punishment is tempered with—or is considered to incorporate—a principle of mercy.

2. Looking to Kant and Dworkin

Retributivists have a reputation for being single-minded about just punishment, despite Moore's advice that "it would be a crude caricature of the retributivist to make him monomaniacally focused on the achievement of retributive justice."[16] Of course, such caricatures in general are common and to some extent understandable; environmentalist scholars can be single-minded about conservation, others who write on animal rights issues can be single-minded about cruelty to animals, and so on. But certainly these people—most of them, at least—are not blind to competing concerns; they simply choose to emphasize an issue they feel is often neglected by the mainstream and argue for more—not all—resources to be devoted to it. So it would be a mistake to say that retributivists in general cannot, on principle, admit the importance of other principles in decisions impacting on punishment issues. (This is not to say that some do not, of course!) They would naturally emphasize and argue for the urgency of justice and desert in such decisions but certainly not to the exclusion of other legitimate concerns (on which they may disagree).

As it so happens, Immanuel Kant suffers from the same misunderstanding. His reputation as an ethicist is one of being demanding, uncompromising, rule-obsessed, and insensitive to context and circumstances. Certainly his rhetoric supports, and is some-what responsible for, this misconception, especially his essay "On the Supposed Right to Lie from Philanthropic Concerns," an exercise in stubbornness which flies in the face of what he wrote at more thoughtful times. After reading the *Groundwork* (with which the study of Kant usually begins and ends in introductory ethics classes), it is clear why this impression is so pervasive; even a wider reading of Kant's ethical writings, such as *The Metaphysics of Morals*, tends to reinforce this.

For instance, despite the popular caricature, Kant opposed a strict adherence to formal rules, regarding them as a threat to true freedom and autonomy: "Dogmas and formulas, those mechanical instruments for rational use (or rather misuse) of [man's] natural endowments, are the ball and chain of his permanent immaturity."[17] As Onora O'Neill writes, "Kant provides us primarily an ethic of virtue rather than of rules," in part because "Kant offers us a form of rationalism in ethics that. . . does not generate a unique moral code, but still provides fundamental guidelines and suggests the types of reasoning by which we might see how to introduce these guidelines into the lives we lead."[18] At most, the categorical imperative and the duties it generates are intended to provide rough guidelines for moral intention and action in real-world contexts, with significant room for flexibility to accommodate the context of individual decision-making situations.

This is where and why judgment is necessary; as O'Neill explains:

> Discussions of judgment. . . are ubiquitous in Kant's writings. He never assumes agents can move from principles to duty, or other principles of action, to selecting a

highly specific act in particular circumstances without any process of judgment. He is as firm as any devotee of Aristotelian *phronesis* in maintaining that principles of action are not algorithms and do not entail their own applications.[19]

Kant had tremendous respect for judgment, writing that "though understanding is capable of being instructed. . . judgment is a peculiar talent which can be practiced only, and cannot be taught. It is the specific quality of so-called mother-wit; and its lack no school can make good."[20] Sullivan emphasizes the never-ending development and growth of our judgment:

> Through simply living, facing ordinary moral problems day by day, we all accumulate a store of moral experience to help us judge how to act; we all develop some sensitivity to the features to which we should attend. Moreover, most of the situations in which we find ourselves are familiar ones, and we do not need to deliberate over how to act. We simply act on maxims that reflect our long-standing commitments and values.[21]

Furthermore, Kant refuses to reduce judgment to higher-order principles or rules, arguing that this would lead to infinite regress: since no rule, even higher-order rules, will be determinate in all situations, one would need yet higher rules to show how to apply them, and then even higher-order rules for those, and so on.[22]

Judgment is essential in most all choice situations but is particularly indispensable when an agent faces conflicting obligations, such as when one has promised a favor to one friend, but answering an urgent call for help from another would make it impossible to honor that promise. In this case, there seems to be a conflict between the duty not to break promises and the duty to help others in need, though Kant is careful about saying that duties themselves never conflict; he insists that because, ethically speaking, duties must be performed, and furthermore that ought implies can, there can only be one duty operative on a person in a certain situation. Instead, he would describe such a situation as a conflict of obligations which, once resolved, culminates in the one and only duty compelling the person to action. The only thing he wrote about such conflicts was to assess the "stronger ground of obligation" but chose not to elaborate on what, precisely, that means.[23]

Without further elaboration, it is fairly clear that Kant is pointing to the importance of judgment in settling conflicts of obligation. As we saw, he writes of the need for judgment in applying the broad dictates of the categorical imperative to real-world decisions—especially, it would seem, conflicts of obligation—recommending an integration of moral principles with seasoned judgment which will enable people to make sound moral decisions in complex situations. For instance, it is clear why "do not lie" is a general duty, but it is not always clear precisely how to follow it in real-world decisions. When is not lying an agent's most important obligation? (Certainly not in the murderer-at-the-door case, most would say.) And when it is not, what should be done instead?

This is where Kantian ethics seems to coincide with the more flexible deontology of W.D. Ross, at least in terms of their practical ethics. (Their respective foundations of moral duties could hardly be more different, of course.) Ross wrote of *pro tanto* duties (which he called *prima facie* duties, a term now considered incorrect given the context of Ross's discussion), which provide contributory but not conclusive reasons for action, to be balanced by our judgment given the circumstances of the situation.[24] If none of Kant's duties, including the perfect ones, is taken as absolutely binding and, instead, is subject to being overwhelmed by another obligation with "stronger ground," then those duties work much like Ross's *pro tanto* duties.

Understood this way, Kantian judgment resembles Ronald Dworkin's model of judicial decision making. In his well-known conception, he distinguishes between policy and principle: generally speaking—for Dworkin acknowledges the distinction is not always clear—policies are goals based on the interests of various groups in society, which are properly deliberated over in a democratic forum such as a legislature, while principles are ideals based on rights of individuals, and as such are not subject to democratic vote, but are best left to the judiciary to apply to specific cases. In doing this, judges weigh competing principles against each other, including not only the substantive principles that ground legal rules but also conservative principles (such as *stare decisis*) that speak to following existing rules. A judge must find the "right answer" to any given case, based on the balancing of principles that best maintains the integrity or character of the legal system as that judge sees it.[25]

If we understand Kantian duties to be akin to principles (as opposed, at the risk of oversimplification, to the consequentialist and contingent nature of policy), we can say that in cases of conflicting obligations, a moral agent will choose the action that preserves the integrity of her character, based on her judgment, informed by her specific life experiences and her understanding of the moral law and the core ideas of dignity and autonomy that ground it. And just like Dworkin's judges, it is entirely possible that two people, both dedicated Kantians facing identical circumstances, would make two different judgments regarding the best action in that particular case because each person's judgment, based on previous experiences and choices, is unique to her.[26]

3. *Pro Tanto* Retributivism and Threshold Retributivism

I argue that this Kantian/Dworkinian model of judgment provides a way to understand the choices that must be made by agents within the criminal justice system—local police administrators, prosecutors, and judges, just to name a few—by considering the balance of principles (including the principles behind policies) at play in real-world retributivism. One such principle (or *pro tanto* duty in the Kantian framework) is the ideal of just punishment, and the balance between this principle and others must be struck in a particular case using judgment based on the legal-political system in which the criminal justice system operates, specifically its practices and core ideals. This understanding allows consequentialist considerations (among others) to enter into deliberations over balancing principles, but only on a secondary level—at the level of balancing itself—and not as a central concern. Nor does it require the quantification of the ideal of just punishment, which is problematic. This conception is also consistent with various methods of justifying retributivism, such as the three principles that Dan Markel proposes in his Confrontational Conception of Retributivism and which he also considers to be contributory but not conclusive reasons for just punishment.[27]

My practical view of retributivism also respects the societal importance of principles other than retributive punishment (without passing judgment on particular ones), acknowledging the necessary trade-offs emphasized by scholars such as Cahill and Markel, but arrives at a balance or compromise in a fashion more palatable to deontological retributivists. For instance, Cahill writes:

> The consequentialist-retributivist (CR) view strikes a balance between adhering to retribution as a force that justifies and drives punishment and recognizing that competing real-world goals prevent an absolute, unyielding commitment to retribution. . . . In fact, the notion of maximizing overall (deserved) punishment seems to accord with the most natural, intuitive response to the problem of how retributive justice would or should work in practice. If the system is unable to impose all deserved punishment all the time, a natural second-best strategy is to impose as much deserved punishment as possible.[28]

Aside from the aspect of "maximizing overall (deserved) punishment" (which I addressed above), I am in complete agreement with this statement; the Kantian/Dworkinian version of retributivism developed herein simply finds this balance in a way that retains respect for the ideal, immeasurable nature of ideal principles, rather than denying this nature through quantifying them.

We can use this concept of *pro tanto retributivism* (for lack of a better term) to think about the two types of conflict that every society must confront due to scarcity: the external problem of how to balance retributivist justice with other uses for its limited resources, and the internal problem of how to balance various retributivist concerns within the criminal justice system itself. Internally, an example would be exercising prosecutorial discretion in the face of limited resources, which often necessitates dropping cases with weaker arguments or entering into plea bargains with a less important defendant to make conviction of a more important one more likely.[29] Externally, the needs of the criminal justice system must be balanced with education, national defense, and other societal needs; all of these priorities may be based on sound principles but nonetheless must be balanced somehow.[30] The model presented herein suggests that they be balanced in a way that reflects the decision maker's impression of the character and integrity of the legal-political system. As Dworkin argues, this maintains the importance of each of the principles at play in the conflict but necessarily weighs them against each other and finds one to be the top priority in the context of the broader system of which the principles are part.

Consistent with the concept of Kantian-Dworkinian judgment, character, and integrity presented above, I offer no formula or algorithm to determine the proper balance of principles in any nontrivial decision-making situation. Different people in different situations will feel that one principle or other has more weight, and for different reasons; each person will recommend a solution stemming from his or her impression of the character of the system—the criminal justice system, in the case of retributivist punishment. A similar approach, focusing on the general efficacy of the law more than its internal character, is offered by Robinson and Cahill, who recommend that when other principles conflict with just punishment (or desert),

> these principles should be weighed, as against the prima facie equally valid principle of desert, according to their *instrumental* merit: the extent to which they maintain the legitimacy of the legal system, thereby promoting respect for and compliance with the law.[31]

This is a practical test based on the particular consequences of principles in terms of legitimacy, which itself can be based on principle. In the Kantian-Dworkinian approach detailed above, consequences may also be used to balance principles, as in the case of the police officer choosing which of two suspects to pursue. This suggests that the problem that many retributivists have with consequentialist retributivism may not be the use of consequences in balancing just punishment internally or with other goals externally, which must be done, but rather the conceptual quantification of just punishment itself (as argued above).

Another way this balance could be reached is suggested by Michael Moore in the form of threshold retributivism (a specific instance of his *threshold deontology*), in which retributivist principles hold until the costs become prohibitively high, at which point they—or, more generally, the consequences—become the controlling factor. This concept has been criticized on several fronts, as I will discuss below,[32] but nonetheless, it seems to correspond with intuitions about how far we should "push" deontological principles, which most people support until they prove too costly and start to detract from other principles or goals.[33] In Moore's work, he considers only the consequences of following retributivist principles, not (explicitly) the conflict of retributivist principles with one or more other principles (resulting in less easily quantifiable opportunity costs). Of course, in a world of scarcity, devoting resources to serve one principle or ideal means less resources available for others, so Moore's emphasis on costs and consequences is not inconsistent with a focus on principles; it merely generalizes from identifying the principles that take precedence if the opportunity costs of another become too high, so the analyst can focus on the costs of following one principle (in terms of unspecified foregone alternatives).

I agree with the other critics who argue that Moore's concept of the threshold at which retributivist (or, more broadly, deontological) concerns give over to consequentialist ones (or, more broadly, other competing concerns) seems too abrupt, what Cahill calls "a discontinuity. . . a binary switch where consequences go from, 'off' (irrelevant) to 'on' (paramount)."[34] Generalizing to a conflict of principles, this implies that one principle is followed until too costly, at which point it is abandoned for another principle, goal, or concern. This serves to minimize (or deny altogether) the importance of the first principle, since it is implied that it is only worthwhile to pursue up to a point and not worthwhile after that. The Kantian-Dworkinian approach would prevent this interpretation, since in such cases, one principle, such as retributivist punishment, need not be abandoned altogether because it is too costly; rather, it can be compromised with regret. Furthermore, such compromises (entering into plea bargains where most beneficial, for instance) may be implemented gradually as opportunity costs start to become prohibitive, eliminating the need for an all-or-nothing threshold point and preserving the sense of balance that Moore's threshold retributivism (or deontology) implies.

The conception of judgment suggested above can also address the criticisms regarding the arbitrariness of the threshold point. In his article "Deontology, Incommensurability, and the Arbitrary," Anthony Ellis makes a convincing argument that any threshold point between deontological principles and consequentialist considerations is necessarily arbitrary because they are essentially incommensurable: one cannot be stated in terms of the other. This analysis would extend naturally to conflicting principles, because there is no way to state one principle in terms of another unless one is indeed subsumed in the other (as the principle of proportionate punishment is included in the principle of just punishment), in which case there would be no conflict.

In such instances of conflict, as Kant and Dworkin argue, judgment is necessary, but Ellis questions the viability of this:

> Slightly more sophisticatedly, people sometimes appeal to the idea of *judgment*. . . There is no *formula* for deciding such matters, it may be said; on the other hand, they do not have to be decided arbitrarily. The virtuous man, or the man of wisdom, will take account of all of the relevant factors and will arrive at an appropriate decision through the exercise of judgment.[35]

Ellis then questions whether there is any basis on which judgment can be made:

> There can be judgment only where there is something to be judged about. And that does not simply mean that there must be an issue to be resolved, but that there must be considerations capable of resolving the issue. . . *And the problem here is to see what considerations could do that.*[36]

Ellis's point is relevant only when such judgment takes place in an ethical vacuum—if the only principles that exist are the ones between which one must decide or judge. But the

Kantian-Dworkinian judgment that drives the balancing process in *pro tanto* retributivism does not encounter this problem, since conflicts involving retributivist principles, internally or externally, take place within a broader legal-political framework, with its own character and guiding high-level principles, and also takes actual real-world circumstances into account.

Also, arbitrariness is not a problem only for systems that attempt to balance incommensurable concerns; it is present too when attempts are made to quantify ideal principles such as just punishment, much less to determine how it would be compared to other goals that society must pursue. For instance, with respect to the quantification of just punishment, Cahill acknowledges

> the significant difficulty of ascertaining how much weight the "goodness" of desert should merit in the overall consequentialist analysis. The very notion of calculating the value of desert along some metric that would enable its comparison to other goods, like crime reduction or cost savings, might seem either odd or patently impossible. Yet almost any cost-benefit analysis inevitably involves difficult or even unsavory apple-orange comparisons of the "how much money is a human life worth" sort. Without minimizing the complexity (and perhaps even the ineradicable moral contestability) of such judgments, they are necessarily made all the time, and recognizing the tradeoffs they involve at least serves to focus attention and debate.[37]

Such comparisons may be necessary if consequential analysis is the chosen decision-making process, but that does not make them less arbitrary or less a matter of judgment, which must ultimately be defended using the same principles used to balance conflicting concerns in *pro tanto* retributivism (or determining the cutoff point in threshold retributivism).[38] Also, avoiding quantification of just punishment renders moot another problem that Cahill anticipates with regard to consequential retributivism, namely, that it, "while having the advantage of offering a feasible *means* for achieving retributive justice in the real world, has the drawback of no longer offering a *mandate* for doing so."[39] As I have argued, *pro tanto* retributivism achieves the balancing needed in a world of scarce resources without compromising the imperative nature of principles (unless those principles are taken to be absolutely binding even in cases of conflict).

4. Conclusion

Consequentialist retributivism has been presented as a solution to the problem of implementing desert-based punishment to the fullest extent consistent with real-world resource constraints. As I hope this chapter has made clear, I wholeheartedly agree with the assessment of the problem, as well as the spirit of balance and compromise necessitated by it, but I prefer an alternative, which I have termed *pro tanto* retributivism. Relying on a concept of judgment drawn from the ethics of Immanuel Kant and the jurisprudence of Ronald Dworkin, this conception of retributivism provides a framework for balancing the ideal of retributivist punishment internally and externally while retaining the immeasurable and incomparable nature of that principle (as well as others held by a given society). While practically oriented in that it address real-world considerations of resource scarcity and competing principles, *pro tanto* retributivism is also consistent with core retributivist ideals of punishing the deserving proportionately to their desert—insofar as this is possible, given other principles and goals that societies rightfully seek to further.

Notes

1 See, for instance, Cahill, "Retributive Justice in the Real World"; White, "Retributivism in a World of Scarcity"; as well as Markel's chapter in this volume (and his previous work cited therein).

2 On the extent and nature of Kant's retributivism, see the chapter by Holtman in this book (and references therein).

3 Dworkin, "Hard Cases," pp. 82–84.

4 See my *Kantian Ethics and Economics*, ch. 1.

5 I see a strong parallel between Kantian judgment and Dworkinian jurisprudence, which I plan to explore in future work; I am dipping my toe into the pond, so to speak, with this chapter (and parts of *Kantian Ethics and Economics*).

6 Cahill, "Retributive Justice," p. 820 n. 14; see also Robinson and Cahill, *Law without Justice*, pp. 137–39, as well as the final section of the chapter by Cahill in this volume.

7 Dolinko, "Retributivism, Consequentialism, and the Intrinsic Goodness of Punishment," pp. 513–15.

8 See, most significantly, Moore, "Justifying Retributivism," pp. 155–59; Cahill, "Retributive Justice" and his chapter in this book; and Markel's chapter in this book (and his earlier work cited therein). Markel's conception is more elaborate than the others, stating that retributive punishment promotes goods internal to, or constitutive of, the practice (such as affirming the moral responsibility of the offender, based on the principle of dignity), rather than external goods (such as deterrence) whose actual promotion is contingent; see, for instance, his "Are Shaming Punishments Beautifully Retributive?," pp. 2192–94, or "State, Be Not Proud," p. 427 ("the good achieved by punishment for an offense is not a contingent good, such as general deterrence. Rather, it is bound up in the practice of punishment itself, so that the practice of punishment has an internal good, and the achievement of that good makes the practice internally intelligible and attractive").

9 Most of the people Dolinko cites as supporting the intrinsic good claim ("Retributivism," p. 516 n. 27) focus on the "intrinsic" rather than the "good," though the "good" is what is needed to support a consequentialist approach, as pointed out by Markel (see, for instance, "Shaming Punishments," pp. 2193–94).

10 Moore, "Justifying Retributivism," p. 156.

11 See, for instance, Wertheimer, "Should Punishment Fit the Crime?"

12 See, for instance, the chapter by Duff in this volume. For another very influential recent discussion of justification, see Berman, "Punishment and Justification."

13 This is similar to the rhetorical travesty of the law-and-economics trope that says society "demands" the level of crime that they cannot effectively deter.

14 For more on the inadvertent punishment of the innocent in the context of capital punishment, see the chapter by Brooks in this volume.

15 As Markel puts it, "Prima facie duties cannot be denied as obligations, but the determination of how and when to discharge those obligations is a prudential matter and these obligations may be set aside when other duties supervene" ("Executing Retributivism," p. 1182 n. 77).

16 Moore, "Justifying Retributivism," p. 34.

17 Kant, "An Answer to the Question: What Is Enlightenment?," pp. 54–55. (All citations to Kant's work will use Academy pagination, standard in all reputable editions.)

18 O'Neill, "Kant after Virtue," p. 161.

19 O'Neill, "Kant: Rationality as Practical Reason," p. 104.

20 Kant, *Critique of Pure Reason*, p. A133/B172.

21 Sullivan, *Introduction to Kant's Ethics*, p. 40.

22 See Sullivan, *Immanuel Kant's Moral Theory*, p. 53.

23 Kant, *Metaphysics of Morals*, p. 224.

24 Ross, *Right and the Good*, pp. 30–32.

25 See Dworkin, "Hard Cases" and *Law's Empire*. This theory has been widely criticized as applied to judicial decision making; see the essays in Cohen, *Ronald Dworkin and Contemporary Jurisprudence* for seminal early criticism. Nonetheless, I argue that his concepts of judgment applied to principles to retain integrity of character to be a valuable one in more general contexts (see next note).

26 I explore this conception of judgment briefly in chapter 1 of *Kantian Ethics and Economics*; in Chapter 3, I argue that a person's unique faculty for judgment (along with her will) defines who she is, and together they compromise her character, which serves as her most essential identity and renders her unique.

27 See the chapter by Markel in this volume.

28 Cahill, "Retributive Justice," p. 861.

29 See ibid., pp. 853–56. As mentioned above, another example is justifying the unavoidable and inadvertent punishment of the innocent, reconciling the dual (positive) retributivist principles of punishing the guilty while not punishing the innocent; again, see the chapter by Brooks in this volume for more on this issue. Yet another example of balancing competing principles within retributivism is the problems with sentencing multiple offenders, detailed in the chapter by Lippke in this volume.

30 See Robinson and Cahill, *Law without Justice*, chs. 2–8, for detailed real-world examples of both types of conflict.

31 Ibid., p. 139; see also Robinson and Darley, "Utility of Desert," for a more abstract elaboration.

32 As a succinct summary and extension of the major criticisms, see Cahill, "Retributive Justice," pp. 858–61; other prominent critics (of either threshold retributivism or threshold deontology) include Dolinko, "Retributivism," Alexander, "Deontology at the Threshold," and Ellis, "Deontology, Incommensurability, and the Arbitrary."

33 Witness recent debates over the use of torture on terror suspects, which, incidentally, motivated Moore's first work on threshold deontology ("Torture and the Balance of Evils").

34 Cahill, "Retributive Justice," pp. 858–59; Moore himself acknowledges this point and offers a response in "Torture," pp. 723–24, which has been taken up by Alexander, "Deontology," pp. 908–09.

35 Ellis, "Deontology," p. 860.

36 Ibid.

37 Cahill, "Retributive Justice," p. 867.

38 This point is supported by Moore's statement that an adherent of consequentialist retributivism, facing the conflict between punishing the guilty and not punishing the innocent, "may easily maximize *both* that those deserving punishment receive it *and* that those not deserving of punishment not receive it. Where in the actual design of punishment institutions the consequentialist-retributivist comes out on this balance need not here detain us. . ." ("Justifying Retributivism," p. 157), suggesting several possible ways of resolving this problem in the subsequent footnote (p. 157 n.11).

39 Cahill, "Retributive Justice," p. 868.

Bibliography

Alexander, Larry. "Deontology at the Threshold." *San Diego Law Review* 37 (2000): 893–912.

Berman, Mitchell N. "Punishment and Justification." *Ethics* 118 (2008): 258–90.

Cahill, Michael T. "Retributive Justice in the Real World." *Washington University Law Review* 85 (2007): 815–70.

Cohen, Marshall (ed.). *Ronald Dworkin and Contemporary Jurisprudence*. Totowa, NJ: Rowman & Allanheld, 1983.

Dolinko, David. "Retributivism, Consequentialism, and the Intrinsic Goodness of Punishment." *Law and Philosophy* 16 (1997): 507–28.

Dworkin, Ronald. "Hard Cases." In *Taking Rights Seriously*, 81–130. Cambridge, MA: Harvard University Press, 1977.

Dworkin, Ronald. *Law's Empire*. Cambridge, MA: Harvard University Press, 1986.

Ellis, Anthony. "Deontology, Incommensurability, and the Arbitrary." *Philosophy and Phenomenological Research* 52 (1992): 855–75.

Kant, Immanuel. "An Answer to the Question: What Is Enlightenment?" In *Kant: Political Writings*, 2nd ed., edited by H.S. Reiss and translated by H.B. Nisbet, 54–60. Cambridge: Cambridge University Press, 1991.

Kant, Immanuel. *Critique of Pure Reason*. Translated by Norman Kemp Smith. New York: St. Martin's Press, 1929.

Kant, Immanuel. *The Metaphysics of Morals*. Translated and edited by Mary J. Gregor. Cambridge, UK: Cambridge University Press, 1996.

Kant, Immanuel. "On a Supposed Right to Lie because of Philanthropic Concerns." In *Grounding for the Metaphysics of Morals*, translated by James W. Ellington, 63–67. Indianapolis: Hackett Publishing Company, 1993.

Markel, Dan. "Are Shaming Punishments Beautifully Retributive? Retributivism and the Implications for the Alternative Sanctions Debate." *Vanderbilt Law Review* 54 (2001): 2157–242.

Markel, Dan. "Executing Retributivism: *Panetti* and the Future of the Eighth Amendment." *Northwestern University Law Review* 103: 1163–222.

Markel, Dan. "State, Be Not Proud: A Retributivist Defense of the Commutation of Death Row and the Abolition of the Death Penalty." *Harvard Civil Rights-Civil Liberties Law Review* 40: 407–80.

Moore, Michael S. "Justifying Retributivism." In *Placing Blame: A Theory of the Criminal Law*, 153–88. Oxford: Oxford University Press, 1997.

Moore, Michael S. "Torture and the Balance of Evils." In *Placing Blame: A Theory of the Criminal Law*, 669–736. Oxford: Oxford University Press, 1997.

O'Neill, Onora. "Kant after Virtue." In *Constructions of Reason: Explorations of Kant's Practical Philosophy*, 145–61. Cambridge, UK: Cambridge University Press, 1989.

O'Neill, Onora. "Kant: Rationality as Practical Reason." In *The Oxford Handbook of Rationality*, edited by Alfred R. Mele and Piers Rawling, 93–109. Oxford: Oxford University Press, 2004.

Robinson, Paul H., and Michael T. Cahill. *Law without Justice: Why Criminal Law Doesn't Give People What They Deserve*. Oxford: Oxford University Press, 2006.

Robinson, Paul H., and John M. Darley. "The Utility of Desert." *Northwestern University Law Review* 91 (1997): 453–99.

Ross, W.D. *The Right and the Good*. Indianapolis: Hackett, 1930.

Sullivan, Roger J. *Immanuel Kant's Moral Theory*. Cambridge: Cambridge University Press, 1989.

Sullivan, Roger J. *An Introduction to Kant's Ethics*. Cambridge: Cambridge University Press, 1994.

Wertheimer, Alan. "Should Punishment Fit the Crime?" *Social Theory and Practice* 3 (1975): 403–23.

White, Mark D. *Kantian Ethics and Economics: Autonomy, Dignity, and Character*. Stanford, CA: Stanford University Press, 2011.

White, Mark D. "Retributivism in a World of Scarcity." In *Theoretical Foundations of Law and Economics*, edited by Mark D. White, 253–71. Cambridge: Cambridge University Press, 2009.

8

HEGEL ON PUNISHMENT: A MORE

SOPHISTICATED RETRIBUTIVISM

Jane Johnson

IN ENGLISH-SPEAKING scholarship, G.W.F. Hegel's view of punishment has received relatively little attention, particularly when compared to the space devoted to his predecessor Immanuel Kant.[1] This is perhaps not surprising, given Hegel's challenging (even obscure) writing style, which has, it seems, also opened his view up to a wide range of interpretations: mixed, reformist, deterrent, and retributivist. By contrast, Kant's position is almost universally regarded to be retributivist,[2] so much so that he is often considered to be *the* paradigmatic retributivist. This interpretation is based on just a few key passages in the *Metaphysics of Morals,* extracted seemingly without difficulty from his broader philosophy.[3]

This chapter will argue that a coherent account of Hegel on punishment—and one that rivals Kant's—can be developed if his (at times) taxing lexicon and broader philosophy are engaged. Such efforts will also be rewarded by a theory of punishment capable of answering a central problem for retributivism: namely, how to ground the concept of desert. To achieve these ends, an interpretation of Hegel on punishment will be sketched, appealing to sources beyond *The Philosophy of Right*, including *The Phenomenology*, *The Science of Logic*, and *The Encyclopaedia Logic*. Armed with this interpretation, it will be apparent that Hegel is a consistent retributivist, enabling alternate views to be briefly acknowledged and dismissed. The nature of the problem regarding desert will be articulated and Hegel's answer to this problem demonstrated. Finally, the chapter will conclude with some comments about how Hegel's view of punishment finds parallels in Kant but is ultimately more rich and interesting than the Kantian view.

1. Hegel on Crime and Punishment

At the outset, it should be acknowledged—and as will become rapidly apparent below—understanding Hegel on punishment is by no means a straightforward task, even for those who are otherwise familiar with and sympathetic to his philosophy. As Dudley Knowles, for instance, notes, "[i]t is fair to say that the theory is complex and unclear,"[4] while Mark Tunick comments that Hegel has a "well-earned reputation for obscurity"[5] and that his theory of punishment has, for some philosophers, come to be regarded as an "object of scorn or ridicule."[6] Similarly, James Doyle argues that although Hegel has the beginnings of a "defensible theory of punishment," his remarks on the subject can be regarded as "needlessly obscure and abstract."[7]

The difficulty of reading Hegel on punishment has surely contributed to its relative neglect in Anglo-American jurisprudence. William Lucy has in fact pointed to what he has called "a strain of intolerance" in Anglo-American linguistic philosophy, which is highly critical of the type of (purportedly metaphysically charged) project Hegel embarks on. This intolerance manifests itself in the familiar (and surely comprehensible) charge that Hegel is obscure but goes further to suggest that this obscurity verges on willful.[8] Considerable effort is undoubtedly required to make sense of Hegel's idiosyncratic expression and draw together the various elements from his vast corpus in order to develop a coherent account on punishment,[9] yet this task is worthwhile and will be embarked on below.

A. HEGEL ON CRIME

Though the treatment of Hegel on punishment is sparse, the attention devoted to his theory of crime is even more limited.[10] Since crime and punishment are however inextricably linked for Hegel, any serious attempt to come to terms with his view of punishment must engage with his view of crime. In the first instance, it needs to be recognized that the link Hegel appeals to between crime and punishment is not merely the straightforward and commonsense manner in which punishment follows crime, nor is it simply the basic point held to by retributivists—that crime deserves punishment, and that its type and amount should be derived from the criminal act. Rather, the connection that Hegel claims is more fundamental than this: it is both logical and necessary. Crime and punishment are just two halves of one whole that cannot be prised apart lest the resulting phenomena be meaningless and even misleading. To understand crime, one needs to understand punishment and vice versa, since punishment is "merely a manifestation of the crime, i.e., it is one half which is necessarily presupposed by the other."[11]

1. Crime and Judgment

According to Hegel, crime is one of three kinds of wrongdoing, the other two being civil wrong and fraud. Each of these forms of wrongdoing corresponds to a different judgment type involving a particular relationship to right, and all these relationships entail a fundamental opposition between right itself and an individual will. According to *The Encyclopedia Logic,* civil wrongs, for instance, correspond to simple negative judgments. These judgments are simple because they only negate the rights of a particular individual in one instance, leaving intact the broader system of right and, in fact, appealing to that system to resolve what effectively is a mistaken rights claim. For example, my neighbor and I disagree over where the boundary between our properties should be drawn, we take the dispute before a court (that is, we stay within the system of right), and the judge decides my neighbor's claim is correct, and mine was erroneous. My mistake was just that, a mistake, not criminal or malicious. Fraud, on the other hand, involves deliberate deception, though it also assumes the system of right. The fraudster relies on this system and pretends to work within it, all the while being deceitful about some aspect of his transaction with others. For Hegel, therefore, fraud is an instance of what he terms a "positively infinite judgment." Such judgments involve a kind of identity claim, but the positively infinite judgment is dubious considered as a form of judgment. For instance, "a rose is a rose" is a positively infinite judgment, but being framed as a judgment is, in a sense, deceitful. The predicate fails to reveal anything about the particular subject in the way in which we ordinarily assume it should in a judgment. The connection to fraud is thus revealed: in fraud, there is an appearance of legality so that the form of legality is adhered to, but adherence to this form is misleading because it does not hold up on close scrutiny.

As with civil wrong and fraud, crime corresponds to a judgment type: the negative infinite one. However, before explaining how crime is like this particular type of judgment, the underlying (and seemingly very odd) idea that an act can be like any type of judgment needs to be explained. For Hegel, there is something to be gleaned from comparing what occurs in a judgment and the kind of phenomenon that a deliberate criminal act represents because in Hegel's view, if someone is to be held responsible, we need to be concerned with their intention, and for Hegel, an individual's intention is revealed through his act. Since an act represents a type of assertion or claim,[12] comparing the criminal's act to a type of judgment makes sense.

In the negative infinite judgment, there is a kind of truth posited but also a kind of absurdity. For instance, while it is undoubtedly the case that the following negative infinite judgments hold, namely, that "the rose is not an elephant" and "the understanding is not a table,"[13] these judgments are peculiar because they attempt to draw together otherwise disparate elements or realms. They are "*correct* or *true*... but in spite of such truth they are nonsensical and absurd,"[14] because any meaningful relationship between subject and predicate is absent. Subject and predicate do not even inhabit relevantly similar realms; they are incommensurable, so (for instance) "table" is not the kind of predicate that could ever be meaningfully ascribed to an understanding, and thus it is no surprise that it can be negated in this context. Although negative infinite judgments appear to be judgments and may even seem to be true, they are not genuinely so because they stand outside the proper system of inferential relations in which judgments play a role.

If we return to consideration of a criminal act as an instance of a negative infinite judgment, such an act "does indeed possess *correctness*, since it is an actual deed, but it is nonsensical because it is related purely negatively to morality which constitutes its universal sphere."[15] Thus, in referring to the criminal act as negative, there is no fanciful suggestion that it did not occur, but rather that the act simply makes no sense since it goes against the very foundations of right. It is like an assertion that although it looks true, actually represents a situation in which the whole ground of the practice of asserting has been undermined.

2. Crime as Negation

As distinct from civil wrong and fraud, crime involves a coercive act by a free and rational agent and represents a threefold negation: of the rights of the victim, the right of the criminal himself (making his act self-contradictory), and right as such (revealing the internally "null and void" nature of the crime). In the preceding paragraphs, this peculiarly Hegelian use of "negation" with respect to judgments passed without comment, but such terminology cannot be glossed over if a more widely palatable interpretation of Hegel on punishment is to be attempted. After all, what could it possibly mean to describe events that have actually occurred as negations? And what could plausibly be intended by what Allen Wood has described as "the baffling claim" that the criminal act and crime's existence is null and void in itself, even contradictory?[16]

What Hegel means by negation is not what contemporary logicians mean when they use this term. The scope of contemporary logic is generally limited to consideration of propositions: their internal structure, relationships, and to some extent, how these propositions relate to the empirical world. Negation, therefore, just concerns propositions or parts of propositions that are not the case—the denial of something. For Hegel, however, negation concerns form *and* content; it is a kind of embedded notion that can reside in processes, objects, and concepts themselves, rather than simply operating at the level of statements about processes, objects, and so on. Negation for Hegel arises out of a relationship of opposition between terms, rather than from the denial of one proposition in counter position to another, or from any sense that a particular term is in itself inherently or absolutely negative. Designation makes one term negative and its opposite positive. This is the result of a decision that could be regarded as arbitrary: that is, the term deemed negative could just as easily be construed as positive and vice versa. Applied to his discussion of crime, negation does not involve making some perverse metaphysical claim of the kind that crime is somehow not a genuine event because it involves negation. As Hegel explicitly states in the *Philosophy of Right:* "[w]hen an infringement of right as right occurs, it does have a *positive* external *existence*, but this existence *within itself* is null and void."[17] Crime actually happens; its negation is not a negation of existence, it is rather that the criminal act entails three types of negative implication.

In the first instance, through crime, the right of a particular individual to be treated as a free and autonomous person is effectively negated, that is, crime results in the victim having her rights actively overturned or ignored.[18] She is treated by the criminal (incorrectly) as if she had no legitimate claims to right. Secondly, Hegel suggests that the very process and concept of crime is bound up with and contains negation: the negation of right. Effectively, the criminal has gone beyond the mere denial of a particular individual's rights in a specific instance and shown a flagrant disregard for rights more broadly—for the very principle of right itself. In refusing to acknowledge the status and rights of an individual, the very basis of civil society is challenged. Crime cannot be regarded as a discrete negation of the individual and her rights but involves a more substantial negation of right, with implications for law and society as a whole.

Hegel elucidates his point in *The Encyclopaedia Logic* through the case of theft. When a thief steals something it is not that he simply denies

the particular right of someone else to this particular thing (as in a suit about civil rights); instead, he denies the rights of that person completely. . . he has violated right as such, i.e., right in general.[19]

As Steinberger puts it, "the criminal act suggests that there is no such thing as property; rather, there are only possessions. . . for the criminal we have these things only as a matter of might or of accident not Right; hence our having them has no normative force."[20]

Finally, Hegel maintains that the criminal also negates his own right. This is perhaps the most counterintuitive of the negations to which Hegel refers, since many would surely regard the criminal to have achieved precisely the opposite: through his act, he has asserted his own rights as superior to that of the victim. Yet Hegel specifically claims the criminal act is self-contradictory and undermines the criminal's own capacity for rights.

At this point, in order to make any sense of this and related claims, it is necessary to draw on what has come to be known as Hegel's "theory of recognition."[21] Hegel's notion of recognition is absolutely central to his account of the legal, political, and social worlds (and thereby to his view of crime and punishment), yet in spite of its significance, recognition generally goes unacknowledged in discussions of Hegel on crime and punishment.[22] This neglect needs to be remedied however, if a tenable account of punishment is to be developed, since it is central to understanding his view of punishment.

Undoubtedly, Hegel's most well-known rendering of recognition is to be found in the master-slave dialectic from the fourth chapter of the *Phenomenology of Spirit*. Here Hegel tells the tale of a struggle between two players that reaches a type of resolution through their tacit agreement to fulfill certain roles—one as master, the other as slave. In mutually accepting and acknowledging each other as occupying these roles, the rules of engagement for their interaction are established. So rather than battling against each other, they have found a way to legitimately coexist by following conditions for their mutual conduct. To be a master or a slave is to fulfill a position and have certain important aspects of interaction already established. This parable-like interchange can be read as an account of how human beings come to be self-conscious, and simply put, for Hegel, it is the notion of recognition that is the key. It is only through our relationship to others, our mutual dependence, and our reciprocal acknowledgement of ourselves as such, that self-consciousness emerges. In Hegel's words, "[s]elf-consciousness achieves its satisfaction only in another self-consciousness."[23] According to Hegel's account, social life must be mediated via social roles like those of master and slave, which are normative. It is only through such circumscribed roles that individuals recognize themselves and others as such. Thus, society is absolutely essential to self-consciousness in Hegel's view.[24]

In the *Philosophy of Right*, recognition finds its most direct expression in Hegel's account of property and contract. Property and (in turn) contract are no mere by-products of civil society for Hegel but are absolutely seminal to how we understand ourselves and others within the social realm, for legitimate claims to ownership are not grounded in either merely possessing or giving form to something.[25] Rather, property requires making a mark or sign that signifies the relationship between the owned object and the will of the owner, and critically this mark must also be recognized as fulfilling such a role by others. In this context, appealing to a sign involves appeal to a phenomenon whose very existence is dependent on recognition.

There are obvious parallels between the functioning of contract and right for Hegel. Contract mediates and controls property transactions while right guides transactions in the civil realm, and both contract and right depend on recognition. In the case of contract, buyer and seller must recognize each other as legitimate participants in an alienation of property and acknowledge contract as the means of mediating their transaction. Similarly, in the civil (or legal) realm, individuals must recognize each other as legal persons, and the whole system of right must be accepted as a framework within which interpersonal legal relations are mediated. A kind of recognitive loop could therefore be thought to underpin civil society, established when individuals mutually acknowledge each other as intentional/self-conscious beings with rights. I only recognize myself in this capacity as intentional/self-conscious in another's recognition of me as such and vice versa. Crucially, rights claims made within such a system only gain legitimacy when those over whom they are purported to hold sway (that is, rights bearers and claimants) recognize these claims as normative.

From these discussions of property, contract, and right, we might articulate a commonly held principle of recognition for Hegel: that our normativity and capacity for rule following depend on our social existence. The master and the slave, the buyer and the seller all furnish models of recognitive exchange inside a social system. Rules and laws only make sense in a public context where individuals mutually hold one another to account.

Returning to the proposition that sparked this exposition—that through his act, the criminal negates his own right—this can now be understood in the context of the recognitive meaning of crime. Criminal wrongdoing can be thought to initiate a disruptive change in the recognitive relations that determine him as a legal person, right bearer, and a self-consciousness. Through an act that failed to properly acknowledge another as right bearing, the criminal effectively cuts himself off from the recognitive loop that underpins society. In refusing to acknowledge and, in fact, undermining the right of another, he has, by extension, violated the more general principle of right, threatening the whole recognitive basis of society. By implication, he has undermined his own claim to right and recognition. So the point Hegel is making in positing crime's three negations is not that crime is some sort of non-act or non-event, but rather that crime simply represents a negation or an effective denial of right on three fronts.

3. Crime as Contradiction

Crime not only involves negation for Hegel but contradiction: the criminal's will is null and void in itself. Claims such as these have attracted even more critical attention and derisive commentary than those associated with negation, and indeed it does seem perverse to suggest that an actual event in the empirical world could possibly embody a contradiction.[26] But this apparent perversion is explicable because Hegel has a different account of contradiction to the one commonly held. On his view, a contradiction is invoked when one of the two sides of a negation and what that negation is grounded in are opposed. For Hegel, contradiction is the soul of life, development, and change in the empirical world and exists in objects and their relations: "[C]ontradiction is the root of all movement and vitality; it is only in so far as something has a contradiction within it that it moves, has an urge and activity."[27] He suggests that those who maintain that contradiction cannot even be thought hold a "ridiculous" position: "What is correct in this assertion is just that contradiction is not all there is to it, and that contradiction sublates itself by its own doing."[28] Contradiction does not remain but must be resolved.

Applying this definition to the example of crime means recognizing, in the first instance, the claim made above that through crime, the criminal wills the negation of a particular individual's rights. This quite specific negation is however grounded in a more general notion of right itself, a universal notion of right. And this is where the contradiction comes into play, since the opposition set up between the particular will of the criminal and the universal notion of right on which that will depends is contradictory for Hegel. In spite of depending on this universal grounding, the individual will goes against the universal and thereby undermines and overturns the very basis on which it exists. Though not referring specifically to the contradiction involved, Lewis Hinchman makes the point well when he states that for Hegel, "the criminal is someone who denies his own status as a person in the act of violating the personality of another. To be a person is to be the incumbent of a *universal* role, but the criminal sees his act in purely particular terms."[29] Likewise, though this time observing the Hegelian contradiction, Reyburn notes that "the notion of crime contradicts itself: it cancels that in virtue of which it is."[30] Thus, by failing to recognize the claims of a legitimate rights holder through his criminal act, the criminal effectively undermines the whole system of recognition on which he in fact depends and makes a claim that was always destined to fail. In Reyburn's words, the criminal's claim here is "intrinsically void."[31]

Many commentators have struggled to understand Hegel on contradiction, in part, because they fail to probe the Hegelian meaning of this term. David Cooper, responding to Reyburn, seems to conclude that, for Reyburn at least, Hegel suggests that crime is a piece of behavior that exhibits an inconsistency between crime as an act of a free man and crime as an attack on free men. And as has been revealed in previous paragraphs, this is basically where the contradiction is located for Hegel: in an act that depends for its grounding on a system of right and freedom which the act itself contravenes. Cooper, however, appears to trivialize or at least downplay the nature of this contradiction, referring to it as simply inconsistency and wondering how it could possibly license punishment. As he states, "[n]o doubt inconsistent behavior should be brought to the attention of the agent—this might be the job of a psychoanalyst—but I do not see how inconsistency per se merits punishment."[32] In suggesting that a psychoanalyst rather than a jailer (for instance) might be of assistance, Cooper is surely trading on a sense of inconsistency that implies a discrepancy between an agent's intentions and actual behavior (or perhaps between behavior and social norms, which might be closer to Hegel's meaning). It is difficult to know precisely what Cooper intends, given his relatively brief and inconclusive thoughts; however, regardless of the details, Hegelian contradiction surely runs deeper than inconsistency, and such terminology underplays the significance of the criminal's act.

B. HEGEL ON PUNISHMENT

Hegel's account of punishment follows directly from his view of crime, with punishment involving a response to each of the negations invoked by crime—of the victim, the criminal, and right itself. In the case of the victim, punishment serves to acknowledge the criminal's mistake in effectively ignoring her rights. Because the criminal has also negated his own right through crime, punishment is required to cancel this move and to bring the criminal back within the fold of civil society. And just like the victim, the criminal has his legitimacy as a right-bearing individual reinstated by punishment. Hegel's way of conveying this notion, however, begins to sound quite odd and even counterintuitive when he speaks of punishment as the criminal's right, something he consents to and even wills. The final negation to be overturned by punishment is the negation that makes punishment rather than restitution or compensation the only reasonable response to crime for Hegel—that is, the negation directed at right itself. Crime must be met by punishment so that the threat to right which crime represents can be shown up for what it is, namely, null and void in itself. As Hegel explains, "[t]he *manifestation* of. . . [crime's] nullity is that the nullification of the infringement likewise comes into existence; this is the actuality of right, as its necessity which mediates itself with itself through the cancellation of its infringement."[33] Not only does punishment make crime's wrong explicit, but right is also rehabilitated to its proper place by punishment; via punishment, the law "restores and thereby *actualizes itself as valid through the cancellation of crime*."[34]

Hegel's use of negation in the context of punishment attracts puzzlement and criticism just as it did in the context of crime. D. J. B. Hawkins mounts a typical attack when he writes:

> Hegelian theory is really excessively obscure. If you could bring the murdered person back to life by executing the murderer, you could truly be said to negate the evil act, and, if you can reform the criminal, you can truly be said to negate his evil will. But how the infliction of a punishment which neither reverses the evil act nor necessarily reforms the evil will can be said to negate the wrong done is surely beyond the comprehension of any literal-minded person.[35]

Beyond concerns about negation, Hegel's account of punishment introduces a new target for critics through his notion of "annulment." David Dolinko, for one, describes as "obscure" Hegel's claim that punishment annuls something that has actually occurred.[36] Likewise, Ted Honderich has referred to the obscurity of Hegelian theory with regard to annulment, stating that although marriages *qua* contracts can be annulled, "crimes cannot be, in any ordinary sense."[37] He goes on to make the point that "[m]y death or imprisonment, after I have killed a man, does not make things what they were before."[38] The obvious question then becomes: "In what way can my death or imprisonment be seen as an annulment?"[39]

Concerns about annulment, namely, that Hegel is somehow claiming that punishment can expunge the very existence of the wrongful act, can be ameliorated to some extent by acknowledging that the term is, in fact, an extremely poor translation of the German word that Hegel uses in this context: *Aufhebung*. *Aufhebung* entails "preserving" as well as "repealing," "raising" as well as "abolishing," "canceling" as well as "bringing out," so that the German word is clearly much richer in meaning and has levels of sophistication entirely absent from this English translation.

When Hegel writes of the annulment of crime by punishment, he is not referring to annulment at the level of the actual existence of the criminal act but rather annulling the broader implications and meaning of crime for the victim, criminal, and right. This is also how we can better understand Hegel's point that punishment represents a negation of a negation. Both the annulment and the negation involved in punishment are about overturning the wrong of crime and rehabilitating right to its proper place, since for the victim, the criminal, and the broader principle of right inside a society grounded on recognition, crime represents a threat that must be addressed. If the challenge to right is allowed to stand, then rights are not real—they have no purchase or meaning. As an idealist, rights can only exist and have legitimacy for Hegel by virtue of their recognition by others as binding; it is through their mutual acknowledgment that rights claims and rights bearers have status. If it were the case that both valid and invalid rights claims elicited the same response, then how would the two be distinguished? Differential treatment is required to effectively mark right from wrong.

When it comes to the seemingly astounding claims that Hegel makes about the criminal and his punishment (namely, that punishment is his right, something he consents to, and even wills), these are in fact only astounding if one ignores their particularly Hegelian meaning. In the first instance, they are not meant to be empirically descriptive claims or to actually capture something about the mindset of the criminal (that he actively claims his right to punishment, intends to be punished, and desires this outcome). This would indeed be preposterous. Instead, the claims Hegel makes are conceptually normative. So given his situation within civil society, the criminal *should* acknowledge retributive punishment as his right. The criminal has the right to be addressed and treated as a rational agent who has chosen to perpetrate a criminal act. If he has not earned this right (for example, if he is mentally unstable or a child), then it is not punishment which is his due. As Cooper explains in his well-known account of Hegel on punishment:

> If a man acts as a free, rational agent, and is aware of himself as such, then he must, in general, wish to be held responsible for the intended results of such actions. He has a right, indeed, to have his actions looked upon in this light. To treat him otherwise is to treat him like an animal or a maniac... To speak to the criminal as Hegel thinks the utilitarian must speak to him would deny him the status of a rational being.[40]

Similarly, the claims that the criminal consents to and wills his punishment are conceptual and normative points. It is not the case, as Michael Mitias maintains, that "[b]efore punishment can be inflicted the criminal must... freely consent to the punishment; he must confess his guilt."[41] If Hegel's points were not conceptual and normative, then he would be in conflict with what he says elsewhere that punishment must be enforced "with or without the consent of individuals."[42] The terms "consent" and "will" are not intended to describe the criminal's psychological state (which is surely impervious to direct scrutiny anyway), but rather they capture what is implicit in his act. It is his consent and will as identified in this external act that is at issue. So as is stated in the *Philosophy of Right*, "the criminal gives this consent by his very act."[43] Regardless of what the criminal might think or even say on the matter, he has committed a criminal act, and so has thereby effectively willed his own punishment, since punishment is a necessary consequence of infringements of right within a society based on recognition. As Jami Anderson notes,

> [t]he criminal may (truthfully) claim that he did not commit a crime with the thought of his punishment in mind, but he cannot deny that he committed a criminal act. And, therefore, Hegel claims that the criminal cannot truthfully claim that he did not will an act that is punishable.[44]

2. Hegel and the Problem of Retributivism

As discussed above, punishment for Hegel concerns acknowledging the various wrongs and injuries to right evoked by crime. The redress to these wrongs establishes the proper place of right in a society grounded on recognition. Armed with this interpretation of Hegel, I want to turn now to situating it in the broader literature on punishment and explaining how it can address the retributivist's problem about grounding desert.

A. SITUATING HEGEL'S ACCOUNT

In order to both locate Hegel's view in the literature and demonstrate how he can meet the challenge of grounding retributivism, it will be useful to appeal to some distinctions with their origin in the work of H.L.A. Hart. Hart famously construed punishment as comprised of a number of distinct but interrelated components: its definition, general justifying aim, and distribution.[45] The general justifying aim of punishment is concerned with reasons that legitimate the very existence of the institution, while punishment's distribution concerns who should be punished, why they ought to be punished, and the amount of their punishment. Although involving a variation on Hart's distinctions, Edmund Pincoffs has examined the justification of punishment in terms of different "addressees": the victim, the criminal and the public.[46] In this chapter, appeal will be made to these same addressees, though "society" will be substituted for "the public."[47]

With respect to these three addresses, I want to argue that Hegel is a consistent retributivist. In order to do so, I want first to engage with some of those who have outlined alternate views. Despite Hegel's explicit rejection of deterrence or reform as appropriate motivations for punishment (since they undermine the criminal's rationality), some philosophers have argued that Hegel is effectively a closet consequentialist. Stanley Benn, for instance, renders Hegel on annulment and right in consequentialist terms, suggesting that possible good ends for the victim and society could justify the practice. For Benn, if punishment did in fact annul wrong, "it would be justified by the betterment of the victim of the crime or of society in general."[48] Similarly, he asserts that, in suggesting that punishment reaffirms right, Hegel is really making a utilitarian point, "for why should it be necessary to reaffirm the right, if not to uphold law for the general advantage?"[49] Wood also questions whether the notion of restoring right is genuinely a retributivist goal and finds Hegel wanting here. As he explains,

> the state's intention to *reassert* the validity of right in the face of wrong looks like an intention not to do justice as such, but to promote a good end, namely the public *recognition* of the validity of right. If there is room for doubt about this, that is largely because the precise nature of the end is rather mysterious. Why is it important for the state to *assert* the validity of right, to *express* its disapproval of crime? Is there any

reason for it to do this apart from its devotion to such consequentialist ends as preventing future crimes and reassuring people that their rights are being protected?[50]

Going as far back in English-speaking scholarship as J. Ellis McTaggart's early but influential view,[51] there have been philosophers who have interpreted Hegel as motivated by the reform and even repentance of the criminal. Gertrude Ezorsky, for one (relying on McTaggart), focuses on the justification that Hegel offers to the criminal and thereby comes to label his account "teleological" because, on her view, it attempts to achieve as its goal an improvement of the criminal. According to Ezorsky, for Hegel "the pain of punishment yields repentance, whereby the criminal recognizes his sin. He does not merely change his ways. Fear of future punishment might yield this superficial reform. He really becomes a better man; thus, Hegel declares, realizes his true nature."[52] Likewise, Paul Griseri argues that the notion that punishment annuls crime only makes sense if interpreted as bearing on the criminal and therefore "the concern to annul collapses into the concern to reform."[53]

A yet more idiosyncratic view of Hegel on punishment has been developed by Mark Tunick. Tunick, sharing with Benn a concern to explain Hegel's point that punishment is about vindicating right, explicitly distances himself from Benn's interpretation, observing that Hegel is no disguised utilitarian. Instead, Tunick maintains that Hegel's account of punishment is retributivist but nondeontic (by which he appears to mean forward looking) because, according to him, "we punish to avoid a future where crimes no longer are regarded as wrong."[54] Punishment is therefore motivated not by some social good as Benn would have it, but simply by the need to have right remain unchallenged as right.

Philosophers who situate Hegel outside the bounds of retributivism seem to have either not looked to Hegel's philosophy directly (for instance, Ezorsky) or have been mistaken about the nature of the claims that Hegel makes in relation to punishment. As observed earlier, some philosophers have been too literal in their attempts to understand Hegel, incorrectly regarding terms like "annulment" as empirically descriptive rather than conceptual and normative. Tunick's point is similarly misguided, as Hegel is not making a temporal and empirical point. It is not the case that punishment is motivated by the future-oriented goal of ensuring that right continues to be distinguished from wrong but simply that conceptually, here and now, right and wrong would be meaningless and nonsensical if punishment were not available to distinguish appropriate rights claims from infringements.

One plausible source of concern for those advocating a thoroughly retributivist reading of Hegel enters via the account of punishment given to the criminal, since Hegel imports consequentialist considerations into the determination of actual punishments. For instance, in discussing the notion that crime may represent a danger to society, Hegel states that

> [a]lthough the view that. . . [crimes] are a threat to civil society may appear to aggravate. . .[them], it has in fact been chiefly responsible for a reduction in punishments. A penal code is therefore primarily a product of its time and of the current condition of civil society.[55]

He clearly maintains that a more stable society can afford to punish more leniently, and conversely, "if society is still inwardly unstable, punishments must be made to set an example."[56] So for Hegel, the actual penalties meted out for particular infringements may vary based on such concerns as the state of the society in which those penalties are disbursed. This does not, however, threaten a retributivist reading since it does not conflict with the broader justification of punishment offered to the criminal. His punishment is still grounded in his act whereby he illegitimately infringed right; it is just that secondary considerations about the social context in which his act occurred (such as the relative fragility of the political system) are brought to bear in determining the amount of his punishment.

Hegel is therefore a retributivist in the relevant sense here, namely, in terms of the justifications that can be given to the criminal, victim, and society (which will be outlined in more detail below). Like retributivists such as Kant, Hegel does not look to motivate punishment through the good ends that it might be possible to achieve, but rather he looks back to the criminal act for the warrant to punish.

B. THE PROBLEM FOR RETRIBUTIVISM

At its most general level, the retributivist position can be thought to revolve around the claim that crime deserves punishment, and from this claim, the retributivist maintains that justifications to society, the criminal, and victim can be derived. When it comes to justifying punishment to the criminal, it is widely accepted that the retributivist is quite successful. In fact, other theories have attempted to harness the retributivist's achievements here: some consequentialists have tried to smuggle retributivist-inspired moral limits into their definitions of what constitutes punishment, while so-called mixed solutions (combining retributivist and utilitarian approaches) generally incorporate retributivist moves to address this issue.[57]

On a purely retributivist account, however, the criminal's punishment is justified as the appropriate response to his criminal act. Punishment respects the autonomy of rational moral agents by holding them responsible for their actions. Since the criminal is treated in punishment simply according to what he did, rather than in terms of some consequentialist agenda, for example, he can be said to be treated justly. A similar and satisfactory justification can be offered to the victim, as punishment seeks appropriate redress for the wrong she has suffered. However, when it comes to providing a broader justification for punishment in terms of society in general, it is widely acknowledged that the retributivist encounters real difficulties, which means that his frequent and confident references to desert may be misplaced. The purported strength and validity of desert simply appears as an unexamined assumption in many retributivist accounts, yet on critical reflection, desert requires further support. It is by no means self-evident, for instance, why it is that for the breach of certain legal prohibitions, the guilty merit punishment, and why, even if this desert can be established, the state can be legitimately charged with enforcing it. In other arenas of life, the existence of a desert by no means guarantees its satisfaction. Perhaps the unfortunate deserve compensation, and the good merit reward; yet there is no state agency entrusted with ensuring that such desert is meted out.[58]

For those retributivists who have attempted to explain their foundational principle, these efforts could be considered (following Ellis[59]) to fall into two categories: desert could be thought to be either an intrinsic value or one that might be explicated further according to principles associated with distributive justice. The former view relies on the surely contentious claim that the connection between crime and punishment is natural, straightforward, and unproblematic. As Jean Hampton describes it, the notion that a lawbreaker merits punishment is on this account simply considered to be a "bedrock intuition."[60] On the second view, in which desert is grounded in a theory of distributive justice, laws are considered to establish a system of burdens and benefits that is disrupted by the criminal's act so that punishment must be applied to rectify balance and order within society.[61] But this approach is also flawed, as a number of commentators (including Hampton) have noted. It is only really plausible to characterize *property* crimes as involving an illegitimate gain on the part of the criminal, and surely the best way of overturning such an inappropriately obtained benefit in such a system would be to remove the benefit and perhaps seek some form of restitution, rather than to punish the offender. When it comes to crimes against persons (not property), some defenders of this view have argued that we *can* make sense of the rapist or murder obtaining an unfair advantage, namely, in terms of the unfettered freedom he has enjoyed at the expense of others. But we might well wonder whether or not this unfettered freedom expressed by the criminal can genuinely be construed as some kind of independently held advantage. Thus, the retributivist account as it pertains to justifying (to society) the institution of punishment harbors major deficiencies, since the two principal ways identified above of explicating desert fall short of satisfactorily accomplishing their task.

C. HEGEL'S GROUNDING OF PUNISHMENT

The way in which Hegel construes punishment as the annulment of three negations—of the victim, the criminal, and right itself—seems tailor-made to justifying punishment in terms of the three addressees (from above). Though the primary interest here is in how Hegel can answer the problem of justifying punishment to society and thereby ground the concept of desert, his view can also bolster retributivism's traditional strengths via the story he can give both the criminal and the victim.

Hegel would, in the first instance, likely reject the way the problem of justifying punishment to the criminal is framed, particularly in liberal theory. Often the problem is put as the need to justify the infliction of harm on an individual by the state. Hegel would find this approach misconceived on a number of fronts. To see the individual as pitted against the state in this way is to misconstrue the nature of our existence within society.

We are not otherwise radically free individuals who stand counterpoised to the overwhelming power and might of the state, but rather ourselves and our freedom only exist within the state. In focusing on the particular criminal and the consequences of punishment (namely, its harm), what Hegel considers to be the absolutely fundamental relationship between punishment and crime and its emphasis on righting wrong is also mislaid. By isolating punishment from its full context, it actually becomes tenable, *contra* the view he holds, to consider punishment as a "purely *arbitrary* association of an evil *with an illicit action*,"[62] and reasonable to question why we should "will an evil merely *because another evil is already present*."[63] Already, in merely stating the problem, we seem to be on the back foot. After all, why should we meet a harm with a harm or an evil with an evil? What possible justification could there be for copying the criminal and committing an immoral act? However, punishment for Hegel is not an independent harm or evil act, but rather it is an integral part of a process initiated by a criminal action, which cannot meaningfully be abstracted from this context. It is not the harm of punishment that should be in the foreground in justification, since harm is just a side effect or consequence of having to punish. It is the connection between crime and punishment that is critical and the role punishment plays within the system of right.

For Hegel, a justification can be addressed to the criminal as someone who has legislated an act by which he has rejected the victim's right, as well as the principle of right more broadly and, in fact, thereby undermined his own standing within society. Society depends on the mutual recognition of rights, and in failing to acknowledge another's legitimate rights claim in a particular case, he has failed to appropriately support and partake in the system of right on which he depends. If he is to regain his place within society's recognitive structure, he cannot stand outside the system and attempt to be some kind of free rider, looking to others to accept his rights claims while he flouts theirs and the system of right more broadly; right must be reinforced and the implications of his act annulled by punishment. Without punishment, the criminal cannot resume his place as a legitimate member of society. Yet in spite of embodying a rejection of his act, the criminal's punishment still acknowledges his status as a rational and autonomous individual. Hegel's retributivism therefore demonstrates an appropriate regard for the individual and his freedom. It does not patronize the criminal with some simplistic "carrot and stick" approach to their choices and behavior nor use them as part of some bigger scheme for society as a whole. The criminal has made a choice, albeit a flawed one, and he should be held responsible for his freely determined act.

It follows that a good justification can also be framed to the victim of crime who can be satisfied that her standing has been reaffirmed and endorsed by punishment of the individual who illegitimately ignored and infringed her rights. Her situation (in which a wrong was unfairly perpetrated against her) has been acknowledged as just that—wrong—a flawed move in the game of rights, and an appropriate response has been formulated in the shape of punishment of the wrongdoer.

Hegel's account is also able to answer the difficulties traditionally associated with retributivism by furnishing reasons why crime deserves punishment, why only infringements of some legal prohibitions merit it, and why the state should enforce punishment. To the first of these, Hegel can respond that the concepts of punishment and crime are inextricably linked or mutually dependent. Our ability to comprehend concepts such as crime and punishment, and right and wrong, depend on appreciating their relation to one another. And further, these connections and distinctions require, for their very existence, appropriate actions and reactions. If the distinction between right and wrong is to have any purchase, it must be borne out in our responses to encounters with right and wrong. Affirmations of right as opposed to its denial must be met differently, lest the contrast between the two be lost. As Nicholson puts it, "[p]unishment, in short, makes the law effective: contrariwise, if there is no punishment laid down and applied, then the criminal's action is condoned (as happens when a law becomes moribund)."[64]

Hegel can also address the related challenge for the retributivist regarding why it is that only some wrongful or illegal activities invoke punishment, and others do not. Hegel can differentiate in a principled and nonarbitrary way those acts that require punishment as opposed to compensation or restitution. If compensation or restitution were the response, then an act would effectively be treated as a civil offense rather than a crime and as something involving only harm to an individual, not also to the perpetrator or to right itself.

Finally, the state must enforce punishment because of its relation to right. Rights originate in and are maintained by our reciprocal recognition of them. Crime threatens the whole structure of right and recognition within society by ignoring or actually subverting the specific rights of individuals, so that it cannot be allowed to pass unchallenged. To genuinely negate the negation of wrong requires the context of the state with its attendant standards and institutions, and this becomes apparent in the distinction that Hegel makes between retribution and revenge.

Punishment is objective, universal, and mediated while revenge is subjective, particular, and immediate. Because of these factors, revenge attains justice, if at all, only by chance. According to Hegel, if the content of revenge happens to coincide with retribution, then it may be fair, but the form of revenge will always be individualistic and misguided. Rather than cancelling crime in a definitive manner, an act of revenge actually perpetuates a potentially infinite series of wrongs. Punitive, as opposed to avenging, justice seeks to genuinely overcome the negation of crime and reconcile right with right. It requires therefore a justice system, that is, certain mechanisms and procedures enshrined within institutions intended to dispense appropriate and retributive punishment. The system of justice that Hegel envisages helps furnish a proper distance between the particularities of the criminal event for the interested parties, enabling a certain formality and a disinterested application of the law. Thus, punishment is no mere reflex (as revenge might be construed); the criminal is independently prosecuted and punished so that the penalty of punishment is both established and carried out by a civil body according to retributivist principles. It is only within the context of a properly constituted society with its recognition of property and personality, its universal and objective standards and institutions, that challenges to right can find their appropriate measure through retributive punishment.[65]

3. Hegel's Relation to Kant

Answering retributivism's central problem and bolstering the justification of punishment to the criminal and victim is also possible using Kantian resources, as I have argued elsewhere.[66] However, this task is made easier by appeal to Hegel's account of crime and punishment, since, although there are similarities between Kant and Hegel on punishment, Hegel develops his account in greater depth, and in particular has more to say on the crucial issue of crime.

The relationship between right, crime, and punishment is similar for both philosophers, as is the context within which punishment occurs. The Kantian system contains a concept that Kant labels "real negation," which is echoed in Hegel's system through the concepts of negation and contradiction; both philosophers in fact appeal to similar examples (journeys in opposite directions and cases of credit and debt) to explain these oppositional concepts. For Kant, real negation involves a relationship between two positive predicates such that one predicate is made or construed as negative by virtue of its relationship of opposition to another, and when considered together, the two predicates work to divest each other of some part or all of their individual effects. For Kant, this concept of real negation captures the kind of opposition he maintains should exist between crime and punishment. The manner in which crime inappropriately impedes the victim's freedom can be cancelled through punishment. Punishment therefore represents a legitimate form of coercion, as he explains:

> if a certain use of freedom is itself a hindrance to freedom in accordance with universal laws (i.e. wrong), coercion that is opposed to this (as a *hindering of a hindrance to freedom*) is consistent with freedom in accordance with universal laws, that is, it is right.[67]

Kant's "hindering of a hindrance to freedom" finds clear parallels, then, in Hegel's "negation of a negation," and for both philosophers, part of what licenses punishment is its fundamental conceptual connection to right, and the fact that through punishment, the impediment to right which wrong represents, is overcome.

Hegel's account of right and recognition also appears to be prefigured in the Kantian concept of community. On Kant's account, community describes the mutuality and reciprocity that underpins the state and sets the scene in which punishment and right operate. Citizens are the component parts of the state whose mutual interaction should be guided and coordinated by laws of right to bring about the harmonious whole that is the civil realm.[68] Reciprocity is an underpinning ideal so that citizens stand in relations of civil equality whereby one citizen does "not recogniz[e] among the *people* any superior with the moral capacity to bind him as a matter of right in a way that he could not in turn bind the other."[69] From this normative ideal of legal community, right is construed thus: "Any action is *right* if it can coexist with everyone's freedom in accordance with a universal law, or if on its maxim the freedom of choice of each can coexist with everyone's freedom in accordance with a universal law."[70] Quite simply, acts are right if they are compatible with every citizen's enjoyment of their legitimate freedom, and conversely, acts are wrong if they impede the exercise of the freedom of one's fellow citizens. Thus, for both Kant and Hegel, to comprehend the concept of right, we must see its relationship to wrong and the connection to punishment licensed by infringements of right. Punishment restores balance to society, not by somehow altering what has actually occurred but by revealing the role it plays in establishing justice. The denial of right that crime entails is reframed and finds its appropriate response through punishment.

The manner in which Kant talks about the criminal's act undermining his own situation also bears similarities to Hegel's view, so that with Kant, we perhaps see in embryonic form what Hegel will develop in much greater depth. For instance, with regard to theft, Kant writes in *The Metaphysics of Morals* that "[w]hoever steals makes the property of everyone else insecure and therefore deprives himself (by the principle of retribution) of security in any possible property."[71] In Hegel's view, the thief fails to acknowledge the marks and signs that signify the relationship between the owner and his legitimate property and thereby fails to recognize the kind of norms that should govern society. Given the context in which the thief's act is perpetrated, this impacts on the criminal's standing, effectively excluding him from the legitimate recognition to which he would otherwise be entitled.

Because of parallels in their accounts, reading Kant in tandem with Hegel on punishment can help clarify and illuminate elements of Hegel's view. For instance, the apparently puzzling claim cited earlier that for Hegel the criminal wills his punishment is one also dealt with by Kant. He explains it thus:

No one suffers punishment because he has willed *it* but because he has willed a *punishable action*. . . Saying that I will to be punished if I murder someone is saying nothing more than that I subject myself together with everyone else to the laws.[72]

Kant therefore supports Hegel's view that willing punishment is not about the criminal's consent; rather it involves understanding the ramifications of his criminal act within the state.

Where Hegel really demonstrates the greater capacity of his account is through his vision of crime. Whereas Kant makes a handful of remarks about crime in the *Metaphysics of Morals*, Hegel devotes substantial sections of the *Philosophy of Right* to the topic, and as a result, Hegel's theory of punishment is underpinned by a well-developed and sophisticated account of wrongdoing that includes crime in addition to civil wrongs and fraud.

Though Kant briefly distinguishes between so-called public and private crimes, with the former including counterfeiting, theft, and robbery and the latter embezzlement and some types of fraud, and in fact claims (similarly to Hegel) that what distinguishes public crimes are that they "endanger the commonwealth and not just an individual person,"[73] nonetheless, Hegel's account is superior. Hegel can, for instance, more neatly and satisfactorily answer the problem in jurisprudence about what constitutes a crime as opposed to a civil wrong, using the conceptual resources outlined above in discussing why some illegal activities merit punishment and others do not. Hegel gives well-grounded reasons for this distinction, whereas Kant appears to assume rather than argue for the distinction between criminal and noncriminal legal offenses.

Hegel's more developed account of crime also facilitates a fuller understanding of punishment. By identifying and addressing three specific negations invoked by crime, Hegel gives a clear indication of the motivations and underpinning of punishment. In acknowledging these three different bases for punishment, Hegel explicitly refers to the situation of the victim. Although Kant and Hegel would likely give similar justifications of punishment to the victim, this is explicitly articulated in Hegel and only implicit in Kant. For Hegel, it is clear that the victim has her status as a right-bearing individual acknowledged and reaffirmed through punishment of an individual who ignored her legitimate claim to right.

4. Conclusion

This chapter has developed a coherent account of Hegel on punishment by examining, rather than dismissing, his at-times difficult concepts and often-puzzling claims. The reward is a view of punishment more sophisticated than the Kantian view traditionally offered up as representing the paradigm of retributivism. The tendency for philosophers of law to focus on Kant over Hegel is perhaps understandable given the more favorable reception accorded Kant in Anglo-American philosophy more generally, but is nonetheless unfortunate as Hegel has much to offer. Philosophers of law might do well therefore to look to Hegel in other areas of jurisprudence too, as his richer more-developed account has enormous and as yet inadequately realized potential.[74]

Notes

1 This is not to suggest that Hegel's view has received no attention at all—Mark Tunick, for instance, has devoted an entire book to this subject (*Hegel's Political Philosophy*)—but rather that this attention is scant when compared to the articles, chapters, and books given over to Kant's view of punishment, and the seminal place it is accorded in retributivist theory. This neglect is long standing and has been commented on in the past by Steinberger, "Hegel on Crime and Punishment," and Dubber, "Rediscovering Hegel's Theory of Crime and Punishment."

2 For exceptions to this view, see Byrd "Kant's Theory of Punishment"; Potter "The Principle of Punishment Is a Categorical Imperative"; Scheid, "Kant's Retributivism"; and Tunick. "Is Kant a Retributivist?"

3 While I do not think it is possible to develop an adequate interpretation of Kant on punishment by considering these passages in isolation (see my "Revisiting Kantian Retributivism to Construct a Justification of Punishment"), nonetheless, it seems that the apparent amenability of Kant's view to such an interpretation has contributed to its popularity.

4 Knowles, "Hegel on the Justification of Punishment," p. 125.

5 Tunick, *Hegel's Political Philosophy*, p. vii.

6 Ibid., p. ix.

7 Doyle, "Justice and Legal Punishment," p. 57.

8 Lucy, "Common Law According to Hegel," p. 687.

9 There is disagreement in the literature over whether or not appeal to Hegel's logic and broader philosophy are required to make sense of his account of crime and punishment. For instance, Steinberger ("Hegel on Crime and Punishment") and Brooks ("Hegel's Ambiguous Contribution to Legal Theory") argue it is essential, while others like Dyde ("Hegel's Conception of Crime and Punishment") and McCraken ("Hegel and the Autonomy of Contract Law") doubt this to be the case.

10 However Nicholson, "Hegel on Crime," gives an excellent account.

11 Hegel, *Elements of the Philosophy of Right*, §101 Addition (H).

12 However, an individual can only be held accountable for descriptions of their act which they recognize as their own. Hegel cites the case of Oedipus, who should not be held responsible for the act of patricide since he would not recognize this term as descriptive of his act (because he did not know that the man he killed was his father).

13 Hegel, *Science of Logic*, p. 642. The kind of examples Hegel points to here are instances of what Gilbert Ryle referred to as "category mistakes."

14 Ibid.

15 Ibid. The translation is slightly misleading here with *Sittlichkeit* being translated as "morality," when it is more accurately rendered as "ethics" or "ethical life."

16 Wood, *Hegel's Ethical Thought*, p. 112.

17 Hegel, *Philosophy of Right*, §97.

18 Throughout the chapter, the criminal will be regarded as male and the victim female.

19 Hegel, *Encyclopaedia Logic*, p. 251.

20 Steinberger, "Hegel on Crime and Punishment," p. 860.

21 Hegel himself does not outline a theory of recognition; this can be constructed from the references he makes to recognition throughout his philosophy.

22 For exceptions to this general trend, see Dubber, "Rediscovering Hegel's Theory"; Redding, *Hegel's Hermeneutics*; and Williams, *Hegel's Ethics of Recognition*.

23 Hegel, *Phenomenology of Spirit*, §175.

24 Clearly, this is a very different concept of self-consciousness to the one found in the Cartesian tradition.

25 In the latter, Hegel departs from someone like Locke for whom legitimate ownership can be secured through transforming land, for example, via one's labor.

26 The idea of contradiction in the normative realm may seem more plausible than when Hegel discusses the existence of contradiction in the empirical world. In the normative sphere, there can

be a discrepancy between the world as it ought to be and the world as it is, whereas it is not as clear that such a contradictory relationship can exist empirically.

27 Hegel, *Science of Logic*, p. 439.

28 Hegel, *Philosophy of Right*, § 119 Addition 2.

29 Hinchman, "Hegel's Theory of Crime and Punishment," pp. 541–42.

30 Reyburn, *Ethical Theory of Hegel*, p. 148.

31 Ibid., p. 149.

32 Cooper, "Hegel's Theory of Punishment," pp. 160–61.

33 Hegel, *Philosophy of Right*, §97.

34 Ibid., §220.

35 Hawkins, "Retribution," p. 16.

36 Dolinko, "Some Thoughts About Retributivism," p. 548.

37 Honderich, *Punishment*, p. 45.

38 Ibid.

39 Ibid.

40 Cooper, "Hegel's Theory," p. 153.

41 Mitias, *Moral Foundations of the State*, p. 171.

42 Hegel, *Philosophy of Right*, §100.

43 Ibid., §100 Addition (H,G).

44 Anderson, "Annulment Retributivism," p. 378.

45 Hart, "Prolegomenon to the Principles of Punishment."

46 Pincoffs, *Philosophy of Law*.

47 It might seem that, as a member of society, the victim does not need to be identified as a separate party needing a tailor-made justification; however, given the victim's special stake in what has occurred, she is not only interested in the *raison d'être* of the institution of punishment as a whole, but how the practice of punishment bears on her particular situation.

48 Benn, "Approach to the Problems of Punishment," p. 65.

49 Ibid.

50 Wood, *Hegel's Ethical Thought*, p. 110.

51 McTaggart, "Hegel's Theory of Punishment."

52 Ezorsky, "Ethics of Punishment," p. xii.

53 Griseri, "Punishment and Reparation," p. 411.

54 Tunick, "Is Kant a Retributivist?," p. 67.

55 Hegel, *Philosophy of Right*, §218.

56 Ibid.

57 For a brief but instructive discussion of these issues, see Lacey, *State Punishment*, pp. 46–53.

58 Markel makes a similar point in his chapter in this volume.

59 Ellis, "Critical Study Recent Work on Punishment."

60 Hampton, "Retributive Idea," p. 113.

61 For an example, see Morris, "Persons and Punishment."

62 Hegel, *Philosophy of Right*, §101.

63 Ibid., §99.

64 Nicholson, "Hegel on Crime," p. 113.

65 See the chapter by Markel in this volume for further discussion of the distinction between revenge and retribution.

66 Johnson, "Revisiting Kantian Retributivism"; see also the chapter by Holtman in this volume.

67 Kant, *Metaphysics of Morals*, p. 231 (Academy pagination).

68 Ibid., p. 313.

69 Ibid., p. 314.

70 Ibid., p. 230.

71 Ibid., p. 333.

72 Ibid., p. 335.

73 Ibid., p. 331.

74 I am indebted to Paul Redding, Simon Lumsden, and Steven Tudor for their invaluable feedback on earlier drafts of this chapter.

Bibliography

Anderson, Jami L. "Annulment Retributivism: A Hegelian Theory of Punishment." *Legal Theory* 5 (1999): 363–88.

Benn, Stanley I. "An Approach to the Problems of Punishment." In *Punishment: Selected Readings*, edited by Joel Feinberg and Hyman Gross, 63–73. Encino, California: Dickenson Publishing, 1975.

Brooks, Thom. "Hegel's Ambiguous Contribution to Legal Theory." *Res Publica* 11 (2005): 85–94.

Byrd, Sharon. "Kant's Theory of Punishment: Deterrence in Its Threat, Retribution in Its Execution." *Law and Philosophy* 8 (1989): 151–200.

Cooper, David E. "Hegel's Theory of Punishment." In *Hegel's Political Philosophy*, edited by Z. A. Pelczynski, 151–67. Cambridge: Cambridge University Press, 1971.

Dolinko, David. "Some Thoughts About Retributivism." *Ethics* 101 (1991): 537–59.

Doyle, James. "Justice and Legal Punishment." *Philosophy* 42 (1967): 53–67.

Dubber, Markus Dirk. "Rediscovering Hegel's Theory of Crime and Punishment." *Michigan Law Review* 92 (1994): 1577–621.

Dyde, S.W. "Hegel's Conception of Crime and Punishment." *The Philosophical Review* 7 (1898): 62–71.

Ellis, Anthony. "Critical Study Recent Work on Punishment." *The Philosophical Quarterly* 45 (1995): 225–33.

Ezorsky, Gertrude. "The Ethics of Punishment." In *Philosophical Perspectives on Punishment*, edited by Gertrude Ezorsky. Albany: University of New York Press, 1972.

Griseri, Paul. "Punishment and Reparation." *The Philosophical Quarterly* 35 (1985): 394–413.

Hampton, Jean. "The Retributive Idea." In *Forgiveness and Mercy*, by Jeffrie G. Murphy and Jean Hampton, 111–61. Cambridge: Cambridge University Press, 1988.

Hart, H. L. A. "Prolegomenon to the Principles of Punishment." In *Punishment and Responsibility*, 1–27. Oxford: Clarendon Press, 1968.

Hawkins, D. J. B. "Retribution." In *Theories of Punishment*, edited by Stanley E. Grupp, 13–18. Bloomington: Indiana University Press, 1971.

Hegel, G. W. F. *Elements of the Philosophy of Right*. Translated by H. B. Nisbet. Edited by Allen W. Wood. Cambridge: Cambridge University Press, 1991.

Hegel, G. W. F. *The Encyclopaedia Logic*. Translated by W. A. Suchting, T. F. Geraets, and H. S. Harris. Indianapolis: Hackett Publishing Company, Inc., 1991.

Hegel, G. W. F. *Phenomenology of Spirit*. Translated by A. V. Miller. Oxford: Oxford University Press, 1977.

Hegel, G. W. F. *Science of Logic*. Translated by A. V. Miller. New York: Humanities Press International, Inc., 1969.

Hinchman, Lewis P. "Hegel's Theory of Crime and Punishment." *The Review of Politics* 44 (1982): 523–45.

Honderich, Ted. *Punishment: The Supposed Justifications*. Oxford: Polity Press, 1989.

Johnson, Jane. "Revisiting Kantian Retributivism to Construct a Justification of Punishment." *Criminal Law and Philosophy* 2 (2008): 291–307.

Kant, Immanuel. *The Metaphysics of Morals*. In *The Cambridge Edition of the Works of Immanuel Kant Practical Philosophy*. Edited by Mary J. Gregor, 354–603. Cambridge: Cambridge University Press, 1999.

Knowles, Dudley. "Hegel on the Justification of Punishment." In *Beyond Liberalism and Communitarianism Studies in Hegel's Philosophy of Right*, edited by Robert R. Williams, 125–45. Albany: State University of New York Press, 2001.

Lacey, Nicola. *State Punishment*. London: Routledge, 1988.

Lucy, William N. R. "The Common Law According to Hegel." *Oxford Journal of Legal Studies* 17 (1997): 685–703.

McCraken, Chad. "Hegel and the Autonomy of Contract Law." *Texas Law Review* 77 (1999): 719–51.

McTaggart, J. Ellis. "Hegel's Theory of Punishment." *International Journal of Ethics* 6 (1896): 479–502.

Mitias, Michael H. *Moral Foundations of the State in Hegel's Philosophy of Right: Anatomy of an Argument*. Amsterdam: Elementa, 1984.

Morris, Herbert. "Persons and Punishment." In *Punishment: Selected Readings*, edited by Joel Feinberg and Hyman Gross, 74–87. Encino, CA: Dickenson Publishing, 1975.

Nicholson, Peter P. "Hegel on Crime." *History of Political Thought* 3 (1982): 103–21.

Pincoffs, Edmund L. *Philosophy of Law: A Brief Introduction*. Belmont, CA: Wadsworth Publishing Company, 1991.

Potter, Nelson Thomas, Jr. "The Principle of Punishment Is a Categorical Imperative." In *Autonomy and Community*, edited by Jane E. Kneller, 169–90. Albany: SUNY Press, 1998.

Redding, Paul. *Hegel's Hermeneutics*. Ithaca: Cornell University Press, 1996.

Reyburn, Hugh A. *The Ethical Theory of Hegel*. Oxford: Clarendon Press, 1921.

Scheid, Don E. "Kant's Retributivism." *Ethics* 93 (1983): 262–82.

Steinberger, Peter J. "Hegel on Crime and Punishment." *American Political Science Review* 77 (1983): 858–70.

Tunick, Mark. *Hegel's Political Philosophy Interpreting the Practice of Legal Punishment*. Princeton: Princeton University Press, 1992.

Tunick, Mark. "Is Kant a Retributivist?" *History of Political Thought* 17 (1996): 60–78.

Williams, Robert R. *Hegel's Ethics of Recognition*. Berkeley: University of California Press, 1997.

Wood, Allen W. *Hegel's Ethical Thought*. Cambridge: Cambridge University Press, 1990.5

Retributivism and Policy

9

ENTRAPMENT AND RETRIBUTIVE THEORY

Mark Tunick

1. Introduction: Problems of Entrapment

IN DECIDING WHETHER to punish someone who violates the law, retributivists consider not whether punishment would deter or prevent future crime, but whether the lawbreaker deserves punishment.[1] It has been said that a retributivist cannot support an entrapment defense. In the criminal law, a defense is a reason why you should not be punished even though you did break the law; examples include insanity, infancy, duress, mistake, intoxication, provocation, and hypnosis. With entrapment, the defense is that one was lured by the police, who manufactured the crime. There are at least two reasons why a retributivist might oppose an entrapment defense. First, those who were enticed to crime by the police still broke the law and, according to at least J.D. Mabbott's version of retributive theory, this alone justifies their punishment. For Mabbott, there is no essential connection between punishment and moral wrong.[2] Even if we thought someone who was lured to crime did not act badly precisely because they were tempted, in Mabbott's view we do not punish criminals because they acted badly or are wicked; good persons who break the law only because they were enticed by police still broke the law; and for that reason alone, they deserve punishment. But other retributivists who, breaking with Mabbott, do see punishment as the expression or communication of blame for acting badly, also have reasons to oppose an entrapment defense.[3] Even they, the argument goes, must insist on punishing entrapped criminals because these lawbreakers still are blameworthy, or culpable, and deserve punishment.[4]

I shall show how a retributivist might support an entrapment defense; I begin by introducing some problems raised by entrapment. Suppose you are driving at the speed limit when a car begins to tailgate you. Intimidated and unable to change lanes, you speed up. To your surprise, a siren sounds from the car, which turns out to be an unmarked police cruiser, and the officer tickets you for speeding. You did break the law but only because the officer tailgated you. Should you be punished? The intuition that you should not lies at the root of the entrapment defense. Some would explain this intuition by arguing that we do not want the state to punish "false criminals," or ordinarily law-abiding people who commit crime only because they were enticed or lured by police, whereas we do want the state to punish "true criminals," those who would have committed the crime without the police inducement.[5] In their view, false criminals can claim entrapment and be acquitted.

But why should being enticed by the police constitute a defense, when being lured by a private individual typically does not? When, in Billy Wilder's 1944 film version of James M. Cain's story "Double Indemnity," Walter Neff was lured by the sexy blonde Phyllis Dietrichson to kill her husband in order to cash in on a life insurance policy, he could not claim as a defense that he was tempted. When private citizen Cain offers you $100,000 to burn down an abandoned building, and that is too good an offer for you to refuse, you cannot claim as a defense that you were tempted. So why should it matter if Cain or Ms. Dietrichson was an undercover agent?

In addition to this problem of private entrapment, those defending an entrapment defense face what I call the general problem of entrapment: when should the defense be granted? There are a number of cases where police enticement seems clearly warranted and is no reason to acquit the defendant: a female undercover agent runs in a park to lure a serial rapist who targets women there, or walks around with a wad of money visible from her pocket in a neighborhood in which pickpockets have struck numerous times,[6] or offers a bribe to a congressman.[7] In the first two cases, defendants who attack the decoy are ready and waiting to commit a crime, and it is just their bad luck that their target is an undercover agent—the police catch true criminals. In the latter case, there is a strong public interest in preventing corruption.[8]

But there are also problematic cases of police enticement where it seems wrong to punish the lawbreaker. One sort of example is entrapment by estoppel, which occurs when the police encourage someone to commit a crime by convincing them that the act is legal though it is not.[9] It is also problematic for police to lure a defendant with romantic overtures.[10] Or suppose that an undercover agent arranges to buy cocaine from you; before accepting the cocaine, the agent demands that you cook it to make crack. His purpose is to enhance your sentence, the punishment for selling crack being ten times greater than the punishment for selling cocaine in powder form. While you should be punished for supplying powder cocaine, imposing the additional punishment for supplying crack seems troubling precisely because the state created that aspect of the crime.[11]

There are still other cases that are less clear cut. Consider two examples:

(1) The shopping mall case: an undercover agent offers to sell drugs to people he randomly encounters in a shopping mall. Most people rebuke him, but one person accepts and is arrested.[12]

(2) The auto theft case: police leave an unlocked car in a public parking lot with its keys in the ignition and lie in wait where they cannot be seen. They arrest a man who tries to steal the car.[13]

In the shopping mall case, the defendant breaks the law without having faced an inducement so great that it would entice a normally law-abiding person—he may be a true criminal. But the case is troubling because the defendant was not looking to commit a crime; he was approached by the police, who had no reason to think him likely to buy drugs. They created the crime. In the auto theft case, the police create the crime by presenting a temptation one does not usually encounter; yet one hesitates to excuse the defendant because most law-abiding people would resist this temptation.

There are two approaches commonly taken to the general problem of entrapment. One approach is motivated by a fear of oppressive agent provocateurs who create mistrust or are abusive, perhaps by targeting people they dislike, such as political enemies, or by pressuring someone whose cooperation they need.[14] Suppose you are law abiding, but your friend is a wanted criminal. By entrapping and then threatening to prosecute you unless you assist them, police might get you to agree to wear a wire and tape your friend incriminating himself. On this approach, called the "objective test," the reason to not punish enticed defendants has nothing to do with their subjective state of mind, culpability, or blameworthiness—it is to uphold the integrity of the judicial system and to deter police misconduct. Whether the defense should be available depends not on characteristics of the defendant or his actions but on the character of the police conduct: if the police act outrageously, or use measures likely to lure an average law-abiding citizen, the defendant should be acquitted.[15]

The other approach relies on the intuition that false criminals should not be punished. It looks at whether the targets of police enticement were predisposed to commit the crime, or ready and willing, so that it is likely they would have committed the crime even absent their encounter with undercover agents. Here a "subjective test" is invoked: what matters is not what measures the police took but how predisposed was the defendant to commit the crime.[16] The entrapment defense is available to those not predisposed. Some have suggested an additional consideration: whether the defendant was in the position to commit the crime. Those who are ready and willing to commit the crime but not able, because they lack the resources or know-how, might not be a real threat, which might reduce the need to punish them.[17]

For most retributivists, we punish criminals because they are culpable, and as the objective test appears to ignore culpability, retributivists are unlikely to want to adopt it.[18]

This is not to say that retributivists would object to measures that limit police misconduct and preserve the integrity of the judicial system. A retributivist might oppose an entrapment defense if he thought police enticement does not exculpate the lawbreaker but defend a bar to trial on the ground that because of its enticement, the state undermines its standing to try the defendant.[19] But in that case, the retributivist who does not think that being caught as the result of improper police methods absolves one from blame would be employing a principle that may be at odds with the principle that deserving criminals should get their just deserts.

The subjective test, in contrast, may seem ideal for most retributivists: lawbreakers who are enticed but not predisposed are granted a defense because their lack of predisposition means they are not culpable. (As we shall see, the subjective test can also be given a utilitarian rationale.) One reason a retributivist might nevertheless object to a subjective test is that to absolve the non-predisposed who are enticed to crime by government, while punishing those who are predisposed, is wrongly to assert that a person's culpability hinges on his predisposition, and wrongly to punish someone not for their present conduct but for their character or past actions—I shall call this the "act-requirement concern."[20] The act-requirement concern is that punishing someone because he is predisposed is to punish him not for an act that took place but for a hypothetical act we think he is likely to commit. Doing so violates the principle that punishment must be for a wrong actually committed.[21] To support an entrapment defense, a retributivist averse to an objective test and wanting to avoid the act-requirement concern may need to show that regardless of one's past actions, the fact that one was lured to crime by the police (and not by a private party) makes one less culpable.

Before proceeding, I must comment on my use of "culpable." Culpability is often used in a narrow sense to refer solely to a subjective or agent-relative factor: a person's state of mind. For example, I am culpable if I purposely or knowingly cause wrongful harm, and I am less culpable if I was merely reckless or negligent, regardless of whether my act actually caused harm. I shall use culpable in its broad sense: deserving punishment or being worthy of blame.[22] One may be culpable in the broad sense merely if one is culpable in the narrow sense, but I shall consider an alternative view, that whether one is culpable in the broad sense depends on at least one nonsubjective factor: whether one risked harm. Those who would commit a crime with purpose or knowledge are not less culpable in the narrow sense merely if they are not in the position to commit the crime for lack of ability or resources. The view I shall consider is that they are less culpable in the broad sense: they are less deserving of punishment because they will not risk harm.

2. Theorizing About Entrapment

Before considering whether being enticed by the police makes one less culpable for one's crime, I want to acknowledge the approach to entrapment taken by utilitarians, for whom the issue of culpability in the broad sense is not central. (Culpability in the narrow sense is relevant for utilitarians because whether a defendant acted with purpose, knowledge, recklessness, or negligence will bear on the defendant's need to be deterred or incapacitated.) The utilitarian asks whether punishing someone who the police entice will yield benefits that exceed the costs of punishing them. Possible benefits include deterring the criminal from committing crimes in the future (individual or specific deterrence), deterring others from committing similar crimes (general deterrence), incapacitating people who pose a threat to society, or reforming them.[23] Punishing a person who the police entice would likely promote general deterrence, but it would yield individual deterrence, incapacitation, and reform benefits only if the police nab true criminals.

One problem for the utilitarian is determining whether someone is a true criminal; to decide that, one might use a subjective test and look at predisposition, including prior arrests or convictions, or other evidence of the person's tendencies. The utilitarian's rationale for using a subjective test would differ from that of a retributivist: for the utilitarian, predisposition is a signal not of culpability but of the need for deterrence, incapacitation, or reform. Alternatively, a utilitarian might use an objective test and look at whether the police offered a below-market price inducement: for example, if an undercover agent offered high-grade marijuana at $1/gram when the going rate is $20/gram, this would be entrapment, regardless of the buyer's predisposition. The utilitarian's rationale, here, would be to promote not judicial integrity but economic efficiency: offering large inducements to people who normally obey the law (false criminals) wastes resources.[24]

In contrast, for retributivists, generally, we punish not primarily to promote economic efficiency, deter, or incapacitate, but to express blame or vindicate the law. They insist we focus on whether the criminal is culpable and deserves punishment. This is true even for Mabbott, who argues that we punish a person solely because he broke the law but adds that to be deemed a law violator, one must be responsible and complicit.[25] Does your being enticed by the police to commit a crime make you less culpable for your crime?[26] I shall consider a few reasons for thinking you may be less culpable. First, you are less culpable insofar as you do not cause harm. There are two senses in which you may not cause harm: the crime you commit is artificial and will result in no harm; and not you but the police cause the crime. A further reason I shall consider is that defendants who were enticed by the police are less culpable insofar as their action was not fully voluntary, the police having in effect coerced them.

A. THE RISK OF HARM REQUIREMENT

One reason a retributivist might regard those who are entrapped as not culpable is that their actions will not result in harm.[27] According to what I shall call the "risk of harm" requirement for culpability, if one does something that will produce no harm, one is not legally blameworthy.[28] When the police encourage a person to break the law as part of a sting or decoy operation, then unless something goes terribly wrong, there is no actual victim and no harm caused. When an undercover agent lures a rapist or mugger, an arrest is made before anyone is hurt; if Ms. Dietrichson were an undercover agent, surely Walter Neff would not have completed a murder; and the politician who accepts a bribe in a sting operation is brought in before he or she can dispense illicit favors, although in this case something bad does transpire (he betrays the public's trust). There are exceptions, however, in which police inducements do result in harm. Suppose the police set up a false fencing operation and entice a person to bring in stolen goods with the promise of huge cash payouts. Here, harm is caused when the defendant steals, so when applying the risk of harm requirement, we would grant an entrapment defense for the crime of attempting to fence stolen goods, but not for the theft, because that act risked actual harm.[29] To hold that defendants are culpable only if they create a risk of harm is, of course, not to require that a person actually cause harm before he can be punished. Criminals who risk harm but are caught before harm results satisfy the risk of harm requirement and may be punished.

Underlying the risk of harm requirement is the idea that we have criminal laws not to test people's character but to avoid harmful conduct.[30] This idea is pivotal to Mabbott's retributivism,[31] and while it appeals to what appears to be a utilitarian framework—that we punish ultimately to avoid future disutility—the idea is compatible with the views of many other retributivists. We should not be confused by the thought that a retributivist appeals to consequences. Many theories that most people would recognize as retributive assume that we legally punish because doing so has desirable consequences, such as reducing harm, expressing disapproval, or promoting human freedom.[32] For example, in Hegel's view, we punish to vindicate or restore right because only in a society that recognizes right are we free.[33] Nor should we assume that retributivists must adopt the view that the severity of legal punishment depends on the depravity of the act and must match the criminal's moral wickedness.[34] They can regard the amount of punishment we inflict in particular cases as a function of other factors, including whether the punishment would deter or incapacitate.[35] Retributivists who appeal to such consequences do not adopt a framework according to which decisions about whether or how to punish are guided solely by the principle of utility, and while I cannot expand on the point here, their theories do not collapse into utilitarianism.[36] We should not assume that retributivists must want to test people's virtue so as to increase the amount of virtue in the world.

The position that we allow an entrapment defense where the lawbreaker will cause no harm solves the problem of private entrapment.[37] In almost all cases where a defendant was induced by a private party and not the government, there is a danger of harm being caused. One exception would be cases of private entrapment in which a private party resembles a state actor in seeking to lure targets in order to turn them over to the police. We might think that in such cases an entrapment defense should be available precisely because there was a controlled environment in which no harm will be caused.

Such were the circumstances in *Topolewski v. State* (1906). Officials of a private meat-packing company, made aware that the defendant hatched a plan to steal from the company, secretly encouraged and were an active participant in the plan, making sure that the company's property was placed on a loading platform so it could be easily taken and ordering its workers not to interfere, with the purpose of ensnaring the defendant. The Supreme Court of Wisconsin reversed the conviction on the ground that the company aided and encouraged the crime, which lacked the essential element of nonconsent. That the defendant came up with the idea of the crime was "not controlling"—what did control was that the company "in practical effect delivered [the property] to the would-be thief."[38] As with government entrapment cases, there was little chance the defendant would cause actual harm, which is not usually the case when someone is enticed to crime by a private party.[39] Absence of nonconsent to the crime is arguably also a feature of most government entrapment cases involving decoys, who invite a crime and hope to become a potential victim. It is for other reasons, which I discuss later, that use of decoys usually will not constitute entrapment.

The argument that, to be culpable, your actions must risk harm may support a positional defense. Unusual circumstances aside, those who are not in the position to commit a crime and can do so only with the assistance of undercover agents will never cause the harm associated with that crime because the only time they will commit the crime, the police will intervene before harm results. When a positional defense is supported, it is usually for utilitarian reasons: society should not waste its resources by punishing someone who lacks the ability to commit a crime.[40] But if one is culpable only if one risks harm, a retributivist could also support this defense.

One objection to a positional defense is that punishment will be meted out unequally for reasons that may seem arbitrary. Suppose a defendant living in rural Nebraska in the 1980s is enticed by undercover agents to purchase child pornography. McAdams supports an entrapment defense in this situation, on the assumption that anyone living in rural Nebraska in the pre-Internet age would not be in the position to commit the crime on his own.[41] It might seem unfair that because someone lives in a city or has access to the Internet, he would be punished for responding to police inducements to purchase child pornography while a rural dweller without Internet access who responds to the same inducements is not punished, though they break the same law. However, if it were impossible to commit a crime because you live in a certain environment, that fact would not be an arbitrary basis for determining if you deserve punishment. But I expect that a greater impediment to this defense will be establishing that one could not have committed the crime without government assistance. In the example, if the government reached the defendant through the mail, presumably private pornography suppliers could as well. This impediment becomes greater as geographical location becomes less important to one's ability to commit crimes.

Entrapped criminals generally do not create a risk of harm because the police have constructed an artificial crime in a controlled environment and lie in wait. But what if the police entice the defendant into committing a crime, planning to intervene, but harm does result because the police fail to stop the crime due to unforeseen circumstances or ineptitude? It seems reasonable to hold defendants responsible for harm they cause that is not directly attributable to the police having induced the crime. For example, even if the police induce a target to provide insider trading information, not the police but the target would be responsible for assaulting a business executive to get that information. But if the only harm is the harm of the specific act the police induced and not secondary acts the police did not proximately cause, entrapped defendants may not be culpable even though their act does result in harm, because the risk of their act causing harm was very small; no harm would have been risked had things gone as the police planned. But a better explanation for their lack of culpability in this case may be that the police and not the defendant cause the harm (a position I discuss below).

It may seem puzzling to rest the defendant's culpability on the conduct of the police and not on the defendant's mental state, but recall that I am invoking a broad and not narrow sense of culpability. The defendant thought they were doing something that risked harm, but the risk of harm requirement is an objective, not subjective, standard, appealing to whether harm in fact was risked. We should not confuse the adoption of an objective risk of harm requirement with acceptance of the objective test of entrapment, according to which a defendant is entrapped if the police used inducements likely to lead the average or normally law-abiding person to commit crime.[42] The police may use inducements that would not lure the average person, yet still lure a defendant into a situation in which no harm is risked; on the objective test, this would not be entrapment, but using the risk of harm requirement, it would be.

Adopting the "risk of harm" requirement, I am culpable even if my act results in no harm, so long as my act risked harm. This position must be distinguished from the position that one should be punished for doing an act that causes no harm if the act is of the sort that tends to cause harm. We sometimes punish anticipatory offenses, such as driving under the influence of alcohol, even though often one commits the offense without harm resulting.[43] McAdams notes that we may punish "proxy offenses" where an instance of the offense causes no harm, so long as there is a high enough correlation between committing that offense and conduct that does cause harm.[44] Bentham argues that we should punish those who fail to pay their taxes even if their failure causes no detriment, because the tendency of not paying taxes, if done by many people, would be detrimental.[45]

But in adopting the "risk of harm" requirement, one takes a different position. We punish persons who attempt to attack decoy agents not because their sort of act tends to result in harm—that might be true of any entrapped person's act. Rather, we punish them because they would have caused harm had the police not been lying in wait. We can assume they would have caused harm so long as the decoy was representative of actual, nonpolice targets in the area. If this condition is met, then the reason decoy operations do not result in harm is not that police created an artificial crime in a controlled situation, but that the police deployed surveillance in a way calculated to increase the likelihood of catching a true criminal. Assuming the above condition is met, decoy cases can be viewed as instances of effective surveillance. In contrast, where there is entrapment, the defendant creates no risk of harm.

1. Objection 1: Punishment and Moral Luck

One objection to the position that an entrapped person has a defense because he creates no risk of harm is that moral responsibility should not be contingent on actual harm caused. Whether one's actions result in harm can often be a matter of luck and, the objection goes, we cannot assign or withhold moral blame for consequences that result from luck.[46] Those who attempt to rape an undercover decoy do not cause harm but only because they happen to be the victim of a decoy operation, so that police prevent them from causing harm. Assassins who miss their target out of luck do not cause the same amount of harm as assassins who succeed.[47] But, according to this objection, their luck in not producing harm is no good reason to reduce their punishment and regard them as less culpable; we blame someone for what lies within their will, and not for what they cannot control.

Joel Feinberg presents this objection when addressing how we should punish the inchoate crime of attempt. Feinberg argues that culpability is determined not by harm actually caused but by harm intended; what matters is whether an act was done purposely, knowingly, recklessly, negligently, out of duress, mistakenly, with provocation, or with good intent.[48] Those who intend to cause harm and fail, he argues, should still feel guilty.[49] While it is fortunate that they harmed no one, they are still morally at fault, and their luck in not causing harm should not be a ground for reducing their punishment. Feinberg would reform the criminal law so that completed crimes and failed attempts are punished the same.[50] He sees an incoherence in basing punishment on moral blame, but then allowing luck, or the amount of harm caused, to determine blameworthiness. He recognizes that people do feel more anger at someone who causes actual harm but argues that such natural feelings are "unsavory emotions" and do not constitute a rational argument for punishing failed attempters less.[51] You are not a better person for not causing harm due to luck.[52]

On Feinberg's view, the assassin who fails because of luck, as when a fly lands on his face and causes him to miss his target, deserves the same punishment as the assassin who succeeds, because luck should not determine one's moral responsibility.[53] As a practical matter, it may be difficult to determine when failure is due to luck and when it is due to contingencies that might have been controlled by someone more skilled, more determined, or better positioned to succeed. A skilled assassin will anticipate more contingencies that could lead to failure, such as flies landing on one's face, and is therefore more deserving of punishment than a bungling assassin. A utilitarian would say such a person should receive more punishment because, being more likely than the inept assassin to cause future harm, they are in greater need of deterrence or incapacitation.

A retributivist might defend more punishment for the skilled assassin on one of two views. Mabbott might say that they deserve more punishment only if the law against successful attempts proscribes harsher punishment than the law against failed attempts, which the law might do for utilitarian reasons. For other retributivists, skilled assassins might deserve more punishment because they are more blameworthy: either because the effort it takes to become a skilled assassin belies a more wicked character, or because knowingly using one's skills for wrongful ends merits more blame the greater one's skills, even if the skills were originally obtained for laudable purposes, in that one's instant act is more likely to risk greater harm. Note that this view and the view Mabbott might adopt both differ from the utilitarian argument that we punish more severely those who are more adept at causing future harm in order to yield greater specific deterrence or incapacitation benefits.

But suppose we know that the reason I caused less or no harm really is luck and has nothing to do with my skill, disposition, or position. Feinberg's view is that I deserve as much legal punishment as the person who succeeds in causing harm: I am as morally blameworthy, and I am not a better person for being lucky. That position has been challenged by others,[54] but even if he were correct about that moral judgment, a retributivist need not hold that ascription of legal responsibility involves the same considerations as ascription of moral responsibility.[55] Ascriptions of responsibility may differ in legal as opposed to nonlegal contexts. If in ascribing legal responsibility, our goal is to reduce harm rather than test people's virtue, we might think the target of a police inducement to crime lacks legal culpability or blameworthiness for breaking the law since their act does not in fact risk harm, even though they intended to risk harm and are therefore morally culpable in the narrow sense of culpability.[56]

One can advocate an entrapment defense for those who do not risk harm without holding that failed attempters should get less punishment than successful ones. The failed attempter intends to cause harm and risks harm but does not cause harm; the entrapped person intends to cause harm but does not in fact risk or cause harm. Both are lucky, but only the entrapped person fails to meet the risk of harm requirement for culpability. If a person induced to crime by the police was predisposed to commit the crime and would have risked harm had the police not intervened, then he may be no less morally (as opposed to legally) responsible merely because he was induced by the police. The retributivist who argues that an entrapped defendant is less responsible morally (and not merely legally) would have to establish this either by pointing to the defendant's predisposition (which raises the act-requirement concern), or by showing that the police inducement amounted to coercion and that one is less morally deserving of blame for acts one was coerced to perform.

2. Objection 2: Victimless Crimes

A further objection to the "risk of harm" requirement for culpability is that some lawbreakers cause or risk no harm to any victim but nevertheless commit what is regarded as a crime deserving of punishment; examples sometimes given of such victimless crimes include adultery, gambling, prostitution, or marijuana use.[57] If one is not culpable or deserving of punishment unless one risks harm, then on a retributive theory we might not be permitted to punish anyone who commits victimless crimes. One response to this objection is to welcome it and reply that indeed the state should prohibit only actions that cause harm.[58] While I am now sympathetic to that position, it is a controversial one that not all retributivists may endorse.[59] But another response is available. We might reconceptualize the "risk of harm" requirement to be a "risk of wrong" requirement, where wrongs are whatever actions the law prohibits regardless of whether the actions risk harm. If the defendant's action risks no wrong because the police will intervene prior to the wrong transpiring, an entrapment defense may be available. The underlying rationale for the "risk of wrong" requirement is similar: the point of legal punishment is to reduce harm or wrongs, not to test people's virtue. But this is not a satisfying response if we regard as a wrong merely possessing an intent to commit a wrong.

A variation of this objection is that one is culpable merely for flouting the law, regardless of the law's content; law in general needs vindication regardless of whether harm was caused or risked by a particular act of lawbreaking. (Mabbott, for example, seems to take that position.) But the objection has force only if we agree that people should be punished merely for breaking the law whether or not there is good reason for the law. I disagree with that assumption, and I am not alone in doing so.[60] But even Mabbott might agree that the state should not test people's willingness to obey the law merely for the sake of increasing the amount of virtue or law abidingness in the world.

B. CAUSATION

So far I have considered just one part of the argument that entrapped persons are not culpable because they do not cause harm: when someone is entrapped, actual harm will not result since the crime is artificial, with no nonconsenting victim. But there is another sense in which they may be said not to cause harm: even if harm were to result, we might think the harm was caused not by them, but by the police who enticed them.

Who causes the crime when police entice the defendant? The crime would not occur if the defendant were not predisposed, unless the police compelled or forced the defendant, but the instant crime would also not occur if there were no police enticement. As Feinberg argues, any ascription of responsibility for a complex event that would not occur but for multiple antecedent causes requires us to decide upon the cause most relevant for our purposes.[61] Not all causes are morally relevant. Oxygen is in a sense the cause of a house fire because it is a necessary condition for the fire; but the more relevant cause is what departs from the normal conditions (such as lighting a gasoline-saturated rag in the basement).[62] If a person's predisposition to crime is strong enough, he has the ability to commit it, and the opportunity to do so normally presents itself to him, then the police enticing that person to commit a crime may not be a departure from the normal conditions.

Predispositions need to be triggered. If my predisposition is easily triggered by common situations, then when the police trigger it they may not cause the crime, provided that my disposition and low threshold are not themselves a result of police manipulation. But if my predisposition is triggered only in rare cases, then when the police trigger it they may well cause the crime and I may not be culpable.[63] Feinberg notes that few of us will commit murder. Yet perhaps all of us are weakly predisposed to murder; we can imagine circumstances when someone causes us such tremendous aggravation and literally ruins our life that we might be driven to kill that person.[64] But the circumstances that would trigger that disposition in most of us are quite rare. For true criminals, they are not that rare. Culpability depends, then, both on one's predisposition and on whether the opportunity presented by the police mimicked opportunities that realistically present themselves to the defendant.

Predisposition, in this view, is relevant to culpability because it may indicate that police enticement was not the departure from normal circumstances that caused the crime, in which case there is no entrapment defense.[65] But there are cases in which someone is predisposed to crime and has a weak trigger but is not culpable. For example, suppose Sherman is undergoing treatment for his drug addiction. Until he successfully completes his treatment, he has a weak trigger when it comes to committing a drug offense. When undercover agents lure him with drugs while he is undergoing treatment, knowing he has a weak trigger, one wants to say they cause the crime and that Sherman should be granted an entrapment defense.[66] It's wrong of police to go after those trying to reform themselves. Someone might have firmly fixed habits of mind that dispose one to crime, yet still the police could be the morally relevant cause if they capitalize on those firmly fixed habits.[67]

The retributivist, in deciding whether to punish, is guided not by "considerations of mere convenience" but by "the essential demands of justice."[68] A person enticed by police may not deserve punishment (is not culpable) insofar as (1) they do not risk harm, or (2) it is not they but the police who cause the crime. Whether the latter is the case depends on how strongly predisposed they were, on how common the triggering situation is, and on whether the police inappropriately capitalized on their target's weakness—although I have not addressed how we are to distinguish appropriate and inappropriate targetings of those with character failings. The argument that an entrapped defendant is not culpable because he did not cause the crime, insofar as it appeals to the character or past actions of the defendant, does not avoid the "act requirement concern"; one fully avoids this concern only when resting the argument that the defendant is not culpable on the claim that no actual harm is risked, or on the next argument I discuss: that the defendant did not act voluntarily.

C. COERCION

The other argument that those who are enticed to crime by the police are not culpable is that they do not voluntarily commit the crime: there is a sense in which they are coerced.

In developing this argument, I draw on Robert Nozick's essay "Coercion." Nozick wants to make sense of the claim that one acts involuntarily when responding to a threat but voluntarily when responding to an offer, in light of some apparently contradictory evidence: (1) that one can choose to do what there is a threat against his doing, just as one can choose to do what there is an offer for him not to do; and (2) sometimes an offer is so tempting that a person cannot reasonably be expected not to go along with it.[69] In saving the distinction between offer and threat, Nozick has us focus on a rational man's preferences both before and after the offer or threat.

Nozick says the rational man will normally welcome credible offers, which he can always decline without being worse off than had the offer not been made (leaving aside the costs of decision making) and will not normally welcome credible threats.[70] He then distinguishes the "pre-situation," the situation prior to the offer or threat, from the situation after a threat or offer is made. The rational man is normally willing to go from the pre-offer to the offer situation and when put in the offer situation, does not normally prefer to be back in the pre-offer situation. But the rational man is normally unwilling to go from the pre-threat to the threat situation and when placed in the threat situation, would normally prefer being back in the pre-threat situation.[71] Nozick then formulates the following principle:

> If the alternatives among which Q must choose are intentionally changed by P, and P made this change in order to get Q to do A, and before the change Q would not have chosen. . . to have the change made. . . and before the change was made Q wouldn't have chosen to do A, and after the change is made Q does A, then Q's choice to do A is not fully his own.[72]

His point is that "[w]e must look also at the (hypothetical) choice of getting (and willingness to get) into the threat and offer situations themselves."[73]

Think of the offer as police enticement to commit a crime, and suppose Q is rational and predisposed and would commit a crime had a nonstate actor made the offer. Does Q prefer to be in the pre- or post-offer situation? If A in Nozick's formulation above is to "commit a crime in which punishment is certain," then, of course, Q would not have chosen to do A. Normally when someone gives you the chance to commit a crime, you are aware there is a potential punishment and will assess the likelihood it would be imposed. But police involvement changes things: had the police used no deception, Q would have known that punishment was certain and assuming the sanction was greater than any benefits of the crime that he would be able to keep, Q would refuse the offer. But with the deception, the offer situation seems preferable to Q because he mistakenly underestimates the probability of getting caught—he does not know it is actually one. If Q knew the actual situation after the offer, he would rather go back to the pre-offer situation. Because of the deception, we might regard the offer as coercive.

When the police entice you, their offer pretends to increase your choices, but unlike the private tempter's, it does not, because punishment is inevitable.[74] Had I not been deceived about the probability of capture, I would prefer the situation before the offer was made to the situation after the offer was made. This makes the choice coercive and, because culpability should be for freely chosen acts, casts doubt on the defendant's culpability. The problem of private entrapment is solved insofar as accepting a private inducement to crime is voluntary, but accepting a police inducement is not.

Because of the deception it involves, entrapment is also unfair. The undercover agents present me with a choice—commit the crime or do not. But it is not a fair choice because they fail to tell me the probability of being caught is one. Being entrapped is not a fair gamble, since there is no chance of keeping the gains—the game is rigged. Larry Alexander argues that using a doomsday machine that would unfailingly exterminate people even for minor offenses such as trespassing is not unfair if there is prior notice, and the machine reacts only to wrongful acts. He argues that "most people would deny a duty to compensate for all injuries stemming from risks undertaken in ignorance of the true odds, especially if it were wrong to undertake the risk in the first place."[75] Even if he is correct about what most people would think, I am not sure the doomsday machine provides a fair bargain. But entrapment is surely unfair because it provides no prior notice of certain punishment.

I think this better explains than some other accounts the sense in which entrapment is not fair. Dillof appeals to fairness to explain why we allow an entrapment defense by arguing that it is unfair to randomly select one particular predisposed target to pay for what everyone benefits from.[76] But that account of fairness does not explain why, if I was entrapped, I do not deserve punishment, since my culpability does not depend on whether the state unfairly singled me out. Linking the unfairness of the deceptive offer to its coerciveness better explains why an entrapped person is not culpable.[77] By articulating this account of why entrapment can be seen as unfair, I do not mean to say that its unfairness best explains why we have an entrapment defense. I am not sure we should compare the criminal justice system to a game of chance.

The argument that those who are enticed by the police do not freely choose to commit their crime does not apply to most decoy cases, where the police do not approach a target with an offer but rather lie in wait, and which are better characterized as instances of police surveillance. In decoy cases, defendants may well underestimate the probability of capture, but they were not lured by an offer, unless the police decoy was not representative of actual, nonpolice targets that the defendant could have encountered.

3. Applications and Conclusion

Entrapment is troubling because the police create an artificial situation in which they test a person's virtue. They use deception to create a crime that will risk no actual harm and lie in wait so that the target will be punished. We may want to entice people to teach them a lesson. The police, for example, may wish to reduce prostitution by having undercover agents solicit customers and issue warnings to any who respond favorably to the solicitation. But it is problematic to entice people in order to punish them, decoy targets being an exception.

Consider the two difficult cases that I introduced in the opening section. Some of the arguments I have presented imply that in the shopping mall case, the person who is approached by an undercover agent and buys drugs was entrapped and should not be punished. His action risks no harm; and the police deception means his choice is not fully voluntary. Whether the defendant or the police caused the crime will depend on whether the police inducement presented an unusual opportunity that is not normally encountered, as well as on the extent to which the defendant was primed to purchase illegal drugs. If people are not generally approached randomly at public places such as malls to buy drugs, or the drugs were offered at a very cheap price, the police may have caused the crime.

The auto theft case may be different in an essential way. It might be regarded as a decoy case, an instance not of police making an offer to the defendant but of effective surveillance, but only if the police have not created an unusual opportunity. If people would rarely encounter the temptation of an unlocked, unoccupied car with the keys in the ignition, then even though most people are weakly disposed to succumb to this temptation, and even if the defendant who does succumb is predisposed and highly primed, we still may conclude that the police caused the crime. The risk of harm requirement for culpability is not met, unless the decoy was representative of actual nonpolice targets in the area so that the case is one of surveillance.

I have not discussed what relative force each of the three arguments I discuss has in deciding whether a police target should be able to invoke the entrapment defense. Nor have I defended a number of assumptions underlying the retributive case for an entrapment defense—for example, I have not defended Nozick's account of coercion, or Feinberg's account of causation—nor have I justified the claim that in punishing, we should be guided by the goal of reducing harm. I also have not attempted to solve the general problem of entrapment. If we categorized the numerous examples of police inducements as either improper entrapment or legitimate crime-fighting strategies, no doubt we would find other factors that matter besides the ones I have considered. What I have tried to show is that a retributivist can defend an entrapment defense insofar as there is something less blameworthy about a defendant who does not risk harm and who is lured into a choice by deception.

I have appealed to a version of retribution that is consequentialist in seeing the point of our criminal justice system as preventing harm. I believe such a version of retribution is necessary because the view that the point of punishment is to make a criminal suffer just as he has caused others to suffer is deeply unsatisfying. Entrapping someone is testing his character rather than focusing on harm prevention, and moral virtue testing should not be the point of our criminal justice system, except perhaps in rare cases such as when we want to ensure that public officials do not betray our trust. The criticism that entrapping is testing moral virtue loses much of its force if the police have probable cause to suspect that their target is a dangerous criminal and have no practical alternative for establishing that.[78]

Notes

1 Compare to Moore, *Placing Blame*; Zaibert, *Punishment and Retribution*, p. 5. There are many variants of retributive theory (see Cottingham, "Varieties of Retribution"), and I shall refer to some versions which justify punishment by appealing to consequences such as reducing harm, although some insist that a theory appealing to such consequences is not retributive (compare to Moore, *Placing Blame*, p. 84).

2 Mabbott, "Punishment," pp. 158, 154–55.

3 Such retributive theories are presented by Feinberg, "Expressive Function of Punishment"; Hegel, *Philosophy of Right*; and Bennett, "Varieties of Retributive Experience."

4 Duff, "'I Might Be Guilty, But You Can't Try Me,'" p. 252; Dillof, "Unraveling Unlawful Entrapment," pp. 843–55; McAdams, "Political Economy of Entrapment," pp. 121–22.

5 McAdams, "Political Economy of Entrapment," pp. 126–29. McAdams notes that this distinction can be misleading since there is seldom a zero probability that one would be a true offender given a large enough inducement, 141; compare to Feinberg, *Problems at the Roots of Law*, p. 62.

6 Daniels v. State, 121 Nev 101 (2005).

7 U.S. v. Kelly, 748 F 2d 691 (1984).

8 Feinberg, *Problems*, pp. 60–2, 76.

9 Yaffe, "'Government Beguiled Me,'" p. 21.

10 Commonwealth v. Thompson, 335 Pa. Super. 332 (1984).

11 See U.S. v. Shepherd, 857 F Supp 105 (D.C. 1994), reversed in 102 F 3d 558 (1996).

12 State v. J.D.W., 910 P 2d 242 (Utah 1995) (not entrapment). Cf. State v. Kummer, 481 NW 2d 437 (N. Dak. 1992) (entrapment when police sell drugs to defendant); superseded by statute, see State v. Murchison, 541 NW 2d 435 (N. Dak. 1995).

13 People v. Watson, 22 Cal 4th 220 (2000).

14 On the potential for abuse, see Carlson, "Act Requirement and the Foundations of the Entrapment Defense," pp. 1101–14, 1120, and Hay, "Sting Operations, Undercover Agents, and Entrapment," pp. 398–39. On inviting mistrust, see Slobogin, "Deceit, Pretext, and Trickery," pp. 797–78, and Schoeman, "Privacy and Undercover Work," pp. 133, 137, 140.

15 Grossman v. Alaska, 457 P 2d 226, 229 (1969); People v. Barraza, 591 P 2d 947, 955 (1979).

16 Having to use a strong inducement might imply the target was weakly predisposed, see Feinberg, *Problems*, 60; compare to Seidman, "Supreme Court, Entrapment, and our Criminal Justice Dilemma," p. 120, and Carlson, "Act Requirement," pp. 1030–31.

17 See U.S. v. Hollingsworth, 27 F 3d 1196 (1994); discussed in McAdams, "Reforming Entrapment Doctrine."

18 Yaffe, "'Government Beguiled Me,'" p. 7.

19 Duff, "Estoppel and Other Bars to Trial," pp. 252–53.

20 Compare to Sherman v. U.S., 356 US 369 (1958), 382; Carlson, "Act Requirement," p. 1041.

21 Compare to Foucault, *Discipline and Punish*, pp. 17–18. Yaffe calls it "monstrous" to base punishment on a prediction of how one might act, but distinguishes doing so from basing punishment on one's past actions ("'Government Beguiled Me,'" pp. 14–5).

22 Compare to Moore, *Placing Blame*, p. 403.

23 Tunick, *Punishment*.

24 See McAdams, "Political Economy of Entrapment" and "Reforming Entrapment Defense Doctrine," pp. 1807–8; Allen et al, "Clarifying Entrapment"; and Judge Merrill's dissent in Greene v US, 454 F 2d 783 (1972).

25 Mabbott, "Punishment," p. 162; cf. p. 158.

26 Carlson argues the entrapped are less culpable as they do not cause harm ("Act Requirement," pp. 1060–65, 1097–101); I develop that idea further in the next section. Park and Yaffe each hold that at least the non-predisposed are less culpable when enticed by police. Park says this "seems obvious" but provides no argument, in "Entrapment Controversy," pp. 240–41. Yaffe does provide an argument: when the non-predisposed are enticed by police, they do not bring the punishment on themselves, because their decision to commit the crime arose "in the wrong way" ("'Government Beguiled Me,'" p. 24). "He brought it on himself" means "the reason-giving force of the act's illegality was included in the calculus of reasons that entered into [the defendant's] deliberation and he nonetheless chose an action that was illegal" (p. 26). Being predisposed implies one had prior deliberations about whether to commit the crime one later commits, and having faced pressure to grant the act's illegality reason-giving force, that one brought it on himself (p. 32). But, Yaffe argues, this does not happen when the government induces me (p. 33). Yaffe assumes the government tracks the target, increasing the temptation until the target succumbs (pp. 33–34)—the target was in effect coerced and therefore did not bring the punishment on himself. (Because private enticers do not track, he argues, this solves the problem of private entrapment; pp. 37–39.) But most entrapment does not involve such extensive tracking. If it did—if the police literally forced you to commit the crime—you would have a defense of coercion. I thank Katherine Mockler for bringing Yaffe's important article to my attention and sharing her insights about it with me.

27 Compare to Carlson, "Act Requirement," pp. 1060–61, 1067.

28 On Michael Davis's version of retributive theory (which draws on Morris, "Persons and Punishment"), we punish to respond to the criminal's taking an unfair advantage, which criminals might do even though they may cause no harm—see his "Harm and Retribution." But the entrapped person will not risk taking an unfair advantage, since he will be caught.

29 Carlon (in "Note: Entrapment, Punishment, and the Sadistic State," pp. 1123–24) favors an entrapment defense for the theft.

30 Compare to U.S. v. Hollingsworth, 27 F 3d 1196, 1203; and Judge Marston, concurring in Saunders v People, 38 Mich. 218 (1878): "Human nature is frail enough at best, and requires no encouragement in wrong-doing. If we cannot assist another and prevent him from violating the laws of the land, we at least should abstain from any active efforts in the way of leading him into temptation."

31 Mabbott says we choose to have laws, and which laws to have, by considering consequences ("Punishment," pp. 161, 163–65); but he denies that we choose to punish for utilitarian reasons (p. 161), or to express moral disapproval (see text accompanying note 2).

32 Feinberg, *Problems*, p. 69; Mabbott, "Punishment," pp. 163–64; Bennett, "Varieties of Retributive Experience"; Husak, "Why Punish the Deserving," p. 451; and on "mixed views"

drawing on both retributive and utilitarian principles, Kaplow and Shavell, *Fairness versus Welfare*, pp. 314–15 n. 46.

33 Tunick, *Hegel's Political Philosophy*; see the chapter by Johnson in this volume for a somewhat different take on Hegel's view of punishment.

34 Rawls refers to this view without himself endorsing it in "Two Concepts of Rules," p. 5.

35 Compare to Hegel, *Philosophy of Right*, Par. 99 Remark: "The various considerations [such as deterrence and correction] are of essential significance… primarily only in connection with the modality of punishment. But they take it for granted that punishment in and for itself is just."

36 Tunick, "Efficiency, Practices, and the Moral Point of View," and *Punishment*.

37 Compare to Carlson, "Act Requirement," pp. 1066–67.

38 Topolewski v. State, 109 N.W. 1037 (Wisconsin, 1906), 1041; referred to in Katz, *Bad Acts and Guilty Minds*, p. 159.

39 See Woo Wai v. U.S., 223 F 412 (9th Cir 1915), 415-16; compare to the "mail sting" cases finding that when government arranges for a defendant to send a letter to a nonexistent person that, if sent to an actual person would violate a statute, there can be no conviction as the law was not actually violated: U.S. v. Adams, 59 F 674 (1894), 676; U.S. v. Matthews, 35 F 890 (1888); U.S. v Whittier, 5 Dill. 35 (1878).

40 McAdams, "Reforming Entrapment Doctrine," p. 1800; compare to Dillof, "Unraveling Unlawful Entrapment," p. 894.

41 McAdams, "Reforming Entrapment Doctrine," p. 1811, referring to Jacobson v. U.S., 503 U.S. 540 (1992).

42 See note 15 and accompanying text.

43 See Husak, "Is Drunk Driving a Serious Offense?"

44 McAdams, "Political Economy," pp. 160–62.

45 Jeremy Bentham, *Principles of Morals and Legislation*, ch. 12, Sec. 17; compare to Carlson, "Act Requirement," p. 1097, and Feinberg, *Problems*, p. 82.

46 Feinberg, *Problems* (discussed below); compare to Parker, "Blame, Punishment, and the Role of Result"; Sverdilik, "Crime and Moral Luck"; but see Moore, *Placing Blame*, ch. 5, and Katz, "Why the Successful Assassin Is More Wicked than the Unsuccessful One."

47 But they still cause harm if we are aware that they made the attempt, by creating alarm and other of what Bentham calls "secondary mischiefs" (*Principles*, ch. 12).

48 Feinberg, *Problems*, pp. 100–01.

49 Ibid., pp. 88–89.

50 Ibid., p. 79.

51 Ibid., 91-94.

52 Ibid., pp. 67–68.

53 Ibid., p. 78.

54 Katz, "Why the Successful Assassin."

55 Feinberg, *Problems*, pp. 344–46, 350–51.

56 Compare to the text accompanying notes 32–36.

57 Carlon, "Note," p. 1098; but see Carlson, "Act Requirement," pp. 1065, 1067.

58 Mill, *On Liberty*; Feinberg, *Harm to Others*.

59 Moore, *Placing Blame*.

60 Tunick, "Moral Obligation to Obey Law"; Smith, "Is There a Prima Facie Obligation to Obey the Law?"; Wasserstrom, "Obligation to Obey the Law"; Moore, *Placing Blame*, pp. 70–72.

61 Feinberg, *Doing and Deserving*, pp. 143, 146.

62 Ibid., p. 143.

63 Ibid., pp. 169–71.

64 Feinberg, *Problems*, pp. 62–63; compare to note 5.

65 Feinberg himself draws this conclusion only with some hesitation and only in his later work. In his earlier work, *Doing and Deserving*, he says it is hard to decide whether an act was coaxed and involuntary (p. 174). If, when police enticement precipitates a crime, we punish only highly primed defendants with loose triggers, but police intervention was necessary for the crime to occur, we would be punishing them for their predisposition and, he argues, intuitively this is disconcerting and unjust (p. 175). But, he notes, from a moral point of view according to which luck is irrelevant, that the predisposed person was unlucky enough to encounter the police should not matter. Feinberg concludes that the entrapment issue is "too complicated to pursue further" (p. 176). In the later *Problems*, he is open to an entrapment defense if the defendant is weakly primed and faces a strong police inducement (p. 60; compare to pp. 74–75), in part because it will keep police honest and promote trust (p. 75).

66 Sherman v U.S., 356 U.S. 369 (1958), ruling entrapment; cf. State v. Lively, 130 Wash. 2d 1 (1996).

67 Feinberg, *Doing and Deserving*, p. 158.

68 Sorrells v U.S., 287 U.S. 435 (1932), at 451.

69 Nozick, "Coercion," p. 460.

70 Ibid., pp. 460–61. He notes some atypical exceptions; for example, P tells Q that he will give Q $10,000 if next week someone threatens Q.

71 Ibid., p. 462.

72 Ibid., p. 463.

73 Ibid., p. 464.

74 I disagree with Seidman, who argues that police enticement merely expands one's choices rather than threatens; see his "Supreme Court," p. 139. Feinberg (*Problems*, p. 57) argues that if a buyer of drugs approaches an undercover seller, there is no entrapment because the defendant is deceived about no element of the crime, and I agree. However, if the undercover agent approaches the defendant with an offer, the deception may make the defendant's acceptance involuntary.

75 Alexander, "Doomsday Machine."

76 Dilloff, "Unraveling Unlawful Entrapment," pp. 874–79.

77 Some English judges also depict entrapment as unfair, saying it violates "English notions of decency and fair play"; see R. v. Loosely, [2001] UKHL 53, at §49; cf. §§19, 53.

78 On a reasonable suspicion or probable cause requirement, see Dworkin, "Serpent Beguiled Me and I Did Eat," p. 33.

Bibliography

Alexander, Larry. "The Doomsday Machine." *The Monist* 63 (1980): 208–27.

Allen, Ronald J., Melissa Luttrell, and Anne Kreeger. "Clarifying Entrapment." *Journal of Criminal Law and Criminology* 89 (1999): 407–32.

Bentham, Jeremy. *The Principles of Morals and Legislation*. Buffalo, NY: Prometheus Books, 1988.

Bennett, Christopher. "The Varieties of Retributive Experience." *Philosophical Quarterly* 52 (2002): 145–63.

Carlon, Andrew. "Note: Entrapment, Punishment, and the Sadistic State." *Virginia Law Review* 93 (2007): 1081–139.

Carlson, Jonathan. "The Act Requirement and the Foundations of the Entrapment Defense." *Virginia Law Review* 73 (1987): 1011–108.

Cottingham, John. "Varieties of Retribution." *Philosophical Quarterly* 29 (1979): 238–46.

Davis, Michael. "Harm and Retribution." *Philosophy and Public Affairs* 15 (1986): 236–66.

Dillof, Anthony. "Unraveling Unlawful Entrapment." *Journal of Criminal Law and Criminology* 94 (2004): 927–96.

Duff, R.A. "'I Might Be Guilty, But You Can't Try Me': Estoppel and Other Bars to Trial." *Ohio State Journal of Criminal Law* 1 (2003): 245–59.

Dworkin, Gerald. "The Serpent Beguiled Me and I Did Eat: Entrapment and the Creation of Crime." *Law and Philosophy* 4 (1985): 17–39.

Feinberg, Joel. *Doing and Deserving: Essays in the Theory of Responsibility*. Princeton: Princeton University Press, 1970.

Feinberg, Joel. "The Expressive Function of Punishment." In *Doing and Deserving: Essays in the Theory of Responsibility*, 95–118. Princeton: Princeton University Press, 1970.

Feinberg, Joel. *Harm to Others*. Oxford: Oxford University Press, 1987.

Feinberg, Joel. *Problems at the Roots of Law*. Oxford: Oxford University Press, 2003.

Foucault, Michel. *Discipline and Punish*. New York: Vintage, 1979.

Hay, Bruce. "Sting Operations, Undercover Agents, and Entrapment." *Missouri Law Review* 70 (2005): 387–431.

Hegel, G.W.F. *Philosophy of Right*. Edited by Allen W. Wood. Translated by H.B. Nisbet. Cambridge: Cambridge University Press, 1991.

Husak, Douglas N. "Is Drunk Driving a Serious Offense?" *Philosophy and Public Affairs* 23 (1994): 52–73.

Husak, Douglas N. "Why Punish the Deserving?" *Noûs* 26 (1992): 447–64.

Kaplow, Louis, and Steven Shavell. *Fairness versus Welfare*. Cambridge, MA: Harvard University Press, 2002.

Katz, Leo. *Bad Acts and Guilty Minds*. Chicago: University of Chicago Press, 1987.

Katz, Leo. "Why the Successful Assassin is More Wicked than the Unsuccessful One." *California Law Review* 88 (2000): 791–812.

Mabbott, J.D. "Punishment." *Mind* 48 (1939): 152–67.

McAdams, Richard H. "The Political Economy of Entrapment." *Journal of Criminal Law and Criminology* 96 (2005): 107–86.

McAdams, Richard H. "Reforming Entrapment Doctrine in *United States v. Hollingsworth*." *University of Chicago Law Review* 74 (2007): 1795–1812.

Mill, John Stuart. *On Liberty*. Edited by David Spitz. New York: W. W. Norton, 1975.

Moore, Michael S. *Placing Blame: A Theory of the Criminal Law*. Oxford: Oxford University Press, 1997.

Morris, Herbert. "Persons and Punishment." *The Monist* 52 (1968): 475–501.

Nozick, Robert. "Coercion." In *Philosophy, Science, and Method: Essays in Honor of Ernest Nagel*, edited by Sidney Morgenbesser, Patrick Suppes, and Morton White, 440–72. New York: St. Martin's Press, 1969.

Park, Roger. "The Entrapment Controversy." *Minnesota Law Review* 60 (1976): 163–274.

Parker, Richard. "Blame, Punishment, and the Role of Result." *American Philosophical Quarterly* 21 (1984): 269–76.

Rawls, John. "Two Concepts of Rules." *The Philosophical Review* 64 (1955): 3–32.

Schoeman, Ferdinand. "Privacy and Police Undercover Work." In *Police Ethics: Hard Choices in Law Enforcement*, edited by William C. Heffernan and Timothy Stroup, 133–53. New York: John Jay Press, 1985.

Seidman, Louis Michael. "The Supreme Court, Entrapment, and our Criminal Justice Dilemma." *Supreme Court Review* 1981 (1981): 111–55.

Slobogin, Christopher. "Deceit, Pretext, and Trickery: Investigative Lies by the Police." *Oregon Law Review* 76 (1997): 755–800.

Smith, M.B.E. "Is There a Prima Facie Obligation to Obey the Law?" *Yale Law Journal* 82 (1973): 950–76.

Sverdilik, Steven. "Crime and Moral Luck." *American Philosophical Quarterly* 25 (1988): 79–86.

Tunick, Mark. "Efficiency, Practices, and the Moral Point of View: Limits to Economic Interpretations of Law." In *Theoretical Foundations of Law and Economics*, edited by Mark D. White, 77–95. Cambridge: Cambridge University Press, 2009.

Tunick, Mark. *Hegel's Political Philosophy: Interpreting the Practice of Legal Punishment.* Princeton: Princeton University Press, 1992.

Tunick, Mark. "The Moral Obligation to Obey Law." *Journal of Social Philosophy* 33 (2002): 464–83.

Tunick, Mark. *Punishment: Theory and Practice.* Berkeley, CA: University of California Press, 1992.

Wasserstrom, Richard. "The Obligation to Obey the Law." *UCLA Law Review* 10 (1963): 780–807.

Yaffe, Gideon. "'The Government Beguiled Me': The Entrapment Defense and the Problem of Private Entrapment." *Journal of Ethics and Social Philosophy* 1 (2005): 1–50.

Zaibert, Leo. *Punishment and Retribution.* Aldershot: Ashgate, 2006.

10

THE CHOICE OF EVILS AND THE COLLISIONS OF THEORY

Marc O. DeGirolami

> Human life and philosophical explanations of it move
> in different planes till the explanation has become so
> complete as not to interfere with the thing explained.
>
> JAMES FITZJAMES STEPHEN,
> A History of the Criminal Law of England, Vol. II (P. 84)

IN THE PROLEGOMENON to his famous work, *Punishment and Responsibility*, H.L.A. Hart observed that many of his contemporaries were skeptical about the possibility that a single "supreme value or objective" could answer, let alone definitively resolve, all of the sundry and disparate questions about the justification of punishment.[1] While Hart acknowledged the dangers of "oversimplification," he was nevertheless much more sanguine. Hart took it to be the very essence of his efforts in criminal theory to counter the skepticism about ultimate justifications and expose it as a muddled, facile, and perhaps even indolent intellectual attitude toward criminal law:

> [W]hat is most needed is not the simple admission that instead of a single value or
> aim (Deterrence, Retribution, Reform or any other) a plurality of different values
> and aims should be given as a conjunctive answer to some single question concerning
> the justification of punishment. What is needed is the realization that different
> principles. . . are relevant at different points in any morally acceptable account of
> punishment.[2]

Hart's call in this passage for order and clarity, for sorting out and tidily classifying whether and how different justifications ought to apply to this or that penological phenomenon, is suggestive of the relentlessly categorical compulsions of legal theory. Over the years since Hart wrote, his careful and nuanced project sometimes became something quite different in the hands of scholars who followed. Post-Hartian criminal law scholarship too often sought—and still seeks—to identify something conceptually pure about each of the "theories of punishment" and to argue that one of them ought to predominate either with respect to a particular theoretical question or to criminal law generally. Such was certainly the aspiration of the chief drafter of the Model Penal Code, Herbert Wechsler, whose utilitarian orientations inclined him explicitly to privilege deterrence as the crucial, though not the absolute, function of criminal law.[3] Even today, criminal law scholarship is beguiled by the idea that notwithstanding the varied and often incompatible purposes of criminal law,[4] there is, in fact, one central aim of punishment around which the criminal law ought to coalesce. A single core aim is not necessarily the same as an exclusive aim, but scholars since Hart seem as a general matter predisposed to give one or another theory of punishment preeminent normative status. And in fairness to his epigones, Hart himself never maintained an Olympian neutrality as between theories of punishment. Like the rest of us, he had his favorites, too.[5]

This chapter explores the project of theoretical reduction in criminal law in a narrow but paradigmatic context: the choice of evils justification or necessity defense. Many scholars take the view that the only conceivable explanation for the choice of evils defense must be purely act-utilitarian. There can be no other fundamental explanation, it is said, for a defense that at bottom always must issue in a particularized cost/benefit analysis—a weighing or comparison of the illegal evil that must be done against the evil that will thereby be avoided—than a concern for increasing, or maximizing, social welfare. More than this, any policy or doctrine that interferes with or obstructs that core function of the defense, it is also commonly claimed, is at best incompatible with the defense, and at worst misguided, confused, or simply the product of clouded and disordered thinking.

Against these views, this chapter argues that some of the doctrines that adorn the choice of evils defense are worthwhile precisely because they instantiate values that are in direct and irreconcilable conflict with act-utilitarianism. It develops this claim by considering one of these adornments: the widely adopted doctrinal rule that an actor who is criminally culpable for causing the conditions leading to a choice of evils should not be permitted to assert the defense. Part I of this essay describes the conventional presuppositions about the act-utilitarian purpose of the choice of evils. In Part II, the essay discusses the nearly universal doctrinal bar on the defense when the actor is criminally responsible for creating the conditions leading to the necessitous act, as well as some of the scholarly reactions (uniformly negative) to that exclusion. The essay offers a retributivist explanation for the exclusion where the actor was purposely and criminally culpable for creating the necessitous conditions and discusses how this justification is in tension with the act-utilitarian aims of the defense. It then considers in Part III whether, in light of this tension, a "hybrid" theory of justification—modeled on hybrid theories of punishment—might best explain the defense. But it rejects that possibility. Hybrid theories, no less than their purebred cousins, are inclined toward precisely the types of totalistic explanations that are seemingly confounded by the culpability-in-causing exclusion. The collision of values highlighted by the problem of the choice of evils intimates a different conclusion, one that is offered in Part IV and that echoes the deep pluralism constitutive of criminal law itself.

The aims of this chapter are modest. No systematic challenge to the feasibility or desirability of purity in criminal theory is mounted here. The essay merely suggests, in a limited context, that the admirable purpose that inspired Hart's Prolegomenon—to develop the "sense of the complexity of punishment"[6]—may not be well served by categorically denying the irreconcilability and inevitable collision of the values of the criminal law.

1.

If there is any criminal law doctrine that appears to admit a straightforward, settled, and uncomplicatedly act-utilitarian explication, surely it is the choice of evils or necessity defense, the affirmative defense that an actor is justified in breaking the law when the social harm resulting from the illegal evil chosen is outweighed by the social harm that would have resulted from the evil avoided. Seizing on this orientation, legal scholars and judges often opine about the ultimate justification of the defense and its theoretical limits. And it is the reductionistic quality of these pronouncements that seems to lend them a certain heft of inevitability.[7] It may be helpful to review a few of them:

Necessity is, essentially, a utilitarian defense.[8]

The necessity defense is a uniquely collective act-utilitarian doctrine. . . These philosophical underpinnings. . . are both inherently radical and provide a one-way ratchet toward certain types of transformative social change. . . [T]he necessity doctrine is a social libertarian's dream.[9]

Justified conduct concerns a theory of utilitarian values, that is, whether the unlawful is commendable and whether society benefits from the act.[10]

Even though transaction costs were not high in the usual sense in Dudley and Stephens,[11] at some point the sacrifice of one person so that others might live must increase social welfare. If in advance of the voyage the members of the crew had agreed to sacrifice the weakest should that become necessary to save the others, there would be no economic argument for allowing the defense of necessity if the agreement had to be performed. It is only one step beyond that to argue that if we are confident that the members of the crew would have made such an agreement if they had foreseen the contingency that materialized, the defense of necessity ought to have been recognized—always assuming that economic efficiency is to be the guidepost for criminal law doctrine.[12]

It is the nature of justified conduct that it either is or is not justified—depending on whether it causes a net societal benefit—regardless of the particular state of mind, past or present, of the actor.[13]

The varieties of act-utilitarian explanation for the choice of evils defense are manifold: "welfarist or nonwelfarist"; if welfarist, "based on an objective list of goods, on satisfaction of preferences, or on hedonic states"; "if preference based. . . the preferences are raw, or corrected for misinformation, and/or laundered of malicious, envious, and other antisocial content, and/or restricted to self-regarding preferences, as to other regarding preferences," eudaimonistic or not, and so on.[14] Yet what these and other perspectives share is a belief that the master value of the choice of evils defense must necessarily be a certain type of act-utilitarian judgment, the outcome of a balancing test with respect to the particular choice of evils confronted. It would be tedious to document that act-utilitarianism holds master value status for many of these theorists. Perhaps it will suffice to offer Shaun Martin's somewhat Manichean observation that either the choice of evils instantiates an all-powerful act-utilitarian value or "the traditional consequentialist principles that lie at the very heart of the necessity defense [must] be discarded in favor of alternative fundamental principles."[15]

2.

Were these reductive visions of the choice of evils defense descriptively accurate, one might expect that the doctrine as it actually appears at common law and in various criminal codes would not be encumbered by rules directly at odds with the act-utilitarian supervalue allegedly at its core. This need not mean that one would not expect to see rules limiting the reach of the defense. For example, the restriction common in many jurisdictions that an actor must avail himself of all effective legal alternatives before confronting the choice of evils is perfectly consonant with the reductive act-utilitarian position.[16] It is more likely to conduce to the greatest social net benefit, one might plausibly claim, if an actor who potentially faces a choice of evils is encouraged to dissolve the dilemma by following a legal and effective alternative course; what could be more socially beneficial, more appealing from the vantage point of the best all-things-considered result, than an act which is both legal and effective?[17] The same may be said for the doctrine that the defense is unavailable where a legislature has made an ex ante judgment that the choice of evils defense ought not to apply to a particular situation—where it has preempted the field of utilitarian calculus.[18]

But there are other doctrinal features of the choice of evils defense that are much more difficult to reconcile with an approach that is exclusively concerned with act-utilitarian net benefits. One of these is the requirement that the actor must believe that his illegal conduct—the evil that he chooses—will be effective in abating the danger. From an intransigently act-utilitarian perspective, what the actor believed at the time that he acted ought to be irrelevant. If, in response to a forest fire, X burns Y's house to create a firebreak so that valuable crops on the other side of Y's house will be saved, why should it matter that X entertained serious doubts that setting the firebreak would abate the danger? Why should it even make any difference that X believed that setting the firebreak would almost certainly not abate the danger, but that it would be thrilling to take the risk—or that it would be a delight to see her neighbor's house in flames—if we are solely and exclusively interested in the social net benefit of X's act measured against the danger that she abated?[19] It is conceivable that a consequentialist might value the utils derived from the pleasure of seeing someone's house burning, utils that would coincide with, and augment, the net utility derived from saving the valuable crops. Yet this point lends additional strength to the argument that the "subjective belief" limitation is problematic for a strictly act-utilitarian view of the choice of evils.[20]

Another doctrine of this kind is the categorical exclusion of the defense in many jurisdictions (but not in the Model Penal Code) where it is used to justify an intentional homicide. This hard-and-fast rule has in it something of what Bernard Williams called "the unthinkable," because it is a doctrine that can only be explained as a kind of rigid resistance to act-utilitarian balancing and trade-offs altogether:

> It could be a feature of a man's moral outlook that he regarded certain courses of action as *unthinkable*. . . . Entertaining certain alternatives, regarding them indeed as *alternatives*, is something that he regards as dishonourable or morally absurd. . . . Logically, or indeed empirically conceivable they may be, but they are not to him morally conceivable, meaning by that that their occurrence as situations presenting him with a choice would present not a special problem in his moral world, but something that lay beyond its limits.[21]

It is not farfetched to suppose that the "unthinkability" of intentionally killing another person is what at least historically grounded this common rule. But consequentialist rationality, as Williams wryly observes, "has no such limitations. . . . [I]t will have something to say even on the difference between massacring seven million, and massacring seven million and one."[22]

A third nearly universal doctrinal frill that is difficult to reconcile with an overriding act-utilitarian value is the requirement that the actor not have been criminally culpable in causing the conditions leading to the choice of evils. For example, suppose X is drunk and purposely shoots V. There being no other legal option that would effectively abate the danger of V dying, X (whether riven by pangs of remorse, or egoistically concerned about being charged with a crime of omission, or for whatever other reason) drives V to the hospital, whereupon he is charged with drunk driving as well as the underlying offense (attempted murder, for example, if V survives). The question is whether X should be able to assert the choice of evils defense as to the drunk driving charge. Almost every American jurisdiction that has considered the question prohibits the defense in those circumstances, as does the Model Penal Code.[23] Many jurisdictions have adopted even more stringent rules (in some cases, indefensibly stringent) barring the defense in cases of "fault in" or "any contribution to" the creation of the necessity.[24]

Elsewhere I have considered the cogency of the various doctrinal rules dealing with the issue of creating the choice of evils and the possible explanations and criticisms of those approaches.[25] In this chapter, I want to make a different point: *If* the causing-the-conditions bar is defensible, it cannot be adequately defended if one takes the act-utilitarian aim of achieving the maximum social net benefit in the weighing of evils to be the master value of the choice of evils defense.[26]

This need not mean that the causing-the-conditions exclusion is entirely incompatible with various rule-utilitarian functions of punishment. A deterrence theorist might well argue in favor of some type of bar where an actor culpably caused the conditions on the grounds of foreseeability, the claim being that the law ought to discourage people from engaging in conduct that they know, or should know, will lead to a choice of evils. This is an especially persuasive argument in the case of what Paul Robinson has called the "grand schemer": the actor who causes the necessitous conditions for the very purpose of engaging in the proscribed but (now) necessary conduct.[27] Suppose Bob wants to kill Gladys, and he knows that Gladys is both deeply attached to her pocket watch and explosively hot tempered. Bob writes a letter to Gladys falsely claiming that he has taken Gladys's watch and that he will not give it back. Bob does this hoping very much that it will incite Gladys to attack him. Sure enough, Gladys storms into Bob's house stark-raving mad and Bob, having no duty to retreat inside his home, shoots Gladys in "self-defense." Excluding the defense of justification in such circumstances might well be explained on grounds of foreseeability alone: not only was it foreseeable that Gladys would attack Bob, compelling him to act in self-defense, but it was, in fact, Bob's self-same strategic purpose that this occur.

Yet while the causing-the-conditions bar might be justified on rule-utilitarian deterrence grounds in the case of the grand schemer, deterrence does not seem adequately to explain the function and value of the bar. As an initial matter, the bar is difficult to reconcile with the idea that the master value of the choice of evils is act-utilitarian. If our overriding concern is with whether Bob's reaction to the choice of evils is warranted at the moment that it occurs, then Bob's state of mind at any point prior to the moment at which he defended himself should be irrelevant. At the moment that he acts, it is beyond dispute that Bob is being attacked by Gladys, and his life is being threatened; would we require that he submit to Gladys's deadly attack? Any value—including deterrence— which might come into conflict with the overriding act-utilitarian calculus (here, the best all-things-considered consequence at the moment at which the choice of evils is confronted) is, on the most common scholarly account of the choice of evils, defeated by it. It is true that if Bob foresees that he will not receive the choice of evils defense, he may be deterred from writing the letter to Gladys in the first place. But what if Bob writes the letter as a grand schemer, but just as Gladys is on the attack, he regrets his grand scheme? Now he is faced with a livid and bloodthirsty Gladys: what reason is powerful enough to deny him the defense in that situation?

Even if one understands the deterrent aims of criminal law more broadly as including the range of activities and behaviors more diffusely connected to any specific act (such as those relating to general deterrence), it is difficult to see how those are sufficiently powerful to defeat the act-utilitarian value of achieving the best all-things-considered result. If A, while drunk, shoots B, why should we want *in any way* to deter A from driving B to the hospital (if we subscribe to the act-utilitarian justification of necessity), even if a causing-the-conditions exclusion for such cases perhaps (who is really to know for sure?) might have the general deterrent effect of inducing others to act more carefully?[28]

But there is a more substantial problem. Every jurisdiction that has directly confronted the question bars the choice of evils defense not only where the actor was a grand schemer but also where he was purposely and criminally culpable for creating the conditions leading to the choice of evils—that is, where he intended the criminal act causing the choice of evils but did not intend the choice of evils itself.[29] And this rule cannot be explained by deterrence or any other consequentialist (act- or rule-utilitarian) justification, because we are now assuming that the creation of the choice of evils is not realistically deterrable.

Indeed, it would be fair to say that most actual culpable causation situations do not involve the rather far-fetched case of grand schemers but more ordinary actors who did not, and could not, have predicted that their actions would have resulted in a choice of evils. As a somewhat extreme case, consider the careful murderer, who plans in exquisite detail the murder of his wife. The careful murderer does everything according to plan, but all of a sudden, after he has dealt the lethal blow and while he is enjoying his third celebratory snifter of cognac, he repents his heinous deed (or he realizes that he has jeopardized the likelihood of receiving his wife's fortune). It is only then that he decides to drive his wife to the hospital (while drunk). Or consider a more common example: Jim gets drunk and punches his girlfriend a single time in the back. As a result, his girlfriend lurches forward, trips over the corner of a rug, and hits her head on the corner of a glass table, opening a serious head wound. While drunk, Jim drives his girlfriend to the hospital. All states would exclude the defense for both drunk driving charges, and here foreseeability is not in issue because the careful murderer could not have anticipated the contingency (he was, *ex hypothesi*, careful), and it is extremely unlikely that a single blow to the back would result in a life-threatening injury.

In these sorts of cases, the only adequate explanation for the exclusion is retributive: an actor who has purposely and criminally caused the conditions leading to a choice of evils does not *deserve* the defense—his conduct, particularly where the criminally causing conduct is grave or heinous, does not merit the defense in the same way as does conduct in response to a blamelessly caused choice of evils, whether by the actor or someone (or something) else.[30]

Ignoring or discounting the import of purposeful and criminal blameworthiness in causing a necessity renders the concept of justified conduct—that is, conduct that is at some level praiseworthy or socially valuable—defective. Just as any adequate theory of punishment must account for the "traditional metaphysics of punishment: that somehow the punishment must address the crime and seek to negate its occurrence,"[31] so must any adequate theory of justification, inversely, explain why fault (and therefore punishment) is inappropriate in the face of socially valuable or praiseworthy conduct.[32] It is this retributivist explanation for the culpability-in-causing exclusion that also does fuller justice to our intuitions in the case of the grand schemer than can the deterrence explanation. Vera Bergelson's grand schemer hypothetical is illuminating:

> Suppose person A hates his enemy B and wants him dead. Knowing that B frequents a certain bar, A spends night after night outside the bar waiting for an occasion. While he is waiting, he witnesses numerous fights, sexual assaults, even murders; however, he never interferes, until finally one day he sees B attacking another patron C with deadly force. Knowing the law of defense of another, A intervenes and kills B. At his trial, A honestly tells his story of patience and determination. Should he be rewarded for these qualities and completely exonerated, even though we know that he would not have defended C but for his desire to kill B?[33]

Bergelson argues that "most of us" would recoil at justifying A's conduct in such a situation, that we would find it "a mockery of justice."[34] I agree, but why?

It is not for any consequentialist reason, but rather precisely that "justification" carries with it more than the mere sense that an act that is normally criminal was, in the event, noncriminal. Since a justified act itself is ordinarily wrongful, the actor must demonstrate that the circumstances in which the act was performed transmuted the wrong into something else entirely: a right, laudable, or praiseworthy act, an act that merits the social judgment that it was justified given the context in which it was performed. And once one focuses on the circumstances in which the act was performed, rather than the split-second moment of decision during which the act itself was chosen, one begins to see that those circumstances may greatly affect whether an actor has earned, and so deserves, the label "justified" for his conduct.

Suppose that A had staged the assault by paying off C to appear outside the bar at a propitious moment so as to incite B to attack him (C). If Bergelson is correct that A's inchoate and noncriminal feelings of hate toward B somehow ought to make a legal difference, so, presumably, should A's purposeful culpability in causing the need for putatively "justified" action. And this remains true even if at the very moment that A is reacting to B's deadly onslaught, he is acting, at least in part but possibly entirely, in true or real defense of C. A may, at some level, actually want to defend C against B's attack, but at another psychological level, he may also want very much to kill B. Or perhaps at the moment that B is attacking C, A repents and is now acting in "pure" defense of C. And if purposeful culpability-in-causing should make a legal difference, so, too, should purposeful *and criminal* culpability-in-causing. Thus, at the least, the culpability-in-causing exclusion seems to implicate both consequentialist and retributivist concerns.[35] But one might go further: the retributivist reasons are the very heart of the explanation for the exclusion.

Alan Brudner once observed that "[c]ommentary on the law of necessity has for centuries been marked by a sharp discordance between the views of philosophic writers on the one hand and those of judges... on the other."[36] This remark is nowhere more true than in the case of the culpability-in-causing exclusion, as scholarly appraisal has unfailingly found it wanting. Most scholars seem to accept Robinson's objectivist judgment that the culpability-in-causing bar is illegitimate in any form because conduct is either justified or not at the snapshot instant that it occurs and entirely without regard to the actor's past or present state of mind.[37] Douglas Husak lumps together the culpability-in-causing exclusion with other doctrinal manifestations of "taint" that he finds indefensible.[38] George Fletcher calls the exclusion "questionable" and doctrinal examples of it "bad law," the result of legislators "confusing the criteria of justification and excuse."[39] Michael Hoffheimer associates the culpability-in-causing bar as of a piece with the archaic, and now largely defunct, requirement that the necessity have been caused by natural (or divine) interventions.[40] Both are rules that, in Hoffheimer's view, "lack substantial authority" in a modern context.[41] The culpability-in-causing exclusion—even for grand schemers or actors who purposely and criminally caused the choice of evils— seems to have no academic defenders.

Yet something seems to have gone awry when a doctrine is so universally accepted in the common and statutory law, and at the same time so steadfastly and intensely reviled by the academic literature. The bare fact that a doctrine has achieved extremely broad popular endorsement is not itself reason enough to accept its legitimacy. Still, one need not go as far as to claim, with James Fitzjames Stephen, that general theories of criminal responsibility are justifiable insofar as they comport with community sentiment, to recognize that such a polarized disjunction between theory and practice may bespeak some defect or lack of understanding.[42]

The answer runs deep. It lies in the overriding act-utilitarianism to which so many theorists of the necessity defense subscribe. While the culpability-in-causing bar is an unwise doctrine in its more extreme forms,[43] more restrained versions are defensible on powerful retributivist grounds and, at least in some cases, on weaker grounds of rule-utilitarian deterrence. But theorists who are fixated on the act-utilitarian traits of the defense are liable to miss those features of the necessity defense that ill fit their theoretical preferences. It seems that even the necessity defense, about which it is so tempting to ascribe a simple and reductive explanation, contains within it values that collide and are incompatible—values that reflect the long-standing conflicts between the retributivist and consequentialist theories of punishment as well as justification.

3.

In light of these tensions and conflicting aims inherent in the necessity defense, perhaps the best explanation for it—the best theory of it—might be modeled on what some theorists have dubbed "hybrid" or mixed theories of punishment. A hybrid theory of punishment is one which incorporates both consequentialist and retributivist features in an effort at reconciliation: "A typical hybrid approach holds that moral desert specifies a range of permissible penalties, and utilitarian considerations should drive the selection of the appropriate penalty within that range."[44] Thus, a mixed or hybrid theory of punishment might posit a "negative" retributivism, one in which retributivism is a necessary but insufficient condition for punishment. For example:

> Punishment's purpose is utilitarian: to reduce crime and thus protect the rights of all to be secure in their persons and property. But that purpose must be pursued within retribution's limits: the state cannot punish someone unless he commits a crime, nor can it punish him disproportionately in relation to the crime he commits.[45]

Alternatively, a hybrid approach that gave primary, or "defining," emphasis to desert might require that, in the main, punishment would be based solely on the seriousness of the offense, but more severe punishments would be permitted when unusually great risks of crime were involved.

Hybrid theories begin with a presumption that philosophical conflict inheres in criminal codes: desert and deterrence may conflict, as when a jurisdiction maintains an insanity defense.[46] Incapacitation and deterrence—two consequentialist functions—may conflict, as when a jurisdiction punishes attempts less seriously than it punishes completed crimes.[47] And there are internal contradictions within individual functions as well. Desert, for example, contains within itself internally contradictory values: the question whether an attempt truly deserves less punishment because it caused no harm generates the subcategories of harm-retributivism and intent-retributivism.

Faced with these conflicts and so many others, hybrid approaches nevertheless insist that a fully rational and justifiable scheme of punishment can be achieved by mixing theoretical explanations in just the right quantities.[48] In an early and influential exposition of a hybrid approach,[49] Paul Robinson urged a "hybrid distributive principle" of punishment:

> Desert is to be given priority over the combined utilitarian formulation, except where it causes an intolerable level of crime that the utilitarian formulation would avoid. At this point, utilitarian arguments can be made, but no utilitarian adjustment can be made if it generates a formulation that imposes an intolerably unjust punishment.[50]

Yet "hybrid" is something of a misnomer for theories like Robinson's and others that claim the label, since the term's natural meaning suggests that two or more philosophies of punishment would be intermingled or blended with unknown and unpredictable effects to create something entirely novel, much as the hybrid Iron Age Pig is the offspring of the blessed union of a domestic pig and a wild boar. A hybrid theory of punishment, in contrast, is "not simply an amalgam of multiple purposes; a hybrid theory illuminates the weight given to different purposes and clarifies which purpose controls when they can't be pursued simultaneously."[51] Or, as has been observed admiringly of Robinson's hybrid approach:

> Policymakers have an understandable wish to combine the various penal policies to the extent they can, but these policies conflict. This makes a principled synthesis essential—one that does not merely "blend" the various aims, but assigns explicit priorities.[52]

The hybrid theory is therefore less the theoretical equivalent of the mule and more that of the recipe: mix two dashes of retributivism with three cups of deterrence, knead and bake the dough just so, and behold the punishment theory cake, as per the cookbook's method.

A better description of the hybrid theory might be that one type of consideration places an "outer limit" or side constraint on a different consideration underlying the theory.[53] A hybrid theory might use "desert as a determining principle and combined utilitarian principles as a limiting principle" where the limiting principle constrains the determining principle in cases where the result would otherwise be "intolerable," a term left conspicuously undefined.[54]

This way of putting it appears on its face to explain the culpability-in-causing exclusion. Just as there may be theories of punishment that mix consequentialist and retributivist functions by placing side constraints of one sort or another on the availability of a defense that otherwise might be completely explained by a pure theory, so too may there be theories of justification (and excuse as well) that place limits on what would otherwise be an unconstrained and altogether too powerful theoretical commitment that underlies the defense.

In the case of the choice of evils, the determining principle would be consequentialist: deterrence (or another consequentialist function) controls unless the limiting, side-constraining principle (retributivism) would be violated in such a way as to be deemed "intolerable."[55] And one might say, if one found grounds to support the culpability-in-causing exclusion at least as to the grand schemer, or as to purposeful and criminal conduct as well, that the exclusion represents a side constraint on the necessity defense to remedy what would otherwise be an "intolerable" violation of the retributivist side-constraining principle. The defense, the argument might go, should in general operate on consequentialist premises of one type or another, but under no circumstances should someone who criminally and purposely caused the conditions leading to the choice of evils be allowed the defense because that would represent an intolerable, deeply unjust outcome.

An example of a hybrid theory of justification may be the view recently offered by Larry Alexander and Kimberly Kessler Ferzan that the choice of evils defense has a "general consequentialist structure" but that there are "deontological constraints on the consequentialist calculus."[56] Alexander and Ferzan are skeptical about the intentionalist "Doctrine of Double Effect"[57] and argue instead that "the deontological constraint on achieving best consequences is means-focused rather than intent-focused."[58] A means-focused constraint explains why it would be unjustified for a surgeon to kill a patient in order to harvest organs that could be used to save the lives of five others, while it is justified to divert a speeding trolley away from a collision with five people and toward collision with a single person[59]:

> This idea of appropriating others—using their bodies, labors, and talents without their consent as the means of producing the beneficial consequences—accounts better than any other theory for our deontological intuitions about the limits on pursuit of the best consequences.[60]

Alexander's and Ferzan's argument seems plausible for the example that they offer, but two points are worth mentioning. First, the deontological side-constrained approach must reject the exclusion for culpability-in-causing—even as to grand schemers. It holds that if the actor can justifiably act at the moment, it is entirely immaterial that he was culpable for creating the choice of evils at some earlier point in time. The only constraint on the justification of the act is deontological; if that constraint is absent, nothing stands in the way of the consequentialist calculus. And it surely is absent in the case of the grand schemer, since the grand schemer may have "appropriated" no one at all. Suppose that X, hoping to gain fame as a local hero, sets fire to a forest knowing that the blaze will threaten valuable crops and that the only way to stop the fire is to create a firebreak by burning his own house down, which he does. Is X appropriating himself? Is he appropriating his own house (and why would that be objectionable, since he owns it)? Perhaps one could say that X is appropriating the crops, but what if they are X's crops? Or what if they are Y's crops, but Y has given X "consent" to use them as part of the grand scheme (that is, Y is in on the plan)? X would not then be "appropriating" Y's crops in the way that seems to matter to Alexander and Ferzan, but it is difficult to see why that should make any difference with respect to whether X ought to obtain a necessity instruction.[61] The culpability-in-causing exclusion is far better explained on the ground of desert, of having failed to earn the justification for one's act based on one's prior conduct.

Second, the deontological constraint also does not explain another common limitation on the defense: its exclusion in all cases of intentional murder (Williams's argument about the morally "unthinkable" is better here).[62] The most that can be said for Alexander's and Ferzan's deontological constraint is that it is one factor—possibly an important one—that affects the judgment whether an act is justified.

Indeed, although I have recently expressed support for something like Alexander's and Ferzan's view of the choice of evils defense,[63] I am increasingly skeptical about it. The problem of the culpability-in-causing exclusion is not effectively answered by recourse to hybrid theories of affirmative defenses. However, the hybrid approach is an improvement in one important sense: it does away with the illusion that the choice of evils defense as it exists in the legal status quo can be properly explained by act-utilitarianism alone. By focusing on the conflicts of theory and confronting squarely the reality that retributivist concerns do play a defensible role in the defense as it is actually practiced, and that those retributivist side constraints conflict with other values inherent in the choice of evils defense and may sometimes (but not always) defeat them, hybrid theories rightly reject the more common view that the defense is justifiable only by recourse to a single master value.

Yet in place of a theory dependent on one overriding value, the hybrid offers an alternative theory that depends on two, each of which is conditional but admits of no deviation. Under a hybrid approach, where the culpability-in-causing exclusion exists, it seems always—at least as to purposeful and criminal conduct—to defeat the consequentialist balancing. Where it does not exist, the consequentialist balancing always defeats all other conflicting values. A hybrid theorist might respond to this criticism, as Robinson has in a different context, with the argument that the determining principle of the choice of evils defense—consequentialism—is not always defeated by the limiting principle—retributivism. It is only defeated by the limiting principle where the determining principle generates "an intolerable injustice."[64] But an intolerably heavy burden then is placed on the word "intolerable" since everything appears to turn on the meaning of what is, surely, a highly contestable and decidedly ambiguous term. Moreover, the asserted utility of the hybrid theory—that it is capable of specifying just how much desert or deterrence ought to be poured into our explanatory mixing bowl—quickly evaporates. And it seems we are left merely with contestable notions of intolerability to assist us in explaining the relationship of the culpability-in-causing exclusion to the choice of evils defense.

Perhaps this is not such a terrible place to be. It may be true that the culpability-in-causing exclusion is defensible in certain cases and for certain actors—for grand schemers, for example, or for actors who purposely commit very serious crimes that give rise to a choice of evils. Yet even in these situations, and certainly for many others that do not fall into these categories, barring the defense inevitably entails substantial and serious loss, even sacrifice, of other values underwriting the choice of evils defense, values about which it would be intolerable, because untrue, to say that they simply do not matter or are irrelevant when an actor has culpably caused the conditions leading to the choice of evils defense. It is entirely coherent, even persuasive, to conclude that even though A watched in the bushes for a propitious moment to kill the hated B and opportunistically used B's attack of C to accomplish his nefarious motive ostensibly in "defense" of C, that A should nevertheless be entitled to the defense of justification. While at one level, our intuitions sense that this outcome would be a "mockery of justice,"[65] at another we still want very much that A come to the defense of C; we still believe that act to be worthwhile, one which the criminal law ought not punish, one which may in fact be praiseworthy. A juror (and therefore a jury) may, in sum, be torn between values that are not capable of commensuration without the sense that something of great worth has been lost in the outcome.

Jurors will need to negotiate the pull and push of these conflicting values. More than this, it is entirely proper that they be compelled to do so, and that different reflections and considerations issue in different outcomes. The collision of values endemic to the choice of evils defense is without a neat theoretical solution: whatever path is chosen, whatever value is elevated in the particular case, will inevitably and rightly entail losses that ought not be denied or dismissed for the sake of theoretical tidiness. I suppose that in the end, I am advocating the Iron Age Pig theory of the choice of evils defense: an amalgam of different purposes, different values, colliding together and coexisting in an uneasy *modus vivendi* to form a creature altogether curious and new.[66]

4.

Hart comments in *Punishment and Responsibility* that justified conduct is "regarded as something that the law does not condemn, or even welcomes."[67] This ambiguous statement is followed in a footnote by a delightfully cryptic anecdote: "In 1811 Mr. Purcell of Co. Cork, a septuagenarian, was knighted for killing four burglars with a carving knife."[68] Is our intuition to praise or tolerate the old man's bloody deed? And how should the criminal law reflect and make sense of those intuitions? Hart does not say. Much will depend on context and the circumstances that led to the killings; perhaps some of these will be circumstances that are not the proper concern of the criminal law.[69] But some—perhaps including the fact of culpable causation—may be, and their existence may make us feel differently about whether conduct that would otherwise merit praise now merits criminal condemnation (or at least something much less than praise) or vice versa.

Whether an act is justified—whether the choice of evils defense ought to apply in any given situation—does not depend upon any procrustean conceptual truth. While it will be possible to specify those theoretical conditions that ought to be considered and that ought to make a difference, there will in the end be a range of plausible negotiations of the predicaments and collisions of theory. That range is in small measure reflected in the great variety of approaches to the choice of evils defense that one finds in different jurisdictions, different negotiations for different locales with different histories and different constituencies.[70] It is reflected, too, in the differing resolutions that juries may reach when faced with the incommensurable conflicts of theoretical explanation for the choice of evils defense. If "justice is conflict," in Stuart Hampshire's memorable phrase,[71] then justification is conflict as well. It is past time for criminal theoreticians to tolerate—dare one say even to celebrate—the collisions of theory reflected in the pluralism of criminal law itself.[72]

Notes

1 Hart, *Punishment and Responsibility*, p. 2.

2 Ibid.

3 Model Penal Code § 1.02(1), Explanatory Note ("the dominant theme is the prevention of offenses").

4 See Kutz, "Torture, Necessity and Existential Politics," p. 251: "Given the disparate goals of criminal law, you might think that theoretical discussions of the necessity defense would recognize the inherent limits of any basically utilitarian mode of argument applied to individual rights."

5 See Hart, *Punishment*, pp. 9–10 (excluding retribution as a "general justifying aim" of punishment) and pp. 230–37 (rejecting any retributive theory of punishment that would make it "morally obligatory" to punish wrongdoers).

6 Ibid., p. 3.

7 A notable exception is Simons, "Exploring the Intricacies of the Lesser Evils Defense," pp. 648–49: "[E]ven if we could agree on the fundamental values that should underlie a very general necessity defense and should, in principle, resolve all cases, the legal task of implementing those principles in a given criminal case would inevitably require the jury (or even the judge) to rely heavily on an intuitive sense of justice, and not merely to apply, for example, a utilitarian social welfare function (or such a function constrained by a specified set of deontological principles)."

8 United States v. Schoon, 971 F.2d 193, 196 (9th Cir. 1991).

9 Martin, "Radical Necessity Defense," pp. 1549, 1557.

10 Carter, "Knight in the Duel with Death," pp. 709–10.

11 Regina v. Dudley and Stephens, 14 Q.B.D. 273 (1884). The well-known *Dudley & Stephens* case involved the murder trial of two men who had killed and eaten a cabin boy while in a lifeboat adrift on the ocean.

12 Posner, "Economic Theory of the Criminal Law," p. 1230; see also Kutz, "Torture," pp. 251–52: "[O]n 'economic' theories of criminal law, where the point of the criminal norm is to block transactions that could, were they Pareto-improving, go through with mutual consent, the necessity defense would, indeed, exemplify the logic of the criminal law in general—a form of 'efficient breach' theory."

13 Robinson, "Causing the Conditions of One's Own Defense," p. 28. I use the term "objective" to mean an approach to the choice of evils that cares only for the universally observable facts at the moment of choice; see Huigens, "Continuity of Justification Defenses," p. 633n. 23.

14 Alexander, Ferzan, and Morse, *Crime and Culpability*, p. 95.

15 Martin, "Radical Necessity Defense," p. 1555n. 26.

16 See, for example, United States v. Bailey, 444 U.S. 394 (1980).

17 An exception might be the case of civil disobedience, where one could claim that the act of disobeying a putatively unjust law is itself part of the "social benefit" of the evil chosen. Yet even here, if one *could effectively* change the objectionable law without violating that law, or another law, it is difficult to see why that would not produce the greatest social benefit.

18 See Model Penal Code § 3.02, cmt. 2. Legislative preclusion might, but need not, be consistent with the overriding act-utilitarian value. A legislature might have considered an explicit exception for a case like the actor's and might have agreed that the actor's choice was in fact the lesser evil, but it might nevertheless reject that exception "because it feared that recognizing an exception would, in the long run, lead to greater evils, as a result of mistaken or fraudulent invocation of the exception" (Simons, "Exploring the Intricacies," p. 674).

19 See Parry, "Virtue of Necessity." A possible counterargument is that someone who believes that her action will abate a danger is usually more likely to be successful at abating it, but that assumes that the belief was reasonable, and not merely subjectively held.

20 It might well be consistent with a rule utilitarian justification for the defense, but rule utilitarianism has not often been used by legal scholars to justify the choice of evils.

21 Smart and Williams, *Utilitarianism: For and Against*, p. 92.

22 Ibid., p. 93.

23 See Model Penal Code § 3.02(2): "When the actor was negligent or reckless in bringing about the situation requiring a choice of harms or evils... the justification afforded by this Section is unavailable in a prosecution for any offense for which recklessness or negligence, as the case may be, suffices to establish culpability." The Code does not state specifically that the necessity defense is unavailable where the actor purposely (or knowingly) caused the necessitous conditions, but it would be anomalous to afford the defense to an actor who purposely caused the conditions but deny it to an actor who recklessly or negligently caused the conditions. The provision therefore has been plausibly interpreted to bar the defense when the actor's culpability for causing the conditions and her culpability for the underlying offense match. See LaFave, *Criminal Law*, p. 534: "Thus, if he intentionally brings on the danger, he may be guilty of a crime of intention; if he was reckless, of a crime of recklessness; of negligence, of a crime of negligence"; and Simons, "Exploring the Intricacies," p. 678, characterizing the Code's approach as "treating fault in creating the necessity as roughly comparable to that level of fault as to the material element of the offense."

24 See DeGirolami, "Culpability in Creating the Choice of Evils."

25 Ibid.

26 In consequence, there is little in the way of normative justification for the culpability-in-causing limitation offered in this essay.

27 Robinson, "Causing the Conditions," p. 31.

28 See Fletcher, *Rethinking Criminal Law*, p. 277: "There comes a point where the deterrent efficacy of a norm is so weak that one might properly think that competing values require that deterrence not be accepted as a justification."

29 DeGirolami, "Culpability in Creating."

30 Putting it this way highlights the point that there may be shades of justification that could be compared, and that one need not immediately jump to excuse, which focuses on the "psychological state of the agent" (Hart, *Punishment and Responsibility*, p. 14). For example, an actor who is negligently, or even recklessly, culpable in causing a necessity has a more meritorious claim on the choice of evils defense than an actor who purposely and criminally causes a necessity. It may be that the actor who is only negligently culpable-in-causing should not be barred from the defense, while the actor who is purposely and criminally culpable-in-causing should be. On "comparative justifications" see Bergelson, "Rights, Wrongs, and Comparative Justifications."

31 Fletcher, *Basic Concepts of Criminal Law*, pp. 33, 138.

32 For greater elaboration of this argument, see DeGirolami, "Culpability in Creating."

33 Bergelson, "Consent to Harm," p. 700.

34 Ibid.

35 Chiu, "Culture as Justification, Not Excuse," p. 1344: "The doctrine of clean hands reflects both retributivist concerns with the decisions of the defendant in bringing about bad circumstances and the utilitarian desire to deter the future occurrence of such circumstances."

36 Brudner, "Theory of Necessity," p. 339.

37 See generally Robinson, "Causing the Conditions."

38 Husak, *Philosophy of Criminal Law*, pp. 69–72. Husak states that the issue of "taint" may derive from the problem of "persons who bring about their own excusing conditions" and he allows that there may be greater justification for "taint" where the actor engaged in a criminal (as opposed merely to immoral) act prior to the related criminal act for which he is being charged.

39 Fletcher, *Rethinking*, pp. 796–98. In the case of excuses, like duress, scholars more commonly (but not universally) support the culpability-in-causing exclusion. See, for example, Dressler, "Exegesis of the Law of Duress," pp. 1341–42; Fletcher, *Rethinking*, p. 798; but see Robinson, "Causing the Conditions," p. 29: "As with justifications, there is a fundamental flaw in an approach that denies an excuse because the actor culpably causes the conditions of his excuse. Just as causing one's defense does not alter the justified nature of otherwise justified conduct, it does not erase the excusing conditions that exculpates the actor for the offense conduct."

40 Hoffheimer, "Codifying Necessity," p. 242.

41 Ibid., p. 241.

42 Stephen, *History of the Criminal Law*, pp. 80–82.

43 See, for example, Colo. Rev. Stat. Ann. § 18-1-702 (imposing the bar when the actor engaged in any conduct giving rise to the necessity); State v. Tadlock, 34 P.3d 1096, 1097 (Idaho Ct. App. 2001) (requiring that the "circumstances which necessitate the illegal act must not have been brought about by the defendant").

44 Ristroph, "Respect and Resistance in Punishment Theory," p. 621.

45 Garvey, "Lifting the Veil on Punishment," p. 450; see also Morris, "Desert as a Limiting Principle," p. 180: "[T]he concept of a just desert properly limits the maximum and the minimum of the sentence that may be imposed, but does not give us any more fine-tuning to the appropriate sentence than that."

46 Excusing the insane might be explained because the insane cannot be deterred, or because the insane do not deserve punishment. But for the harm-retributivist, insanity ought to be inexcusable.

47 I am assuming that those who favor incapacitation as a theory of punishment (do such theorists exist?) would support longer periods of incapacitation for those who complete their crimes than for those who do not.

For a classic argument for punishing attempts on grounds of deterrence, see Hart, *Punishment and Responsibility*, pp. 128–29: "[T]here seems a clear case for the use of punishment as an individual deterrent in the cases of unsuccessful attempts to commit crimes; for the accused has manifested a dangerous disposition to do all he can to commit a crime, and the experience of punishment may check him in the future, since it may cause him to attach more weight to the law's threats. . . . [T]here seems to be no difference in wickedness, though there may be in skill, between the successful and the unsuccessful attempt[.]"

48 See Robinson, "Hybrid Principles for the Distribution of Criminal Sanctions," pp. 20–21.

49 Mitchell Berman writes that one of "the most famous" hybrid approaches was Hart's—that "the 'general justifying aim' of the institution of punishment [i]s crime reduction but. . . that pursuit of this consequentialist goal is constrained by a principle of 'retribution in distribution' that permits imposition of punishment only on 'an offender for an offense'" ("Punishment and Justification," p. 259). As Berman acknowledges, however, Hart's hybrid view is rather lopsided at least as to the underlying justification of punishment, assigning a very crucial role to consequentialism and a much less consequential role to retributivism.

50 Robinson, "Hybrid Principles," p. 38. Robinson believes that he has dissolved all conflict between the respective consequentialist functions because each of these has "the same goal" (efficient crime prevention) and a single currency," money (p. 32). This is what he describes as the "combined utilitarian formulation." Setting aside the plausibility of the unitary explanation that Robinson offers for the consequentialist pastiche—and there are good reasons to doubt it (whether rehabilitation or incapacitation can be explained purely monetarily is dubious)—the more important "hybrid" point deals with the relationship between the retributivist and consequentialist functions.

51 Hofer and Allenbaugh, "Reason Behind the Rules," p. 45.

52 Von Hirsch, "Hybrid Principles in Allocating Sanctions," p. 72.

53 See Chiu, "Culture as Justification," p. 1344.

54 Robinson, "Hybrid Principles," p. 38. For criticisms along similar lines, see Blumstein, "Search for the Elusive Common 'Principle,'" p. 50: "[Robinson's] final hybrid distributive principle seems to suggest that desert should overcome utilitarian concerns when you don't care about the utilitarian issues. While that is clearly unobjectionable, it seems to beg the primary question."

55 Robinson, "Hybrid Principles," pp. 30–31.

56 Alexander, Ferzan, and Morse, *Crime and Culpability*, pp. 94–103.

57 Ibid., pp. 96–97.

58 Ibid., pp. 98–99.

59 These examples are of course variations on older themes; see, for example, Thomson, "Killing, Letting Die, and the Trolley Problem."

60 Alexander, Ferzan, and Morse, *Culpability and Crime*, p. 100.

61 For Alexander and Ferzan, this type of grand schemer situation is better addressed by the mechanism of a culpable omission; that is, X may, as a result of his culpable causation, now be under a duty to act to rectify the situation (email of Larry Alexander to the author, October 14, 2009). But other types of grand schemer situations—the defense of others example discussed earlier may be one—may not lend themselves to a culpable omission analysis.

62 It may be that Alexander and Ferzan do not accept these doctrinal limitations on the choice of evils defense. I should add that the means-based limitation *would* rule out the utils or satisfaction derived from another person's suffering (or, as in the earlier example, of seeing someone's house in flames): "[e]ven if Deborah gets a huge thrill from imposing risks on others, that thrill should not be capable of tipping the consequentialist balance in favor of her risk impositions" (*Culpability and Crime*, p. 99 n. 28).

63 See DeGirolami, "Culpability in Creating," p. 601 (calling the culpability-in-causing exclusion a "retributivist check" on a defense that is otherwise consequentialist).

64 Robinson, "Hybrid Principles," p. 38.

65 Bergelson, "Consent to Harm," p. 700.

66 Even Simons, who is unusually sensitive to the competing values implicated in the choice of evils defense, suggests that the normative justification for the defense is either purely consequentialist or "some hybrid theory, such as consequentialism constrained by retributive or other deontological principles" ("Exploring the Intricacies," p. 646).

67 Hart, *Punishment and Responsibility*, p. 13.

68 Ibid., p. 13n. 6.

69 See Greenawalt, "Perplexing Borders of Justification and Excuse," p. 1906 (arguing that the law of justification, and the criminal law generally, do not impose a perfectionist ethic).

70 See DeGirolami, "Culpability in Creating."

71 Hampshire, *Justice Is Conflict.*

72 For learned comments, I thank Larry Alexander, Vera Bergelson, William Berry, Samuel Bray, Thom Brooks, Vincent Chiao, Chad Flanders, Mark Movsesian, Kenneth Simons, and Mark White.

Bibliography

Alexander, Larry, Kimberly Kessler Ferzan, and Stephen Morse. *Crime and Culpability: A Theory of Criminal Law*. New York: Cambridge University Press, 2009.

Bergelson, Vera. "Consent to Harm." *Pace Law Review* 28 (2008): 683–711.

Bergelson, Vera. "Rights, Wrongs, and Comparative Justifications." *Cardozo Law Review* 28 (2007): 2481–503.

Berman, Mitchell N. "Punishment and Justification."*Ethics* 118 (2008): 258–90.

Blumstein, Alfred. "The Search for the Elusive Common 'Principle.'"*Northwestern Law Review* 82 (1987): 43–51.

Brudner, Alan. "A Theory of Necessity."*Oxford Journal of Legal Studies* 7 (1987): 339–68.

Carter, Derrick Augustus. "Knight in the Duel with Death: Physician Assisted Suicide and the Medical Necessity Defense." *Villanova Law Review* 41 (1996): 663–724.

Chiu, Elaine. "Culture as Justification, Not Excuse."*American Criminal Law Review* 43 (2006): 1317–74.

DeGirolami, Marc O. "Culpability in Creating the Choice of Evils."*Alabama Law Review* 60 (2008): 597–647.

Dressler, Joshua. "Exegesis of the Law of Duress: Justifying the Excuse and Searching for its Proper Limits." *Southern California Law Review* 62 (1989): 1331–86.

Fletcher, George P. *Basic Concepts of Criminal Law*. New York: Oxford University Press, 1998.

Fletcher. *Rethinking Criminal Law*. New York: Oxford University Press, 1978.

Garvey, Stephen P. "Lifting the Veil on Punishment." *Buffalo Criminal Law Review* 7 (2004): 443–64.

Greenawalt, Kent. "The Perplexing Borders of Justification and Excuse."*Columbia Law Review* 84 (1984): 1897–927.

Hampshire, Stuart. *Justice Is Conflict*. Princeton: Princeton University Press, 1999.

Hart, H. L. A. *Punishment and Responsibility: Essays in the Philosophy of Law*. New York: Oxford University Press, 1968.

Hofer, Paul J., and Mark H. Allenbaugh. "The Reason Behind the Rules: Finding and Using the Philosophy of the Federal Sentencing Guidelines." *American Criminal Law Review* (2003): 19–85.

Hoffheimer, Michael H. "Codifying Necessity: Legislative Resistance to Enacting Choice-of-Evils Defenses to Criminal Liability." *Tulane Law Review* 82 (2007): 191–244.

Huigens, Kyron. "The Continuity of Justification Defenses." *Illinois Law Review* 2009 (2009): 627–95.

Husak, Douglas N. *Philosophy of Criminal Law*. Lanham, MD: Rowman& Littlefield Publishers, Inc., 1987.

Kutz, Christopher. "Torture, Necessity and Existential Politics." *California Law Review* 95 (2007): 235–76.

LaFave, Wayne R. *Criminal Law*. 4th ed. St. Paul: Thomson/West Publishers, 2003.

Martin, Shaun P. "The Radical Necessity Defense." *University of Cincinnati Law Review* 73 (2005): 1527–607.

Morris, Norval. "Desert as a Limiting Principle." In *Principled Sentencing: Readings on Theory and Policy*, edited by Andrew von Hirsch and Andrew Ashworth, 180–84. Oxford: Hart Publishing, 1998.

Parry, John T. "The Virtue of Necessity: Reshaping Culpability and the Rule of Law." *Houston Law Review* 36(1999): 397–469.

Posner, Richard A. "An Economic Theory of the Criminal Law." *Columbia Law Review* 85 (1985): 1193–231.

Ristroph, Alice. "Respect and Resistance in Punishment Theory." *California Law Review* 97 (2009): 601–32.

Robinson, Paul H. "Hybrid Principles for the Distribution of Criminal Sanctions." *Northwestern Law Review* 82 (1987): 19–42.

Robinson, Paul H. "Causing the Conditions of One's Own Defense: A Study of the Limits of Theory in Criminal Law Doctrine." *Virginia Law Review* 71 (1985): 1–63.

Simons, Kenneth W. "Exploring the Intricacies of the Lesser Evils Defense." *Law and Philosophy* 24 (2005): 645–79.

Smart, J. J. C., and Bernard Williams. *Utilitarianism: For and Against*. Cambridge: Cambridge University Press, 1973.

Stephen, James Fitzjames. *A History of the Criminal Law of England, Volume II*. London: MacMillen and Co., 1882.

Thomson, Judith Jarvis. "Killing, Letting Die, and the Trolley Problem." *The Monist* 59 (1976): 204–17.

von Hirsch, Andrew. "Hybrid Principles in Allocating Sanctions: A Response to Professor Robinson." *Northwestern Law Review* 82 (1987): 64–72.

11

RETRIBUTIVE SENTENCING, MULTIPLE OFFENDERS,

AND BULK DISCOUNTS

Richard L. Lippke

ONE OF THE more vexing problems in sentencing theory is posed by individuals who have pled or been found guilty of numerous criminal offenses and face sentencing for all of them at once. The problem is not solely a theoretical one, as many of the individuals who offend do so in multiple ways. When individuals are convicted of multiple crimes, should we require them to serve the sentences for each of them one right after the other—that is, consecutively? Or should we require them to serve only one of their sentences, presumably the longest one, effectively subsuming the rest of them under it? The former option will produce spectacularly long sentences for some multiple offenders; the latter will make it seem as if multiple offenders are no different than single ones. The unpalatable implications of these two alternatives naturally spur us to search for some middle ground between them.

But is it possible to find and defend such a middle ground? My aim in this chapter is not only to do so but to do so from within a retributive sentencing framework. Such a framework poses its own difficulties, not the least of which is its reputation as an uncompromising approach to punishment's justification. Some would have us believe that retributive sentencing theory's implications are straightforward: Punish offenders proportionately with the seriousness of all of their crimes, and be done with it. But a properly developed retributive sentencing approach must accommodate competing principles. This, I contend, points us toward assigning multiple offenders sentences that are longer than those assigned single offenders but shorter than the ones multiple offenders would serve if they had to serve all of their sentences in succession. Further complicating matters, however, is the variety of multiple offenders. Some victimize many people by a single act or coordinated series of actions. Others victimize people sequentially, as in the case of serial murderers, arsonists, and rapists, and yet we often find ourselves sentencing them on one occasion for several of their offenses. Still others commit a more or less coordinated series of criminal acts and so on. Once their diverse character is understood, it is not obvious that all multiple offenders should be treated alike when it comes to sentencing.

Furthermore, there is considerable uncertainty about what a proportionate sentencing scheme should look like, apart from its addressing the problems raised by multiple offenders. Some progress has been made by theorists when it comes to ranking the comparative severity of offenses and sanctions (what Andrew von Hirsch has termed the problem of "ordinal" proportionality).[1] But the sticking point remains the anchoring point of the entire sentencing scale (which von Hirsch refers to as the problem of "cardinal" proportionality)—in particular, whether we should favor a "decremental strategy" that brings overall sanction levels down significantly from their current levels or some other strategy which might not bring them down quite so much.[2] I shall not have much to say about specific sentence lengths for the various kinds of offenses in the discussion that follows. The problems raised by multiple offenders are likely to persist unless we move overall sentencing levels in one of two extreme directions: toward exceedingly mild sentences or exceedingly lengthy ones. In the former case, consecutively served sentences might not add up to much, so the problem of what to do with multiple offenders will become moot. In the latter case, there would be little point to concerning ourselves with the impact of multiple sentences if all offenders, whether multiple or not, were sentenced to draconian prison terms. So long as we imagine that overall sentencing scales remain somewhere in between these extremes, as they are likely to do, the problem of what to say about the sentencing of multiple offenders will be a live and interesting one.[3] Still, uncertainty about how the sentencing scale is anchored is bound to affect, to some extent, our thinking about what to do with multiple offenders.

In urging a middle ground in the sentencing of multiple offenders, I avoid introducing considerations that seem largely extraneous to retributive sentencing approaches. Some would argue for minimizing the sentences of multiple offenders on grounds of mercy or parsimony. The former, it seems to me, is too individualized to serve as the basis for a general policy of not assigning multiple offenders consecutive sentences.[4] We might reduce sentences for particular offenders out of mercy based on their peculiar characteristics or circumstances, but most multiple offenders will not share those characteristics or circumstances.[5] Parsimony, if understood as a principle designed to limit sentences to "no more than necessary to achieve the aims of punishment," seems empty without some independent account of whether consecutive sentences are needed to achieve punishment's aims.[6] If parsimony in punishment is understood differently—as a requirement that we reduce punishment when the broader social conditions of just punishment are not satisfied sufficiently, or when sanctions cannot be kept in conformity with retributive constraints on just punishment—then I believe, and have argued elsewhere, that it can serve as a basis for reduced sentences.[7] However, parsimony, so understood, is an independent ground of diminished punishment which should not, in my view, be confused with the question of whether the cumulative impact of sentences on multiple offenders should likewise serve as a ground for reducing them. Simply put, even in societies that are reasonably just and employ sanctions consistent with treating offenders as morally self-governing beings, the question whether multiple offenders should have to serve all or only some part of all of their several sentences will have to be addressed.

1. Laying Out the Options

Let us call the approach to the sentencing of multiple offenders in which they have to serve the sentences for all of their crimes in succession "Strong Consecutivism." If, for instance, an individual was convicted of five murders and assigned a life sentence for each of them, then Strong Consecutivism would have us assign him five consecutive life sentences. Many will regard such an approach as absurd on its face: no one should be sentenced to several hundred years of imprisonment, even if for only symbolic purposes. Yet Strong Consecutivism seems troubling even if we set to one side the extreme case of successive life sentences. Suppose that an individual, in a coordinated series of actions, defrauds 100 people of $10,000 each. Suppose also that the sentence for defrauding a single person of that sum is three months of confinement. Strong Consecutivism would have us sentence the perpetrator of the mass fraud to 300 months in prison. That, too, seems excessive, even if not quite absurd.

Strong Consecutivism goes against what has been termed the "Totality Principle," a principle according to which the total sentences assigned multiple offenders must not be allowed to become excessive or disproportionately severe.[8] Those who favor a crime reduction approach to the justification of legal punishment would seem to have a relatively easy time defending some version of the Totality Principle, for there is scant evidence linking longer sentences with greater marginal deterrence.[9] Longer sentences will, admittedly, incapacitate offenders for more extensive periods of time, but it is well known that there are diminishing crime reduction returns on lengthy prison terms.[10] At some point, most offenders "age out," meaning that they naturally desist from further offending. Continued imprisonment of such individuals is costly and produces few benefits. Further, there seems little reason to believe that long prison stints serve any sort of rehabilitative purpose. Indeed, quite the opposite seems likely—that the longer the prison terms served by individuals, the less likely that they subsequently will be able to forge productive lives in society.[11]

Those who defend retributive approaches to legal punishment have also sought to defend some version of the Totality Principle. The problem they face is that the standard retributive requirement that sentences be proportionate with the seriousness of crimes does not, it seems, provide unequivocal support for the principle. That requirement, as it is usually interpreted, pertains to the punishment of individual offenses. But what if someone has committed numerous and quite serious offenses and is being sentenced for them all at once? How then does proportionality work to set an upper limit on the amount of overall punishment that he or she is to be assigned? There may be answers to these questions that retributivists can offer, but it takes some work to uncover them. Furthermore, some of the answers that desert theorists have put forward seem singularly unpersuasive.

At the other end of the sentencing spectrum is what we might term "Strong Concurrentivism," according to which individuals convicted of multiple offenses should serve the sentence for their most serious offense, with sentences for any equivalent or lesser offenses served concurrently. Though Strong Concurrentivism is unlikely to yield excessively long sentences, at least under otherwise defensible sentencing schemes, it too has implications that are unsettling. Under such an approach, the perpetrator of the mass fraud might have to serve only a three-month sentence, with the 99 additional three-month sentences served concurrently. In effect, such a multiple offender would be given a huge "bulk discount" in spite of the fact that she victimized many people.[12] Her first victim "costs" her three months imprisonment, but her other 99 are, as it were, "free." Yet surely a defensible sentencing scheme would have us punish more severely someone who victimizes many people as opposed to a single person.[13] Again, crime reduction approaches seem adept at accommodating this point. We should create stronger disincentives (in the form of longer sentences) for those tempted to victimize many people. Moreover, multiple victimizers are probably more dangerous, on average, than single ones, and so more suitable candidates for lengthier incapacitation. They may likewise be more in need of rehabilitation or perhaps less amenable to it and so should simply be kept locked up for longer periods of time.

Retributive theorists would seem to be on firm ground in defending longer sentences for multiple rather than nonmultiple offenders, especially given their tendency to focus attention on the victims of crimes and the injustices done to them. Strong Concurrentivism runs contrary to a principle requiring us to acknowledge each direct victim of a crime in a multiple offender's sentence.[14] Subsequently, I term this the "Each Victim Counts" (or EVC) Principle. By the "direct victim" of a crime, I refer to the person assaulted, stolen from, injured, or killed by the criminal offender. Direct victims are to be distinguished from "related victims" (that is, those individuals affected by crimes, sometimes quite dramatically, due to their close personal relationship with direct victims) and "indirect victims" (that is, members of the general public who fear victimization or have to bear some of the costs of apprehending, convicting, and punishing offenders). Retributive theorists have typically ignored related and indirect victims in developing their approaches to sentencing, though it is not clear whether it is appropriate for them to do so.[15] However, to simplify things, I will adhere to the common practice of focusing exclusively on direct victims.

There are different ways in which retributivists might have multiple offenders' sentences acknowledge their direct victims. Strong Consecutivism would do so in a particularly robust way, since in theory it would require multiple offenders to serve cumulative sentences that reflect the wrongs done to each of their victims. Yet such punishment outcomes are, as we have seen, at odds with the Totality Principle. Fortunately, other options may exist for retributivists. For instance, we can imagine a scheme of modest bulk discounts, according to which multiple offenders would have to serve a substantial portion of the sentence for the crimes against each of their direct victims, though not the whole sentences. Perhaps the offender who defrauds 100 victims would have to serve a two-month sentence for each fraud or a one-month sentence for each of them. We might term such an approach to sentencing "Moderate Consecutivism." Like its pure counterpart, it runs afoul of the Totality Principle, though not quite as badly.

Alternatively, we can envision a scheme of more generous bulk discounts, according to which multiple offenders would have to serve only a small portion of what would be the typical sentence for each crime that they committed. The mass defrauder might serve 100 10-day sentences, for a total of less than three years imprisonment. We could term such an approach to sentencing "Moderate Concurrentivism." Like its more stringent counterpart, it seeks to limit dramatically the impact of multiple sentences. Further complexity is introduced by the possibility of granting increasing sentence discounts for each additional offense. Thus, for instance, the mass defrauder might receive a three-month sentence reflecting the harm done to her first victim, a two-month for her second, and so on down to a very brief sentence reflecting the harm done to her one-hundredth victim.

Given the many complexities raised by the sentencing of multiple offenders, the conclusions I reach are no more than tentative. I contend that neither Strong Consecutivism nor Strong Concurrentivism is attractive. As between Moderate Consecutivism and Moderate Concurrentivism, some version of the latter seems preferable, especially if a convincing account of the Totality Principle can be produced. However, there are positions available in between the two moderate views that would have to be considered in any more comprehensive treatment of the problems raised by multiple offenders.

2. Interpreting and Defending the Totality Principle

Again, the impetus for rejecting Strong Consecutivism is that it would sometimes produce cumulative sentences for multiple offenders that seem excessive, perhaps stupendously so. As I have already noted, there are competing ways of interpreting such a presumptive upper limit on multiple offender sentences and rationales for it. In this section, I survey some of the accounts of the Totality Principle put forward by those with retributive sympathies, show why they seem inadequate, and sketch an alternative account. I also address an important objection to having such a principle at all. Given space limitations, my remarks will have to be more brief than the subject matter warrants.

Andrew Ashworth notes a version of the Totality Principle that has been adopted by the British courts and which appears to be grounded in the notion of ordinal proportionality. The court, in assigning sentences, "is to consider the overall sentence in relation to the totality of the offending and in relation to sentencing levels for other crimes."[16] What this means is that judges are not to permit the total sentence served by a multiple offender to bump up her sentence from one appropriate for a less severe crime to one appropriate for a more severe one. For instance, if an offender is being sentenced for multiple residential burglaries, we should assign her a sentence that is greater than the one we would assign to someone guilty of a single such burglary. However, we should not let the enhanced sentence bump her total sentence up into the range that would be appropriate for someone convicted of a more serious crime such as armed robbery or aggravated assault. The idea seems to be that no matter how many crimes of a given type an offender has committed, it is a violation of ordinal proportionality to allow her sentence to become one appropriate for a more serious offense.[17] But what if an offender has committed a diverse group of crimes for which she is being sentenced at a given time? The answer, one surmises, is that her overall sentence should not bump her punishment up into a range that exceeds the sentence for her most serious offense.

This version of the Totality Principle seems somewhat arbitrary in stipulating that the total sentence of someone who has committed numerous lesser crimes should never exceed the sentence of someone who has committed a single, more serious one. Given that offense seriousness is a matter of degree, there could be two offenses that are not only adjacent on the crime seriousness scale but such that one is only slightly worse than the other. Ashworth's Totality Principle says that multiple offenses of the lesser kind should never be allowed to nudge an offender's sentence into the range for the slightly more serious kind of offense. But why should that be true no matter how large the number of (slightly) lesser crimes? Even if we consider offenses that are further separated on the crime seriousness scale, this version of the Totality Principle does not seem wholly convincing. Rape is, I assume, a less serious offense than manslaughter, and certainly a less serious offense than second degree homicide. But is it really plausible to say that someone who has committed ten rapes should not be assigned a total sentence that puts it up in the range that we would reserve for manslaughter or even second degree homicide? It is, admittedly, hard to discern how we should go about making comparisons among the harms suffered by individual crime victims.[18] But rape surely inflicts serious harm on its victims, though they remain alive and will (hopefully) eventually recover from the physical and emotional trauma, along with the severe affront to their dignity, that rape inflicts. Similar things obviously cannot be said about manslaughter or second degree homicide victims. Yet, if a serial rapist inflicts severe harm on many, many victims, is it persuasive to claim that what he has done is less bad, and so deserving of less punishment, than the perpetrator of a single manslaughter or second degree homicide? I, for one, am not at all confident about that judgment.

A different Totality Principle can be gleaned from Ashworth's and Andrew von Hirsch's defense of a decremental sentencing scheme, one that aims at reducing current (by their lights, excessive) levels of sentencing.[19] Ashworth and von Hirsch contend that sentences exceeding five years imprisonment should not be assigned, except for the most malicious kinds of homicide. The reason for this, they argue, is that the moral message that legal punishment is designed to convey to offenders will be obscured or undermined by the prospect of lengthy penal confinement. Offenders facing terrifyingly long prison terms may not be able to comprehend much beyond their own fears; such sentences are therefore inconsistent with addressing them as moral beings. Whether von Hirsch and Ashworth would urge such a conclusion for multiple offenders, especially the more serious kinds of them, is unclear. Yet it is hard to see how they could avoid doing so. After all, if we must steer clear of lengthy prison terms because they will produce mind-numbing fear in nonmultiple offenders, then this presumably will be true, as well, for multiple offenders, unless we make the questionable assumption that multiple offenders are less inclined to come into the grips of such fear. Of course, von Hirsch and Ashworth could consistently maintain that multiple offenders ought to receive somewhat longer sentences than nonmultiple ones. But presumably the bulk discounts given multiple offenders would have to be rather steep, or else their cumulative sentences would quickly exceed the limits set by the need to preserve punishment's expressive role. For instance, a serial rapist with many victims might receive a three- or four-year sentence, while a rapist with just one victim would receive some lesser sentence (say, a year or two). According to this version of the Totality Principle, then, multiple offenders' sentences should not be allowed to jeopardize offenders' abilities to perceive punishment's censure of their conduct.

Von Hirsch's and Ashworth's argument in defense of a robustly decremental sentencing approach, and by implication, a fairly powerful version of the Totality Principle, seems unpersuasive for a number of reasons. Leave aside the worry that the exceedingly mild sentences that von Hirsch and Ashworth would have us employ against even the most serious offenders appear to run the risk of trivializing their crimes.[20] Von Hirsch's and Ashworth's intuitions about what is necessary to censure deliberate murder are, I have to say, decidedly different than my own. The deeper problem, in any case, is that they offer little to convince us that sentences longer than five years imprisonment undermine the moral message punishment is meant to convey. Is their claim that individuals sentenced to more than five years imprisonment somehow lose their abilities to comprehend the moral condemnation expressed by their sentences? That would seem to be a proposition that is, in part, subject to some empirical testing. It would not be surprising to find out that many people, facing a prison sentence of any length whatsoever, are deeply traumatized by it. Indeed, the evidence suggests that the initial adjustment to prison life is a difficult one for most novices to imprisonment.[21] But the evidence also suggests that most prisoners make the adjustment after some period of time and do not suffer catastrophic mental breakdowns of the sort that we might reasonably believe will compromise their abilities to understand and act on the censure expressed by their sentences. Veterans of the prison system might not have to go through the initial adjustment (or readjustment) period at all or will get through it more quickly. Even if some individuals sentenced to prison are completely undone by the prospect or are unable to make the adjustment to prison life without debilitating breakdowns, this will not help von Hirsch and Ashworth much. They do not, after all, advocate the abolition of imprisonment for serious offenses, only reductions in sentence lengths. That suggests that they might be prepared to accept the severe traumatization of those few offenders who simply cannot cope with prison life. Von Hirsch and Ashworth could conceivably argue that any long-term imprisonment is so damaging to the capacity for moral self-governance that it is incompatible with the continuing comprehension of the moral condemnation that punishment is meant to convey. But again, we might reasonably doubt such a claim or at least insist on being provided some evidence for it. It could turn out to be true that particularly harsh forms of imprisonment have such debilitating effects, but that more humanely organized forms of it do not.[22] Yet von Hirsch's and Ashworth's argument shows little sensitivity to such variations among prison regimes, and that limits its credibility.

Anthony Bottoms sketches a third interpretation of the Totality Principle that he believes retributive theorists might be able to accept. By his account, we should have mercy on a multiple offender whose cumulative sentence would deprive him of "a high proportion of the prime years of his life."[23] Bottoms cites the example of a very active residential burglar who is being sentenced, all at once, for 100 burglaries, the cumulative sentence for which would add up to 50 years of imprisonment. Bottoms claims that the court might reasonably have "some mercy" on such an offender and others like him who face horrifically long sentences. Bottoms does not attempt to specify the magnitude of the bulk discounts that he is willing to have the courts bestow, but he assures us that a willingness to be similarly merciful with other multiple offenders means that granting them bulk discounts need not lead to widespread inequities in sentencing.[24]

There is, however, a crucial ambiguity in Bottoms's account of the Totality Principle. Is it that we are not to allow sentences in multiple offender cases to take too high a proportion of the prime years of offenders' lives come what may or relative to the seriousness of their crimes? The former interpretation seems implausible. It would not explain why we should give bulk discounts to older offenders, ones who are already past the prime years of their lives, perhaps well past. More importantly, it would seem to suggest that no offender should be sentenced to a prison term exceeding 15 to 20 years, no matter how terrible any of his crimes or how numerous. Even offenders sentenced in their late teens or early twenties would seem destined to lose too high a proportion of the prime years of their lives if sentences longer than 15 or 20 years were imposed. But if they have committed several brutal murders, then I am not quite sure why we should be reluctant to take away most if not all the prime years of their lives. The way to avoid these difficulties is to interpret Bottoms as requiring us to weigh the impact of cumulative sentences against the seriousness of the offenses committed by individuals. What seems wrong with sentencing the high-rate residential burglar to 50 years imprisonment is not the simple fact that it takes too many of the prime years of his life, but also that no one of his crimes was anywhere near so grave as to warrant a 50-year sentence. Sure, the victims of his crimes had important interests that were set back in various ways, but presumably they recovered in relatively short order. The burglar's life, by comparison, would be almost entirely ruined by a 50-year sentence. But then it is not so much mercy that should lead us to abjure such a sentence as disproportion. This points us toward a different version of the Totality Principle, one that grounds it in a comparison of the harms inflicted on multiple offenders by legal punishment with those suffered by the direct victims of their crimes.[25]

This fourth version of the Totality Principle says that multiple offenders should not be made to endure penal losses and deprivations the total impact of which exceeds, by too significant a margin, the harms which they culpably inflicted on any one of their victims. On this interpretation of the Totality Principle, multiple offenders could be assigned longer sentences than nonmultiple ones. But multiple offenders should receive bulk discounts, sometimes substantial ones, in order to keep the overall impact of their sentences from becoming obviously disproportionate with the harms that they culpably inflicted on any one of their victims. Granted, whether the overall impact of sanctions is "obviously disproportionate" with victim harms or exceeds such harms "by too significant a margin" are matters about which there will be dispute. But similar disputes occur when it comes to judging the proportionality of sentences for nonmultiple offenders. There is no precise metric for making judgments of proportionality, given the ways in which they require us to make both comparative and noncomparative evaluations of justice. Nonetheless, it will be clear to most observers that some sentences are clearly excessive, others are probably so, while still others are closer (and hence more debatable) calls.[26] Indeed, if we refuse entirely to compare victim harm and penal harm in making such judgments, it is hard to see what other basis exists for determining proportionality.

It might be objected that we cannot really weigh and compare the harms suffered by crime victims with those inflicted by legal punishment. The physical and emotional injuries inflicted on crime victims, in particular, cannot meaningfully be compared with the losses and deprivations inflicted by legal punishment in the form of imprisonment. I concede that making such comparisons is not easy and that our attempts to do so inevitably will be somewhat crude. I have argued elsewhere that we might try to simplify such comparisons by focusing on the ways and extent to which crimes defeat the abilities of victims to live decent lives of their own choosing and the corresponding ways in which criminal sanctions, including humane imprisonment, have similar effects.[27] Serious crimes make victims' lives very difficult and sometimes do so for many years. Such crimes may also, of course, deprive victims of their lives entirely. This points us toward the use of imprisonment, perhaps extended imprisonment, as the appropriate sanction for such offenses, especially on the assumption that those who committed them acted with a high degree of culpability. Still, many crimes, including some currently treated as serious offenses in some countries, do not do much to impede victims' lives and, as a result, should not be punished very severely. Many property crimes, for instance, inflict temporary losses or setbacks upon victims from which they recover fairly quickly (especially when their property losses are covered by insurance). Given the substantial harms wrought by even short terms of imprisonment, such a comparative approach cautions us against its overuse, and that seems an important point in its favor.[28]

According to this fourth version of the Totality Principle, a serial rapist should receive a longer sentence than a nonserial one, but he should receive a bulk discount so that his total sentence will not be devastating to his ability to at some point go on with his life. Rape is a serious crime, but the victims of it do recover after some period of time and presumably go onto have decent lives. Hence, even serial rapists should not, for the most part, be sentenced to death or life imprisonment or even to prison terms above a certain range (say, 10 to 15 years), especially if we assume that the sentence for a single rape should not exceed five years imprisonment. Still, the principle could be treated as presumptive.[29] Perhaps a rapist with 50 victims would have to be assigned a sentence that was destructive of his life prospects though no single one of his rapes was comparably destructive to the life prospects of his victim. But such high-rate serial offenders would presumably be the exception, not the rule.

Those who favor Strong or Moderate Consecutivism might contend that it is sometimes appropriate for legal punishment to ruin offender's lives or deprive them of most of the prime years of their lives, though they have done nothing comparable to the lives of any of their victims. Consider in this regard ordinary recidivists, by whom I mean individuals who continue to commit crimes of greater or lesser magnitude though they are repeatedly arrested, charged, and punished proportionately for each of them. Such individuals' entire lives might be spent in and out of prisons, although mostly in them. As a result, their capacities for living decent lives of their own choosing will be severely impaired, at least by comparison with those of free citizens living in civil society. Yet, there seems little reason to try to lessen the impact of penal sanctions on them, no matter how devastating it might turn out to be.[30] Why, then, should we attempt to limit the cumulative effects of multiple offenders' sentences? Is there all that much difference between them and ordinary recidivists?

We might despair at the prospect of ordinary recidivists' lives being ruined by their successive punishments. But I agree that we should not regard the cumulative impact of their sentences as constituting a reason for reducing their sentences as we continue to assign them. Yet this does not show that we should opt for Strong or Moderate Consecutivism in sentencing multiple offenders. Why not? Because we might reasonably view each of ordinary recidivists' convictions (and the sanctions endured for them) as opportunities for them to mend their ways—to bring their conduct into conformity with the law and (let us suppose) the underlying moral norms that it aims at enforcing.[31] Yes, their lives have been ruined by the cumulative impact of the sanctions assigned them for each of their offenses, and yes, it may be the case the no one of their offenses came remotely close to ruining the life of anyone else. Nevertheless, the responsibility for ordinary recidivists' sorry lives is all or at least mostly on them.[32] Multiple offenders, by contrast, are sentenced all at once for their several crimes. No official state censure of their conduct has intervened between their offenses, even if some time has elapsed between them; neither have they had the opportunity punishment affords of reassessing their conduct and the difficult path it is leading them down. We might therefore reasonably seek to limit the overall impact of their deserved punishment upon their lives in ways that we do not for ordinary recidivists.[33]

3. Acknowledging Each Direct Victim

The second sentencing principle relevant to multiple offender cases has already been identified: the sentences of multiple offenders should acknowledge and therefore reflect the harms done to (or threatened against) each of the direct victims of their crimes. Again, I term this the "Each Victim Counts" (or EVC) Principle. The basic intuition behind the EVC Principle is that there is something unseemly about sentencing multiple offenders as if they directly harmed only one victim when, in fact, they harmed several of them. Similarly, if a single individual is victimized in more than one way (say, she is raped and robbed), then the multiple victimizations should be acknowledged in the offender's sentence.[34] All of an offender's victims or victimizations should be reflected somehow in the offender's sentence, not just the first or the most serious one.

The EVC Principle might be disputed by Strong Concurrentivists. They could argue that so long as separate sentences reflecting the harm to each victim (modified appropriately by the culpability of the offender in inflicting them) were pronounced by the courts, that would sufficiently acknowledge each victim, even if the sentences were served concurrently. In other words, at the time of sentencing, the judge would note and thereby officially condemn the wrongs done against each victim, but offenders would actually have to serve only the sentence for their most serious crime. There is something to be said for this proposal, but I do not ultimately find it convincing. Under such a sentencing policy, offenders who had five or ten or fifty victims would presumably receive no greater punishment than offenders who had only one, and that does not seem an attractive position. Again, it suggests that the offender must only "pay" for the one victim, while the others (no matter how many) are "free."

In response, it might be argued that the sentence actually served could be viewed as the appropriate penal response for any one of the victims, assuming that it adequately reflected the harm done and the culpability of the offending agent. The sentence would presumably do so as long as it was based on the offender's most serious crime. We should not get too hung up on the notion that the sentence appears to be the appropriate penal response to only one of the victims, as if they rest did not matter. The sentence could be viewed as fitting if we focus exclusively on the first, fifth, tenth, or fiftieth victim. There is, after all, no "super-victim" to whom the harms done by the multiple offender collectively accrue, only each separate victim with the harms he or she suffered.

But this response seems to work only if we are willing to resort to some sleight of hand in thinking about these matters. It just does seem worse for an offender to have multiple victims, and perhaps many of them, even if each of them suffers roughly the same harm and the offender's concurrent sentence is calibrated to the worst harm any one of them suffered. Surely we should have some way to distinguish the rapist who has a single victim from the serial rapist who when apprehended and convicted of one rape confesses to four others. Admittedly, we could say to each of his five victims that his actual penalty served (in the case of a concurrent sentence) reflects the severity of the harm he did to each them, but is hard to ignore the nagging thought that we are being somewhat dishonest in saying this. The rapist with a single victim has done a terrible thing; the serial rapist has done something much worse, and his punishment should reflect that. One way for it to do so would be to assign the serial rapist a sentence for a single rape and then supplement it with additional increments of penalty, one for each of his further victims. Since it is somewhat arbitrary which of his victims counts as the "first" one, each of them could view the initial sentence as one fitting, given his crime against them. And since the serial rapist's sentence could be made to exceed, by some nonnegligible margin, the sentence assigned to a nonserial rapist, we could then plausibly say to each of the serial rapist's victims that he was being punished for the wrong done to each of them.

Predictably, the Strong Consecutivist will at this point object that the only way to fully acknowledge each victim (or victimization) is to assign multiple offenders a sentence for each crime and then simply total up the sentences. Indeed, the Strong Consecutivist appears to favor a more demanding version of the EVC Principle, which we might term the "Each Victim Counts Equally Principle" (or EVCE Principle, for short). Since the EVCE Principle appears to preclude the Totality Principle having any effect on the sentencing of multiple offenders, consecutivists could compromise and opt for Moderate Consecutivism, according to which only modest bulk discounts would be available to multiple offenders. Moderate Consecutivism would often yield quite lengthy sentences, since multiple offenders would have to serve close to the full sentence for each of their offenses and do so successively. Under it, multiple offenders might wind up serving sentences that take far more from them than they took from any one of their victims. That seems prima facie unjust and a consideration in support of Moderate Concurrentivism. Notice this also: Moderate Concurrentivists could take something from the EVCE Principle. Multiple offenders could be assigned a sentence reflecting the gravity of their offense against the (arbitrarily stipulated "first") victim, and then assigned further sentence increments (though substantially bulk discounted ones) for each of their additional victims. Instead of increasing bulk discounts, Moderate Concurrentivists could insist on fixed ones. That way, further victims and the wrongs they suffered at the hands of multiple offenders would be, to some extent, acknowledged equally. Moderate Consecutivists could not consistently object that such an approach does not fully count all victims equally; only Strong Consecutivism does that.

Nonetheless, some middle ground position between Moderate Consecutivism and Moderate Concurrentivism might be staked out and defended. Even if we believe that the former gives too little weight to the Totality Principle, it is possible to conceive of bulk discounts that are somewhere in between modest and substantial. It is tempting to assert that such a middle ground position likewise gives too little weight to the Totality Principle. But that is an argument that would have to be developed more fully, and doing so may not be easy. Indeed, it is not preposterous to believe that we have arrived at a juncture at which retributivists simply have deeply conflicting intuitions about sentencing that may not be amenable to much in the way of rational resolution.

The EVC would seem to have a corollary, one that retributivists could accept in order to limit multiple offender sentences. This corollary principle invokes the well-known, though not always precise, distinction between *mala in se* and *mala prohibita*. Many multiple offenders will be convicted or plead guilty to both types of offenses. The corollary principle enjoins us to allow sentences for multiple offenders' *mala prohibita* crimes to be served concurrently with the sentences for their *mala in se*. With *mala prohibita*, there are typically no identifiable victims of the crimes, and thus no one whose interests must be acknowledged in multiple offenders' sentences. It is not that violations of *mala prohibita* are unimportant, or that individuals who violate such provisions should not be punished. But the sanctions for *mala in se* will typically be more severe, as they should be, since they constitute wrongs to direct victims. Hence, individuals whose multiple offending consists in both types of offenses will already receive substantial sentences. Moreover, the primary reason that the criminal law exists is to protect the vital interests of members of society in their lives, liberty, property, privacy, and dignity.[35] *Mala prohibita* play, at most, indirect roles in securing and protecting such interests and would often not exist at all but for their prohibiting conduct that aids and abets the commission of *mala in se*. It thus makes sense to view punishment of conduct that violates *mala prohibita* as subordinate to the punishment of conduct that violates *mala in se*. We can therefore refer to this corollary principle as the "Subordination Principle."

A weaker version of the Subordination Principle would permit us to augment the sentences of individuals who commit *mala in se* if they also violate *mala prohibita* but require steep bulk discounts for such violations. It arguably is worse to illegally acquire income through theft or fraud and to lie to the authorities about doing so when interrogated. But the former should be our main focus, and so punishment of the latter might be mostly symbolic, perhaps adding vanishingly small increments to offenders' sentences.

4. Further Application of the Sentencing Principles

In the discussion so far, I have sketched the implications of Moderate Concurrentivism, the position which I favor, for the subset of multiple offenders who are serial offenders. Again, by "serial offenders" I refer to individuals who commit multiple *mala in se* over a period of time but who face sentencing for them all at once. Such offenders should be given longer sentences than nonserial ones, in recognition of the fact that they have victimized numerous individuals. The additional sentence increments assigned to serial offenders should be fixed and substantially bulk discounted. Still, I would concede that such offenders present the most troubling challenges to concurrentivism because they are most similar to (though arguably distinguishable from) ordinary recidivists, whose successive sentences should not be limited by the Totality Principle. Also, serial offenders' direct victims have a powerful call upon us when it comes to sentencing.

There are other kinds of multiple offenders, and it is useful to explore the implications for their sentencing of the principles that we have identified. Like others who have examined the bulk discount question, I do not have a high degree of confidence in some of the claims about to be expressed. My strategy will be to point to subtle differences among multiple offenders in an effort to marshal support for extending one type of bulk discount to them rather than another. But I shall work with only rough categories of multiple offenders, and I am fully aware that other multiple offenders exist who do not fall neatly into any of the categories. Even for those who do fall neatly into one of the categories, different approaches to the bulk discounting of their sentences can be envisioned.

A. MULTIPLE OFFENDING AROUND A SINGLE ORGANIZING OFFENSE

Multiple offenders in this group were also alluded to earlier. They commit a central offense but one that is preceded by other offenses (for example, conspiracy if there is more than one perpetrator involved and the main offense was not spur-of-the-moment) and succeeded by others. It is not uncommon for offenders to flee pursuing police, lie to them, or otherwise attempt to conceal their crimes, resist arrest, illegally possess a firearm, and the like. The prior and subsequent offenses would not occur or come to light if not for the central organizing offense, and so arguably that primary offense ought to be the main focus in sentencing. Some of the prior and subsequent offenses will involve violations of *mala prohibita*. Sentences for these should either be served concurrently with the sentence for the primary offense or should be quite steeply discounted, due to the absence of any direct victims. Of course, if in resisting arrest, an offender assaults, or worse, injures a police officer or other official, things are different. Depending on the gravity of the injury attempted or completed, the offender's sentence should be augmented. A further complication involves the commission of multiple offenses, no single one of which can be plausibly described as a single organizing one, preceded and followed by other offenses. The multiple offenses, assuming there are victims in each of them, necessitate treatment along the lines of serial offending discussed previously, though sentences for associated violations of *mala prohibita* might still be served concurrently.

B. COMPLEX SINGLE TRANSACTION OFFENSES

Some crimes involve a series of criminal transactions, no one of which inflicts more than modest or moderate harms on victims but the cumulative harms of which are substantial. For instance, the crime of embezzlement often involves an employee or official misappropriating small amounts of property over an extended period of time. In making decisions about how to deal with such offenders, prosecutors have the choice between treating them as, in effect, multiple offenders, charging them with numerous counts of embezzlement, or as single offenders charged with one count of embezzlement exceeding a certain amount. I would urge the latter, as it makes eminent good sense to view the embezzler's actions as a single, though complex, transaction. It is, we might say, in the nature of embezzlement for it to occur in smallish amounts over a period of time so as not to call undue attention to the crime. A rational sentencing scheme should recognize different levels of embezzlement, depending on the overall amount misappropriated, and punish more and less serious embezzlers accordingly. Such a graduated scheme is likely to produce sentences considerably lower than those meted out to offenders charged with multiple counts and thus better accord with the Totality Principle.

C. DIVERSE MULTIPLE OFFENDERS

A more troubling kind of multiple offender is one who is to be sentenced for having committed several different offenses, many of them *mala in se*. For instance, individuals involved in organized crime rings may plead or be found guilty of numerous serious offenses. There is, in such cases, no single organizing offense or even a small number of them. And although the multiple offenses might be viewed as part of an overall criminal plan, it is a stretch to view them as a single transaction. What unites them is not a single criminal purpose but their role in some complex scheme of criminal activity. Unlike serial offenders, the crimes of such individuals may be quite diverse, ranging from homicide to racketeering to extortion to drug dealing. Such individuals may also have violated numerous *mala prohibita*, ones that cannot reasonably be viewed as subordinated to a single, more serious *mala in se* because they stem from or support a number of such offenses.

Consistent with the approach sketched with other kinds of multiple offenders, we might first consider the *mala in se* committed by multiple offenders in this group. The initial sentence might be set by reference to the most serious of these, with bulk discounted increments added to the initial sentence in recognition of each of the victims of the other *mala in se*. The magnitude of the added increments might have to be adjusted to ensure that the overall sentence accords with the Totality Principle. This might require fairly steep bulk discounts if a given offender's *mala in se* were numerous. Once a total was reached for the *mala in se*, the sentences for the *mala prohibita* would have to be factored in. Again, the sentences for the *mala prohibita* could be subordinated to the total for the *mala in se*, in which case the sentences for them would be served concurrently, or they could function so as to add further, presumably quite small, increments to the overall sentence.

Conceivably, diverse multiple offenders could wind up serving very long prison sentences, especially if among their crimes were one or more homicides. Even if sentences for homicide were lower than those currently employed in many countries, an overall sentence for multiple homicides (with bulk discounts included), combined with other bulk-discounted sentences for other kinds of crimes, could still turn out to be quite lengthy. That is an implication of a retributive sentencing approach that we might simply have to live with.

5. Concluding Remarks

The retributive sentencing of multiple offenders requires us to balance two principles that point in opposing directions. The Totality Principle, however it is ultimately interpreted and defended, would have us limit the overall impact of punishment in multiple offender cases. The EVC Principle requires us to acknowledge each direct victim in multiple offenders' sentences. The former principle pushes us in the direction of shorter sentences, thereby implying that both the Strong and Modified versions of Consecutivism should be avoided. The EVC Principle implies that Pure Concurrentivism is indefensible. However, it need not be interpreted as precluding bulk discounts, though it is arguably more consistent with having fixed rather than declining ones.

These conclusions will not sit well with many penal theorists. There is a widespread sense that penal sanctions in many countries are too long and harsh to begin with. Anything short of Pure Concurrentivism, they might claim, will only make things worse. If retributive sentencing theories suggest otherwise, then so much the worse for them.

To this, retributive theorists can, consistent with their accounts of sentencing, offer several responses. First, they can support efforts to reduce sentences, more or less across the board. Relatively few criminal offenses impose substantial harms on direct victims that are comparable to those wrought by a year or two in prison. Most property and drug offenses surely do not do so, violations of *mala prohibita* rarely do so, and even some crimes against persons have mostly insignificant long-term effects. Imprisonment of any kind is damaging to individuals both in the short and longer term. Still, a few crimes do dramatically impair the lives of direct victims or deprive them of their lives entirely, and the individuals who commit such crimes often act with a high degree of culpability. We might all wish that this were not so and that we could find ways to prevent or forestall such horrific crimes so that we do not have to resort to punishing those who commit them. But if we are to stick with a retributive sentencing scheme, it seems somewhat arbitrary, in the face of crimes of these kinds, to stubbornly insist that legal punishment must be short lived, no matter how many victims an offender racks up whose lives are devastated by what he or she has done to them.

Secondly, retributive theorists could point out that in some countries, the excessive punishment of offenders is partly a function of the practice of strategic overcharging by prosecutors. Strategic overcharging is made possible by the proliferation of overlapping and redundant criminal prohibitions and is typically motivated by the desire of prosecutors to convince criminal defendants to plead guilty in exchange for charge or sentence concessions.[36] In theory, plea negotiations between prosecutors and defense attorneys will eventually bring charges and sentencing recommendations back in line with more reasonable estimates of what offenders merit for their crimes, but in reality, such happy outcomes do not always or consistently eventuate. While Pure Concurrentivism would render strategic overcharging moot, by depriving prosecutors of the bargaining edge such a strategy gives them, it would have the unfortunate consequence of insulating offenders who have badly victimized several people from having to serve longer sentences than their nonmultiple offending counterparts. We would do better to search for ways of discouraging strategic overcharging that do not have this result.

Finally, as I earlier indicated, retributivists can support reduced levels of punishment for reasons that have to do with the failure of many societies to establish or maintain the social conditions of responsible citizenship (especially through their tolerance of severe social deprivation) or devise penal sanctions that are consistent with preserving the capacities of offenders for moral self-governance. To the extent that societal neglect of some of its members' welfare—both outside and inside of prisons—plays a role in generating criminal conduct, no clear-thinking retributivist can happily endorse punishing all individuals as if their offending was fully voluntary or reflective of bad choices made by otherwise morally responsive beings. Importantly, however, the grounds for reducing punishment that societal neglect provides apply to single and multiple offenders alike. They are therefore logically separable from the debate about multiple offenders and bulk discounts.

Notes

1 Von Hirsch, *Censure and Sanctions,* p. 18.

2 For discussion of the "anchoring problem" and the "decremental strategy," see von Hirsch, *Censure and Sanctions*, pp. 36–46. See also von Hirsch and Ashworth, *Proportionate Sentencing*, pp. 141–43. For a nonretributive approach to the decremental strategy, see Braithwaite and Pettit, *Not Just Deserts*, pp. 140–45.

3 Concerns about the overcriminalization of conduct and frequency with which imprisonment is resorted to as a sanction are also distinct from those raised by sentencing multiple offenders, though they are likely to overlap.

4 But see Bottoms, "Five Puzzles in von Hirsch's Theory of Punishment," pp. 63–70 for a defense of sentence reductions grounded in mercy. (I discuss Bottoms's account in the third section.)

5 See also Ryberg's discussion of mercy as a basis for bulk discounts in his "Retributivism and Multiple Offending," pp. 226–31.

6 Ryberg makes this point in ibid., pp. 218–19.

7 See my "Retributive Parsimony."

8 See Ashworth, *Sentencing and Criminal Justice*, pp. 248–49.

9 See von Hirsch et al., *Criminal Deterrence and Sentence Severity*, p. 47, and Doob and Webster, "Sentence Severity and Crime."

10 See Nagin, "Deterrence and Incapacitation," p. 364.

11 See Mathiesen, *Prison on Trial*, pp. 27–54.

12 The notion of a discount for bulk offending comes from Ashworth, *Sentencing and Criminal Justice*, p. 249. See also Jareborg, "Why Bulk Discounts in Multiple Offence Sentencing?" For an illuminating discussion of the bulk discount issue, see Ryberg, "Retributivism and Multiple Offending."

13 Strong Concurrentivists might be able to avoid this implication of their approach in some cases. They could suggest that the perpetrator of the mass fraud should be charged with (and punished pursuant to) a more serious crime reflecting the overall sum of money stolen from her victims. Yet it is easy to conceive of cases in which such a strategy will not work: Consider the serial rapist who is being sentenced all at once for the five rapes he has admitted to committing. It seems imperative to not let such an offender get off scot free for his second, third, fourth, and fifth victims, each of whose rights was unjustifiably violated. But unlike the mass fraud case, there is no feasible way of "summing up" the harms that the serial rapist perpetrated and so charging him with (and punishing him pursuant to) a worse kind of rape.

14 By similar logic, multiple discrete victimizations of the same person should be acknowledged in an offender's sentence.

15 I advanced some tentative thoughts about the incorporation of related victims into a retributive sentencing scheme in *Rethinking Imprisonment*, pp. 34–35.

16 Ashworth, *Sentencing and Criminal Justice*, p. 248.

17 Ashworth also identifies a rehabilitation rationale for keeping total sentences from becoming too long; see ibid., p. 252.

18 For one thoughtful attempt to compare the harms wrought by crimes, see von Hirsch and Jareborg, "Gauging Crime Seriousness."

19 Von Hirsch and Ashworth, *Proportionate Sentencing*, pp. 142–43; see also von Hirsch, *Censure and Sanctions*, pp. 42–46.

20 Von Hirsch has conceded that legal punishment communicates with persons other than offenders—in particular the victims of crimes and the larger community (*Censure and Sanctions*, p. 10).

21 See Bonta and Gendreau, "Reexamining the Cruel and Unusual Punishment of Prison Life." For a more pessimistic view of the effects of imprisonment on individuals, see Liebling, "Prison Suicide and Prisoner Coping." Still, Liebling does not suggest that most prisoners suffer loss of the capacity to respond to moral considerations.

22 Super-maximum security confinement apparently does have debilitating effects on inmates. See Haney, "Mental Health Issues in Long-Term Solitary and 'Supermax' Confinement." I defend more humane and less restrictive forms of confinement in *Rethinking Imprisonment*, especially chs. 7–10.

23 Bottoms, "Five Puzzles," p. 66.

24 See ibid., pp. 68–70.

25 I defend a retributive approach to sentencing that keys sentences to direct victim harms (though tempered by offender culpability) in *Rethinking Imprisonment*, pp. 50–59.

26 A sobering example of a clearly disproportionate punishment is given by Douglas Husak, citing the United States Supreme Court's upholding of two consecutive 25-year sentences for possession of approximately $200 worth of marijuana ("Recreational Drug Use and Paternalism," p. 355).

27 See my *Rethinking Imprisonment*, pp. 50–59. It is important to note that my account is not a "harm for harm" one, since offender culpability must also be factored into attempts to gauge crime seriousness.

28 See ibid., ch. 3.

29 In other words, this version of the Totality Principle does not impose a ceiling on legal sanctions. For the problems with ceilings, see Ryberg, "Retributivism and Multiple Offending," p. 222–23.

30 Indeed, von Hirsch has defended a distinctive form of "recidivist premium," one in which repeat offending warrants assigning individuals sentences higher in the relevant sentencing range for their subsequent offenses. See von Hirsch and Wasik, "Section 29 Revised."

31 Granted, we might have qualms about such a conclusion in a few cases. Some recidivists probably suffer from psychopathic personality disorder or other mental disorders that significantly impair their capacities for moral self-governance. Such offenders may not be appropriate candidates for retributive punishment with its characteristic blaming dimension.

32 Still, we might worry that penal institutions have a substantial role in producing recidivism, and especially that the longer individuals spend in such institutions, the more likely it is that whatever capacity for moral self-governance they had to begin with is eroded over time. Whether individuals who have so devolved, so to speak, are appropriately punished for their further offenses is a difficult question. True, they may no longer be quite capable of moral self-governance because of what our prisons have done to them. But assuming that they once were capable of it, they surely must be seen as having some responsibility for getting themselves to where they now are. In any case, I doubt that all recidivists have been so degraded by their imprisonment as to be no longer capable of moral self-governance. Some may simply prefer lives of crime for the thrills or expected benefits. Even if our prisons were dramatically improved, it seems unlikely that recidivism would wholly disappear.

33 Of course, if a multiple offender subsequently multiply offends again and faces sentencing, it could be argued that her bulk discounts should be reduced.

34 In some cases, it may be possible to combine multiple victimizations of a single person into one more serious offense. For instance, we could have an offense of "aggravated robbery" for those who both rob and batter their victims.

35 Consider in this context Joel Feinberg's distinction between "primary" and "derivative" crimes: the former involve natural wrongs, while the latter would not be wrongs at all or to a very great extent except for the need to prohibit the former. (See his *Harm to Others*, pp. 19–21.)

36 See Stuntz, "Pathological Politics of Criminal Law," especially pp. 529–38.

Bibliography

Ashworth, Andrew. *Sentencing and Criminal Justice*. 4th ed. Cambridge: Cambridge University Press, 2005.

Bonta, James, and Paul Gendreau. "Reexamining the Cruel and Unusual Punishment of Prison Life." *Law and Human Behavior* 14 (1990): 347–72.

Bottoms, Anthony E. "Five Puzzles in von Hirsch's Theory of Punishment." In *Fundamentals of Sentencing Theory*, edited by Andrew Ashworth and Martin Wasik, 53–100. Oxford: Oxford University Press, 1998.

Braithwaite, John, and Philip Pettit. *Not Just Deserts: A Republican Theory of Criminal Justice*. Oxford: Clarendon Press, 1990.

Doob, Antony N., and Cheryl M. Webster. "Sentence Severity and Crime: Accepting the Null Hypothesis." *Crime and Justice: A Review of Research* 30 (2003): 143–95.

Feinberg, Joel. *Harm to Others*. Oxford: Oxford University Press, 1984.

Haney, Craig. "Mental Health Issues in Long-Term Solitary and 'Supermax' Confinement." *Crime and Delinquency* 49 (2003): 124–56.

Husak, Douglas N. "Recreational Drugs and Paternalism." *Law and Philosophy* 8 (1989): 353–81.

Jareborg, Nils. "Why Bulk Discounts in Sentencing?" In *Fundamentals of Sentencing Theory: Essays in Honour of Andrew von Hirsch*, edited by Andrew Ashworth and Martin Wasik, 129–40. Oxford: Clarendon Press, 1998.

Liebling, Alison. "Prison Suicide and Prisoner Coping." *Crime and Justice: A Review of Research* 26 (1999): 283–359.

Lippke, Richard. *Rethinking Imprisonment*. Oxford: Oxford University Press, 2007.

Lippke, Richard. "Retributive Parsimony." *Res Publica* 15 (2009): 377–95.

Mathiesen, Thomas. *Prison On Trial*. 2nd ed. Winchester, UK: Waterside Press, 2000.

Nagin, Daniel S. "Deterrence and Incapacitation." In *The Handbook of Crime and Punishment*, edited by Michael Tonry, 345–68. New York: Oxford University Press, 1998.

Ryberg, Jesper. "Retributivism and Multiple Offending." *Res Publica* 11 (2008): 213–33.

Stuntz, William J. "The Pathological Politics of Criminal Law." *Michigan Law Review* 100 (2001): 505–600.

von Hirsch, Andrew. *Censure and Sanctions*. Oxford: Oxford University Press, 1993.

von Hirsch, Andrew and Andrew Ashworth. *Proportionate Sentencing: Exploring the Principles*. Oxford: Oxford University Press, 2005.

von Hirsch, Andrew, et al. *Criminal Deterrence and Sentence Severity: An Analysis of Recent Research*. Oxford: Hart Publishing, 1999.

von Hirsch, Andrew and Jareborg, Nils. "Gauging Crime Seriousness: A 'Living Standard' Conception of Criminal Harm." *Oxford Journal of Legal Studies* 11 (1991): 1–38.

von Hirsch, Andrew and Wasik, M. "Section 29 Revised: Previous Convictions in Sentencing." *Criminal Law Review* (June 1994): 409–18.

12

RETRIBUTION AND CAPITAL PUNISHMENT

Thom Brooks

SHOULD RETRIBUTIVISTS REJECT capital punishment? It is easy to see how those holding different theories of punishment might oppose it. For example, a deterrence proponent could argue that capital punishment lacks a deterrent effect, and thus, it is unjustified. This seems a far more difficult task for a retributivist.

There are many different versions of retributivism.[1] Some versions would hold that retributivist desert for a crime is necessary but not sufficient for punishment. This view of *negative retributivism* would allow for consequentialist considerations to inform whether a given punishment is justified. Instead, let us focus our attention on *positive retributivism*, in which desert is both necessary and sufficient to justify punishment. Therefore, if someone deserves punishment, that punishment is justified to the proportion that it is deserved. A classic formulation of this view is offered by Immanuel Kant:

> whatever undeserved evil you inflict upon another within the people, you inflict upon yourself. If you insult him, you insult yourself; if you steal from him, you steal from yourself; if you strike him, you strike yourself; if you kill him, you kill yourself.[2]

The greater the wrongfulness of a crime, the greater its punishment. This positive retributivist position could easily justify capital punishment as seen by Kant: the murderer deserves death on account of the gravity of his crime.

However, I will argue that retributivists should reject capital punishment for murderers.[3] I will accept several concessions before making my argument. First, I accept that capital punishment may be proportionate to the crime of murder. Thus, my claim is not that capital punishment should be rejected because it is disproportionate to murder.[4] Second, I accept that capital punishment need not be cruel nor unusual punishment. This is an area of wide disagreement, but I do not wish to be distracted by these debates here. Note that I am not defending any particular method of execution; I simply assume that a method may be found that could be satisfactory. Third, I also accept that capital punishment is not barbaric or uncivilized.[5] Some philosophers, such as Kant, rejected punishments for certain crimes on the grounds that doing so might itself be a crime against humanity.[6] This is another area of wide disagreement that I wish to avoid. In summary, I accept these three concessions up front purely for the sake of argument. My claim is that retributivists should have rejected capital punishments for murderers even if they believed it proportionate for murderers, it was not cruel or unusual to impose capital punishment on murderers, and capital punishment was not barbaric or uncivilized.[7]

The structure of this chapter is as follows. First, I will discuss previous attempts at explaining why retributivists should reject capital punishment offered by Daniel McDermott and Stephen Nathanson. I believe these attempts have been unsuccessful on several grounds. I will then discuss what I believe is a more promising argument presented by Jed Rakoff in *U.S. v Quinones* before concluding with some reflections on the implications of this position.

1. Two Arguments Against Capital Punishment

First, let us consider two arguments meant to explain how retributivists might reject capital punishment. I believe they both fail, in part, because they are not properly *retributivist* objections to capital punishment. A more satisfactory alternative will be offered in the next section.

One attempt to demonstrate how retributivists might reject capital punishment is offered by Daniel McDermott.[8] He argues that retributivists should hold that any punishment they would accept is morally legitimate, and that the punishing institution ought to be morally legitimate as well. Capital punishment might then be a legitimate sanction for murder, all things considered, but its legitimacy as a penal option also rests on the legitimacy of the punishing institution.[9]

McDermott presents us with the following case:

Imagine, for example, that a vicious murderer has been sentenced to death and placed on death row. He has exhausted all of his appeals, he has gotten his affairs in order, and now it is just a matter of days before he gets what he deserves: a lethal injection that will cause his death. Now imagine that the guards at the prison decide that this business of a formal state execution is just too costly an affair and that they should do everybody a favor and take care of the job themselves. That night, they slip into the murderer's cell and give him a lethal injection while he sleeps. The murderer never feels a thing and is dead within minutes.[10]

The argument is that even if the murderer deserved death by lethal injection, it is unjustified for the guards to execute him in this way. The example is meant to show us that the legitimate infliction of capital punishment on murderers requires a legitimate authority. For McDermott, the United States lacks this authority because of the role that race plays in the capital sentencing process. He says:

> If race is *always* going to play a significant role in the capital sentencing process, then our government can *never* have the moral legitimacy necessary to satisfy these desert claims, and therefore its executions will *always* be illegitimate.[11]

In other words, he argues that capital punishment is illegitimate because its use is distributed to deserving persons disproportionately. Thus, the retributivist could support the use of capital punishment if, and only if, the punishment's distribution is fair.

I do not believe that McDermott's argument works. One reason is that the U.S. criminal justice system is not akin to prison guards occasionally killing prisoners in their cells. Since *Gregg v Georgia*, trials for capital crimes have involved a two-step process in which we first ascertain guilt and then (assuming a finding of guilt) and, secondly, we decide whether capital punishment is deserved.[12] According to this process, all executions follow a specified procedure depending upon jurisdiction, and none are like McDermott's prison guards.

A second criticism of McDermott's argument is that it is not a retributivist argument. It is undeniable that race plays a significant role in capital sentencing.[13] Persons with different races may be sentenced to death at different rates for similar crimes, and this is clearly an injustice. However, the retributivist is primarily concerned with whether murderers are punished to the degree that they deserve. For McDermott, desert is not at issue: his argument is not that we should reject capital punishment because it is imposed on persons who do not deserve it. Instead, the concern is that the punishing authority may lack moral legitimacy to inflict such a punishment on the grounds that *not all* persons who deserve death are given death sentences. The retributivist reply should not be to say that we should punish no one to the degree he deserves because our system currently fails to sentence all persons to the punishment they deserve. Instead, the retributivist should reply that the problem is that we are not sentencing *enough* murderers to death row. If race has played a significant role in capital sentencing, and too often white murderers fail to be sentenced to death as often as nonwhite murderers, then the system should aim to sentence more white murderers to death if we concede that murderers deserve capital punishment.[14]

Stephen Nathanson offers a similar attempt at demonstrating how retributivists might reject capital punishment.[15] He uses the example of supposing that highway patrol officers select motorists for speeding tickets on account of whether they have beards.

He argues that "[w]hether one is treated justly or not depends on how others are treated and not solely on what one deserves."[16] The claim is that the criminal justice system may make some people more likely to be sentenced to death than others. The only feature that seems to explain why some are treated differently than others is their race, and race is just as arbitrary at determining who should be sentenced as would be the presence of a beard. If it is wrong to select persons because of the presence of beards, then it is also wrong to select persons because of their skin color; therefore, we can reject capital punishment.

I do not believe this argument works either. The claim is not that we should reject capital punishment because it is disproportionate to a particular crime, such as murder. Additionally, the claim is not that we should reject capital punishment because the persons, however selected, are innocent of a crime whose punishment was the death penalty. Instead, the claim is that we are only choosing *some* deserving persons, not all, and our selection discriminates between persons on illegitimate grounds. Nathanson is wrong to believe that the best response is to then say that we should reject capital punishment, nor is this a retributivist argument against the practice. Retributivists believe that murderers should be punished to the degree they deserve. If murderers deserve capital punishment, and not all murderers are sentenced to death, then (again) the retributivist response would be that we should execute more murderers and not that we should not execute any murderers. The evidence of racial discrimination is convincing, but again, if race has played a significant role in capital sentencing and too often white murderers fail to be sentenced to death as often as nonwhite murderers, then the system should aim to sentence more white murderers to death if we concede that murderers may deserve capital punishment.

Neither McDermott nor Nathanson rule out the justifiability of death for murderers. Their objection with capital punishment lies not with the injustice of its being a proportionate penalty for murder. Instead, both are concerned with the significant role that racial discrimination has played in the U.S. criminal justice system. While I entirely agree with this concern, it does not offer us a satisfactory *retributivist* argument against capital punishment. The fact that not all deserving murderers are sentenced to death is reason to try to sentence more to death, not abandon punishing any murderer to the degree he deserves.

There is a wider problem. This problem of racial discrimination in sentencing affects not merely capital sentencing but sentencing more generally; yet neither McDermott nor Nathanson claim that we should end sentencing altogether. For example, Nathanson says:

> To do away with punishment entirely would be to do away with the criminal law and the system of constraints which it supports... if we abolish capital punishment, there is reason to believe that nothing will happen.[17]

His argument is that capital punishment should be rejected because of the presence of racial discrimination and that murder rates might not become worse upon abolition.

Punishments for all other crimes should remain because their abolition would be socially disastrous. These are not retributivist arguments, which are our focus. We should not judge the justice of a punishment on the grounds of which consequences may be most likely; rather, our concern is whether a person deserves a particular punishment. If murderers deserve capital punishment, and not all murderers are being sentenced appropriately, then the problem with this picture is that we should sentence more murderers to death. Moreover, it is not a retributivist argument to claim that only one form of punishment should be singled out to be abolished on grounds, such as racial discrimination, which affect other forms of punishment because the former is unlikely to lead to worse consequences.

2. The *Quinones* Argument against Capital Punishment

In the last section, we examined two attempts to offer us a retributivist argument against capital punishment. I argued that their arguments are unsatisfactory as retributivist arguments, although this is not to say that they are not compelling on other grounds. I will now offer what I believe is a more satisfactory retributivist argument against capital punishment, which can be found in the *U.S. v Quinones* decision written by Judge Jed Rakoff.[18] Rakoff argues the following:

> What DNA testing has proved, beyond cavil, is the remarkable degree of fallibility in the basic fact-finding processes on which we rely in criminal cases. In each of the 12 cases of DNA-exoneration of death row inmates referenced in *Quinones*, the defendant had been guilty by a unanimous jury that concluded there was proof of his guilt beyond a reasonable doubt; and in each of the 12 cases the conviction had been affirmed on appeal, and collateral challenges rejected, by numerous courts that had carefully scrutinized the evidence and manner of conviction. Yet, for all this alleged "due process," the result in each and every one of these cases, was the conviction of an innocent person who, because of the death penalty, would shortly have been executed (some came within days of being so) were it not for the fortuitous development of a new scientific technique that happened to be applicable to their particular cases.[19]

Rakoff concludes that the conviction of numerous innocent persons is then unavoidable. Therefore, we cannot guarantee that those we convict of murder genuinely possess retributivist desert despite the fairest of trials and subsequent appeals, because advances in scientific testing may always reveal that we have mistakenly convicted innocent persons despite our best efforts.[20] Thus, even if we did accept that murderers deserved capital punishment in theory, we should reject capital punishment in practice because we cannot be satisfactorily certain that a convicted murderer is guilty of the crime. Scientific advances may always show beyond doubt that our greatest certainty posttrial is misplaced.[21]

Unlike the ones previously surveyed, this argument is a sound *retributivist* argument against capital punishment. McDermott's and Nathanson's opposition to capital punishment did not stem from a concern over the genuine desert of those convicted of murder. Instead, we have seen that their opposition mistakenly centred on nonretributivist concerns. The argument in *Quinones* is a more satisfactory argument against capital punishment because at its heart is a claim about the absence of desert. We have granted the retributivist many concessions at the start of our discussion, such as that capital punishment may be proportionate to the murderer's desert. However, the argument in *Quinones* is that we will always be unable to know another's retributivist guilt in practice even if the presence of such guilt would warrant the death penalty in theory. Thus, the retributivist should reject capital punishment because she cannot be satisfactorily certain that a person possesses sufficient desert.[22]

The argument that we cannot know the true desert of another in practice is not an uncommon view among retributivists. For example, Kant argues:

> The real morality of actions, their merit or guilt, even that of our own conduct, thus remains entirely hidden from us. Our imputation can refer only to the empirical character. How much of this is ascribable to the pure effect of freedom, how much to mere nature, that is, to faults of temperament for which there is no responsibility, or to its happy constitution, can *never* be determined, and upon it therefore no *perfectly* just judgements can be passed.[23]

A determination of punishable desert may be substantially a determination concerning the state of mind of another. We cannot read the minds of others, but we can bear witness to their actions against an explanatory narrative that may give us some insight into why another did what he did. The claim here is not that we can never grasp guilt, but that our certainty is always in doubt.[24] This does not mean that retributivism cannot justify punishment because it can offer us "no perfectly just judgments."[25] However, it would mean that capital punishment is especially problematic. When we impose capital punishment on a convicted murderer, there cannot be any room for error since the murderer can never be brought back to life afterward if error is discovered at some later date. If there remains a substantial risk of error, as demonstrated by advances in scientific testing in cases where a person has been sentenced beyond reasonable doubt in a fair trial, then we have good reason on retributivist grounds to reject capital punishment in favor of an alternative sanction.

The *Quinones* argument offers a satisfactory retributivist argument to reject capital punishment. Unfortunately, this argument was not found satisfactory for different reasons by an appellant court.[26] The arguments against the decision were that the United States Supreme Court has upheld capital punishment on many occasions and its legitimacy was part of settled law. Moreover, there is no violation of due process when a defendant is sentenced beyond a reasonable doubt. We cannot rely on the possibility that a defendant may be innocent in theory, but only that a defendant is innocent in fact—as best we can.

My own view is that the original *Quinones* judgement is compelling. We know that persons have been condemned who were innocent; we know that future scientific evidence can overturn the seemingly most safe of convictions; and we know that we could easily avoid such problems in adopting an alternative sanction, such as life imprisonment. Therefore, we knowingly, foreseeably, and avoidably sentence innocent people to death row if we continue to endorse capital punishment, and this would remain true even if capital punishment were a just sentence for murderers. Together, this offers a compelling argument, in my view, to reject capital punishment on retributivist grounds. While it is highly unfortunate that the original *Quinones* decision was overturned, it still inspires a compelling retributivist argument against capital punishment.[27]

3. Possible Objections

We have rejected two attempts to offer a retributivist argument against capital punishment, and instead we have favored a third attempt derived from Judge Rakoff's decision in *Quinones*, which rejects capital punishment on epistemic considerations regarding our inability to know the desert of another with satisfactory safety. In this section, I want to consider possible objections to this view and why I believe these objections are unsuccessful.

Perhaps the classic discussion of retributivism and the problem of wrongfully executing innocent persons is offered by Larry Alexander.[28] He offers two arguments why this problem should not lead us to reject capital punishment. In setting up the first argument, he asks us to accept two conditions: (1) retributivism is only satisfied by punishment of the guilty, and (2) human beings make mistakes when sentencing. If we accept these conditions, and if we were to reject capital punishment on these grounds, we must reject punishment altogether: "[t]he retributive injunction concerns *punishment* of the innocent, not just *execution* of the innocent."[29] If punishment of the innocent is always wrong, and we will inevitably punish some innocent persons by mistake, then punishment of anyone for any crime should be opposed. Such an argument against capital punishment throws out the baby with the bath water.[30]

I do not believe this challenge is successful. The problem is not that we might wrongfully convict innocent persons in any case. We should expect mistakes to be made on occasion with any public policy; human beings are fallible. However, such mistakes should be mitigated appropriately. For example, perhaps it is inevitable that some persons will be charged the wrong amount of tax. The correct way to mitigate this problem is to allow these taxpayers opportunities to correct this mistake. Likewise, the argument that innocent persons may be wrongfully convicted of a variety of crimes need not lead to the conclusion that punishment is wrong. Instead, this problem can be mitigated by permitting opportunities for the wrongfully convicted to correct this mistake through an appeals procedure.

Nevertheless, this argument remains a reason to oppose capital punishment in particular because a condemned person will be unable to appeal post-execution. The critic might then respond that my view fails to account for the fact that we regularly permit those sentenced to death opportunities for appeals. My response would be that these opportunities for appeal do not satisfactorily address the problem. A person on death row may have opportunities for appeal, perhaps numerous ones, but these opportunities will be finite. Furthermore, we know of several cases where these opportunities for appeal were exhausted and, yet, advances in scientific testing demonstrated that such persons were wrongfully condemned. The problem is that when we execute a person, he or she lacks a procedure to mitigate any mistake made. Therefore, we can acknowledge our fallibility in sentencing and concede the retributivist's demand that we only punish the innocent in opposing capital punishment, but this need not push us to oppose punishment *tout court*.[31] Thus, I do not believe Alexander's first challenge is successful.

The second important argument put forward by Alexander involves a distinction between weak and strong retributivism. "Weak retributivism" holds that desert is non-comparative, and treating a person *worse* than she deserves is different in kind from treating her *better* than she deserves.[32] Weak retributivists would say that we have a "moral injunction" to ensure that we avoid treating the innocent worse than they deserve.[33] Alexander argues that weak retributivists would fall victim to his first argument: if it is always wrong to punish the innocent, and if this will often happen by mistake, then (all) punishment should be opposed. As he writes, "[w]eak retributivism, far from being a theory of punishment, condemns all punishment in the real (fallible) world."[34] I have already argued that this is mistaken; we can honor any such "moral injunction" by ensuring that such problems can be mitigated by providing opportunities for such mistakes to be corrected. We can allow most punishment but reject capital punishment, since only it would fail to offer a sufficient chance for remedy for any inevitable mistakes.

Alexander distinguishes this understanding of weak retributivism from what he calls "strong retributivism." This view holds that it is just as wrong that a guilty person not get what he deserves as it is that an innocent person is wrongful convicted.[35] This is a more forceful rejection of my argument. Why think retributivists care only about the innocent? Of course, the inadvertent punishment of the innocent is a wrong, and the wrongful execution of the innocent is a particularly grave wrong. However, criminals are also wronged when they are not given their just deserts. According to the strong retributivist, the correct response to the problem of the possibility of wrongful execution of innocent people is *not* to argue that we should oppose capital punishment because we make mistakes, because doing so would generate even more failures to give just deserts.

Let us accept our earlier concession that the death penalty is proportionate to the crime of murder, so that murderers deserve death for their crimes. If we did not punish anyone with death for fear we might wrongfully execute an innocent person, then we fail to punish murderers as they deserve. If we were to assume that most of the persons we condemn are genuinely guilty with a relatively small handful of exceptions, then we would fail to give all murderers their just deserts in order to avoid wrongfully punishing a small number of innocent persons.[36] Therefore, the strong retributivist might argue that we should not oppose capital punishment even if we were certain to make mistakes because far more people will receive their just deserts than what might otherwise have been the case. In other words, one unjust result is the wrongful execution of innocent persons, but another unjust result is murderers not receiving their just deserts. If it is in fact inevitable that there will be unjust results whatever we do, then our preference should be for the choice that generates "fewer unjust results."[37]

This is a powerful rejection, but I believe it is also unsuccessful. It is mistaken in that it claims that the two injustices are equal in value, but they are not. Desert is not simply a binary value where it is either present or absent; it also comes in degrees. The murderer and the thief may both possess "desert," but their desert will not be of similar values, and the former has more than the latter. Alexander takes the following cases as symmetrical:

Wrongful execution. An innocent person is executed for a murder he did not commit.

Not condemned murderer. A murderer is not executed for a murder that he did commit but receives life imprisonment.

For Alexander, each case is as unjust as the other, but I disagree. The problem with the wrongful execution case is clear: an innocent person is wrongfully executed for a crime he did not commit. This person does not receive the treatment he deserved, which included that he not be executed for this crime. Note that this person is wronged in two ways: he is wronged when convicted for the crime in the first place and then wronged again when executed. He deserved neither imprisonment nor execution.

Now let us consider the case of the "not condemned murderer": is it "equally unjust" as Alexander claims?[38] No, it is not. The murderer is not wronged when convicted (as is the innocent person). The only unjust result in the murderer's case is that he does not receive his *full* desert (namely, execution), but he does receive at least *some* desert. Moreover, if life imprisonment without parole may be understood as a kind of "social death," then it would appear that the murderer *almost* receives his full desert. This is quite different from the first case in which the wrongly executed innocent person received *none* of his full desert. The two cases are then not alike, and therefore we would do more injustice in supporting capital punishment than rejecting it. If we reject it, then all innocent persons would receive *all* the treatment they deserve, and all murderers would receive *almost all* the treatment they deserve.[39] However, if we did not reject capital punishment, then all innocent persons would *not* receive the treatment they deserve although all murderers would receive *all* the treatment they deserve. The difference is that the injustice for the wrongfully condemned is worse than any injustice suffered by murderers given life sentences. I agree with

Alexander that "if unjust results are inevitable whether we punish or not, our preference is for fewer unjust results."[40] However, I hope I have explained clearly why this preference should lead us to reject capital punishment.

A different critic might respond with a further challenge, something like the following. We have said that murderers deserve execution, and innocent people do not deserve execution, but we have neglected to consider one important party: the dead victims. If we were to sentence murderers to life imprisonment, then it may well be that they receive nearly all their just desert, but the problem remains that their victims receive none of their just deserts. Their lives have been wrongfully ended, and justice is demanded in return. If we were to end capital punishment, the victims are not treated justly. The injustice of this situation, combined with the injustice of murderers, punished less than they fully deserve outweighs any injustice to the relatively few innocent persons who might be wrongfully executed.

This challenge is also unsuccessful. Murderers deserve a sanction as grave as capital punishment on account of their having wrongfully killed their victims. A murderer's desert is then already a reflection of his or her wrong, as well as the wrongfulness of his or her act. Therefore, the unjust treatment of victims is already taken into account when we determine a murderer's desert, so we cannot then try to add such factors twice. It remains the case that the injustice accruing to wrongfully executed innocent persons would be greater than that accruing to murderers given life imprisonment. If we prefer a scenario in which we have fewer unjust results, then again, retributivists should oppose capital punishment.

4. Conclusion

In the last section, I responded to several possible objections to my position, explaining not only the force of these objections but also the reasons why these objections are unsuccessful. This is further evidence why I believe my retributivist argument against capital punishment is more compelling than earlier accounts. However, I will conclude this chapter by explaining why this may be an imperfect argument against capital punishment given one further challenge regarding the issue of uncertain guilt.

I have argued that a retributivist should reject capital punishment for murderers because we can almost never be certain that the convicted person really is a murderer. However, I leave open the possibility that we may be certain in some cases. For example, the British politician David Davis has argued that the death penalty would be justified in those cases where someone has been convicted of two or more murders.[41] The reason is that our doubt over his innocence would be substantially less, and we would be particularly more certain that the convicted person actually did commit one of the murders of which he was found guilty. Thus, the epistemic challenge of knowing another's retributivist desert might be overcome. It might seem then that my retributivist argument against capital punishment scores only an imperfect and partial victory in leaving open this possibility.

In closing, I believe there would remain several reasons why we should oppose capital punishment, even in these cases.[42] One reason is that while we may be more certain that someone convicted of multiple murders is genuinely guilty of at least one, some doubt may remain. Such a response may seem to be implausible, especially in cases of persons who have been found guilty of killing several persons, but we may never be perfectly certain of any actual guilt. A second reason to oppose capital punishment might be that it would make little sense to defend the gallows for use against such a very small number of people; very few murderers are convicted of murdering more than one person.[43] Finally, there may be additional reasons, including the desire of the families of the victims to gain answers from the murderer for why their loved ones were killed, or that it would be beneficial to keep such persons alive so that the state could learn more about why they did what they did in the hopes that it might better address such behavior in the future.[44]

Even against the multiple murderer argument, I maintain that retributivists should reject capital punishment for murderers, even if they accept that murders may deserve capital punishment (and the other concessions made at the beginning of the chapter). Those wanting to endorse the death penalty must look elsewhere for justification.[45]

Notes

1 For example, see Cottingham, "Varieties of Retribution."

2 Kant, *Metaphysics of Morals*, p. 332 (Academy pagination).

3 Throughout, I shall speak of retributivism as *positive* retributivism. My claim is that if I can demonstrate that positive retributivists should reject capital punishment then negative retributivists have reason to reject it as well. For more on positive and negative retributivism, see my "Is Hegel a Retributivist?", *Hegel's Political Philosophy*, and *Punishment*.

4 For the claim that retributivism cannot justify capital punishment solely on the grounds that such a punishment fits the crime, see Roberts-Cady, "Against Retributive Justifications of the Death Penalty." I will concede this claim in my argument, although I do not believe that Roberts-Cady successfully rejects it, because she has an impoverished understanding of what retributivist desert is, one that I doubt her opponents would accept. My aim is to be far more charitable and offer several concessions that together I hope will make my argument more persuasive to opponents.

5 I accept this claim for the sake of argument.

6 See Kant, *Metaphysics of Morals*, p. 363.

7 I will also avoid the question of whether it is more justified for a jury and not trial judge determine whether a defendant should be sentenced to death; see *Ring v Arizona*, 536 U.S. 584 (2002) (June 24, 2002). On fair trials, see my *Right to a Fair Trial*.

8 See McDermott, "Retributivist Argument against Capital Punishment."

9 Ibid., p. 318.

10 Ibid., p. 322.

11 Ibid., p. 326.

12 See Gregg v Georgia, 428 U.S. 153 (1976).

13 See Baldus et al., "Racial Discrimination and the Death Penalty"; see also Blume et al., "Post-*McCleskey* Racial Discrimination Claims in Capital Cases."

14 See my "Retributivist Arguments against Capital Punishment," pp. 189–90. One concern might be that our attempt to sentence more white murderers may lead to greater sentencing mistakes, including our condemning a greater number of innocent people. I do not disagree. My argument is that a retributivist can respond to the racial discrimination objection. I will argue shortly that a better *retributivist* argument against capital punishment will concern mistaken convictions more generally.

15 See Nathanson, "Does It Matter if the Death Penalty is Arbitrarily Administered?"

16 Ibid., p. 158.

17 Ibid., p. 162.

18 See *United States v Alan Quinones*, et al., 205 F. Supp. 2d. 256, 2002 WL 1415648 (S.D.N.Y.) (July 1, 2002).

19 Ibid., p. 264.

20 See Gul, "Truth That Dare Not Speak Its Name," and Scheck et al., *Actual Innocence*.

21 An objection might state that this argument can go the other way. DNA evidence may help cast strong doubt, but it might also remove doubt. My reply would be that this evidence is not timeless and unchangeable: there is no reason to believe that the evidence we have today may not be understood differently in light of further scientific advances. We must always be prepared for the evidence to support a person's future innocence even if it would appear unlikely today.

22 I have added the qualifier of "satisfactorily certain" purposefully. It need not be a count against other forms of punishment that we may be mistaken. This is because with forms of punishment other than the death penalty, we may have the opportunity to redress any wrongs we may have made mistakenly. However, more certainty is required in cases of capital crimes because this opportunity is much less or perhaps all but absent.

23 Kant, *Critique of Pure Reason*, A552/B580 (emphasis added).

24 For example, see my "Kant's Theory of Punishment" and "Kantian Punishment and Retributivism."

25 Kant, *Critique of Pure Reason*, A552/B580.

26 See U.S. v Quinones, 313 F. 3d 49 (2d. Cir. 2002) (December 10, 2002).

27 For arguments pertaining to United States law on the constitutionality of capital punishment, see Bentele, "Does the Death Penalty, by Risking the Execution of the Innocent, Violate Substantive Due Process?," and Lugosi, "Executing the Factually Innocent."

28 See Alexander, "Retributivism and the Inadvertent Punishment of the Innocent." See also Duus-Otterström, "Fallibility and Retribution."

29 Alexander, "Retributivism," pp. 234–35.

30 See ibid., p. 245: "if knowingly risking punishing the innocent is morally equivalent to knowingly punishing the innocent, *we can never punish anyone.*"

31 Alexander states in a footnote that "not all convictions of the innocent will be detected and overturned. At best, imprisonment rather than execution improves the chances of such detection. It does not guarantee it" (ibid., p. 235 n. 3). This is correct and supports my view above. Executing a person limits the opportunities for detecting a condemned person's innocence. If all public policies may be enacted fallibly, we need not oppose *punishment* because mistakes will be made,

because there will be satisfactory opportunities to address them. However, we should oppose *capital* punishment because satisfactory opportunities to address mistakes are not possible.

32 Ibid., p. 238ff.

33 See ibid., p. 238.

34 Ibid., p. 244.

35 Ibid., p. 238; see also Alexander, "Crime and Culpability," pp. 27–28.

36 On the conviction and execution of innocent persons, see Kirchmeier, "Dead Innocent," and Tushnet, "Politics of Executing the Innocent."

37 Alexander, "Retributivism," p. 238.

38 Ibid.

39 Of course, innocent persons can still be falsely convicted and punished short of execution, which would still be less than they deserve, but at least in that case they would have the opportunity to seek to correct this error and thereby (belatedly) receive their full desert (an opportunity which, as indicated above, is not available after execution).

40 Ibid.

41 See "Tories' Davis Backs Death Penalty."

42 I recognize that these further reasons to reject capital punishment are not, in fact, retributivist reasons. However, together these reasons may offer a compelling position against capital punishment for retributivists when viewed in combination.

43 On recidivism rates and sentencing, see Cullen and Newell, *Murderers and Life Imprisonment*.

44 See also other important reservations offered in Green, *Lectures on the Principles of Political Obligation*, §205.

45 My most sincere thanks to Fabian Freyenhagen, Claire, Hobson, William O'Brian, Fabienne Peter, Zofia Stemplowska, Victor Tadros, and Mark White for very helpful comments on previous versions.

Bibliography

Alexander, Larry. "Crime and Culpability." *Journal of Contemporary Legal Issues* 5 (1994): 1–29.

Alexander, Larry. "Retributivism and the Inadvertent Punishment of the Innocent." *Law and Philosophy* 2 (1983): 233–46.

Baldus, David C., et al. "Racial Discrimination and the Death Penalty in the Post-*Furman* Era: An Empirical and Legal Overview, with Recent Findings from Philadelphia." *Cornell Law Review* 83 (1998): 1638–1710.

BBC News, 2003. "Tories' Davis Backs Death Penalty." BBC News, November 16, 2003 (http://news.bbc.co.uk/2/hi/uk_news/politics/3274245.stm).

Bentele, Ursula. "Does the Death Penalty, by Risking the Execution of the Innocent, Violate Substantive Due Process?" *Houston Law Review* 40 (2004): 1359–86.

Blume, John H., Theodore Eisenburg, and Sheri Lynn Johnson. "Post-*McCleskey* Racial Discrimination Claims in Capital Cases." *Cornell Law Review* 83 (1998): 1771–1810.

Brooks, Thom. "Kant's Theory of Punishment." *Utilitas* 15 (2003): 206–24.

Brooks, Thom. "Retributivist Arguments against Capital Punishment." *Journal of Social Philosophy* 35 (2004): 188–97.

Brooks, Thom. "Is Hegel a Retributivist?" *Bulletin of the Hegel Society of Great Britain* 49/50 (2004): 113–26.

Brooks, Thom. "Kantian Punishment and Retributivism: A Reply to Clark." *Ratio* 18 (2005): 237–45.

Brooks, Thom. *Hegel's Political Philosophy: A Systematic Reading of the Philosophy of Right.* Edinburgh: Edinburgh University Press, 2007.

Brooks, Thom (ed.). *The Right to a Fair Trial.* Aldershot: Ashgate, 2009.

Brooks, Thom. *Punishment.* London: Routledge, 2011.

Cottingham, John. "Varieties of Retribution." *Philosophical Quarterly* 29 (1979): 238–46.

Cullen, Eric, and Tim Newell. *Murderers and Life Imprisonment: Containment, Treatment, Safety and Risk.* Winchester: Waterside Press, 1999.

Duus-Otterström, Göran. "Fallibility and Retribution." *Law and Philosophy* 29 (2010): 337–69.

Green, Thomas Hill. *Lectures on the Principles of Political Obligation.* London: Longmans, Green and Co., 1941.

Gul, Saad. "The Truth That Dare Not Speak Its Name: The Criminal Justice System's Treatment of Wrongly Convicted Defendants Through the Prism of DNA Exonerations." *Criminal Law Bulletin* 42 (2006): 687–700.

Kant, Immanuel. *Critique of Pure Reason.* Translated by Norman Kemp Smith. London: Macmillan, 1929.

Kant, Immanuel. *The Metaphysics of Morals.* Translated and edited by Mary Gregor. Cambridge: Cambridge University Press, 1996.

Kirchmeier, Jeffrey L. "Dead Innocent: The Death Penalty Abolitionist Search for a Wrongful Execution." *Tulsa Law Review* 42 (2006): 403–35.

Lugosi, Charles I. "Executing the Factually Innocent: The U.S. Constitution, Habeas Corpus, and the Death Penalty." *Stanford Journal of Civil Rights and Civil Liberties* 1 (2005): 473–503.

McDermott, Daniel. "A Retributivist Argument against Capital Punishment." *Journal of Social Philosophy* 32 (2001): 317–33.

Nathanson, Stephen. "Does It Matter if the Death Penalty is Arbitrarily Administered?" *Philosophy & Public Affairs* 14 (1985): 149–64.

Roberts-Cady, Sarah. "Against Retributive Justifications of the Death Penalty." *Journal of Social Philosophy* 41 (2010): 185–93.

Scheck, Barry, Peter Neufeld, and Jim Dwyer. *Actual Innocence: When Justice Goes Wrong and How to Make It Right.* New York: Penguin, 2000.

Tushnet, Mark V. "The Politics of Executing the Innocent: The Death Penalty in the Next Century?" *University of Pittsburgh Law Review* 53 (1991): 261–69.

Index